AF653305

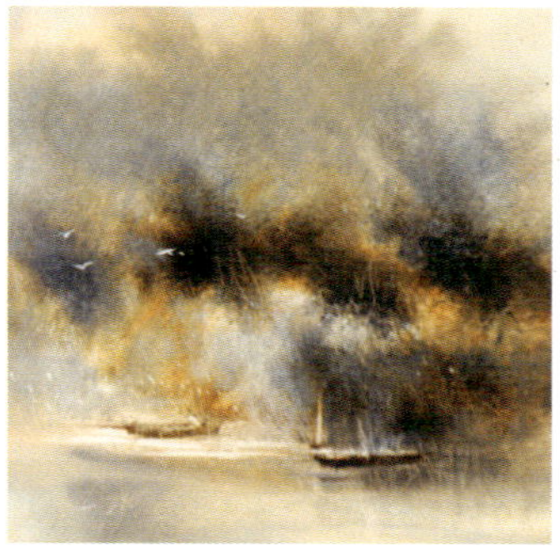

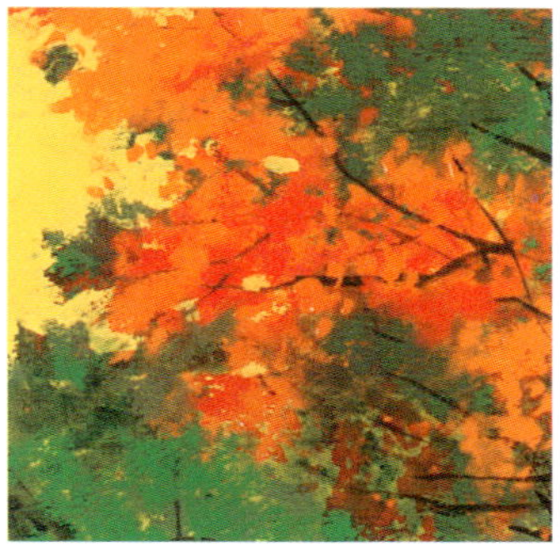

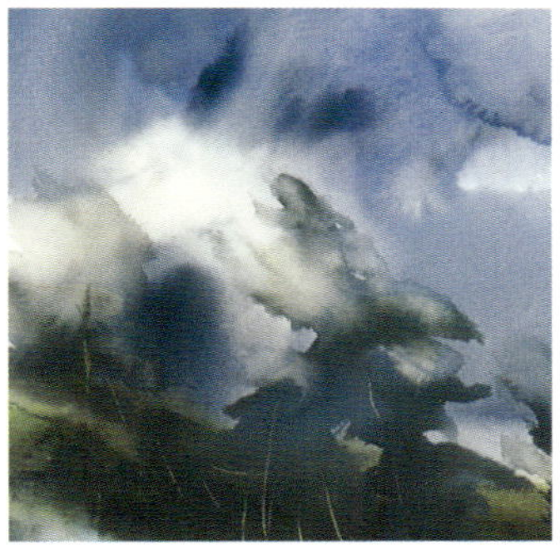

SATISH CHANDRA

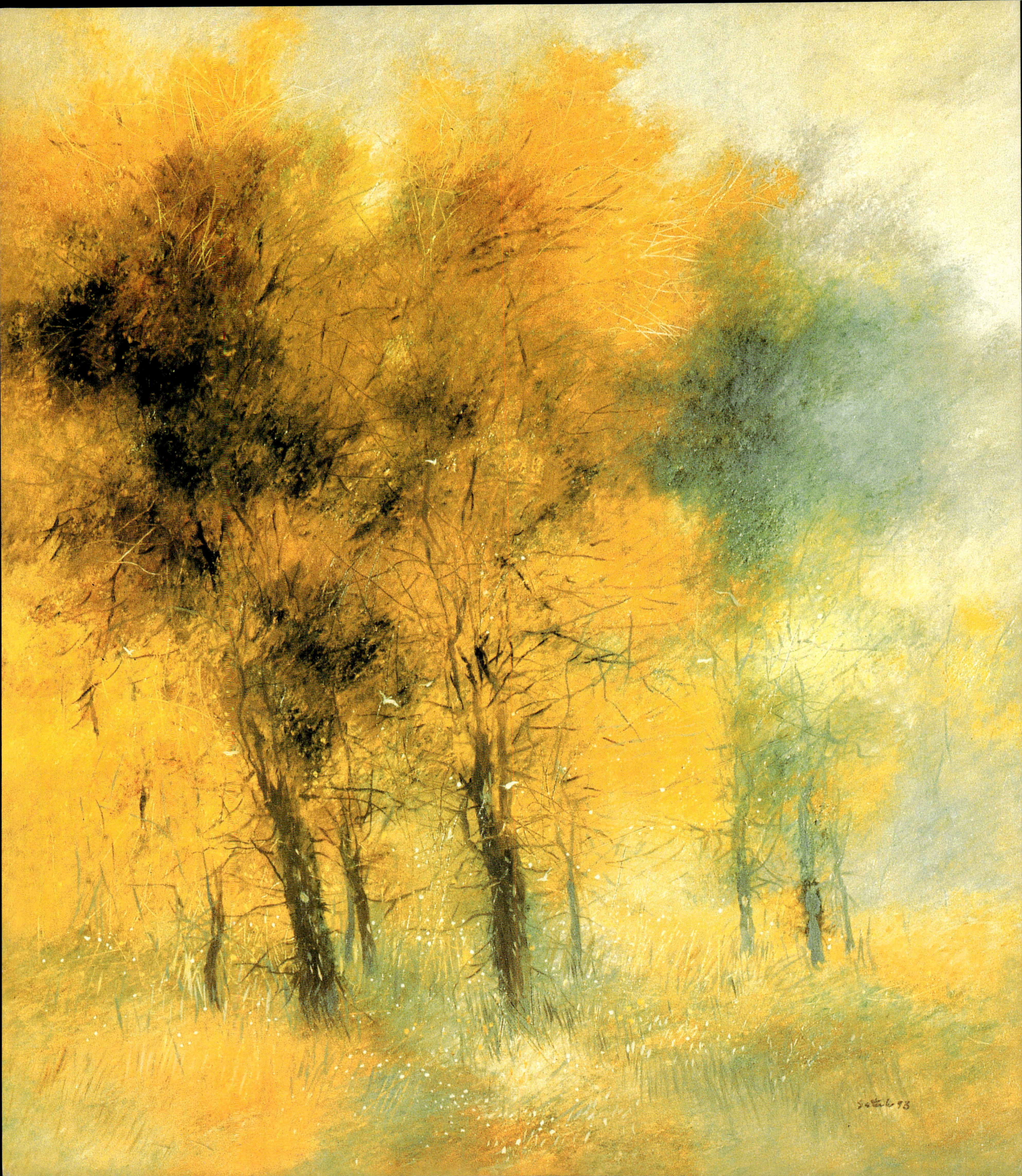

Master of Atmospherics

SATISH CHANDRA

MEENAKSHI CHANDRA

Lustre Press
Roli Books

To

Satish,

My

Soulmate

Preceding page 2: Oil on canvas, 1993.
Oil on canvas, 2001.

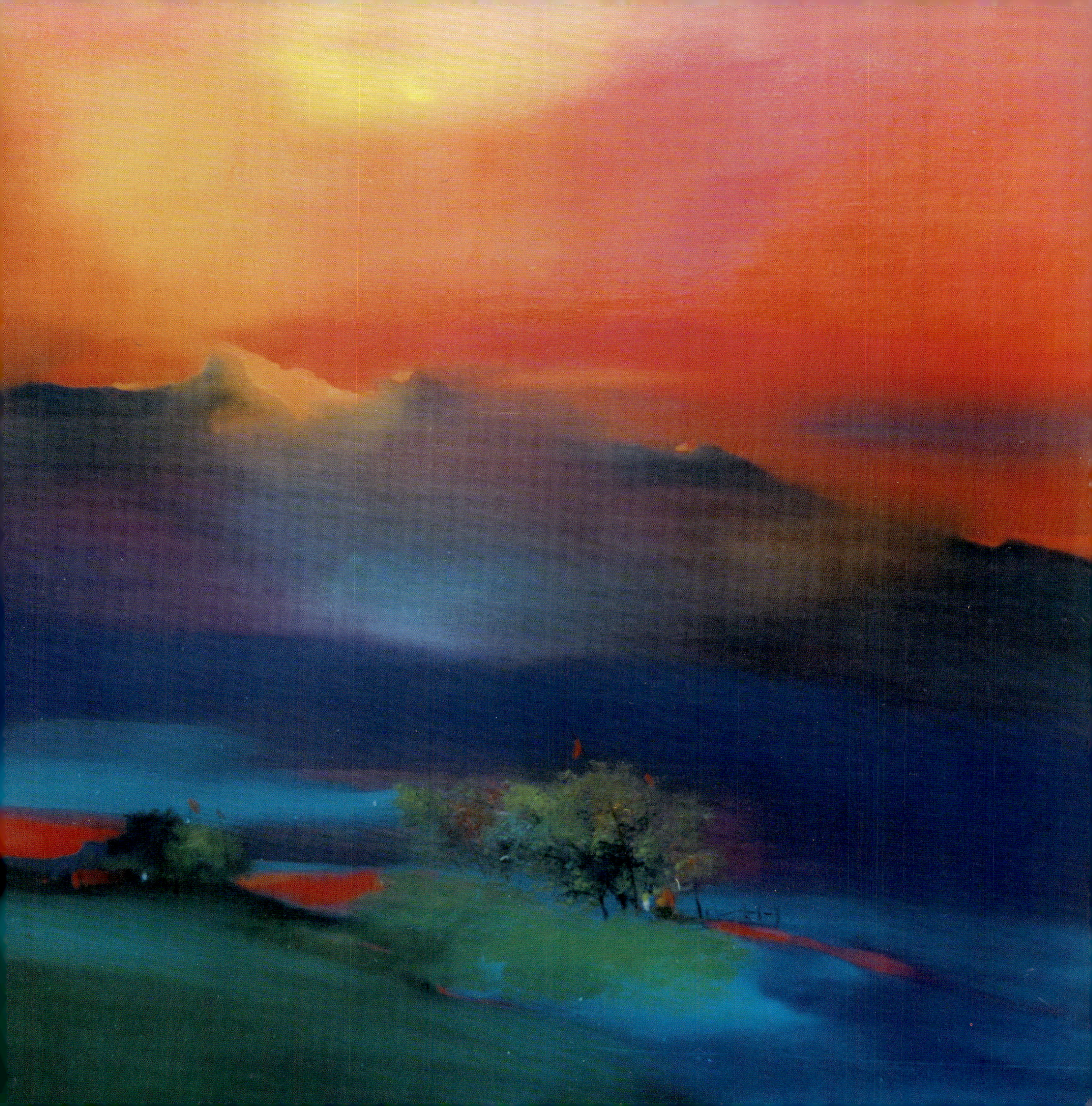

Acknowledgements

The author would like to thank Shobha Bhatia of Gallerie Ganesha for all her support.

All rights are reserved. No part of this publication may be transmitted or reproduced in any form or by any means without prior permission from the publisher.

ISBN: 81-7436-437-4

©Text and illustrations: Meenakshi Chandra 2006
© Design and layout: Roli Books 2006

Published in India by Roli Books Pvt. Ltd.
M-75, Greater Kailash-II Market, New Delhi-110 048, India.
Phone: ++91-11-29212271, ++91-11-29212782. Fax: ++91-11-29217185
Email: roli@vsnl.com; Website: rolibooks.com

Editor: Amit Agarwal; Design: Arati Subramanyam
Layout: Naresh Mondal; Production: Naresh Nigam

Printed and bound in Singapore

Contents

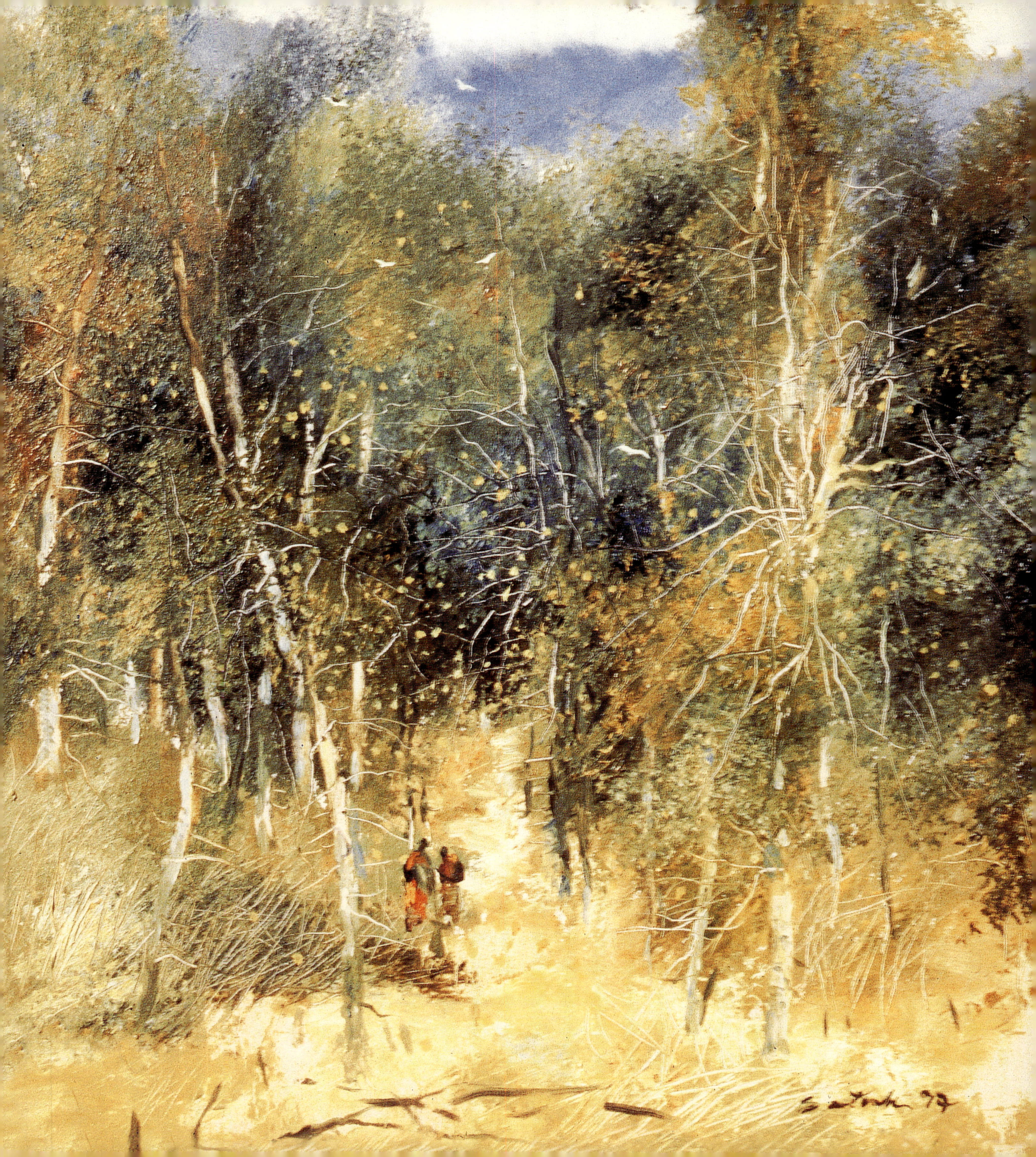

Foreword

Flowers grow everywhere, climbing up trellises, spilling over the railing of our terrace garden. The heady scent of 'mogra', 'raat ki rani', 'harsingar' and roses perfumes the air. Afloat in countless streams of thought, wading through different currents of emotion, I find my vision blurring with tears. Losing my husband, Satish Chandra, is a devastating blow – a loss that can never be recompensed.

Yet, I still cannot accept that he is not around. I can imagine him in his studio, in our bedroom, in his pooja room, or just standing beside me – looking at me with his tender loving smile, reassuring me that he will always be there with me. As I listen to the tune of Nature, the physicality of separation crumbles like illusions. My eyes span the vastness of the sky above and I can feel Satish's spiritual presence in the form of a divine light reflected in its crystal prism, turning from sapphire to gold to a ruby glimmer, surrounding me like a spring of energy. I gain strength and courage from the immense love, wisdom, hope and faith with which Satish has left me enriched. He lives on through everything he has touched, loved and created, filling my life with a depth and meaning it did not have before.

I started writing this book seven years ago, when Satish was still alive. It was fun listening to him talk about himself and his passion in life – landscape painting. Perhaps, it was more than that – I wanted to delve into the deepest crevices of his mind, where remained hidden some of the most magical, poignant and intense moments in time. Or maybe, I wanted to touch his soul and bask in its light, which drew people to him like a magnet.

I completed this book a few months before Satish passed away and I have decided to let it remain this way. It is written in the present tense and, very often, in the first person, as Satish speaks of his journey through life – his loves, hopes, faith, convictions, nightmares and dreams.

We see that as Satish grows, he evolves for himself another way of life – instead of breaking down under the pressures of life and its countless challenges, he learns to conquer them. And as Satish evolves, so does his work – it becomes a powerful mode of expressing his innermost feelings and experiences of life at a higher level, a vehicle to seek the ultimate truth. For the language of an artist is his work.

Satish believed that Nature is a window to reconnect with our inner selves. It is a source of spiritual inspiration for it makes us think about the Creator and his creation, allowing us to tune into our highest selves.

Satish lived life to the fullest, seeking harmony and inner peace. He would often say, "You have to be a part of Nature to enjoy its music lest it passes by unheard and unobserved."

To be able to understand and appreciate Satish's work, it is necessary to understand the person himself – all that went into the moulding of his personality. This is what I have attempted to do in the following pages.

– Meenakshi Chandra

Facing page: Oil on canvas, 1997.

A Master of Atmospherics

"Counted among the practitioners of a genre so vulgarised by academists as the traditional landscape, Satish Chandra appears as a distinct and notable exception.

Using the same implements available to the academists – those of light and shade, of external and tonal ranges – this artist fashions inspired portrayals of nature, which, in oils, possess all the delicacy of an *aquarelle*.

Chandra's forests are an ensemble of deftly scuffed foliage, scumbled undergrowth, and brambles and long grass that the knife has scratched across the canvas. Figures appear occasionally, losing their way in the shrubbery.

The motif of wings, to mark the migrations of birds, is another shorthand device to indicate animal life

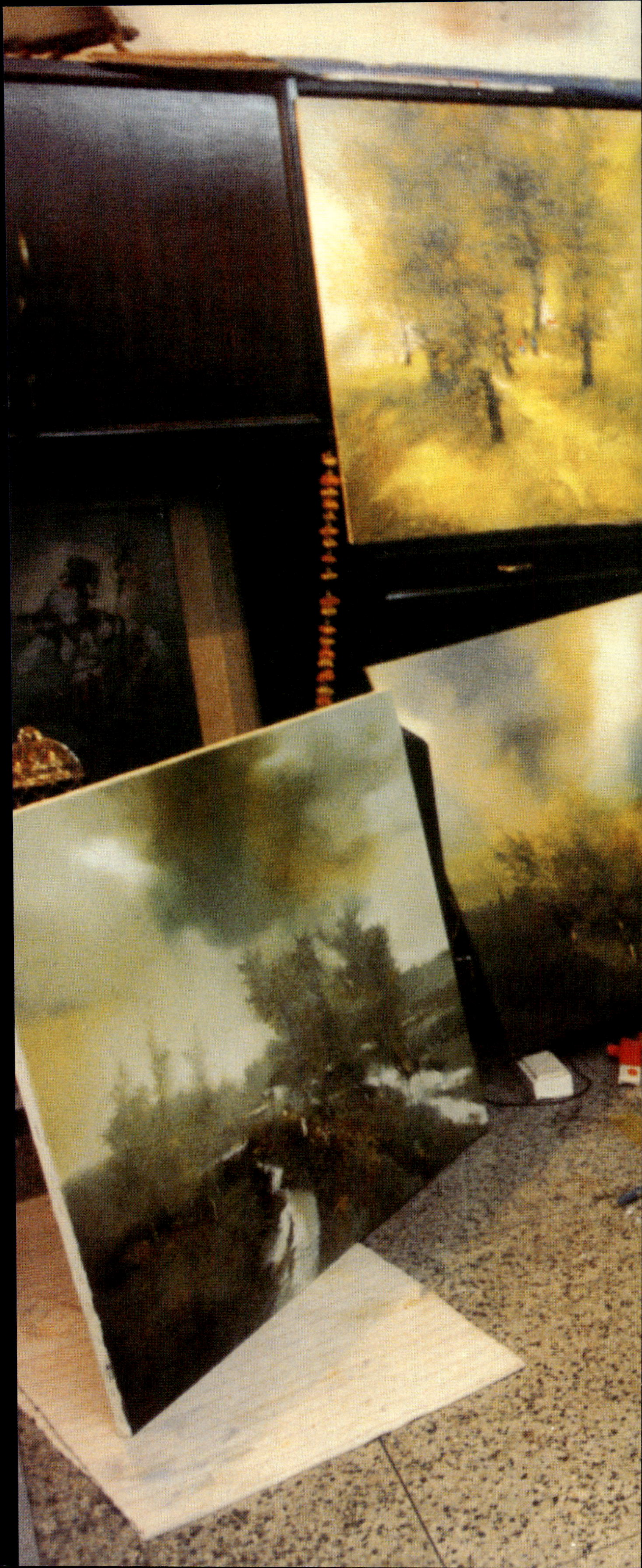

Satish in his studio surrounded by his signature landscapes.

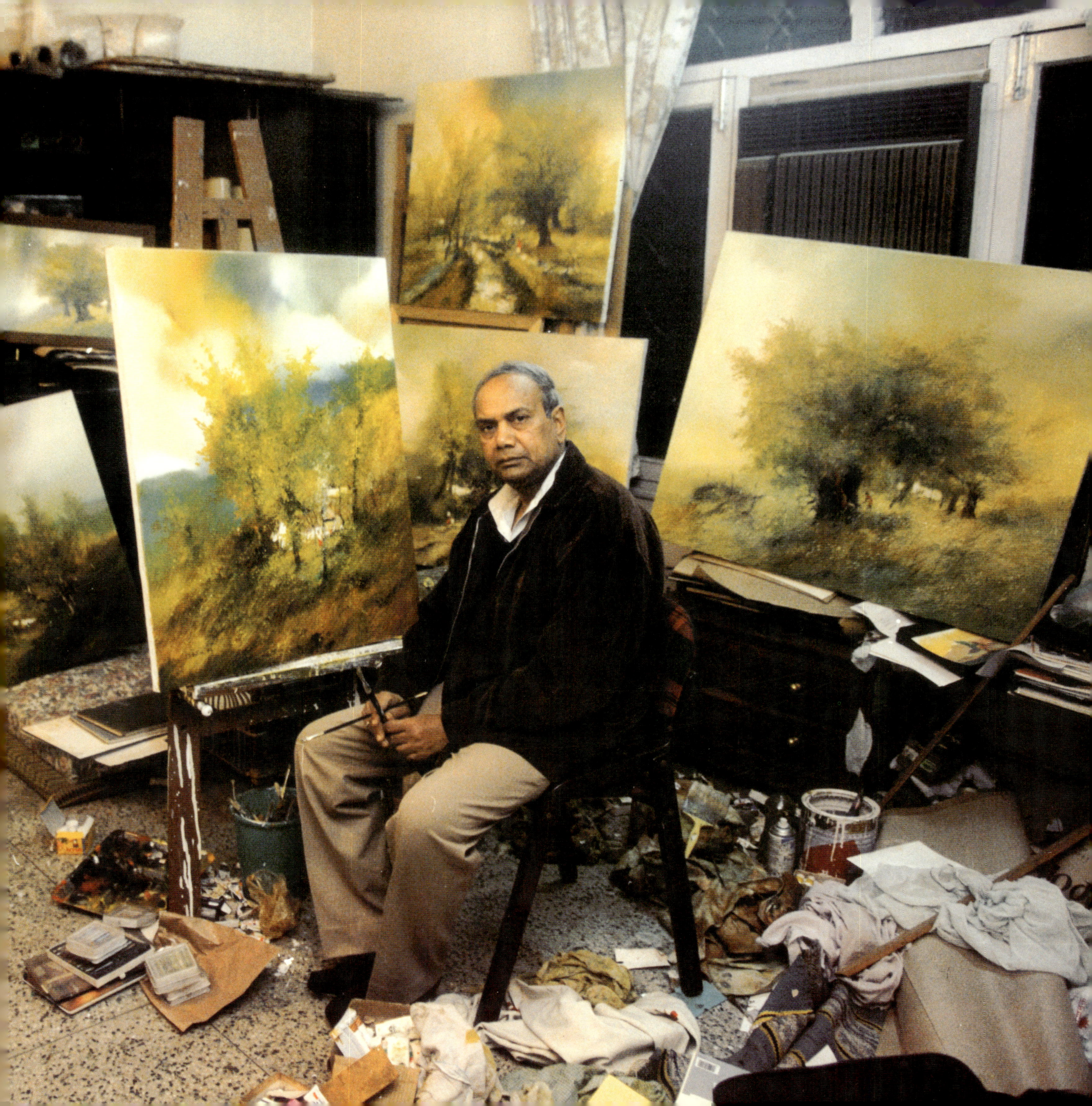

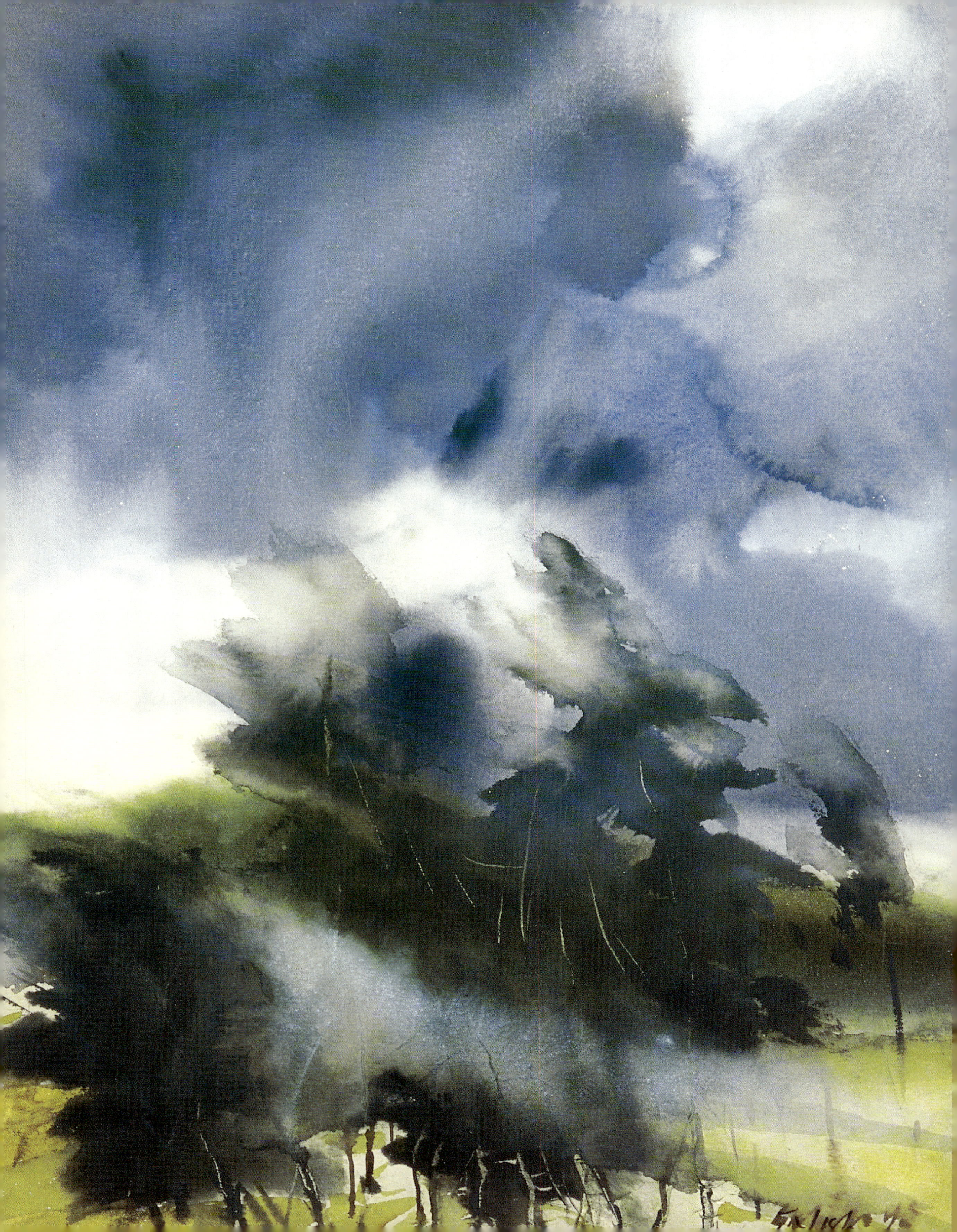

in this otherwise unchallenged realm of the arboreal.

The ghosts of Corot, of Turner and Gainsborough animate these paintings: the misty air, the treatment of the leaves – which sweep upwards like flames – the russett and flame-orange that dominate each work, attest to the continuation of a great tradition.

A master of atmospherics, Satish Chandra lures the sleeping earth into springing up in fire: smouldering orange soil sears into auburn bushes, which themselves spread into tree-bursts, the viridian tinged with bronze where the autumn light catches it.

A quivering motion effects magical changes in the landscapes – a marsh and a tree exchange colours; tracks which, from one angle, seemed to be leading out of a copse, begin to point fiercely into it, with a slight shift in the viewer's position.

The cumulative impression of Satish Chandra's landscapes is one of splendid isolation; and yet, this is neither a celebratory nor a joyous splendour.

Most obviously in his images of desolate moorland – its blizzard riding down a slate-grey horizon – and more subtly in the muffled explosions that bathe the meadows in mustard, one senses the cultivation of a distance in time, between the scenes described, and the viewer.

We are not allowed to participate in the rites of spring and autumn; we are held apart, remote from a roar and a swish that we cannot hear, that are stilled by the sobering touch of grey.

And when we see this, our exile from the scenes of sylvan glory, we know that we are not presented with a facile, theatrical encapsulation of nature for urban consumption, but a deeply poignant knowledge of what we have lost."

– Ranjit Hoskote
The Times of India, Bombay
31 March 1990

Facing page: Watercolour on paper, 1996.

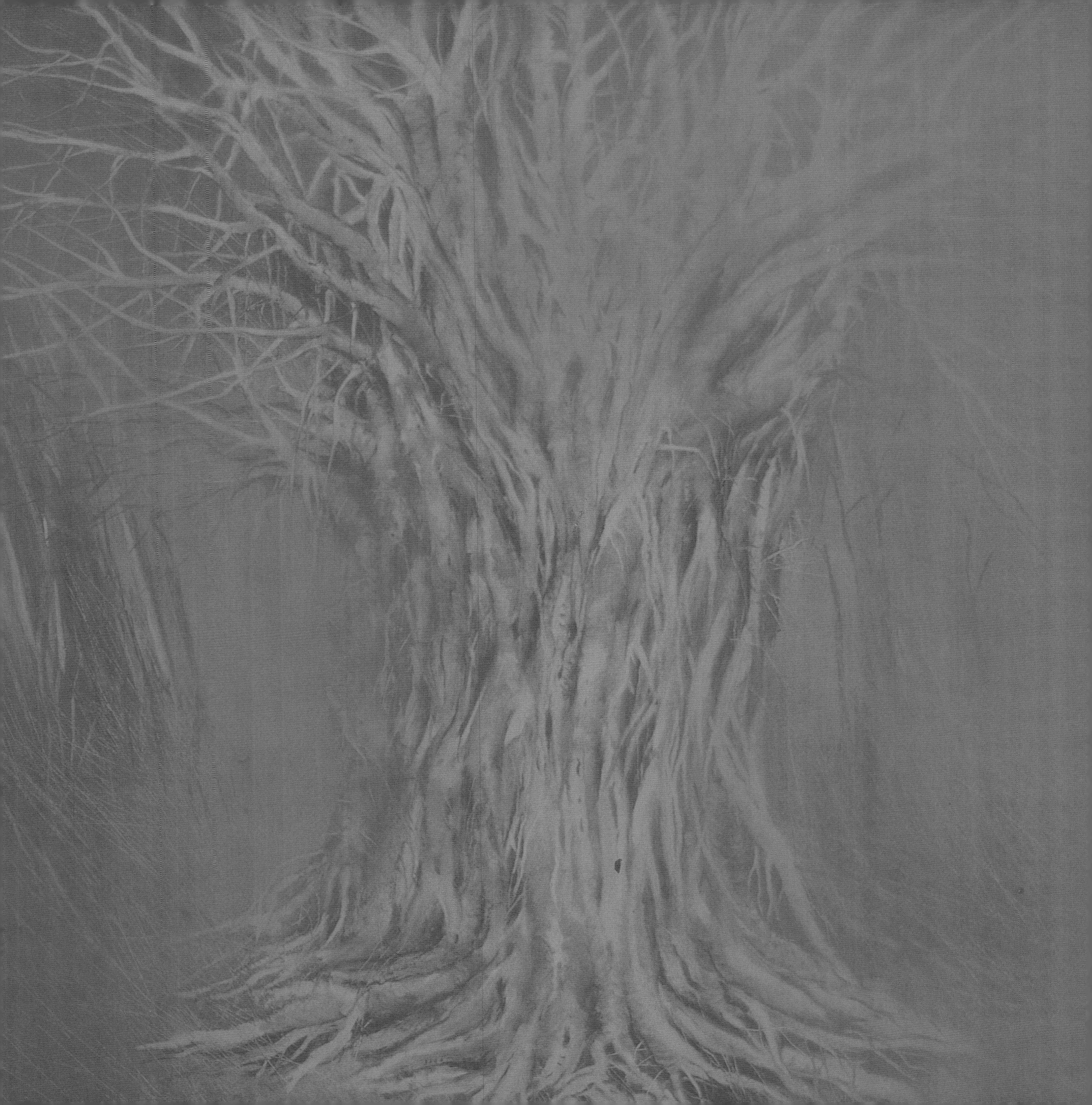

Childhood and Education

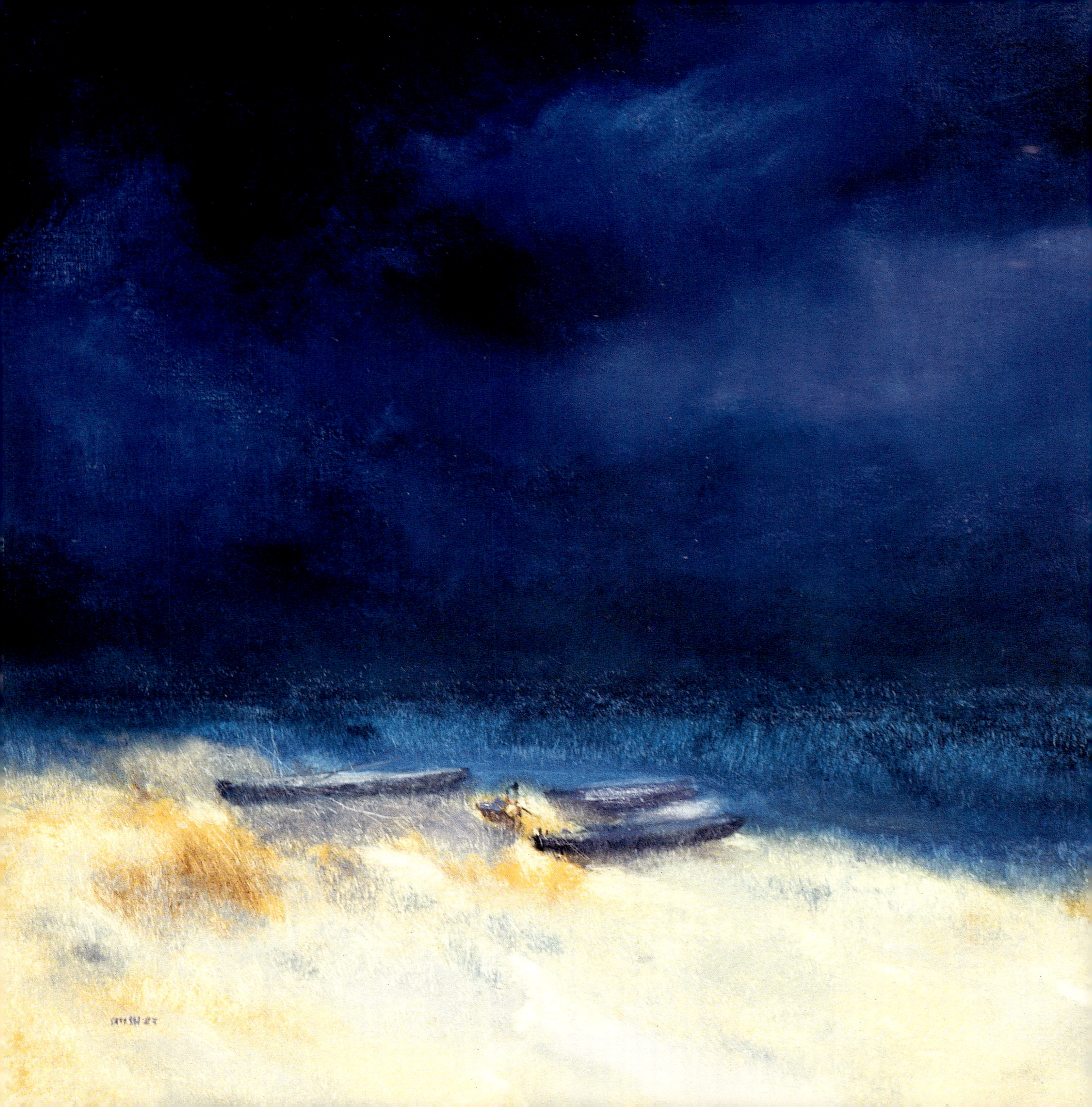

Satish Chandra was born on 5 June 1940 in Ghaziabad. His father, late Manohar Lal Aggarwal, was an officer in the Indian Railways, and Satish was the fourth child among nine brothers and sisters.

Satish's childhood was spent in Khurja, in Uttar Pradesh, where his family lived with his great-grandparents and paternal uncles and aunts in their ancestral haveli known as the 'Patthar Wali Haveli'. Built in 1840, the beautiful haveli, with its intricate carvings in wood and stone, still stood in all its splendour a hundred years later, with elephants at the entrance gates and 'buggies' pulled by horses.

Khurja is a tehsil which, at that time, abounded in natural beauty. It was surrounded by lush green fields, lakes and rivulets, rich fruit orchards, mango groves and rolling meadows, the very air crisp and fresh, laden with the sweet scent of flowers and foliage. Satish grew up in the lap of Nature – and it left its indelible mark on him.

Shyama Devi, Satish's mother, hailed from Jhengirabad, a tehsil in Bulandshahar. Petite, fair and good-looking, she was the daughter of a prosperous cloth merchant. Her marriage to Satish's father was arranged through a matchmaker. She was only fifteen at the time, ten years younger to her husband. After marriage, her husband had brought her to Khurja to live in their ancestral haveli.

Being a railway officer, Satish's father was transferred every two years to a new district or tehsil. Satish's mother decided to stay back in Khurja with the children so as not to disturb their schooling. Like many of his generation, Satish's father was seldom openly affectionate. So the children, specially Satish, did not feel very comfortable with him. "I met Pitaji only when he came home to celebrate special occasions and festivals like Holi and Deepawali with us in Khurja. Since I was with him for short spells only, I hardly got to know him or to feel like I was with my father. He was

Facing page: Watercolour on paper.

a well-built man, 6'-3" tall. He was a disciplinarian and I found him formidable."

But his bond with his mother was deep and unseverable. Even now I can see how much he must have loved Amma, for every time he speaks about her his eyes cloud over and his voice becomes wistful and husky, as if he misses her presence even after all these years. "I spent a lot of time with Amma when my elder brothers were at school or out of town. In a way she was my best friend in those years. I had not started going to school and so I would hold onto Amma's pallu, and follow her all over the haveli, even into the kitchen! She was a very simple woman with a heart of gold. She worked hard all day, catering to the needs and comfort of a big family like ours. The day would leave her exhausted. Yet she was always full of love."

Lying with his head in Amma's lap, nibbling on his favourite home-made 'besan ka laddoo', Satish would listen to stories from the Ramayana and the Mahabharata. In her softly lilting voice she would also talk to him about the sun, the moon, the stars, and their Creator.

It is not surprising that Satish always had a natural tendency towards introspection, for Amma often found him meditating under a bargad tree in

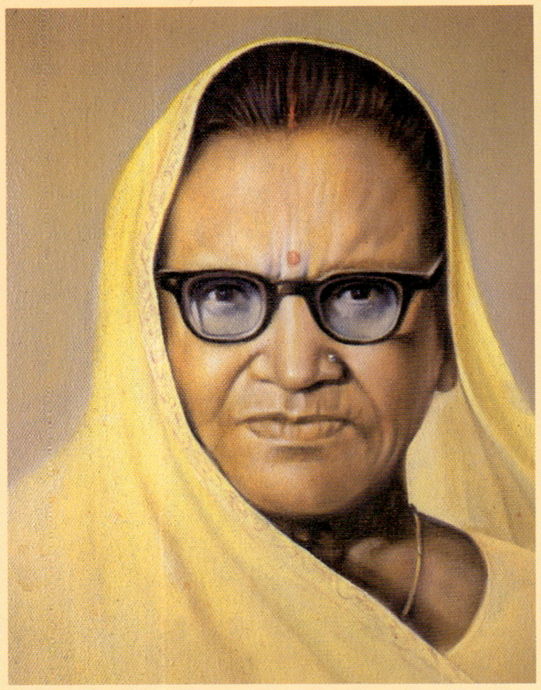

Shyama Devi, Satish's mother. Satish's bond with his mother was deep and unseverable.

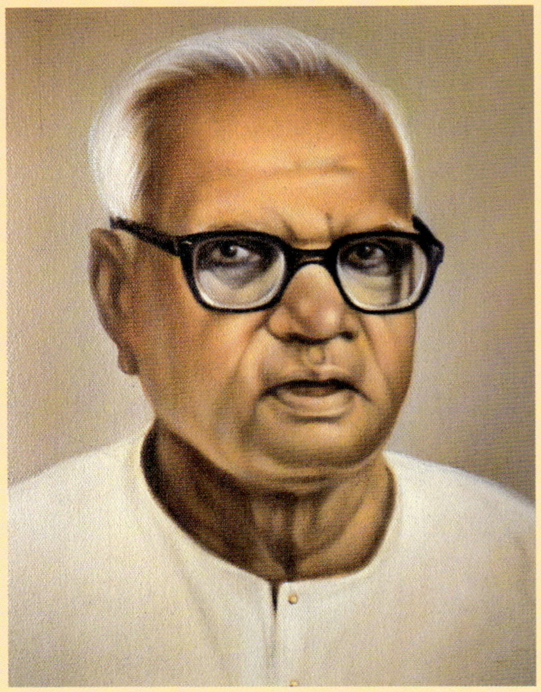

Manohar Lal Aggarwal, Satish's 'formidable' father.
Facing page: Oil on canvas, 2000.

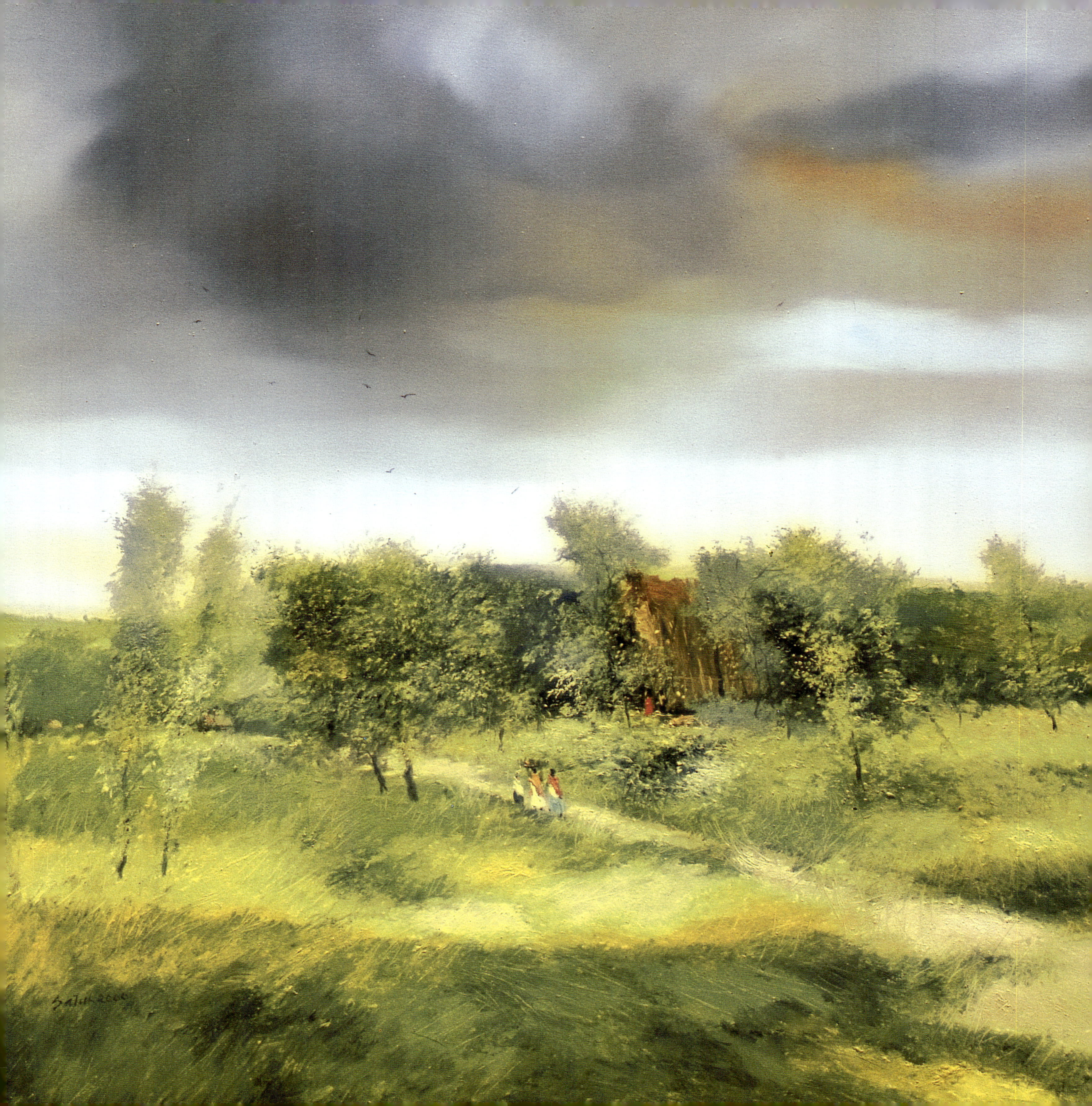

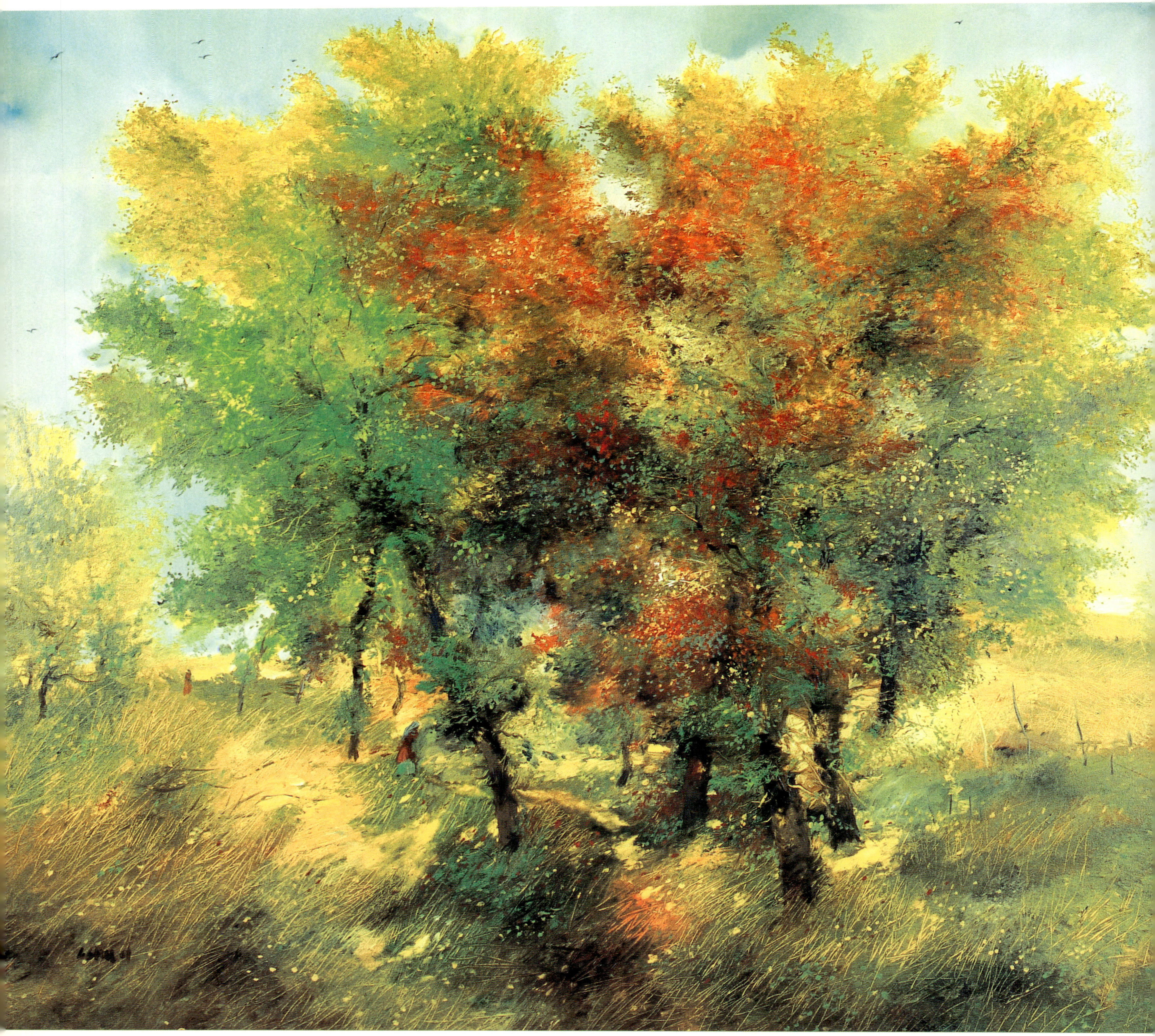

the compound of the haveli, even at the tender age of three.

Over the years, one of the things that has kept him strong is his belief in God and his unwavering faith in the power of prayer and meditation. The pooja room in our house is accessible through a door in Satish's studio and to get to it one has to walk past brushes, colours, the palette and his paintings. Sometimes I take a peek into his studio and find him in a deep trance – his face full of concentration, eyes fixed on a distant spot in space – oblivious to the world. At times, with bated breath, I have crept closer to make sure that he is still breathing!

Satish's sharp and vivid memory makes him fondly recall his childhood days, which he holds so dear to his heart even today. As we sit, holding hands on the swing in our terrace – he likes doing that when he is not busy – he is like a little boy again. With an impish smile that makes his eyes glow softly, he goes down memory lane, back to his childhood days in Khurja. He tells me, "When I was a kid, I dreamed such great dreams. Often I visualized myself as a sports hero or as a famous actor, writer or artist. I really believed that I could do, have and be whatever I wanted to be." I could see that his dreams came from his heart's deepest desires. Over the years he never lost sight of his dreams, fanning the tiny inner sparks into flames of achievement. His zest for life, his deep conviction and trust in himself to create the kind of life he wanted, has its roots in his childhood. "I had a wonderful childhood", he says. "Fun

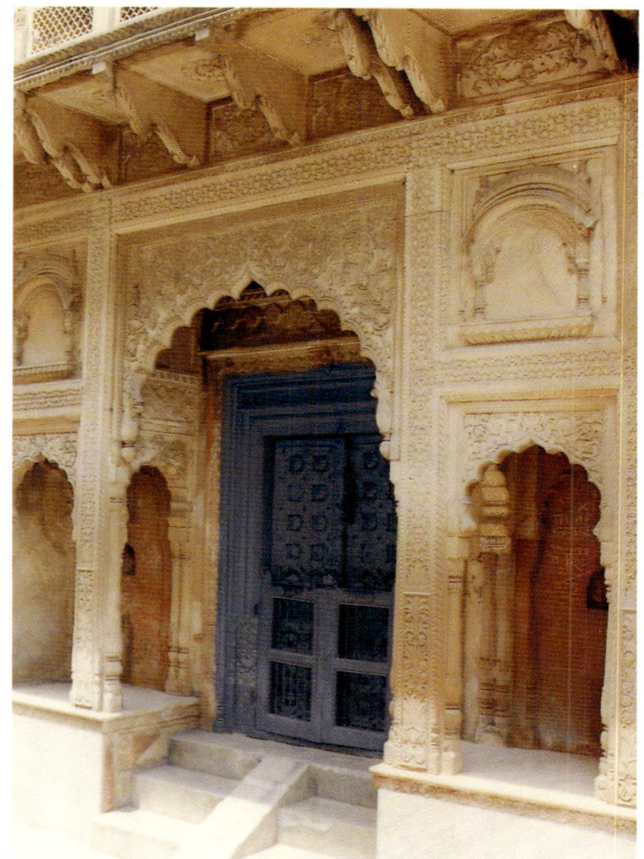

Entrance to Patthar Wali Haveli: Satish's childhood was spent in this beautiful ancestral house in Khurja in Uttar Pradesh.
Facing page: Oil on canvas, 2001.

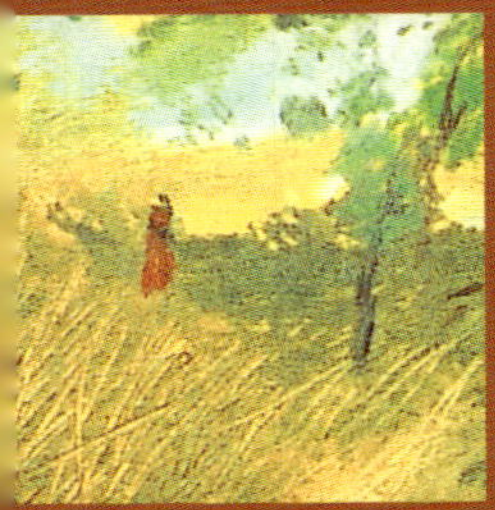

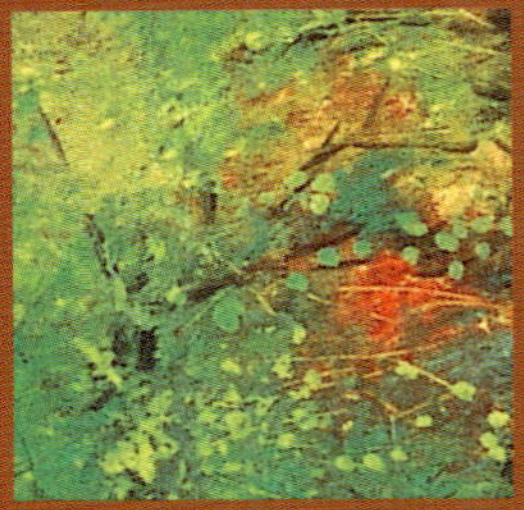

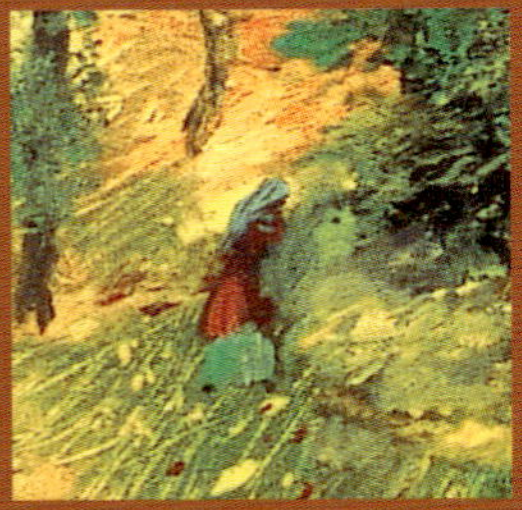

came in the form of simple pleasures. Fun was spending a glorious afternoon skinny-dipping in a canal, splashing around, letting droplets of water drip into my mouth. Or, riding through the woods on my bicycle. Fun was plucking fresh ripe fruit like apples, guavas and mangoes from our orchard and the mango groves, and eating these perched on the branch of a tree. Or the delight of chasing and catching butterflies, bumblebees and grasshoppers and then letting them go again. Or then, tracing the course of the sun across the sky from sunrise to sunset. The feeling of freedom and the sheer joy of being alive was intoxicating."

He continues to reminisce, "Driven by a thirst to absorb the beauty of Nature, I would often gather my friends in the neighbourhood during the early hours of the morning. We would then walk along a barely visible path amidst the thick grass, tall trees and exotic flowers until we arrived at a clearing. At the edge of the clearing was a lake of crystal clear aqua-blue water covered with pink, white and purple lotuses. And rolling away into the distant horizon were green fields. We would bend on our knees, look into the water, make a wish and pray for it to come true. I honestly believed that God was somewhere there, listening to me. We would then return home wending our way through the fields, plucking and eating the sweet green peas, tomatoes or carrots that grew there in abundance – and we had to reach school on time!" The little-boy smile is there again as he tells me, "I had such a curiosity for life. I was an adventurer."

This curiosity for life and the spirit of adventure are an integral part of Satish and have affected his life in more ways than one.

From the age of six, Satish had a penchant for copying the form of things. By the age of ten he was somehow able to fathom the growth patterns of plants and trees and the structure of birds, animals, insects and fish. His copies would be filled with such drawings. "At the same time, my favourite games in school were hockey, 'kabaddi' and wrestling," he tells me enthusiastically.

As memories of his childhood waft into Satish's mind, he remembers one incident in particular, the impact of which left him shocked and bewildered. It was 1947. He was barely seven years old. One day, as he sat with his brothers eating sandwiches and drinking milk, he overheard snatches of conversation between his father and the other elders of the family. "I gathered that the heart of our town had been caught in a surge of communal frenzy – a sort of epidemic had gripped the Hindus and the Muslims. All of us were told to stay indoors and not stir out of the haveli. Suddenly I heard screaming and shouting interspersed with hysterical shrieks which grew louder and louder as people ran down the street shouting, 'Kill! Kill!'

"Curiosity got the better of me and I ran up to the roof-top. Ducking behind the parapet, I peeped through its jaali work. I could see the street below littered with dead bodies, heads rolling. Men were being hung from trees and strangled. Blood flowed in rivulets all around. Petrified, my heart thudding against my chest, I wanted to get away. I found myself transfixed to the spot, unable to move. With bated breath I looked up at the sky. The sun was losing its noontime glow. The shadows of the trees along the compound wall had lengthened across the paved path. To me they looked like swords and daggers strewn on the ground. A stone came hurtling through the air towards me, missing my head by inches. I found my feet and stumbled down the stairs back to my room. In the mirror on the wall I caught a glimpse of myself – dishevelled hair, face smudged with tears. I went into the bathroom and splashed cold water on my face." Satish looks at me, there is pain in his voice, "It was a nightmare. How I wish I could blot out the memory of it all."

Childhood is the most impressionable stage in life and this incident had a profound effect on Satish's heart and mind. It is one thing to talk about secularism, but Satish actually lives the life of a secular person. He does not believe in caste discrimination. He does not even use his surname, Aggarwal. Very few people have a network of so many and such loving friends as we do, irrespective of their caste and creed. Satish dotes on them for "they are fine human beings – and that is what really matters."

When Satish was around twelve years old, his father was posted at Ghaziabad. During the summer vacation his mother would, along with the children, join her husband. They lived in a big bungalow, close to the Ghaziabad station. "My passion for railways goes deep. It is a passion I first felt when I was very young and obviously nostalgia keeps it alive," he tells me. I believe him for I have myself seen his sense of excitement at

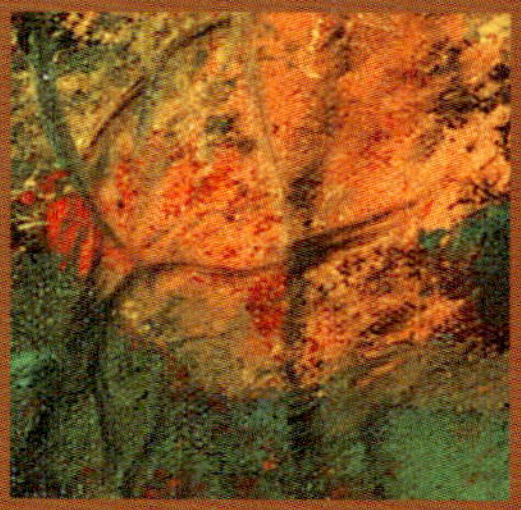

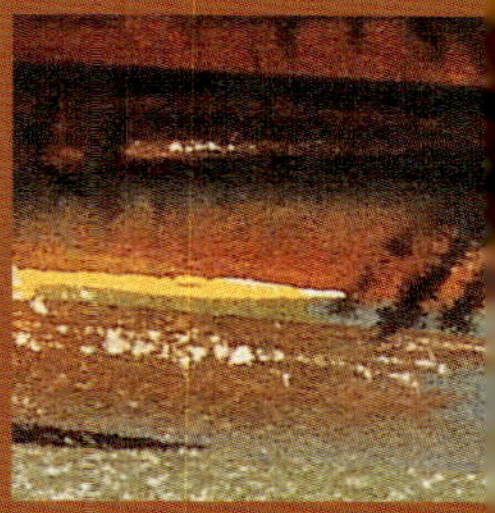

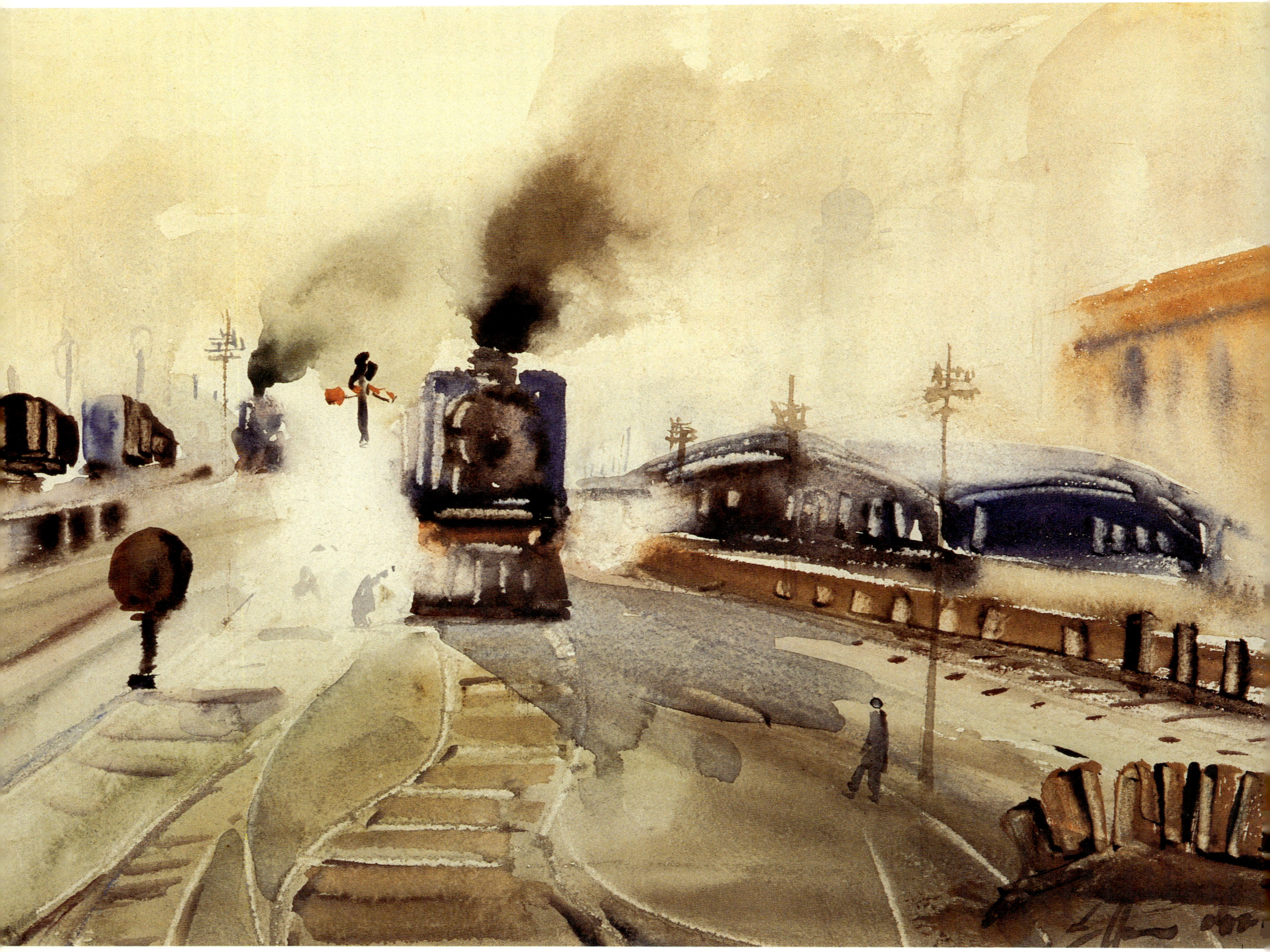

By the age of ten he was somehow able to fathom the growth patterns of plants and trees and the structure of birds, animals, insects and fish.

railway platforms as he will watch a train hurtling towards him, the distant rumbling rising to a thundering climax as the train roars through the station and screeches to a halt – and then the excitement of bagging the seat next to the window, and eating food once the train started moving! Excited like a child, he tells me, "I remember jumping on and off the train, hanging out of the window to watch the brave little engine blowing its heart out puffing up whirls of smoke as it chugged along the track. The sound of the wheels on the rails – steel on steel – and the sensation of speed, left me enthralled."

This passion for trains, speed and movement can be seen in the many in-depth studies of trains and railway tracks he did in charcoal, pen and ink and watercolour during his student days at the Government College of Arts and Crafts, Lucknow.

Later, as Satish grew older, trains became a symbol of a journey through life, "always moving forward, telling me that no matter how much I love the past there has to be movement and change." His convictions and his passion for life have given him the inner strength to avoid stagnation and overcome hurdles in life.

Satish enjoyed watching movies with his sisters and brothers as much as he enjoyed taking part in the 'Ramlila' held during Dussehra every year. The children had built an open-air stage in the fruit orchard, where they would invite their family and friends and enact scenes from the Ramayana, the Mahabharata and other plays and skits.

He recalls an incident that amuses him even today. Once, after watching the film *Jhansi Ki Rani*, he came out of the theatre highly impressed with a scene where the Rani jumps off a moving train straight onto horseback, and gallops away. "The scene generated a sense of great power, arousing the 'hero' within me! Unable to find a good horse, I managed to catch hold of a donkey and requested my friend to run with it alongside a moving train." The two boys found a zig-zag portion of the train's journey when the train had a maximum speed of 12 mph.

Facing page: Watercolour on paper, 1962.

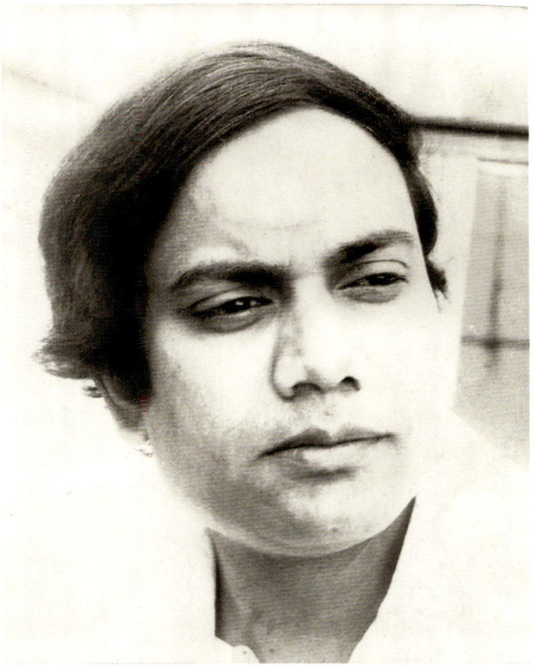

A young Satish: Satish's versatility was evident in his teens itself, when he gave various artistic disciplines a try. *Facing page:* Oil on canvas, 2002.

"From here I decided to jump off the train onto the donkey's back and gallop away. To my surprise and chagrin, I heard a heavy thud as I fell to the ground and rolled into a ditch.... The donkey had let me down! I felt so silly!" I burst out laughing trying to picture the scene. But then, seeing the naughty look in his eyes, it really wasn't all that surprising!

Satish showed an early talent for drawing but this was not encouraged by his father, who had planned a career for him as an engineer. In 1956 he was sent to J.S. Inter College, Khurja to further his education. Here he was encouraged by his drawing teacher, who suggested that he should draw outdoors, observing Nature first hand. Intrigued, the young boy snatched every opportunity to sketch and draw.

Good at academics as well as co-curricular activities, Satish was selected the captain of J.S. Inter College hockey team, and they did not lose a single match. "The experience of winning a match was exhilarating. I would return home with a boxful of 'gajar ka halwa' to share with the whole family. After dinner we would gather around 'angeethis' in the huge 'aangan' of our haveli and there would be singing, dancing and merry-making to celebrate the occasion. The orange glow of the burning coal in the 'angeethi', the leaping and dancing flames radiating light and warmth, the spluttering sparks like flecks of golden yellow and the twinkle of the stars studded in the deep blue velvet of the sky above, fascinated and excited me, tugging at my heart strings more than the strains of the songs.... and then, instinctively, I would look at Amma." Satish's eyes cloud over, there is a catch in his voice as he says, "my eyes would fill with wonder, what was there in that face – the sun, God or a messenger of God? No face could be more beautiful than my mother's, which was lit by dreams and the light of love for me."

Around this time, something very strange happened. One day there was a knock on the door. Satish opened it. An ascetic with a long flowing beard stood in the doorway. Refusing to enter the haveli, he asked Satish to bring a few grains of rice. Satish brought a big bowl of rice and offered it to the sage. The sage picked out just a few grains. He then sent for Satish's mother and told her that this boy had taken birth in the wrong family and would very soon leave them and go away. Saying so, the ascetic started walking away from the haveli and as mother and son stood watching, he suddenly just disappeared. "Silently, I looked at Amma from the corner of my eye. Tears streamed down her cheeks as she

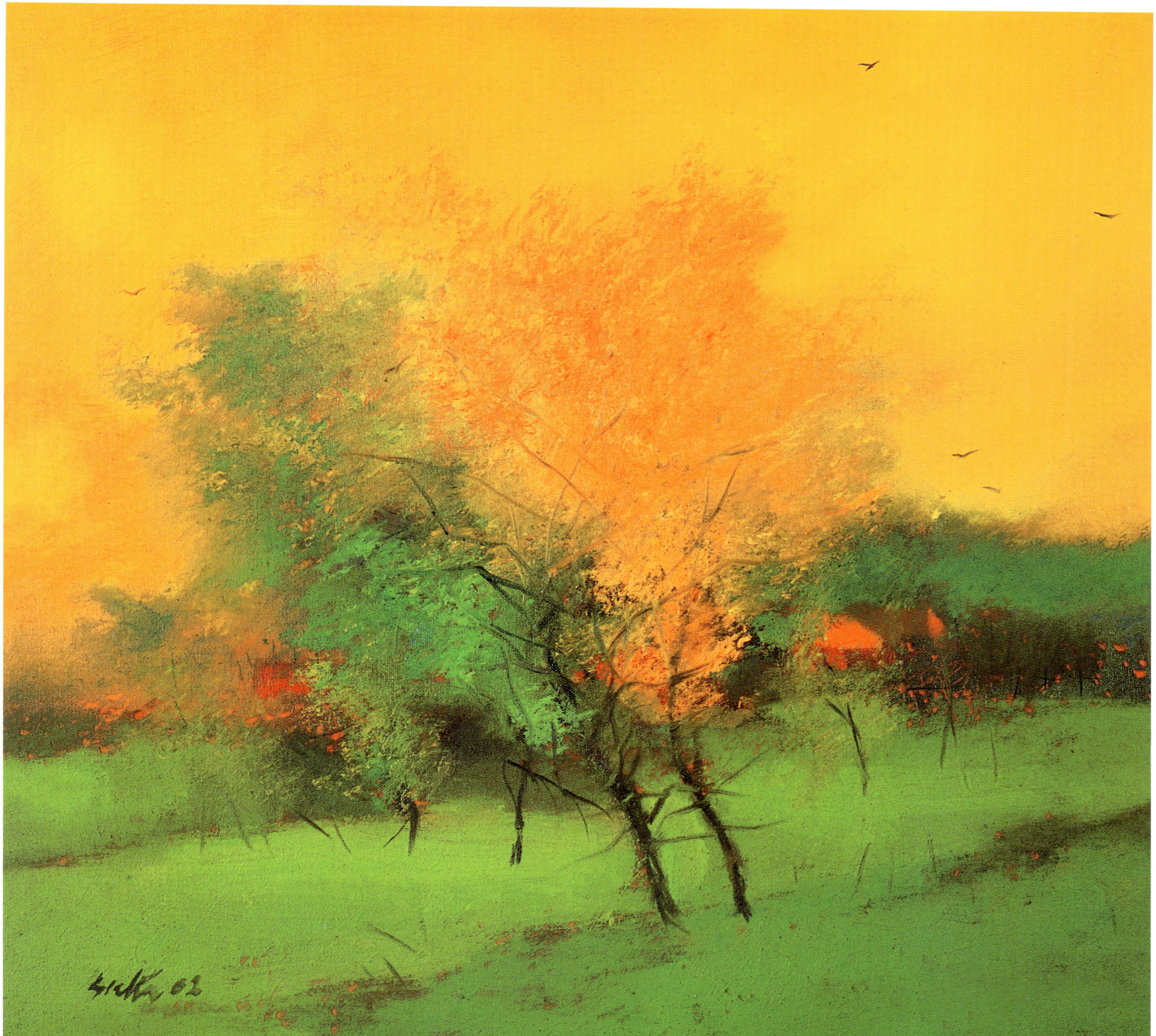

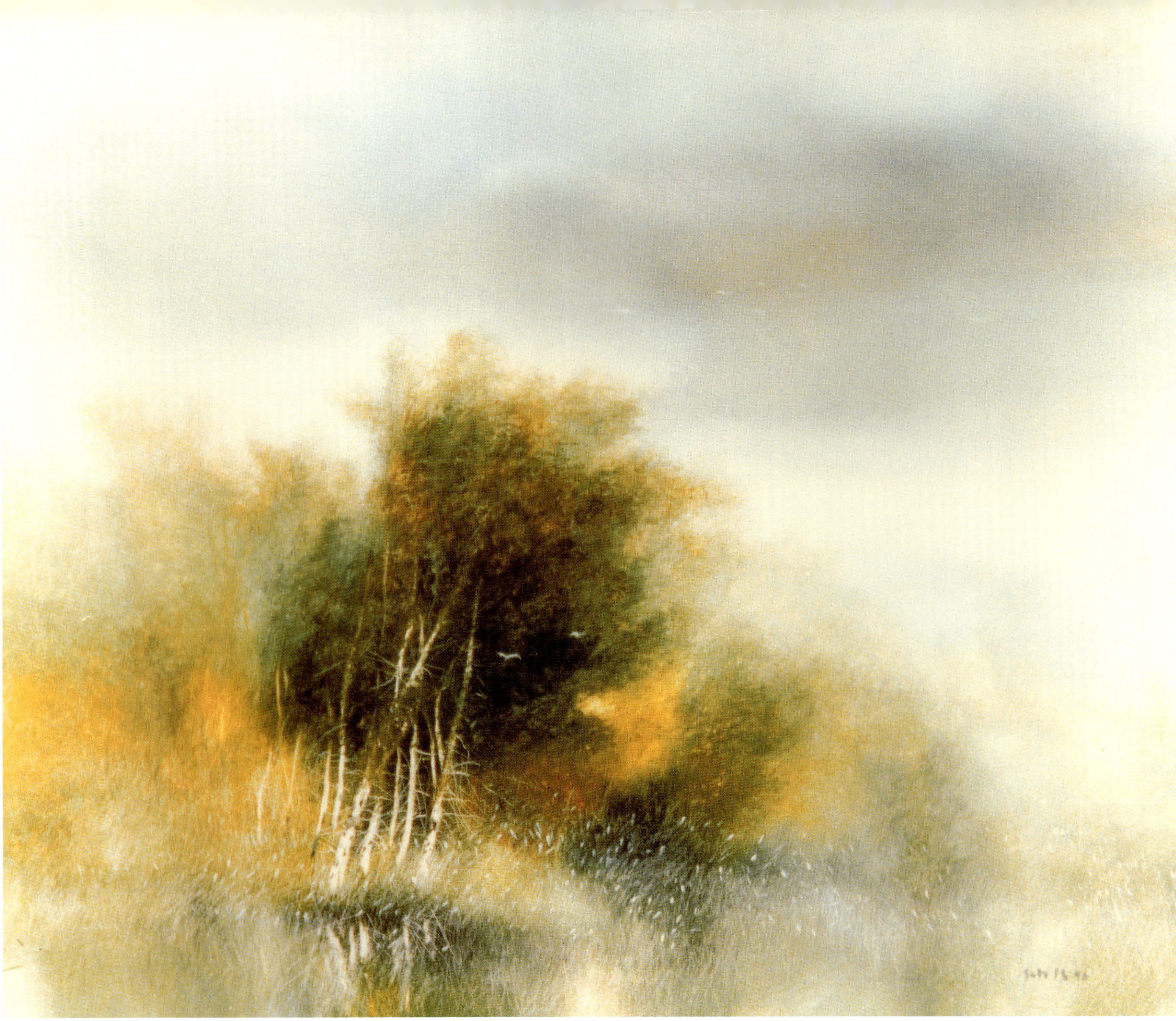

quietly turned and went back into the haveli."

While he was still in his early teens, a love of cinema gripped him. He decided to go to Bombay and try his luck in the world of celluloid. He went directly to the famous film personality, Jagirdar, and appeared for an audition, during which he delivered fiery and powerful lines from *Prithviraj Chauhan*. "As I came to a halt, there was pin-drop silence. I thought perhaps I had lost my chance to be a hero on the movie screen. And then I saw Jagigrdar 'dada' moving towards me with outstretched hands. As I bent down to touch his feet, he pulled me up and clasped me to his chest. I had passed the test! Breathless which excitement, I rang up my parents to

Oil on canvas, 1998.

tell them the news. 'Pitaji' took the call. He yelled at me to return home immediately. There was no point in trying to convince him otherwise, for he firmly believed that children from good families did not go into films."

Obediently, Satish returned home, disappointed, disturbed and a little confused. "I wanted to be a movie star!" he said to his mother. Quiet but intelligent, his mother understood. By now she knew this young boy was a versatile genius and needed to get away from his domineering father. During the school's summer vacation, she sent him to Delhi to his paternal aunt. Here, Satish encountered writers and artists from the fields of drama,

Oil on canvas, 1998.

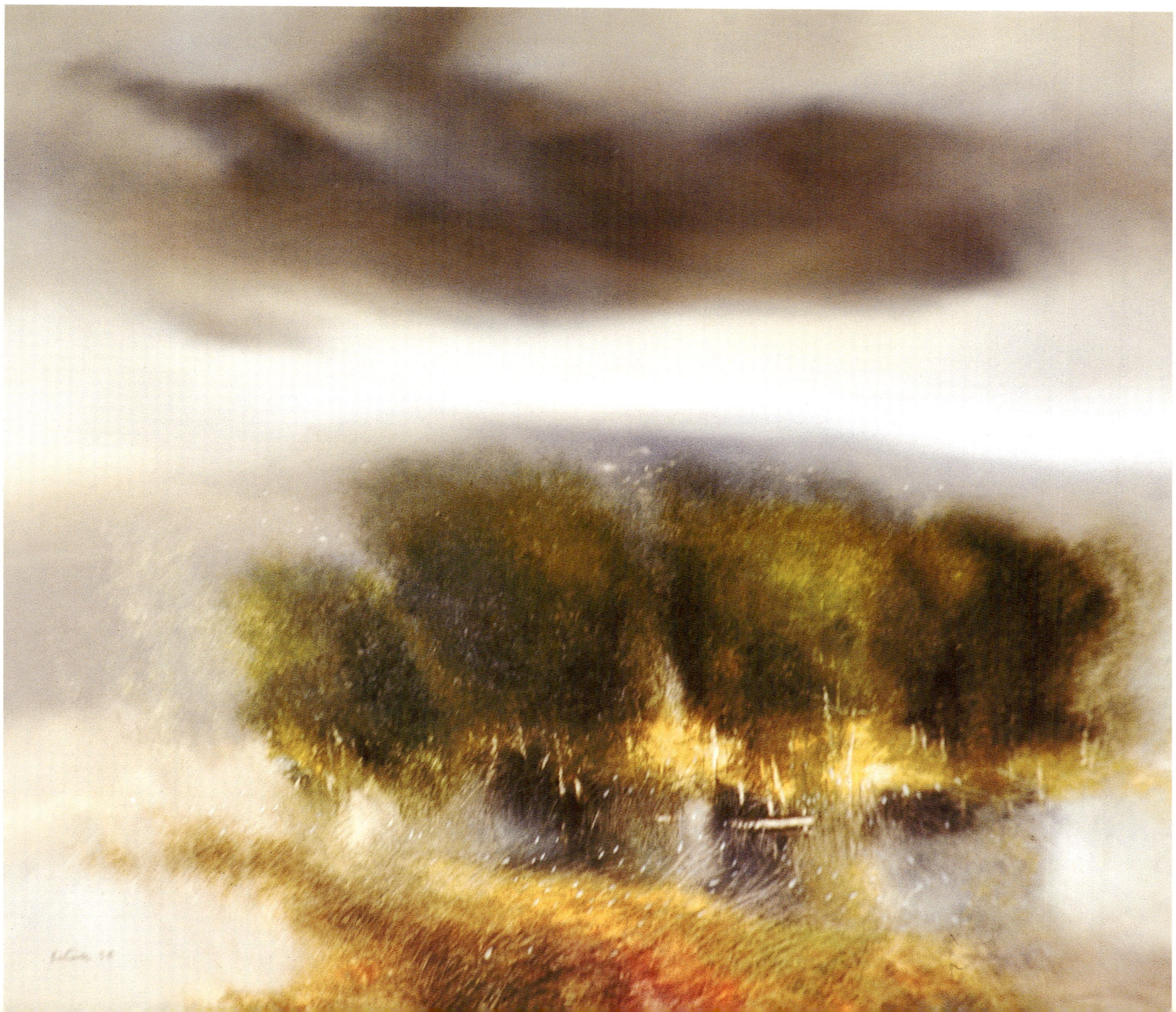

The search for satiation within him continued... and then he found an avenue to express himself, one that gave him satisfaction, a sense of joy and completeness and that brought out his genius – landscape painting.

painting and sculpture. Enamoured by them, he decided to give all disciplines a try. He tried dabbling in poetry and even theatre. However, he soon gave these up. The search for satiation within him continued... and then he found an avenue to express himself, one that gave him satisfaction, a sense of joy and completeness and that brought out his genius – landscape painting. Summer vacation was coming to an end. He returned home. He had found his passion in life.

Around this time, Satish's father was transferred to Kanpur, and the family moved in with him.

By the time he completed his schooling from Government Higher Secondary School at Kanpur, his father was still refusing to accept that his son's talents could not be suppressed. Nevertheless, in 1958, Satish boarded the train to Lucknow, appeared for the competitive entrance examination at the Government College of Arts and Crafts, Lucknow and was selected and admitted there. He stayed as a boarder and worked hard at academic painting, but his instincts led him towards Nature, its first-hand observation, and landscape painting.

During this time period, Satish was driven by an unquenchable thirst to

Facing page: Oil on canvas.

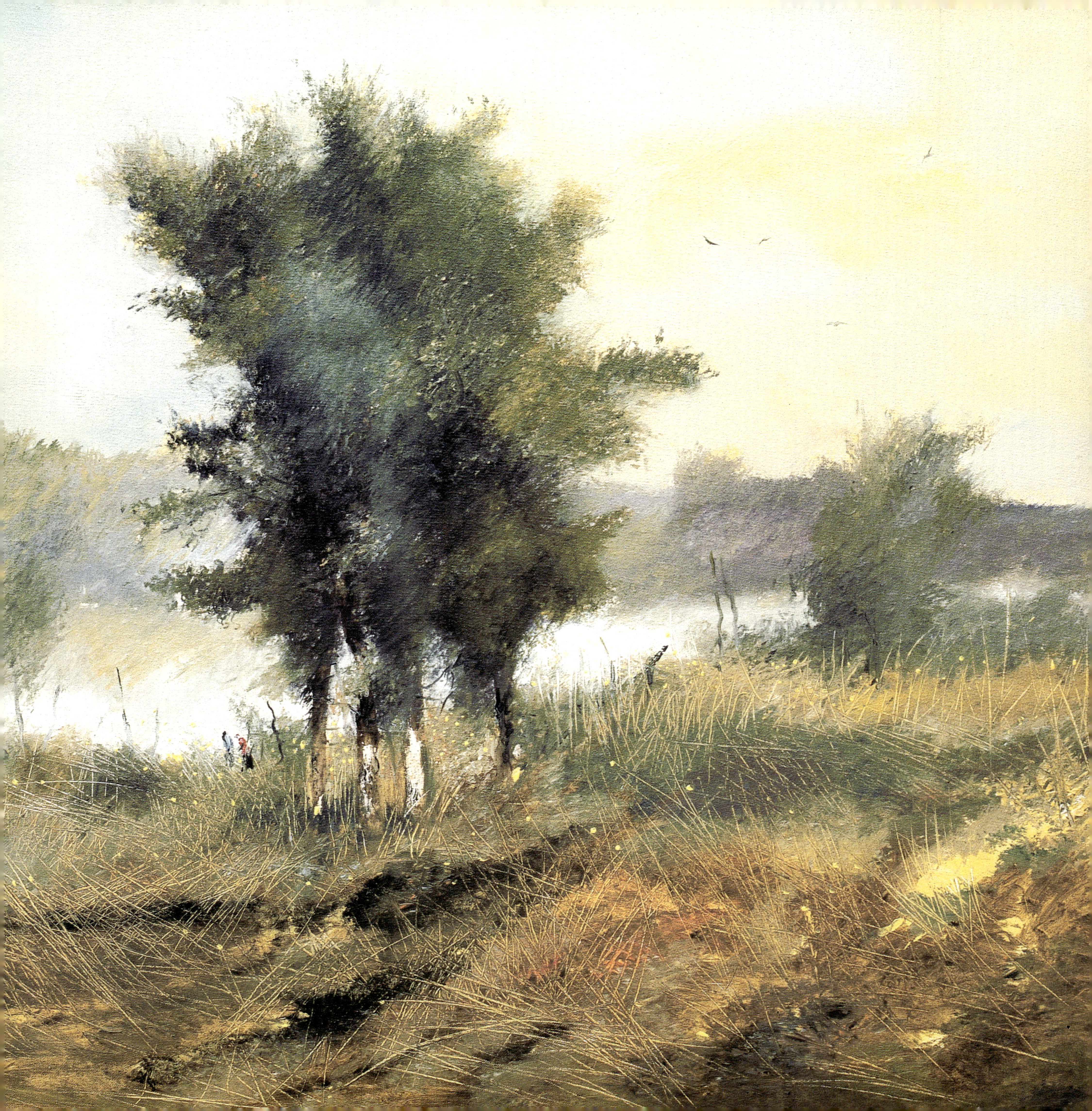

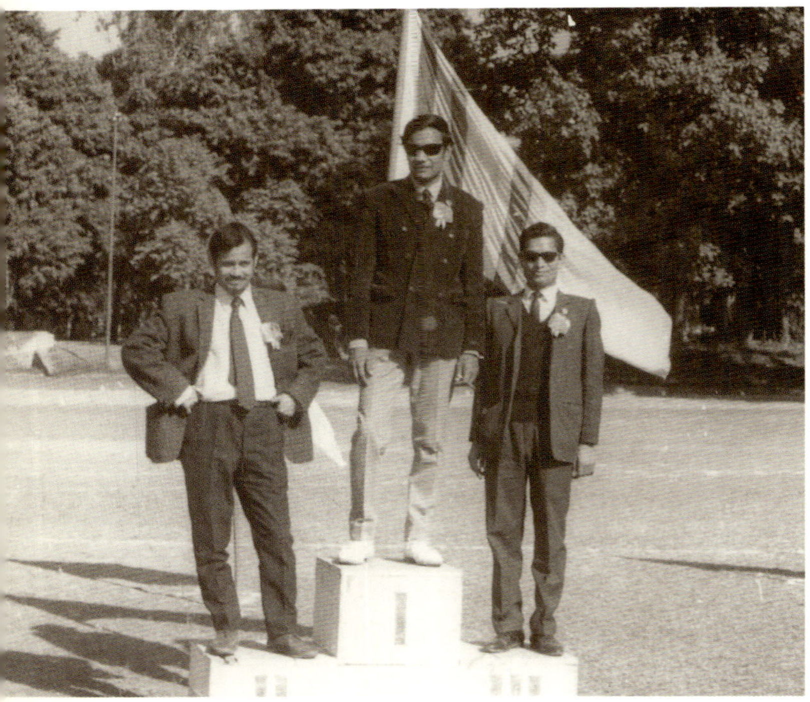

Satish (centre) at the Government College of Arts and Crafts, Lucknow. He was good at academics as well as co-curricular activ ties.

absorb knowledge in the field of painting. Day after day, year after year, Satish learned from his veteran gurus, who were well-known and established artists. Satish's dedicated study under Sudhir Khastagir (who was the principal of the College of Arts and Crafts), Nityanand Mahapatra, B.N. Arya, R.S. Bist and M.L. Nagar, combined with his endless creativity, perhaps bewildered and unnerved some of his teachers. While some remained indifferent, others were encouraging.

Sudhir Khastagir saw the genius in Satish and encouraged him at every step. He would tell Satish, "Baba, mark my words, you will be a great artist one day." This gave Satish the strength and courage to study relentlessly, following a staggering routine of working upto eighteen hours a day. This required discipline, absolute surrender and total dedication. Before and after attending classes, he would go around on a bicycle or on foot, sketching and painting old historical monuments, bridges, stations and trains, marketplaces, and Nature. He believed, and still believes, that the process of learning is never-ending. His work started attracting art lovers and collectors.

Satish graduated from the College of Arts in 1963. He then did his post-graduation in landscape and specialization in watercolour from the same institution, in 1964.

The time had now come for Satish to grow individually and step out of the shadow of his gurus. He was also looking for work to support himself even as he devoted his time to landscape painting.

In 1965 he joined the Roorkee University as an artist in the Department of Architecture, where he worked till 1967. Soon, he realized that he was wasting his time. "I felt very stifled in Roorkee because drawing straight lines was not what I had aspired for. Besides, the staff had to be immaculately dressed in a suit at all times... in the class room and while teaching students, in the mess during meals, and even at the club! At that time my favourite game was billiards but I could not enter the billiard-room without a suit and bow-tie. All this was very different from what I was used to at that time. I began to miss my freedom." In 1968 he returned to his beloved Lucknow and joined the College of Arts and Crafts as lecturer in the department of fine arts, where he simultaneously pursued his first love, landscape painting. Lucknow has remained his base over the years.

Around this time the city was becoming a focal point for an influential group of writers, poets, musicians, journalists and critics who met daily at the Coffee House. Satish came into contact with the leading members of the group – Anand Narayan Mullah, Bhagwati Charan Verma, Amritlal Nagar, Satish Batra, Fanah Kanpuri, Kamleshwar, Surendra Chaturvedi, Birju Maharaj, Bismillah Khan, Ilyas Khan, Ram Lal, S.C. Kala, Vidyasagar, Chandra Dutt Tiwari, Bishan Kapoor, Ramesh Pahalwan, Chandrashekhar, Ram Manohar Lohia, Atal Behari Vajpayee, Sipt Razi,

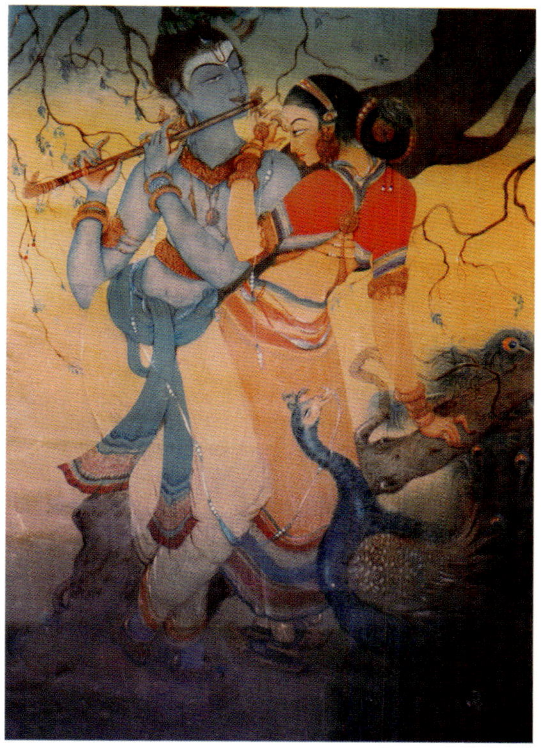

Radha-Krishna in the wash technique, done by Satish during his student days.

Honing his talent: Satish at the Government College of Arts and Crafts, Lucknow.

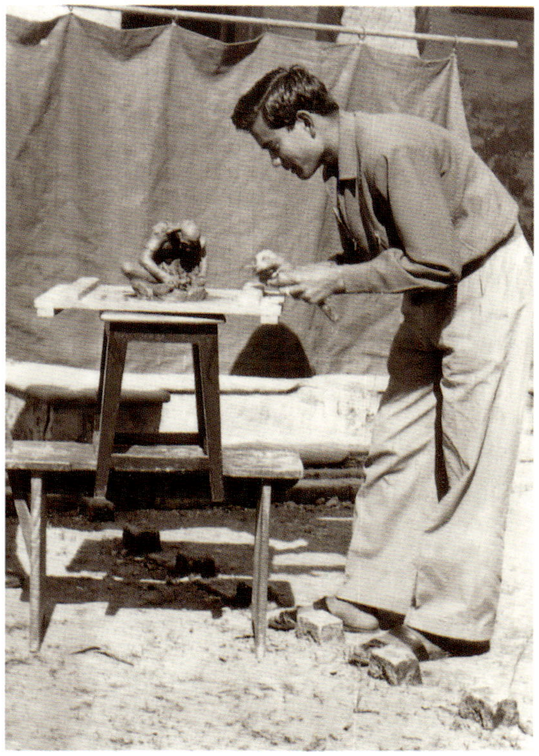

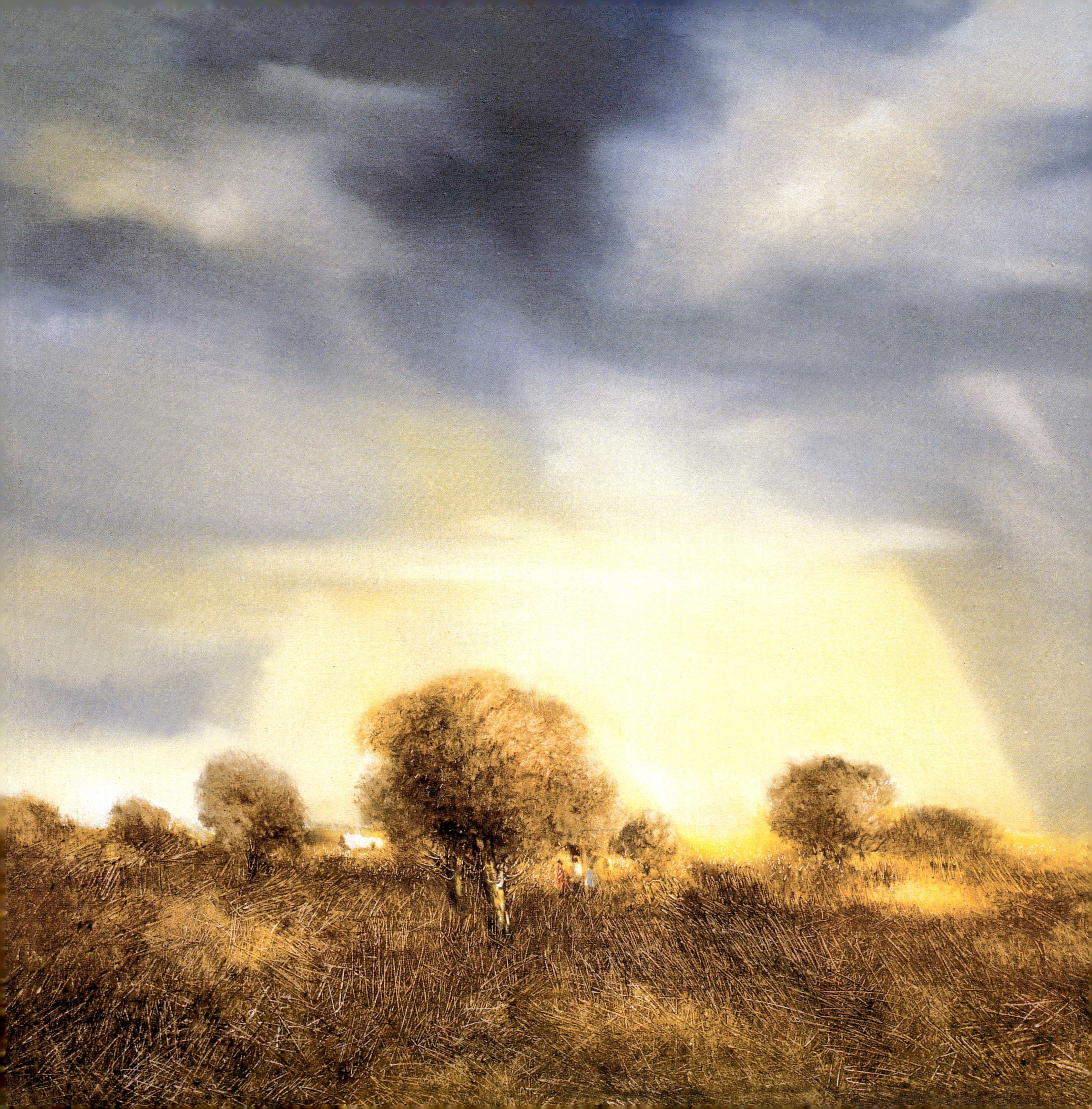

Justice Raza. He quickly absorbed their ideas. It was a time when abstraction in landscape painting had become de rigueur, but Satish clung tenaciously to his original creativity and is credited with establishing the 'Romantic' form in an era of abstract modern art.

Still in his early twenties, of regal disposition, well-dressed, full of warmth and generosity, Satish possessed the unusual and appealing quality of attracting others towards him. He quickly endeared himself to this group. Lovingly, they called him 'Prince'. Many of these figures frequented his home – a small cottage with a beautiful garden filled with flowers and surrounded by gulmohar, amaltas and eucalyptus trees. This cottage was on the college campus. Though small in size, Satish had done up the interior tastefully, making it cosy and comfortable, and friends called it 'the doll's house'. The cottage became a sanctuary where Satish's friends would sit for hours on end writing poetry and fiction. The writer Srilal Shukl wrote his famous novel *Raag Darbari* here.

Satish himself became a voracious reader and read not only the popular books and classics of Indian literature, but also the Bengali poems and writings of Rabindra Nath Tagore. Besides mythological classics like the Ramayana and the Mahabharata, he also read the Gita, the Bible, the Koran and Sufi writings, specially those of Bulle Shah, Rumi and Amir Khusro.

Satish's home was an open house and he never locked it even when he went out of Lucknow. A versatile cook in the kitchen looked after his friends' every need when he was away.

Facing page: Oil on canvas.
Following pages 36-37: Watercolour on paper, 1973.

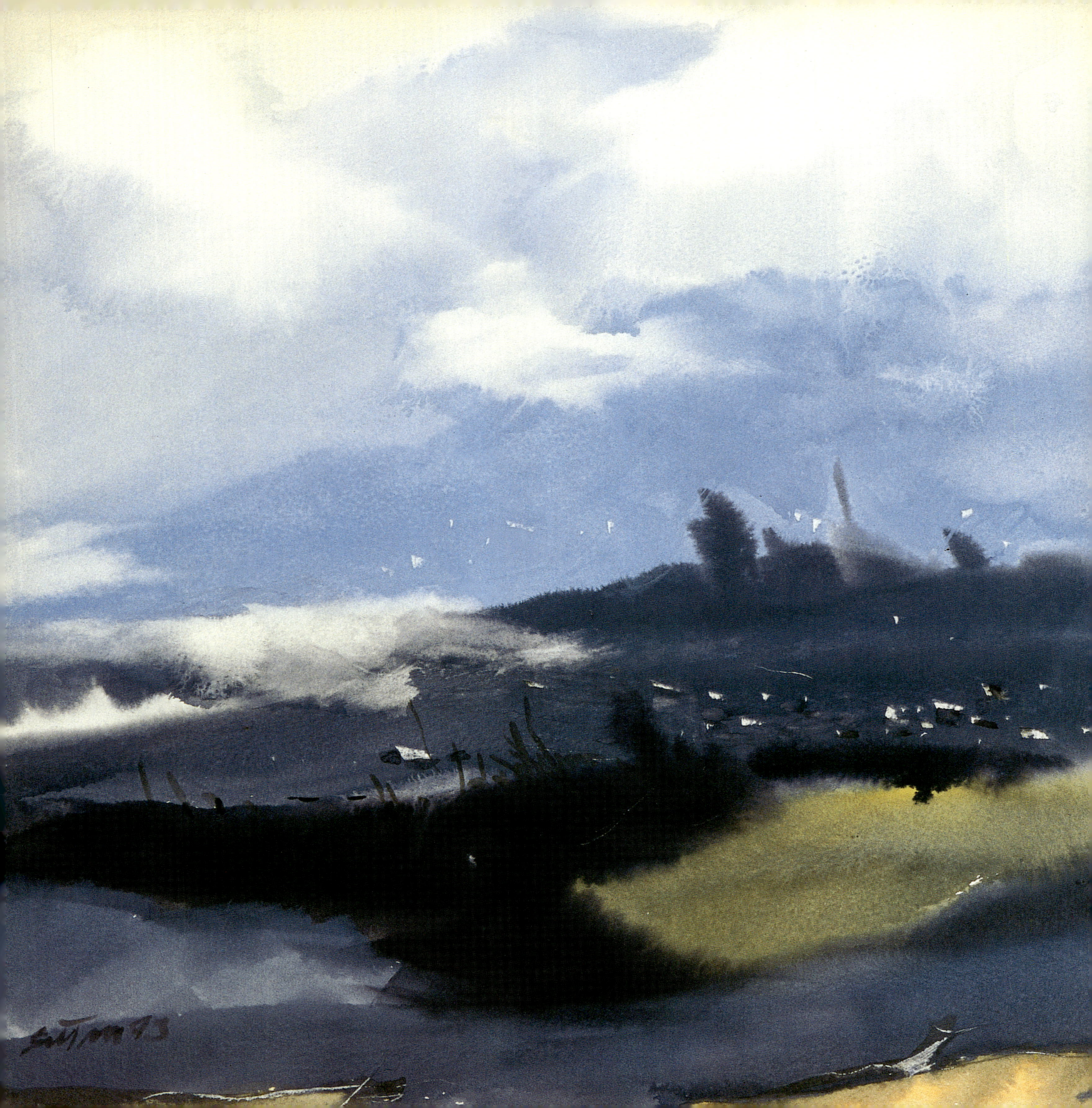

In Kanyakumari and Mahabalipuram... I would invariably go far out into the sea in a dug-out canoe or on a raft, along with a guide. It was a wonderful experience. I learnt a lot about the sea and the wind. How a shift in the winds is marked by a shift in the mood of the sea. I learnt to listen to its sounds and to watch it change its colour.

– Satish Chandra

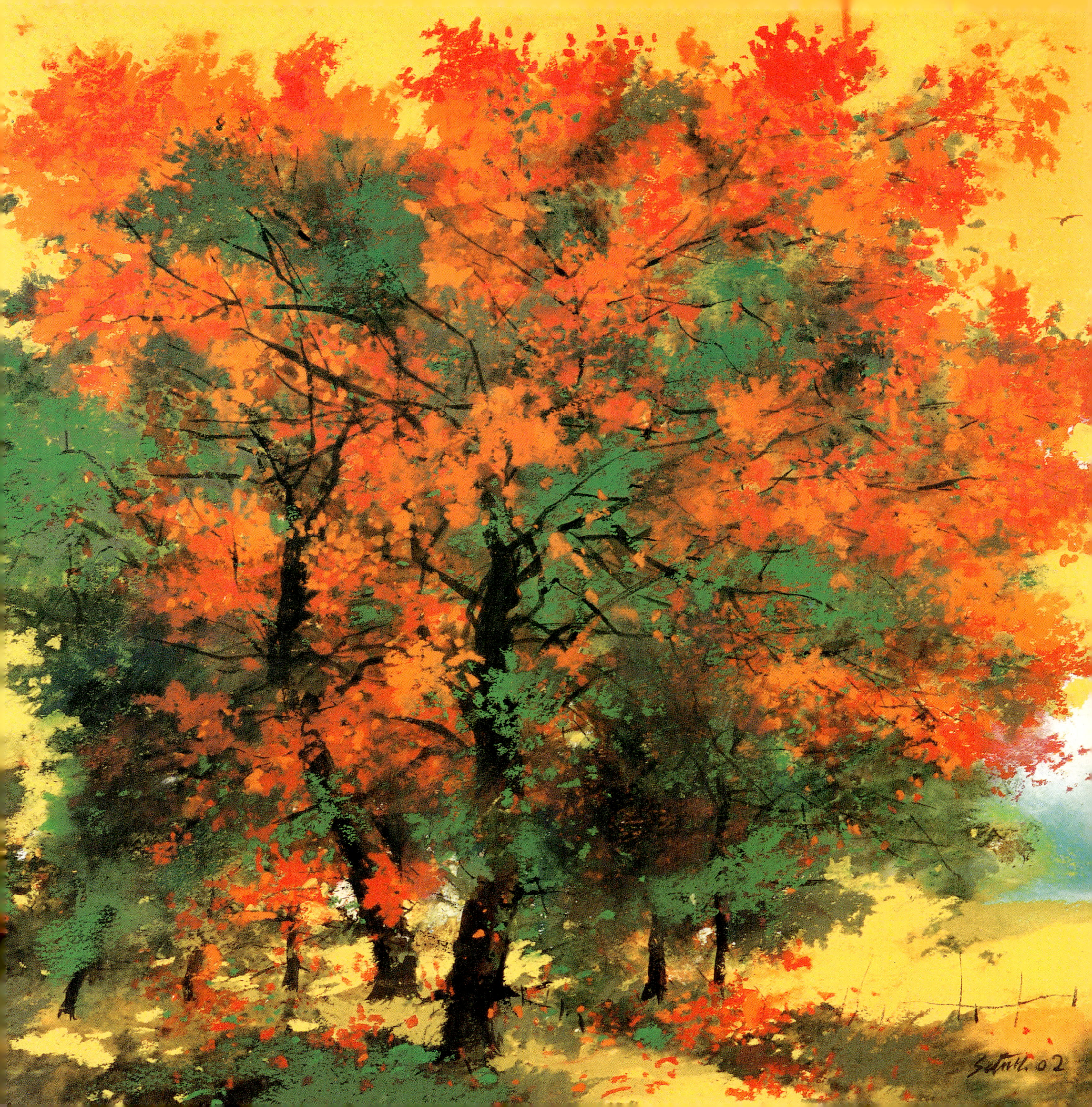

Early Years of Struggle

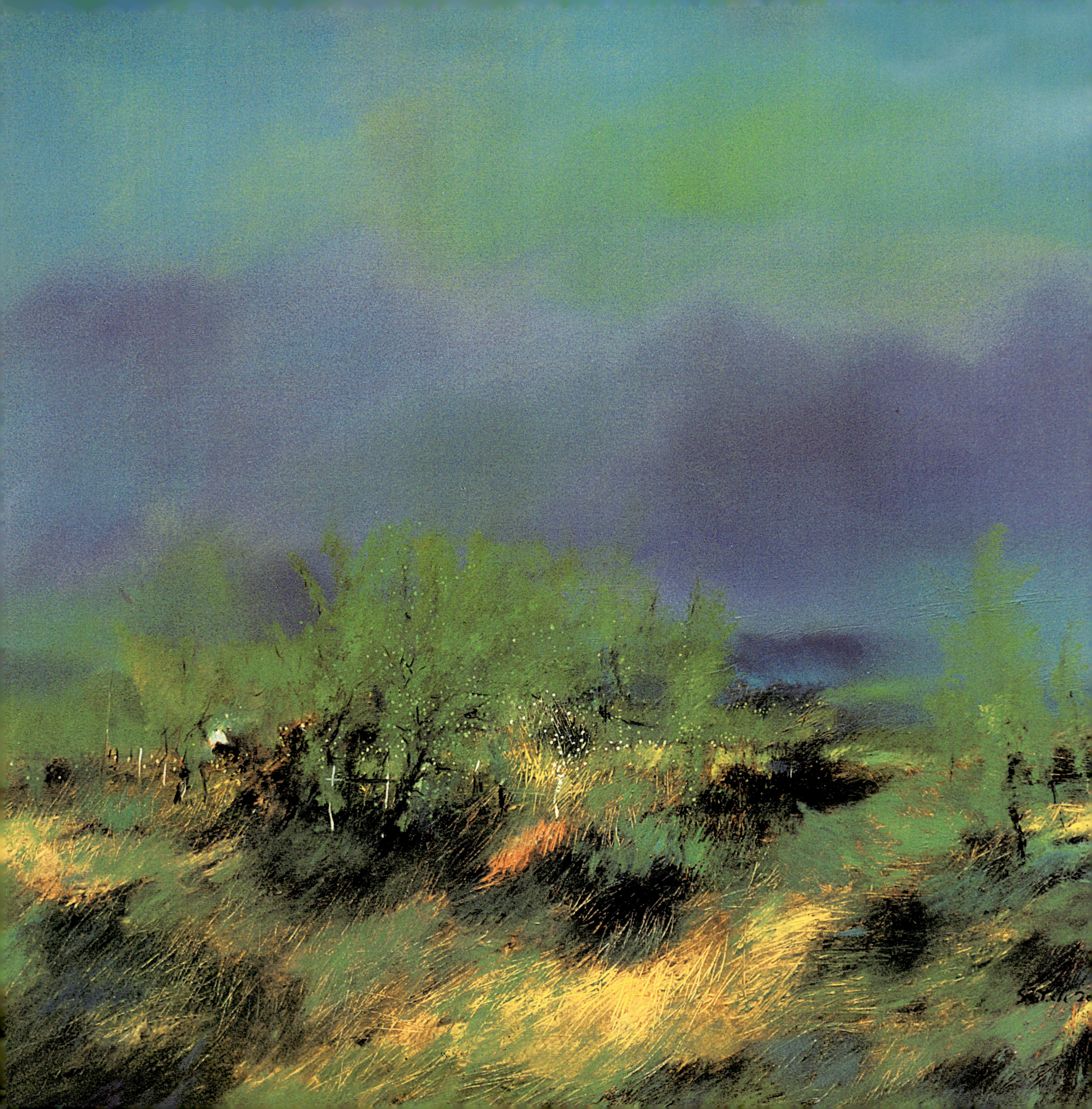

The nomadic habit and the desire for fresh experience, so deeply ingrained in Satish, can be seen in his drawings and sketchbooks, which reveal the surprising extent of his travels in India.

On these tours, he would invariably stop overnight in temples and gurdwaras. He actually lived with the tribals, the fishermen or the natives he met en route. With his simplicity and his child-like smile, he found his way into their hearts. He ate the food offered to him, laughed, sang and danced with them. He studied their everyday life. He observed minutely an incredible range of details relating to the inhabitants and how their environment influenced them. He rejoiced with them in the lap of unspoiled Nature, enjoying this chance to know the people. At times conversation was not possible, for Satish could not speak their language. He would use subtle gestures to make himself understood. "It was enthralling to see them dance – whirling around the bonfire in their colourful tribal dress, their jewellery and beads jingling rhythmically to the beat of the drums. These were places where time seemed to have stopped hundreds of years ago. The landscape was pure like the people who had adapted themselves to it," says Satish.

All that he saw found its way into his sketchbook – the people, their houses made of wood and stone, the temples with their bells of different shapes and sizes, and the boundless beauty of Nature. Most of this work was bought by tourists and by the owners of 'gift-shops' during these travels.

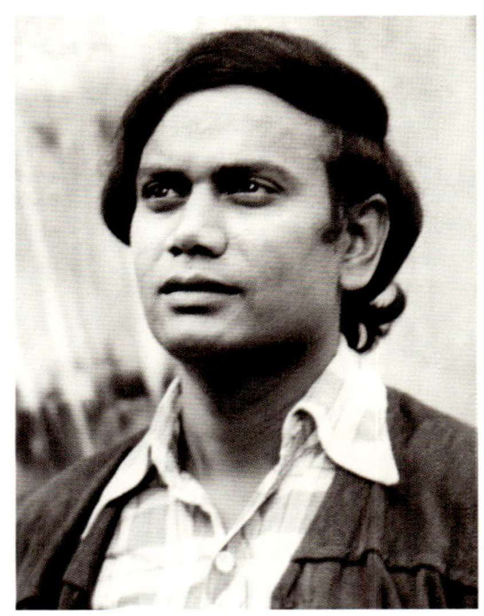

Bitten by the travel bug: In his twenties, Satish travelled all over India painting mountainscapes and seascapes.
Facing page: Oil on canvas.

The year 1958-59 took Satish to a 'basti' of fishermen in Bombay and he lived with them in their environment and painted seascapes. In 1964, Satish travelled to Pathankot, Kangra, Dharamsala, Kullu and Manali, and Kashmir. This journey into the mountains became a turning point in his life. It was a journey which was both physical and of the psyche. It took him not just from place to place but also affected him from the periphery of his consciousness to the inner core of his being.

Of a religious bent of mind, Satish started his journey from the temple of Jwalaji in Kangra, a place of worship in the mountains. "From Kangra I proceeded to Dharamsala. I found myself in a world of bright skies with shades of blue, silvery ranges and vivid slopes shadowed by clouds. The vastness of the land took my breath away. I was bewildered and enchanted by the changing colours of the horizon through the day as the sun paved its path across the sky. All day, I walked in Nature's awesome theatre, sketching and painting to my heart's content.

"From there I travelled to Kullu and Manali. I found myself enveloped in an aura of red and yellow, filled with blossoming flowers. It was like a path leading to Heaven. The atmosphere left me intoxicated. I let the colours flow, arresting these moments on paper.

"I then walked to the 'Sholong Valley', 12 km from Manali. As the sun cast its spell of colour on the snow-covered peaks, they glittered with a heavenly light. By now, my thirst to

Facing page: Watercolour on paper, 1993.

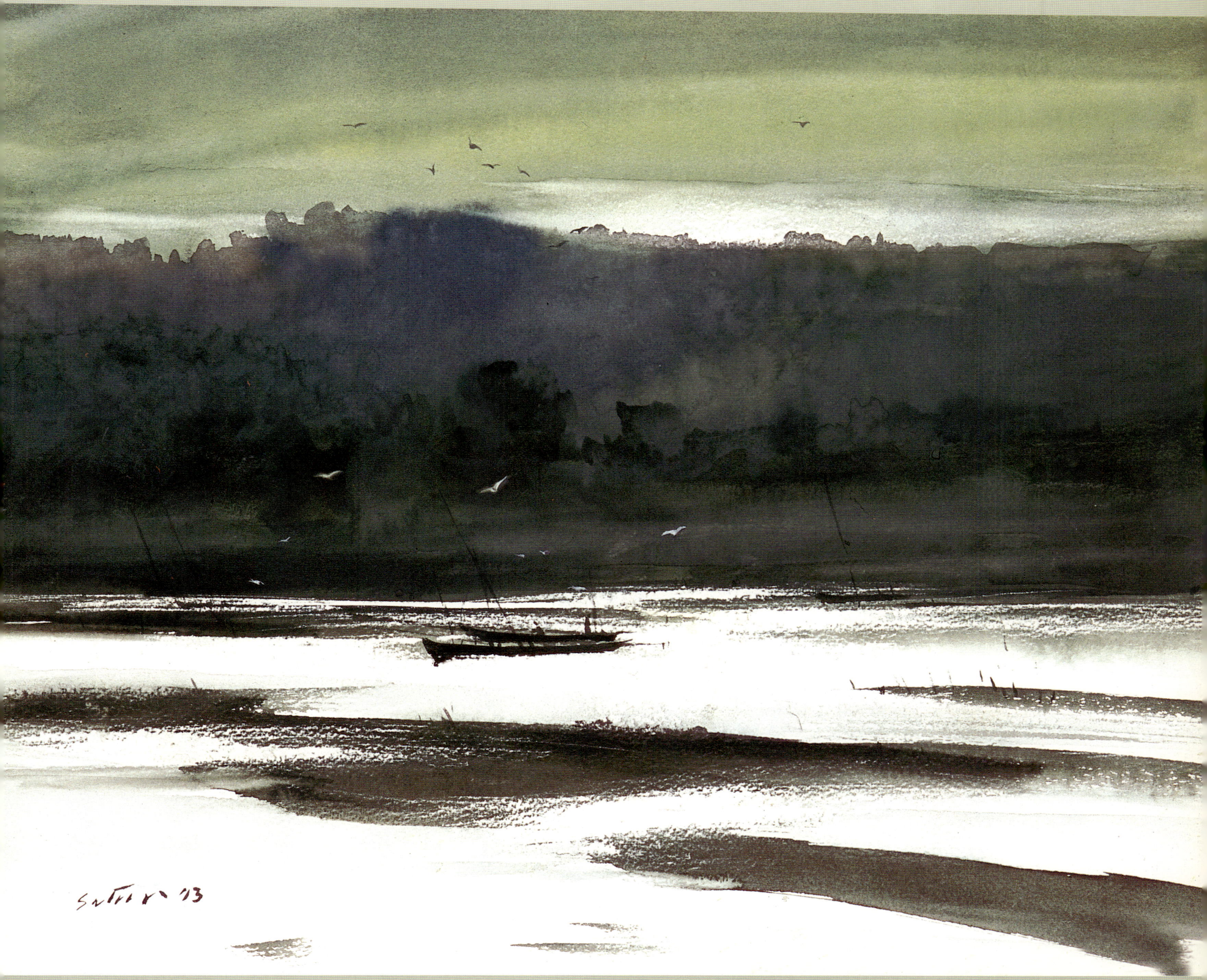

Top: Manali bridge, watercolour on paper, 1960s.
Bottom: Naggar valley, watercolour on paper, 1960s.
These are black and white photographs of the original watercolours done on the spot.

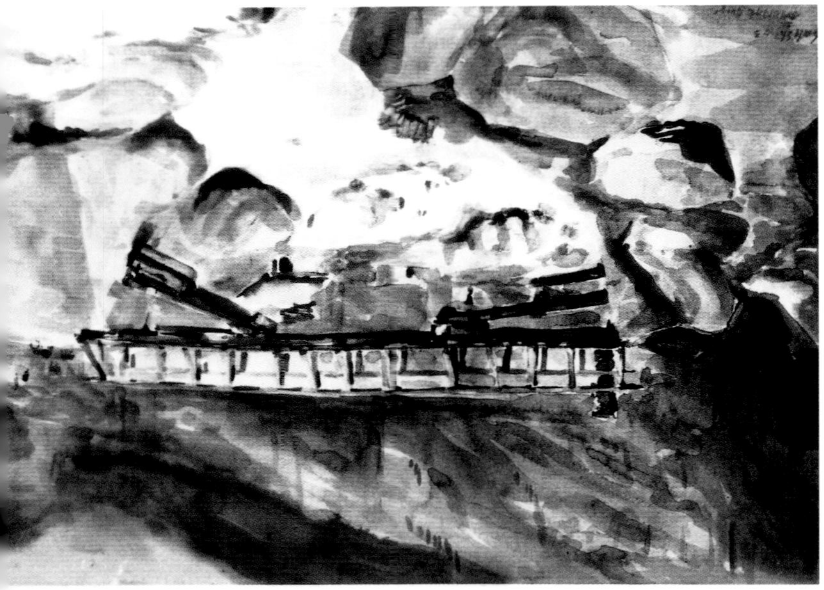

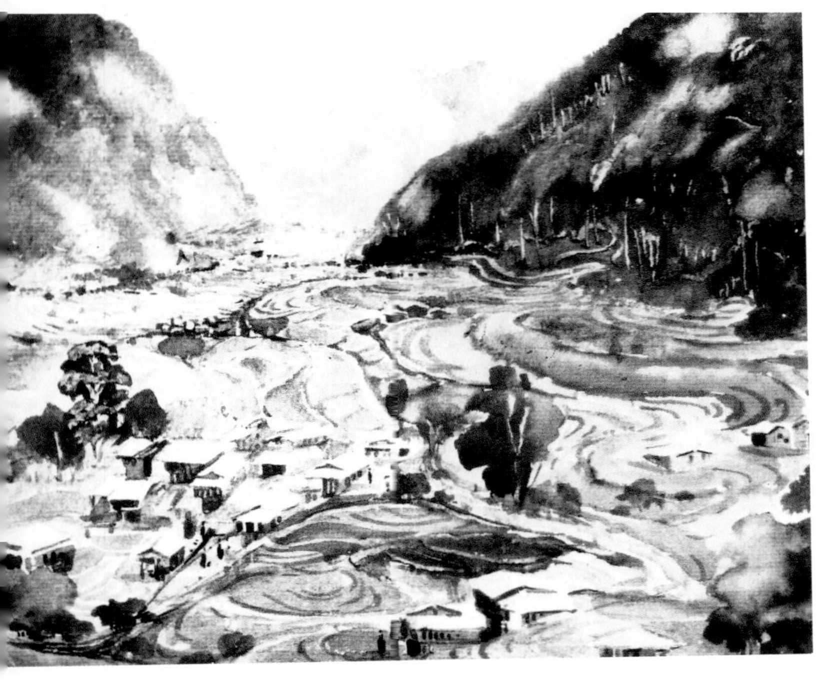

paint Nature in this enchanted realm of God was insatiable."

In these mountains Satish discovered waterfalls. He studied and painted the transparency of water – as it cascaded down the mountain-side, reflecting light – and its spray, as the winds played with the water.

Satish returned to Manali. From there he started his journey on foot again. He went upto Naggar Valley, painting the mighty Himalayas in different moods. He was struck by the effect of light and shade on the snow and ice. "It is a world of great heights and depths, a home of light and shade. The atmosphere filled my whole being with love for the Creator. It energized me, sweeping away fatigue."

Satish succeeded in rendering the feeling of snow-whiteness not by means of a uniform white, but by strokes of various colours to get the desired effect. "Where the sunlight fell directly on these ranges, they turned a golden yellow, a hidden treasure of the Almighty. I let the watercolours flow on paper to capture this sight."

Satish returned to Manali and then started his climb to Rala, 10,500 feet above sea level, on foot again. He found himself in a world of snow-covered mountains and icy winds. "The fresh mountain air cleared my mind and buoyed my spirit. I felt joyous, exhilarated and carefree. I still remember the words that were going through my mind up there – I thought that ultimately life was all about choices and that I had made the right one." Without having the benefit of a guide or a map, Satish reached Rohtang, 14,500 feet above sea level, and from there travelled to the Tibet plateau and onward to Lahaul Spiti – famous for its flower valleys. "It was like I had some sort of inner compass, nudging me gently towards my destination. I don't think I could have stopped climbing even if I had wanted to," Satish tells me excitedly.

High places, the rarefied air of the mountains, the abode of the Gods, an

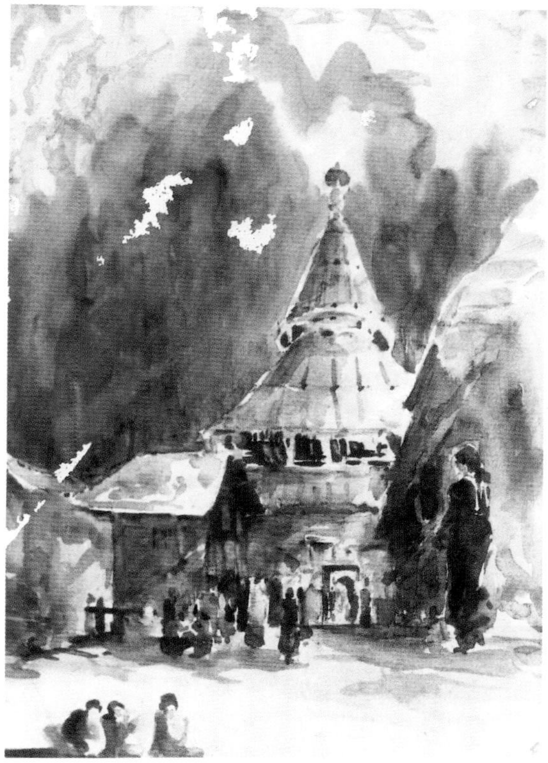

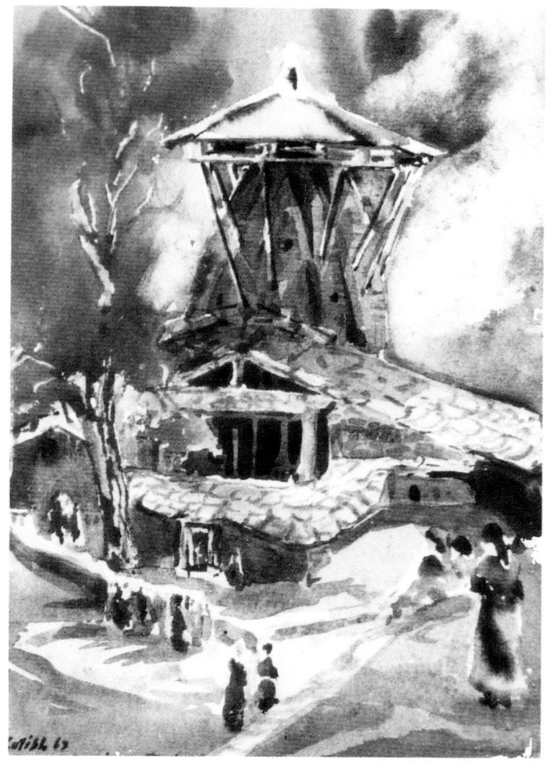

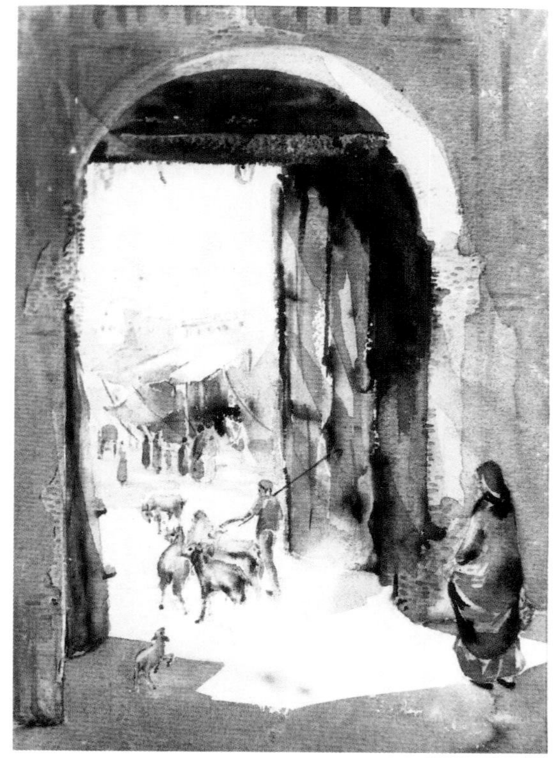

Left: A temple in Tibet, watercolour on paper, 1960s.
Centre: Naggar temple, watercolour on paper, 1960s.
Right: Sheesh Mahal, Lucknow, watercolour on paper, 1960s.
These are black and white photographs of the original watercolours done on the spot.

altitude too high for permanent human habitation – these have been associated with human aspiration since time immemorial. This is the zone of the sacred, the goal of ardous pilgrimage. As feelings and emotions ripple through Satish, there is nostalgia in his voice. He continues to tell me more about his trek into the mountains.

"The narrow path seemed impossibly steep and precarious, stones rolled from under my feet. Step by step, I plodded on, leaving rivers and towns far below. The mountain fell away sharply with deep ravines on both sides of it. This is known as the 'Valley Of Death'. It was then that I noticed the trail left behind by mules and I started stepping on these for a foothold, a stick in one hand for support. Due to dearth of oxygen, I felt myself slipping through the gyre of sense and sensibility. The mountain ranges swam before my eyes. Perception was reduced to breathing. I started reciting a prayer, placing each step to its rhythm. I kept reminding myself that I had to reach the 'Valley of Flowers'. Gradually, a sort of euphoria set in and the joy of walking took over. I felt one with the mountainscape. A sense of well-being cleared my mind and vision. As I climbed higher, centuries seemed to melt away. I found myself alone in an archaic world. I was walking on the soil of antiquity, glorified and graced by God. This was the soil once known

In the peace and solitude of the mountains, at the age of twenty-four, Satish had come closer to an understanding of life. . . He was filled with a serene contentment he had never known before. He knew at last what he was meant to be, what he wanted to do most – he would paint Nature to the end of his life.

more intimately to ancient peoples than to those who have ventured there since.

"I followed the winding path until, with unexpected suddenness, I stepped into a lost world. There lay the 'Valley of Flowers' before me, shimmering like gold in the rays of the sun. The mountains stood in all their magnificence, illuminated by the ethereal light. The effect was breathtaking and utterly baffling. For a few minutes I stood transfixed to the spot, gazing at the sight, inhaling and absorbing it into myself with every deep breath I took, for I knew I might never come back here again in this lifetime. My whole being responded in silent adulation and admiration of the Almighty and his creation. I was experiencing Nature in its purest form. I bowed in homage to the Master. If Nature is the body, then God is its soul. I felt my own nothingness in the eternity of those moments. A strong feeling of renunciation enveloped my whole being. It was an intoxication of the soul. A voice deep within myself seemed to tell me that life's journey is nothing but a process of clearing the rust from my soul. That every prophet and every saint has a way, but all lead to God. All ways are really one." In the peace and solitude of the mountains, at the age of twenty-four, Satish had come closer to an understanding of life. His fears and worries about the future vanished. He was filled with a serene contentment he had never known before. He knew at last what he was meant to be, what he wanted to do most – he would paint Nature to the end of his life.

'I shook myself out of the trance and looked for a vantage point. So I climbed up to a ridge commanding a

Facing page: Oil on canvas, 2003.

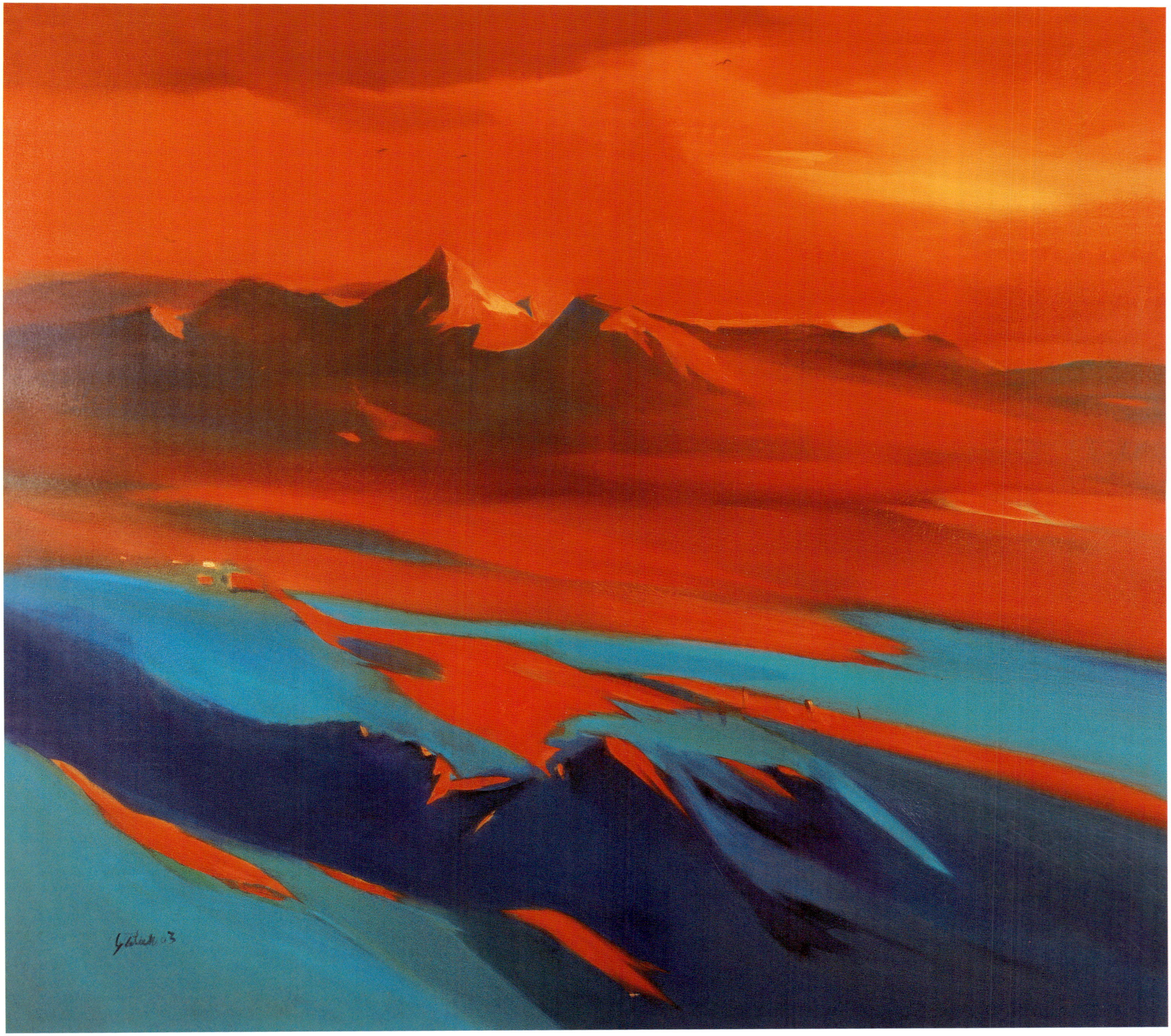

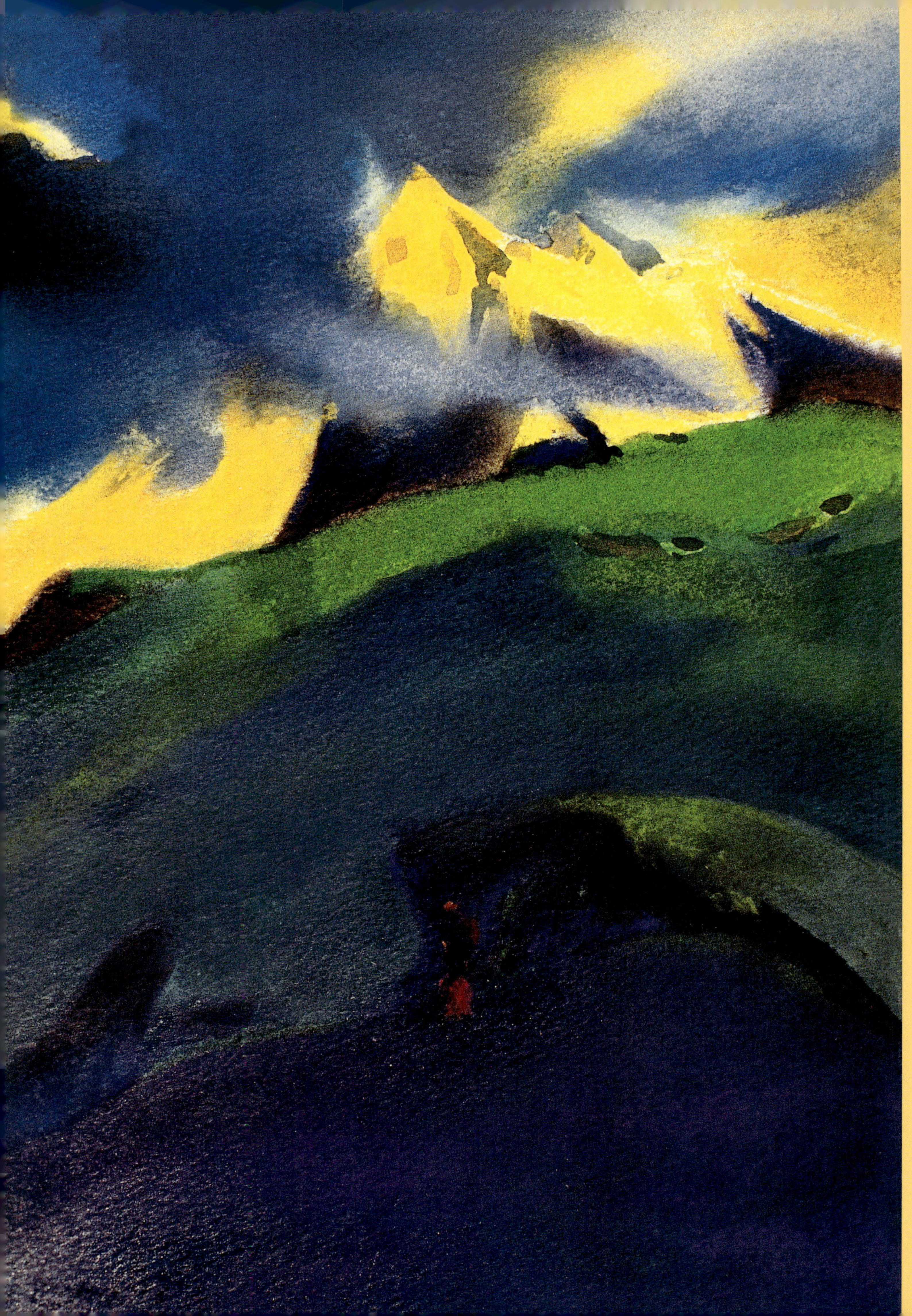

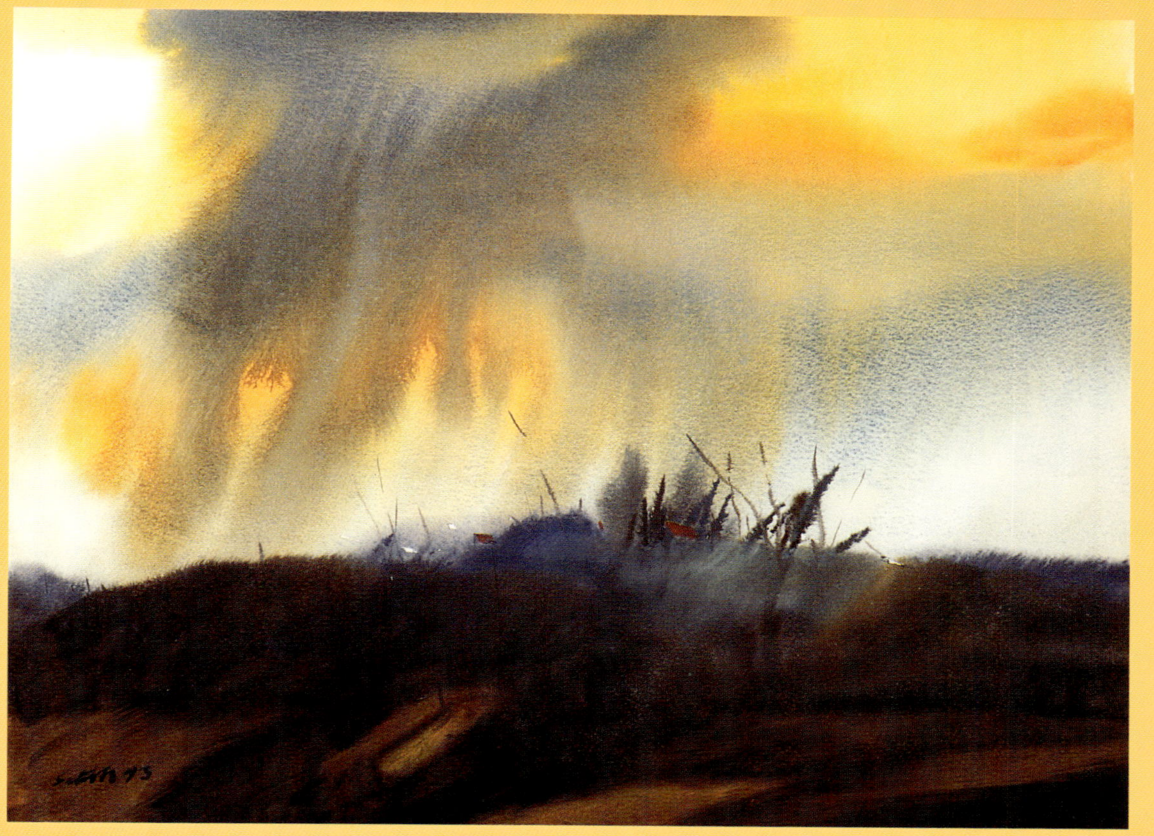

panoramic view of the valley – it was like a sacred enclosure of ethereal beauty. I sketched and painted the golden valley of flowers and the mountain ranges in watercolour, from many different angles."

Later, a series of paintings in oil followed, depicting the mountains with sweeping horizontal and vertical brush strokes, careering across the rock surface with the very breath of life.

That naughty twinkle is there in his eyes again and that elfish grin lights up his face as he tells me, "Once, I was caught in a tremendous thunderstorm which swept down without any warning and caught me in the worst possible place to be – a sloping mountain with no shelter at all and no way of speedy escape either. Suddenly the temperature fell and after a few minutes of deafening thunder, a vigorous snow-storm rolled in, blotting out all landmarks. A 'sadhu' came hurtling down the mountain towards me, a bundle of saffron, crying for help, caught in the white fury of wind and snow. I was absolutely petrified. Luckily, there was a humpbacked rock nearby. I lay down and clung to it for dear life as my legs flailed around helplessly in the ferocity of the wind. Just as suddenly as the storm had come, it vanished, leaving behind an eerie stillness. I tried to stand up. To my consternation, I fell down for my legs were numb with cold. I sat on the rock and rubbed my legs vigorously to bring life back into them. I then stood up and, undeterred, continued to climb. I did not regret this initial ordeal, for it made me more aware of

Watercolour on paper, 1993.
Facing page: Mixed media on paper.

the different moods of the mountains." Satish looks at me quizzically and quips, "Never say die... you do, and you miss out on so much more that life has to offer!"

Seeing both aspects of the mountains – the formidable as well as the gentler, greener side – sharpened Satish's perception and brought a new

glow and richness to his palette, colours like red, chrome yellow, yellow ochre, cadmium yellow, sap green and chrome green alongwith cool colours like grey, mauve and cobalt blue. "Trekking in the mountains helped me get a feel of the spiritual atmosphere: the 'atman-sphere'." As a result, says Satish, he was able to moderate the emotional turbulence within by showing sensitivity towards others.

This tour of two months resulted in the creation of four hundred watercolours and a thousand sketches in charcoal, pen and ink and pastels. These sketches and drawings reveal the astonishing extent of his research into the properties of light and colour, and the expressive freedom that accompanied his habit of close observation. He created numerous studies of clouds and the sky, exercises in black and white, in blue and white – passionate, penetrating studies of Nature in motion. Each landscape, a symphony in colour.

Between 1965 and 1968, Satish toured and painted Saurashtra, Maharashtra, Madhya Pradesh and Rajasthan – then went down south to Kodaikanal, Ooti, Kanyakumari and Mahabalipuram. Each tour gave birth to a new series of landscapes, seascapes and hillscapes. During this tour, Satish specially wanted to study the character and moods of the sea.

Facing page: Oil on canvas.

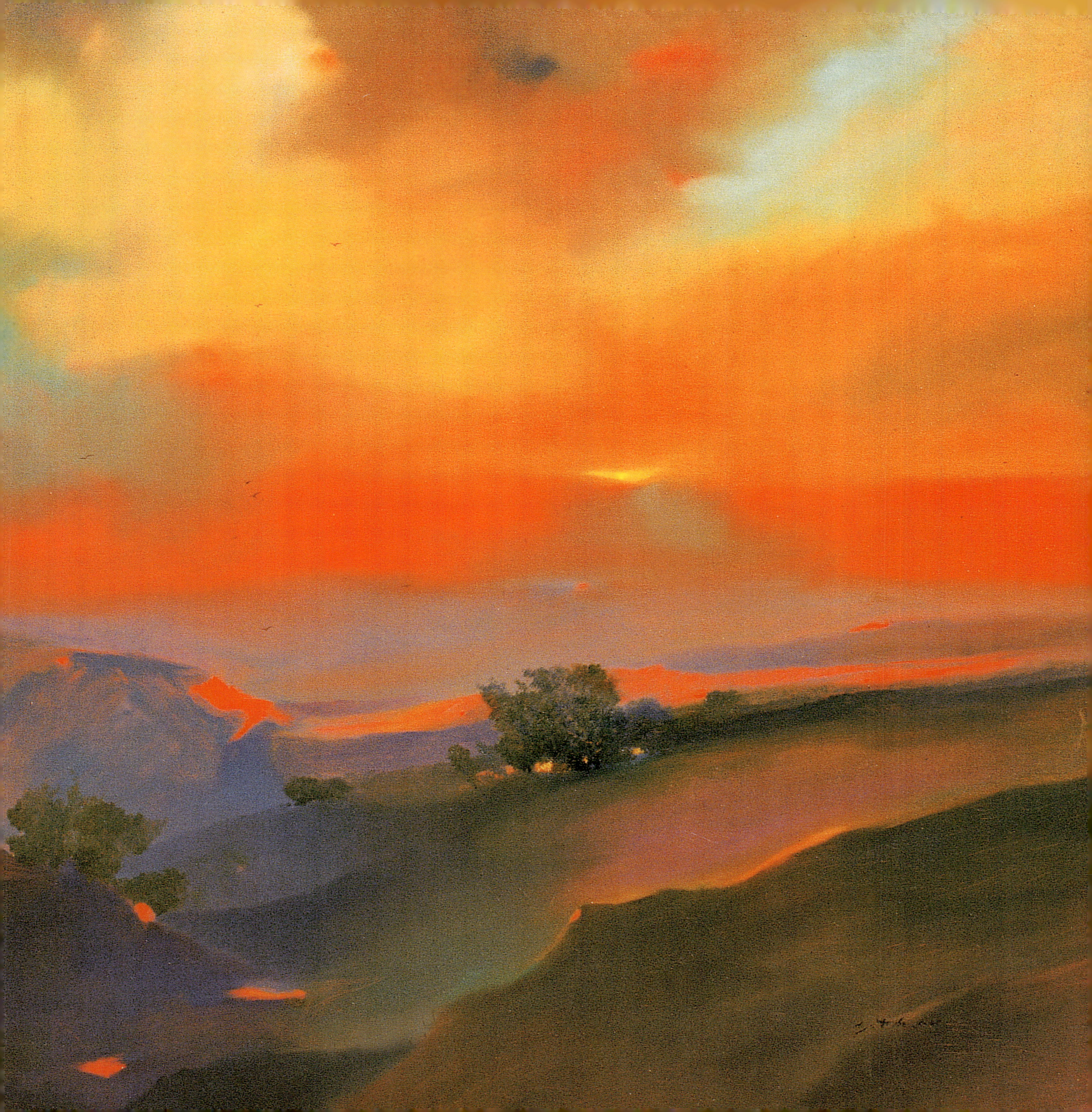

"I felt like a bird flying through flashes of lightning, intoxicated by the electric storm, blinded by the light and spray of the sea water. . . I found myself drowning and then emerging from the depths of the water, delirious and dizzy."

Reminisces Satish, "In Kanyakumari and Mahabalipuram, I would wake up early in the morning to walk on the quiet beach. I would invariably go far out into the sea in a dug-out canoe or on a raft, along with a guide. It was a wonderful experience. I learnt a lot about the sea and the wind. How a shift in the winds is marked by a shift in the mood of the sea. I learnt to listen to its sounds and to watch it change its colour.

"The day dawned when I had to return to Lucknow. I still had two hours left to board the train. I rushed to my guide and asked him to accompany me out to sea, just once more. He tried to dissuade me as a storm was expected within the hour. I looked up at the sky. It was marine-blue and the soft ripples of water looked inviting. I managed to persuade my guide to lend me his raft, which he did, reluctantly.

"Soon, I was in the middle of the sea water, reflecting the sky above, the sun a red spot in the aqua-blue. I could feel the sea breeze in my hair and on my face – a feeling of exhilaration and freedom possessed me. I started to whistle a tune in gay abandon. I think I lost all sense of time. Suddenly, there was a change in the atmosphere – the horizon darkened, bringing with it a gloomy premonition of disaster. Before I could turn the raft around, it inclined at a dangerous angle and I had to make a superhuman effort to remain on board. The waves began to rise and fall with a turbulent motion. My raft plunged through wave upon wave, my breath taken away by the wind, my clothes drenched with water. I felt like a bird flying through flashes of lightning, intoxicated by the electric storm, blinded by the light and spray of the sea water. The wind had shredded the water, making it go up in bright smoke. The next moment, I found myself drowning and then emerging from the depths of the water, delirious and dizzy. The feeling was one of dream-like hallucinatory sea captivity.

"I do not know how I survived the storm, or how my raft was pulled ashore... Yet, I learnt a lot about the sea, and the colours that represent its moods."

From 1968 to 1971, Satish's indefatigable urge for travel took him

Facing page: Watercolour on paper, 1996.

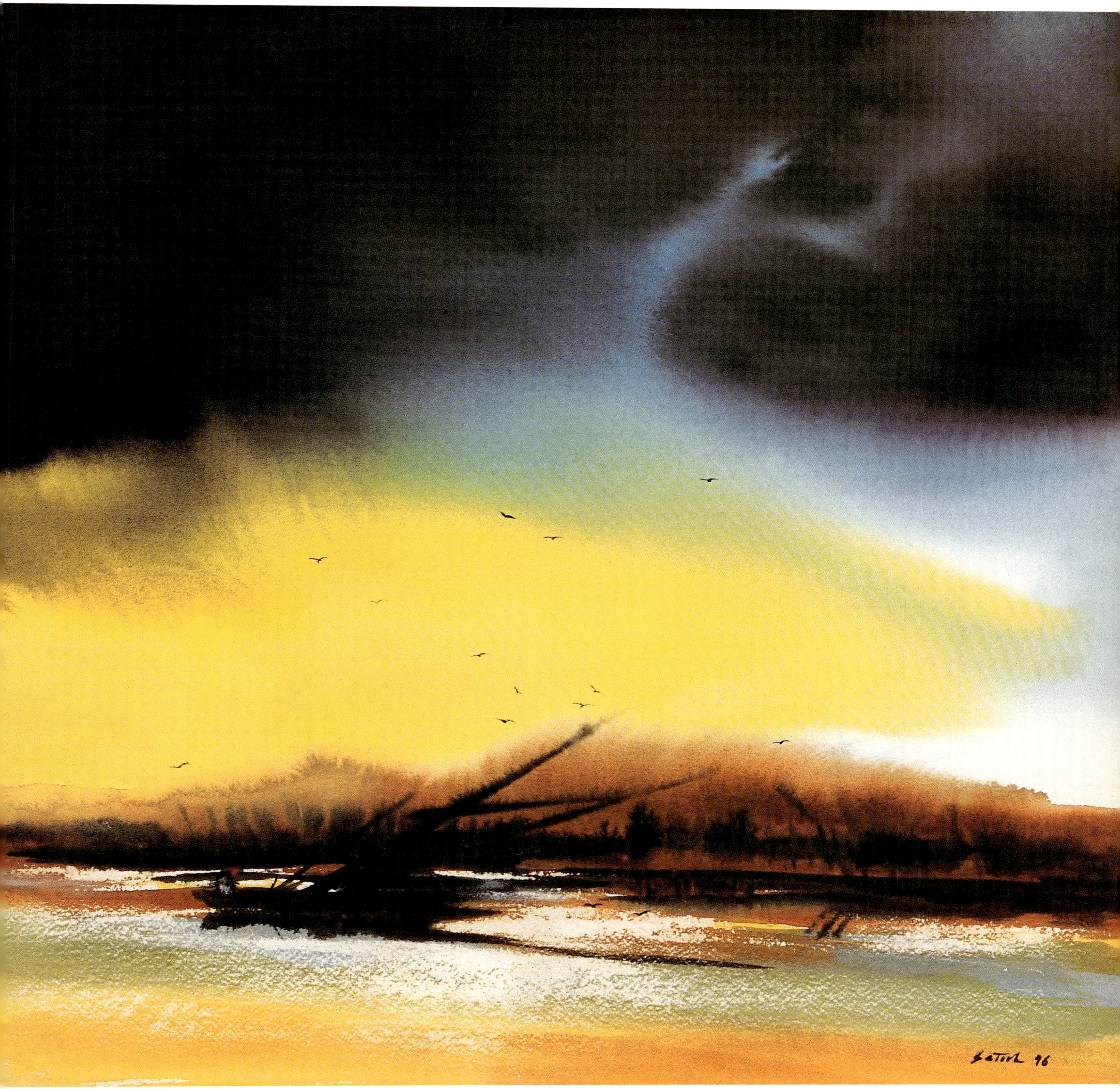

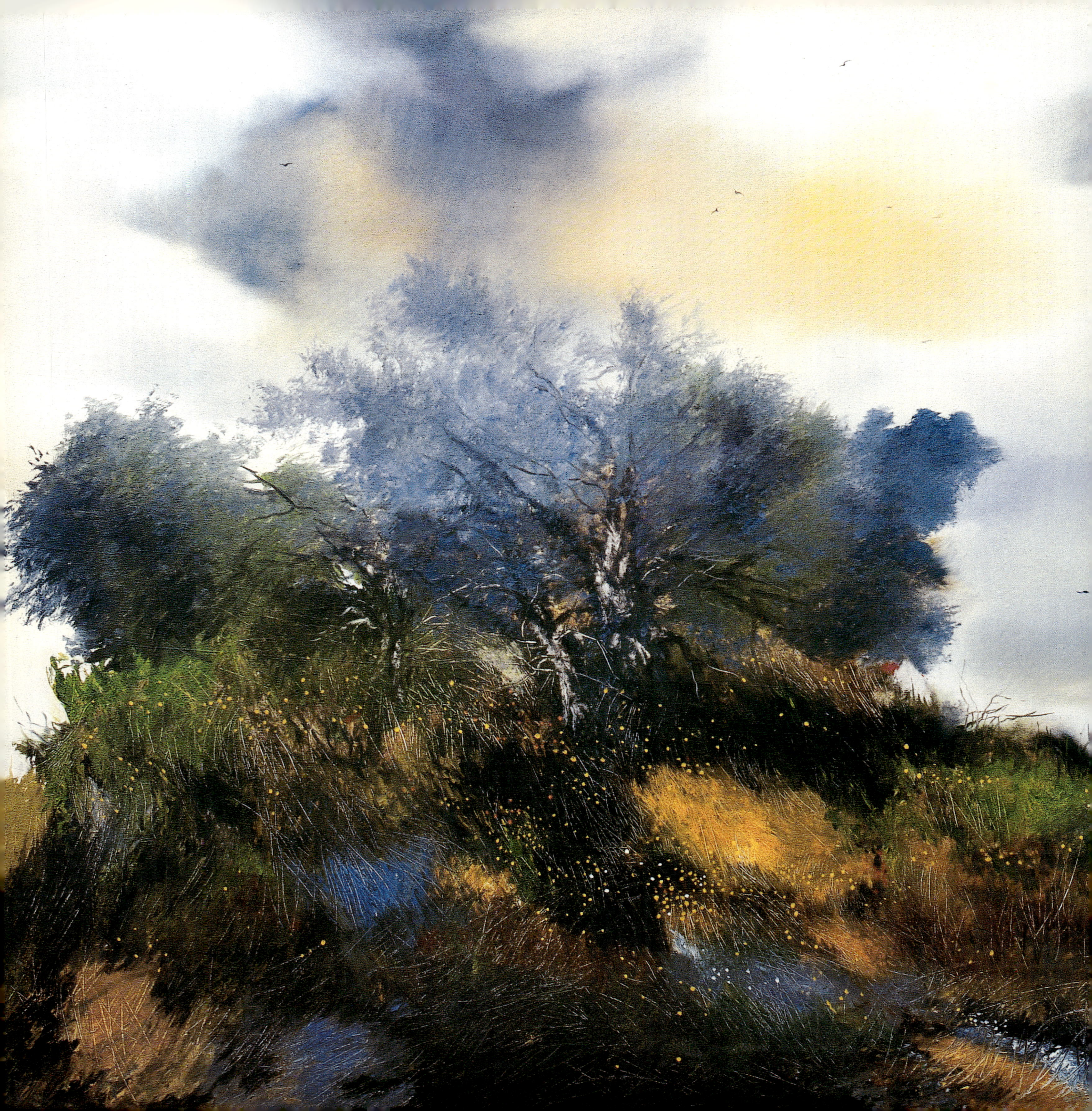

all over Uttar Pradesh – into its villages and to Garhwal Kumaon hills.

To be seen in the resulting pile of sketches, drawings and watercolours are towers of ancient brick and stone blanketed in the mist and rain, ships, chimneys, railway stations and moving trains, the light of lanterns piercing the dimness. An awakened interest in the past of his beloved Lucknow brought forth a series of paintings of old buildings of villages and towns in picturesque decay. He painted the Residency, the Imam Baras, the Roomi Gate and the Ghantaghar; the narrow lanes of Chowk, Kaiserbagh and Nakkhas. There is an air of transparency and fluidity whereby the solid architectures have become translucid spectres. Satish's style has a certain ease and casual grace, but this simplicity is the result of a profound and in-depth study of Nature.

The technique by which Satish floats on the canvas the most delicate films and mists of colour prove him to be a prodigiously great poet of colour. Although he works mainly in water-colour and oils, Satish uses watercolour not only by itself but also with pastels, pen and ink and acrylics. His water-colour is not dependent on outline, but is infused with a strength of colour that compares well with his oil paintings.

Satish's treatment of watercolour allows the white of the paper to be perceived, thus conferring on the painting an unusual transparency. Satish spreads over moistened paper the colours of the mountains, the brightness of the sky in the twilight, the dampness of the atmosphere during monsoon, or the slowly unfurling winter mist. He applies the devices of his watercolours to his oils as well.

Facing page: Oil on canvas.

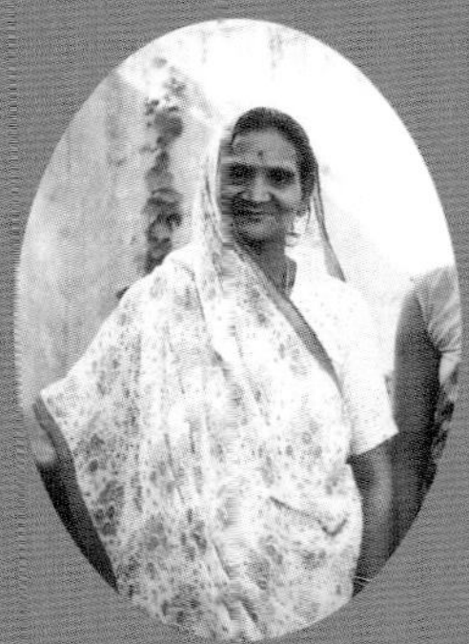

Tragedy strikes: His mother's death in 1971 was a devastating blow to Satish.
Facing page: Oil on canvas, 1993.
Following pages 60-61: Mixed media on paper.

Satish's parents had settled down in Kanpur after his father retired. In the year 1971, tragedy struck the Aggarwal family. On 2 March, Satish received a call from his father asking him to come to Kanpur. "I had bought a silk saree for Amma as a 'Holi' gift. I decided to take it along with me. I was excited at the thought of meeting Amma again. As I climbed into a taxi, clouds were gathering in the sky, slowly blotting out the sun. Normally, on my arrival, there would be excited banter and questions about my bohemien lifestyle. Cool sherbet, sweetmeats and food specially prepared for me by Amma followed. But that day I saw everyone sitting there silent and glum. When I entered my mother's room the silence deepened. My father moved towards me but before he could say anything, I saw Amma lying on the bed, her eyes closed, and I knew that she had died," Satish says quietly. Amma had passed away due to a heart attack, for her heart had grown weak over the years. She was just fifty years old. This was a devastating blow to Satish. He was closer to his mother than anyone else, and loved her very deeply.

I can see him choking. His eyes are misty with tears, but he wants to share his suffering with me and I let him speak. "Disoriented and numb, I came out of the room as the reality of my loss engulfed me. The storm raged outside even as it raged within myself. I stood outside in the pouring rain, crying bitterly like a lost child, letting my tears flow freely. After the cremation ceremony, plunged into the depths of despair, I returned to Lucknow. Restless, unable to regain balance, I was haunted by memories of my mother's tender presence in my life. For the first time I experienced the fear of being alone. I needed my family and I returned to Kanpur. My brothers, sisters and I comforted one another, locked in our love for Amma. I stayed with them for two weeks. On my return to Lucknow I immersed myself in my work and in my quest for identity and meaning."

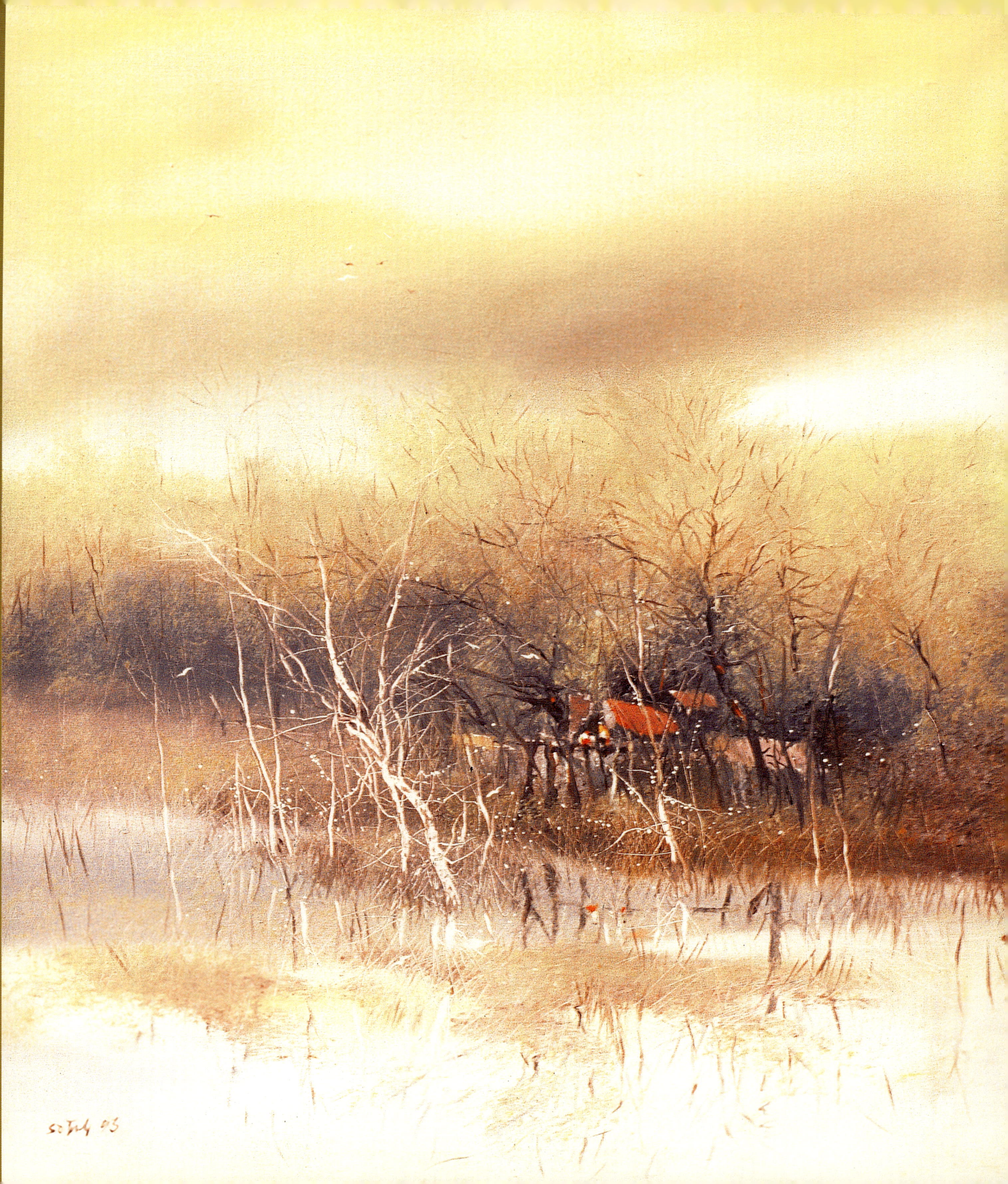

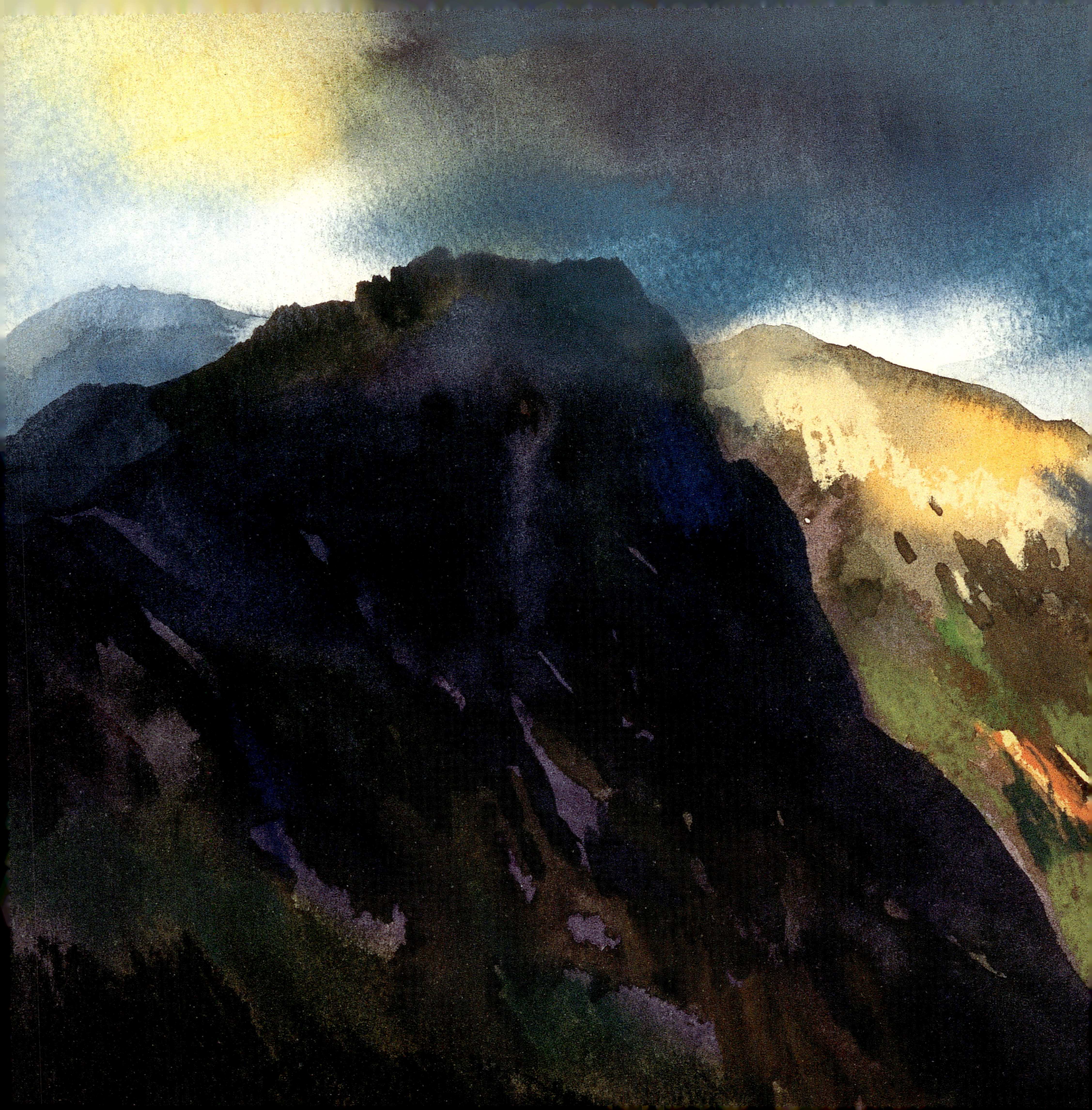

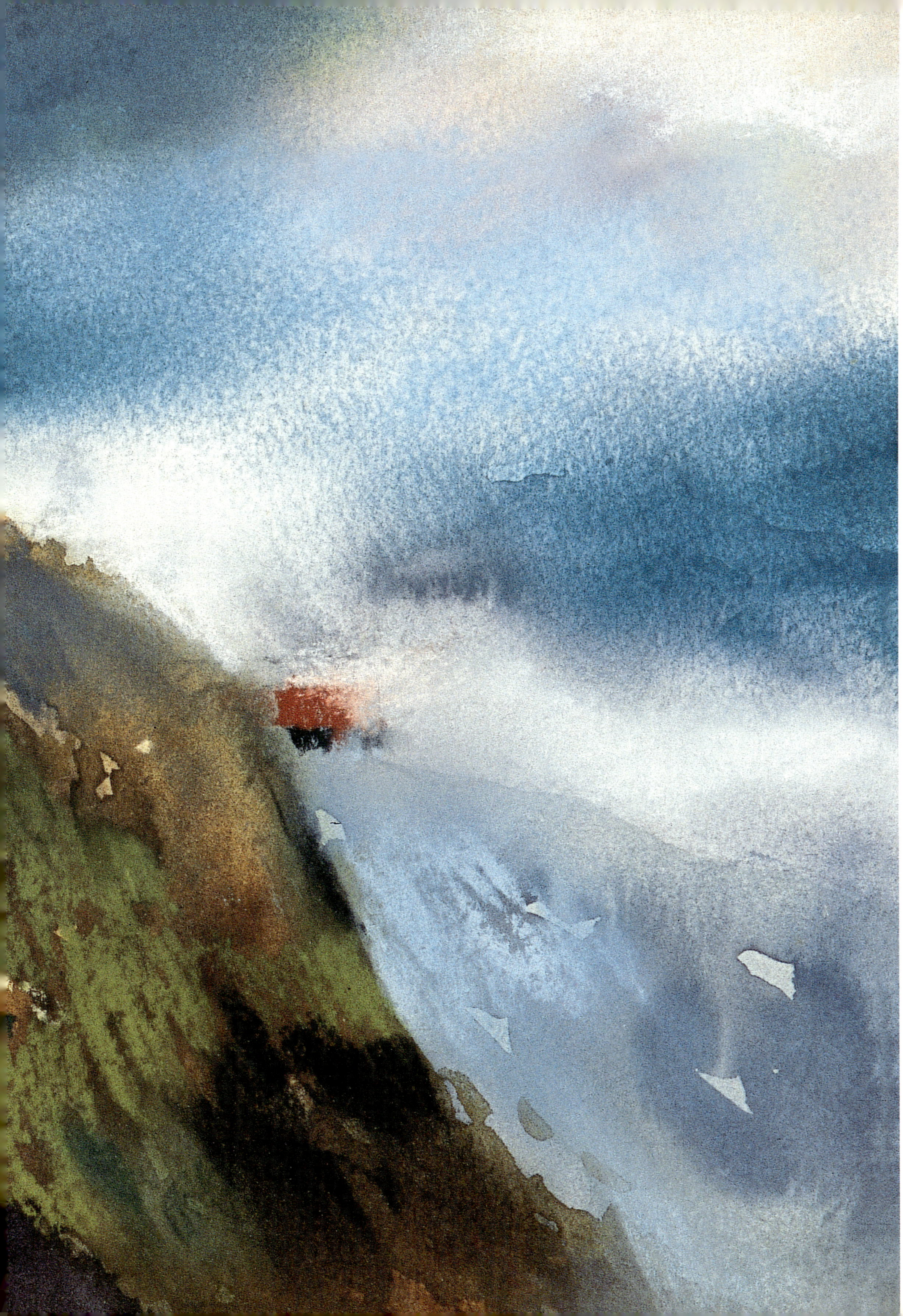

I followed the winding
path until, with
unexpected suddenness,
I stepped into a lost
world... The mountains
stood in all their
magnificence, illuminated
by the ethereal light... For
a few minutes I stood
transfixed to the spot... for
I knew I might never
come back here again
in this lifetime.

– Satish Chandra

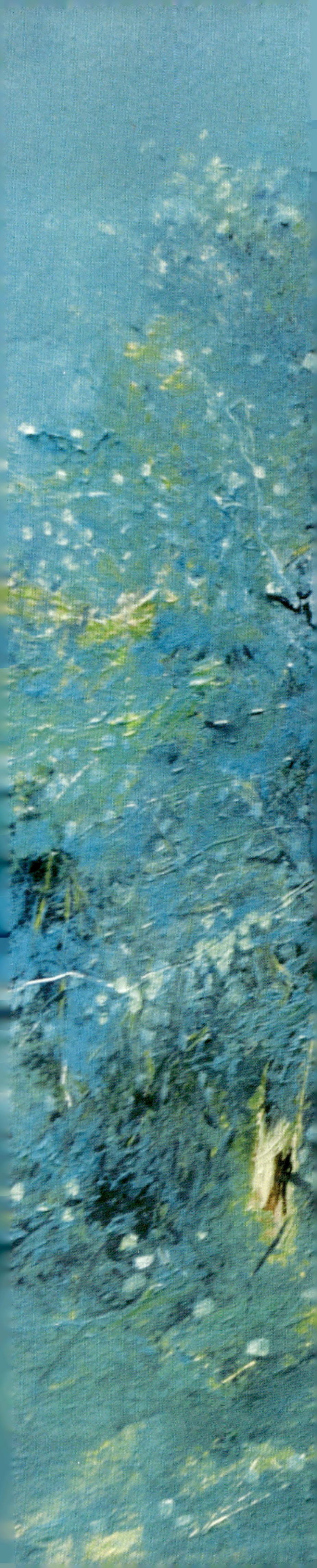

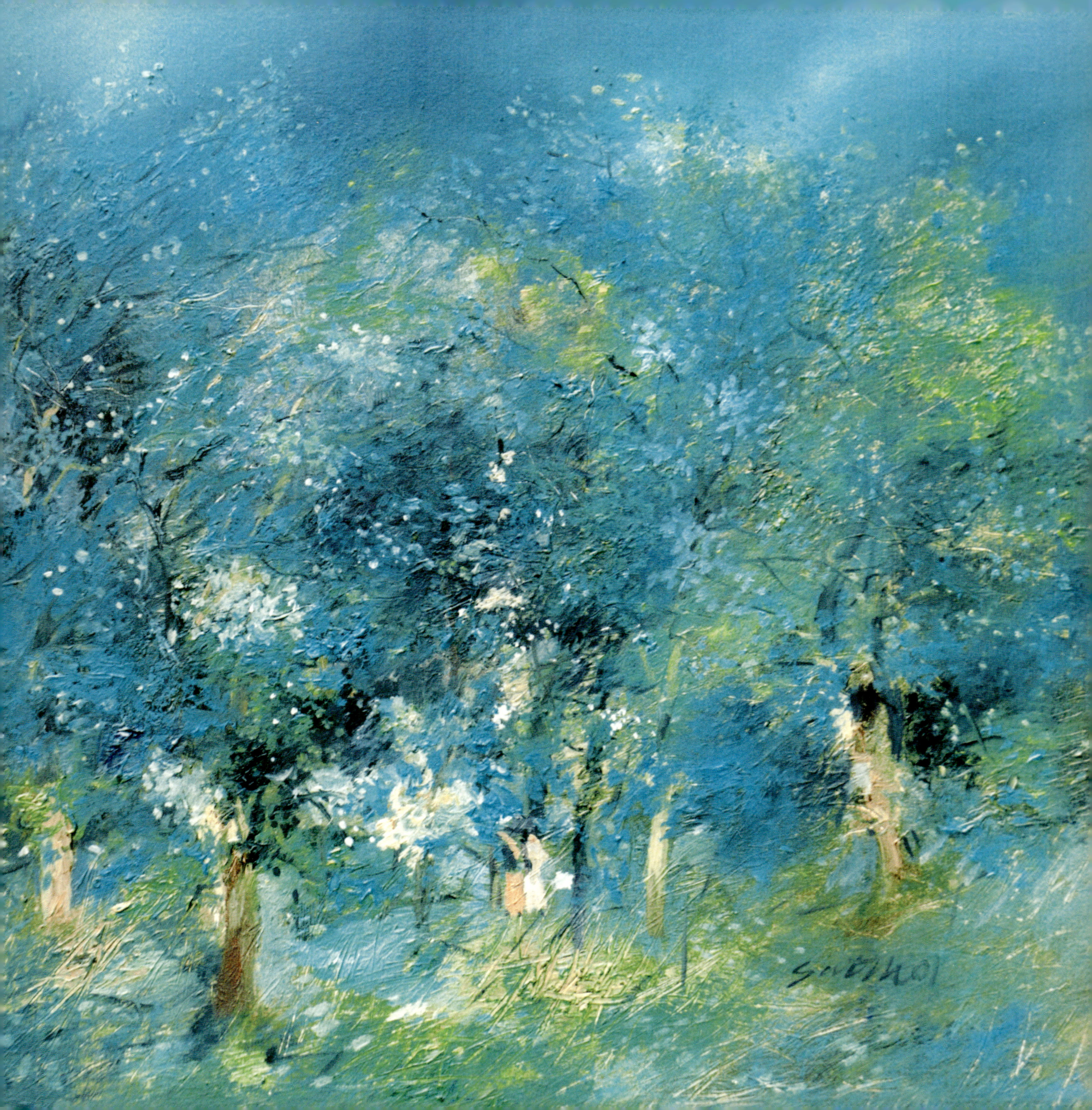

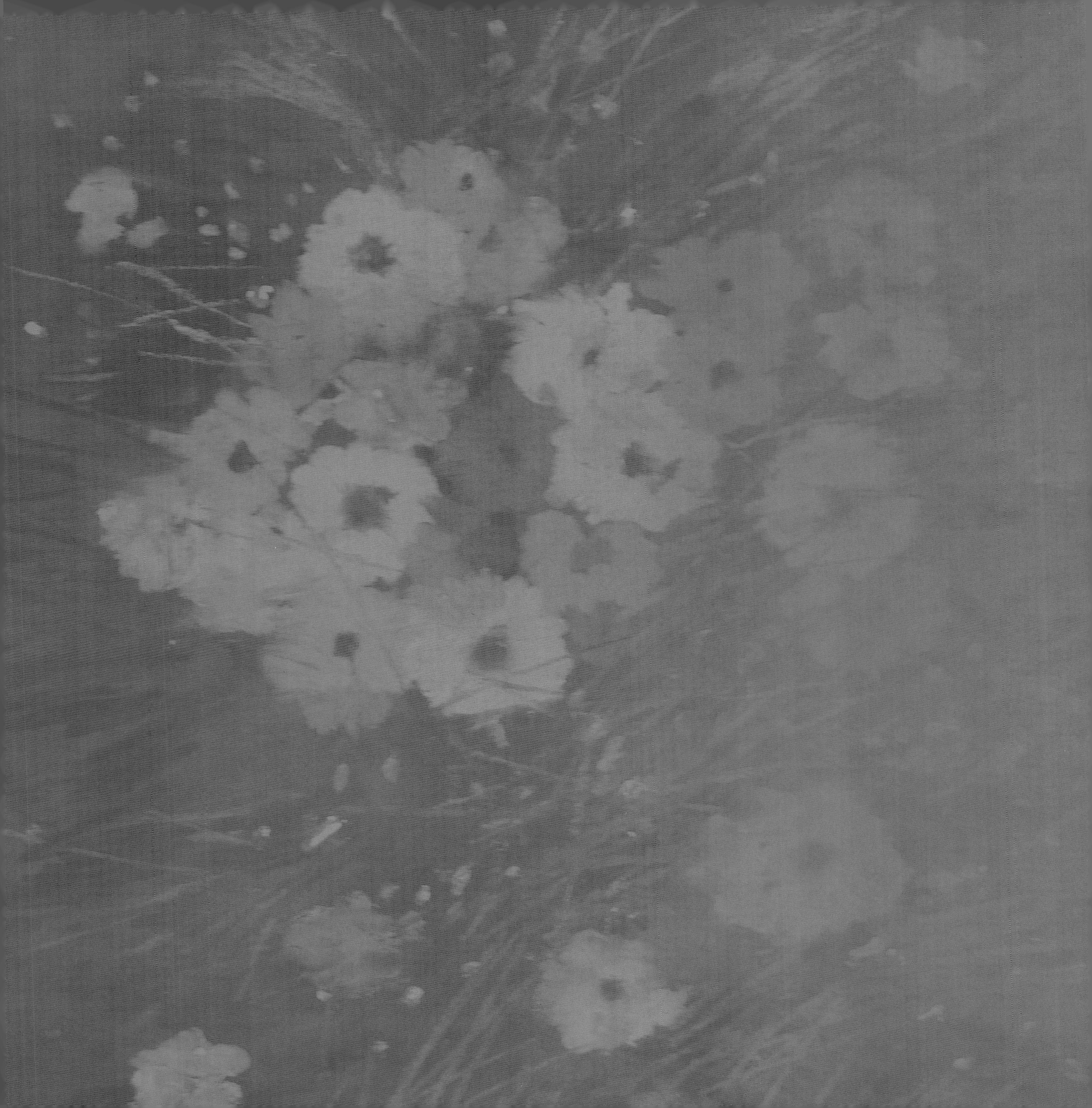

A Relationship Blossoms

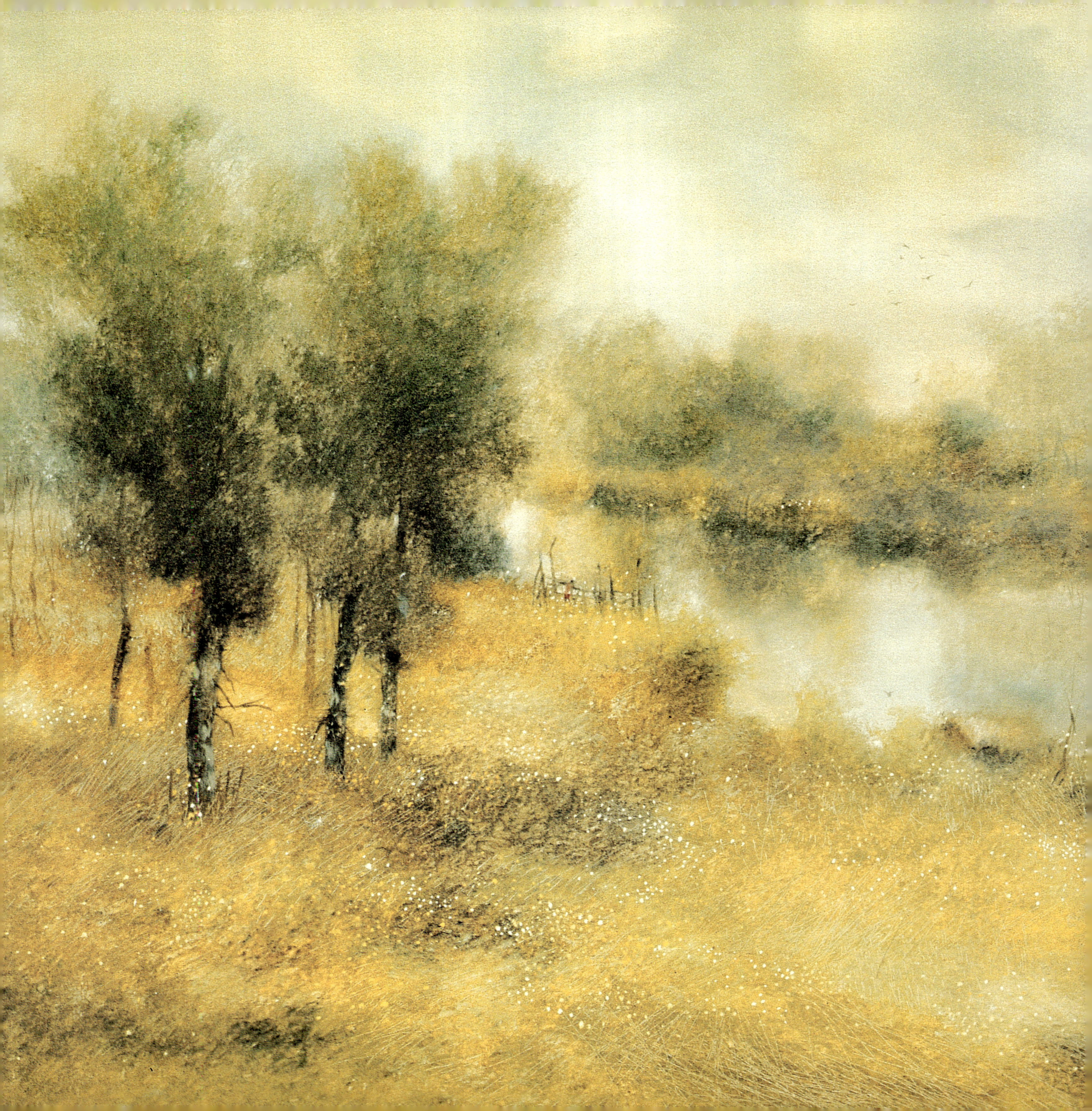

Satish nurtured his passion for flowers in his cottage garden, which won the first prize for small gardens in an annual competition organized by the governor of Uttar Pradesh. The governor would himself visit Satish to look at his paintings and to relax with him over a cup of coffee in the garden. This is the cottage in which we lived after our marriage.

My mind goes back to a spring-kissed morning of 1970. A soft breeze whispered sweet nothings to the trees burgeoning with flowers, soaking the air with their fragrance, and the birds twittered joyously. I saw a young man in his twenties moving towards me. He was tall, lean and masculine, radiating an abundance of vitality and energy. There was more to him than his youthful good looks. An underlying peacefulness gave him an almost divine presence. And his eyes – luminous black eyes, radiating light – looked deep into my soul. A soft honey smooth voice addressed me, "Hello, I am Satish Chandra. May I know your name?" Even as I stretched out my hand in answer, "Hello! call me Meenakshi," a strange sensation tickled the pit of my stomach – as if I had touched something familiar, something old, something deep – and a voice within whispered, 'friends once more to be?'

Intrigued and somewhat perturbed by my own emotions, I wanted to know more about this man. We became friends. He met my parents and became a frequent visitor in our home. Of an enticing and magnetic personality, full of wit and good humour, intelligent, a glib and bright conversationalist, Satish soon found his way into the hearts of my parents.

Over the next few months he drew us further into his world of landscape painting – "my first love!", he quipped, his soft smile bringing a glow to his face. This time, his eyes twinkled – did I see stars in his eyes? He invited us to a one-man show of his paintings held at 'Soochna Kendra' and at the famous Carlton Hotel, which was second home to him.

Facing page: Oil on canvas, 1992.

By this time Satish was well-known in the art world and critics and art-lovers were of the view that he had made a mark within the first few years of his career as a landscape artist.

One day, Satish took permission from my parents to make my portrait. We were in the College Of Arts and Crafts – I, a student, he a teacher. It was during those sessions that he popped the question: "Will you marry me?" Confused and shy, I had asked him to repeat himself and he had promptly said, "Yes, I said what you heard...!" That naughty simplicity is special to him. I asked him to give me time to think. I spoke to my parents. My mother was happy and gave her consent, for a quick and deep bond had developed between Satish and her. My father, a bureaucrat, had planned to marry me off to a government officer. However, my mother convinced him into yielding.

On my twenty-first birthday, my parents invited him over to dinner. He came, a bouquet of red roses in one hand and in the other a gift with bright blue, silver, lavender and sunny-yellow

A group of students that Satish taught. Meenakshi is standing second from right, middle row.

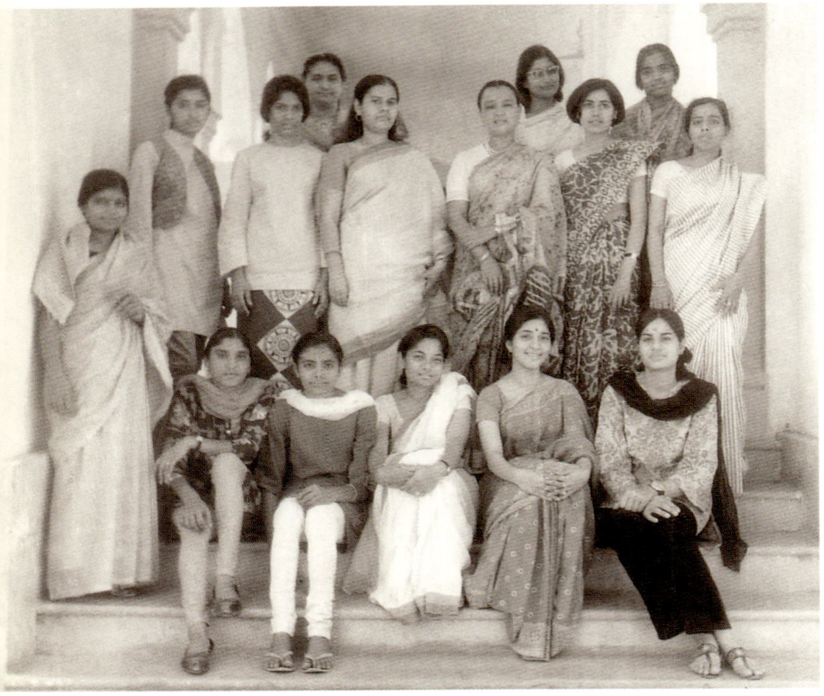

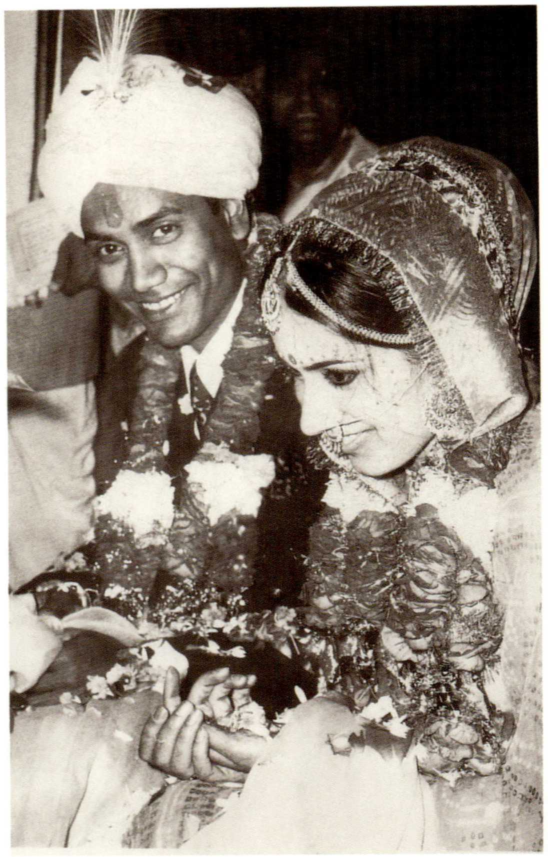

Roses all the way: Satish and Meenakshi on their wedding day.

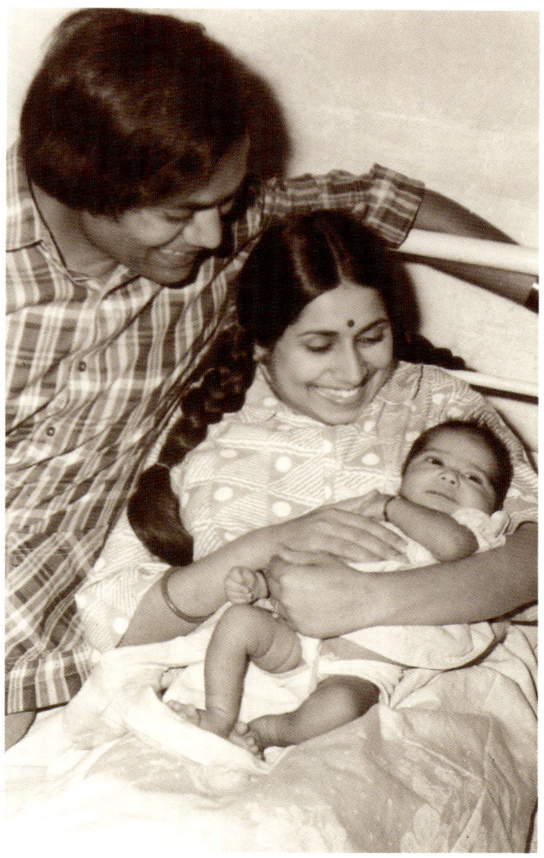

Satish and Meenakshi with their new-born, Siddharth: The kind of love the father and son shared was unique.

ribbons wrapped around it. As he looked at me his eyes seemed to say "Come home" – and I knew my answer, for only the eyes know how to lead you into the mind of the one they gaze upon; only the mind knows how to lead you into the heart of the one with whom you have found a mental affinity; only the heart knows how to lead you into union with the soul of the one you love; and only the soul is well aware of how to lead you then into the ecstasy of oneness.

We got married on 31 January 1972 and were blessed with a son in 1975, whom we named 'Siddharth Chandra'. Satish's son became the centre of his universe and the kind of love they shared was unique. Neither could bear to see the other unhappy even for an

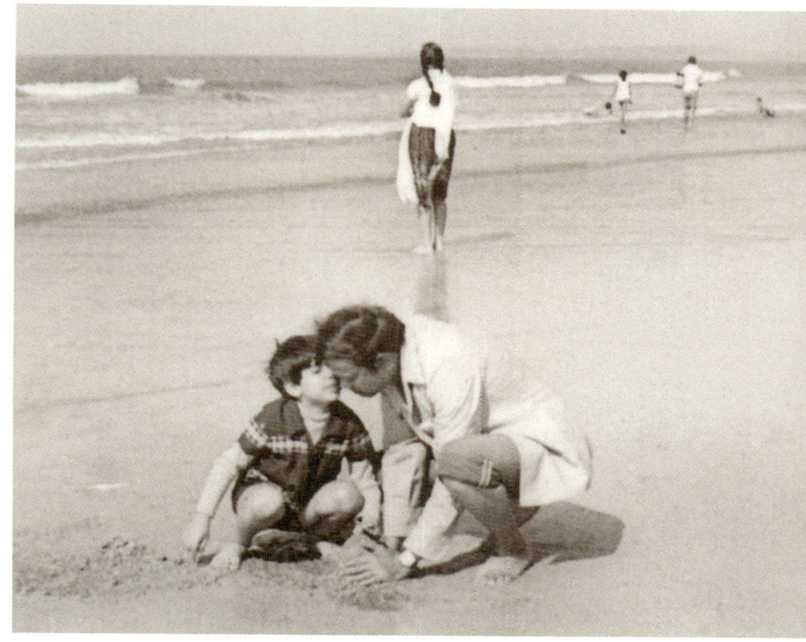

At the beach: Siddharth quickly became the centre of Satish's universe.

instant. But then Satish was an ideal father. From the beginning, he involved himself in his child's growing up. Never stifling Siddharth's curiosity, initiative and confidence, he helped his son develop his own personality.

Living with Satish enriched not just my life but my entire being. He was not just my husband but my best friend, mentor and guide. It was from him that I learnt that happiness and fulfilment result from the small steps we take in the direction of our dreams.

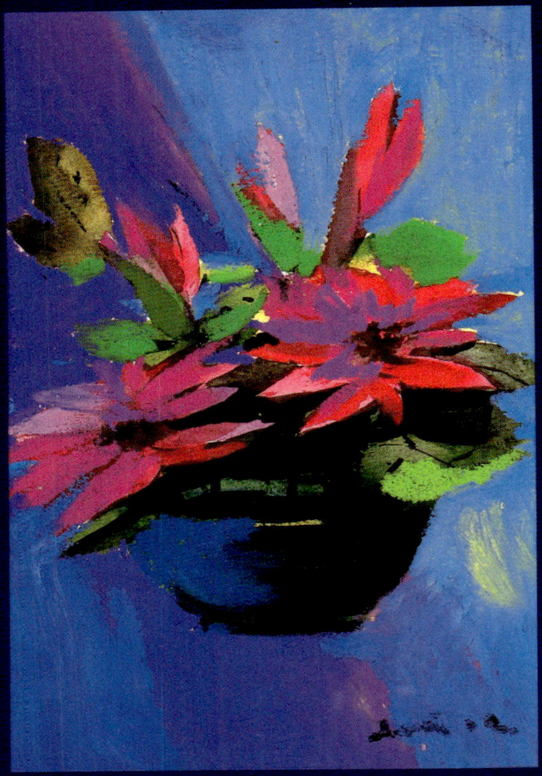

Watercolour on paper, 2002.
Facing page: Watercolour on paper, 2002.

In our lives the fragrance and beauty of flowers has come to stay. Satish's love for flowers can be traced back to his childhood. "Flowers are the moment's representations of things that are in themselves eternal," he says, as he lovingly gives me a flower every morning, after first offering flowers at the feet of Lord Shiva in our 'pooja room'. Though a gardener tends the garden, Satish finds great joy in caressing the plants and talking to them softly. He has green fingers, for I

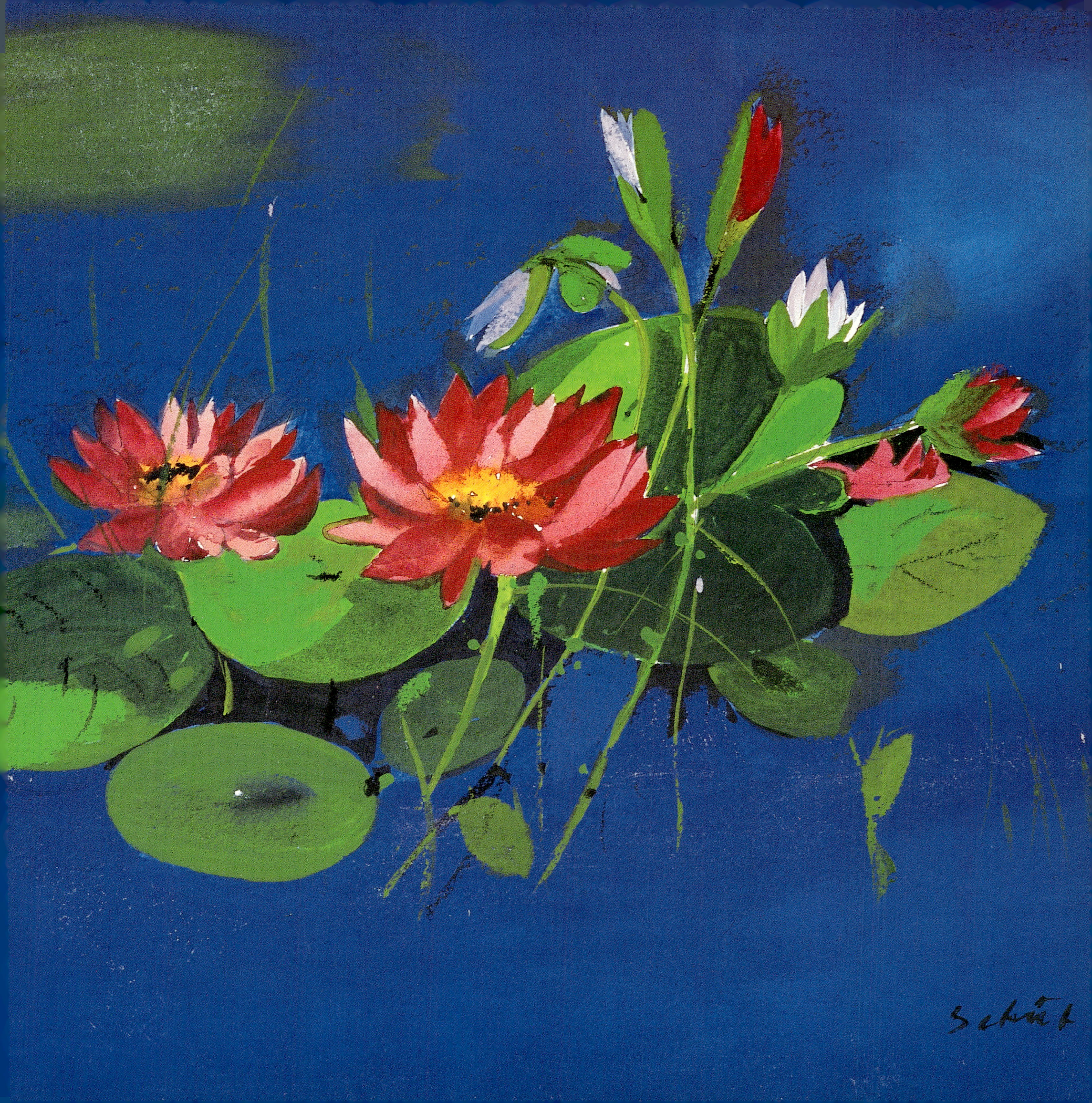

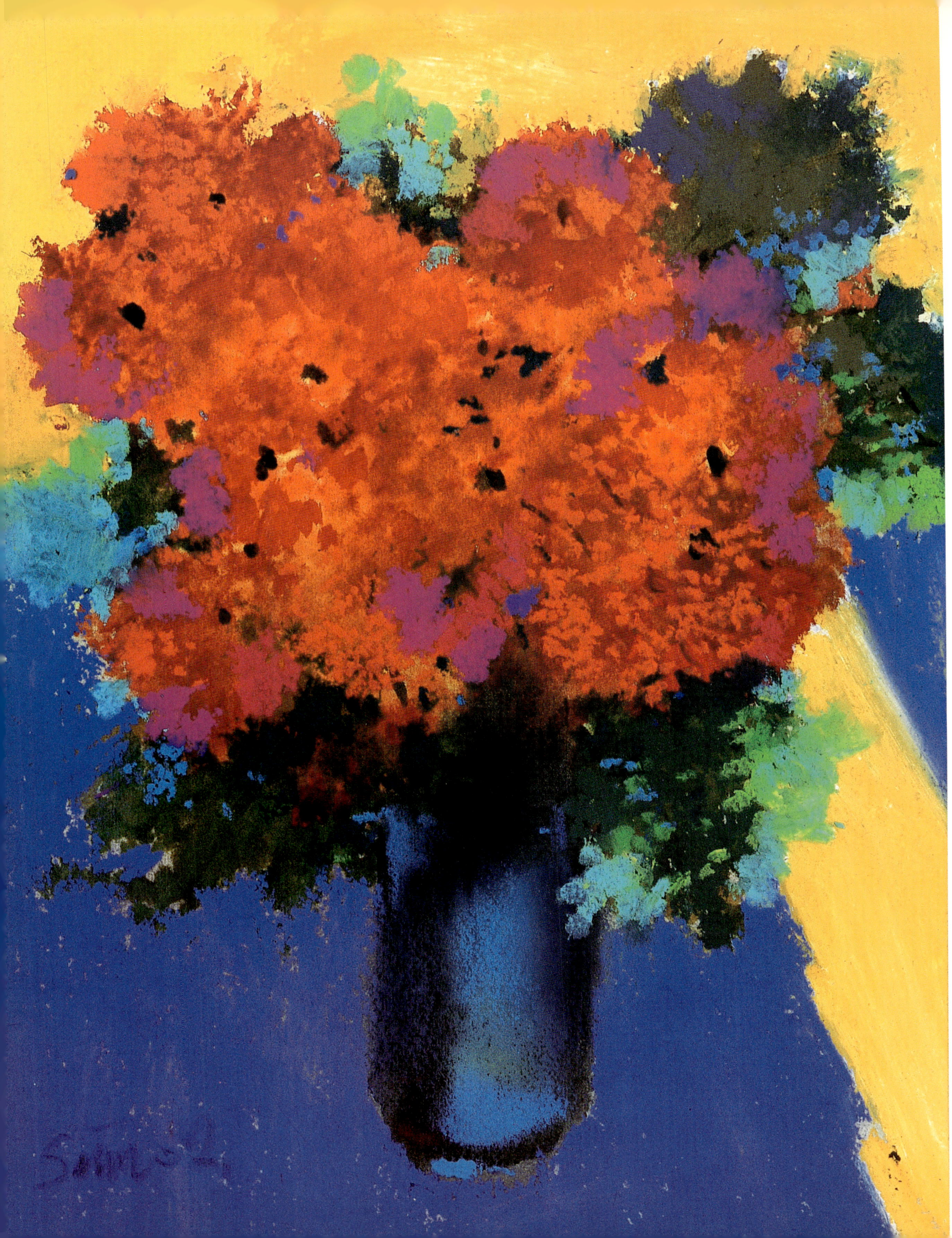

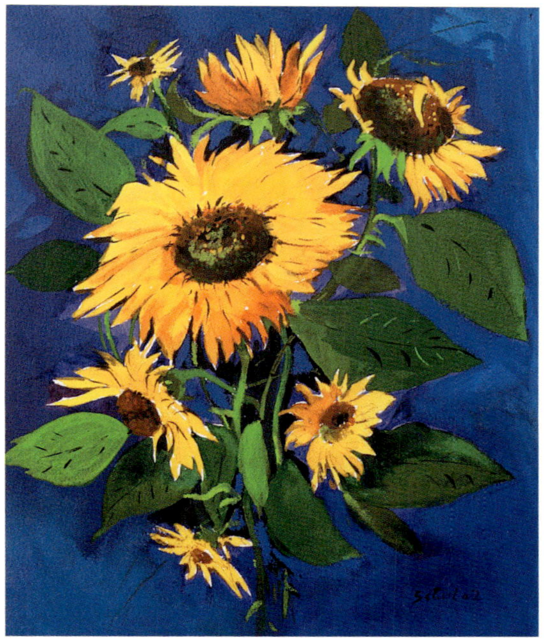

Watercolour on paper, 2002.
Facing page: Watercolour on paper, 2002.

"Flowers are the moment's representations of things that are in themselves eternal... The best way to open ourselves to the influence of flowers is to love them."

have seen sick plants recover completely under his care. And if he pays them a compliment by words or by feelings, if he admires them, well, I have seen them hold up their head – with vanity!

Over the years his passion for flowers has poured forth on paper in watercolour and in mixed-media. Clusters, fistsful or bunches of flowers, under his touch, bloom and blossom out on paper in all their splendour and glory. Satish paints delicate clusters of white, pink, light blue, mauve or light yellow flowers set among velvety foliage – they seem to envelop and conquer us by their sweetness and beauty.

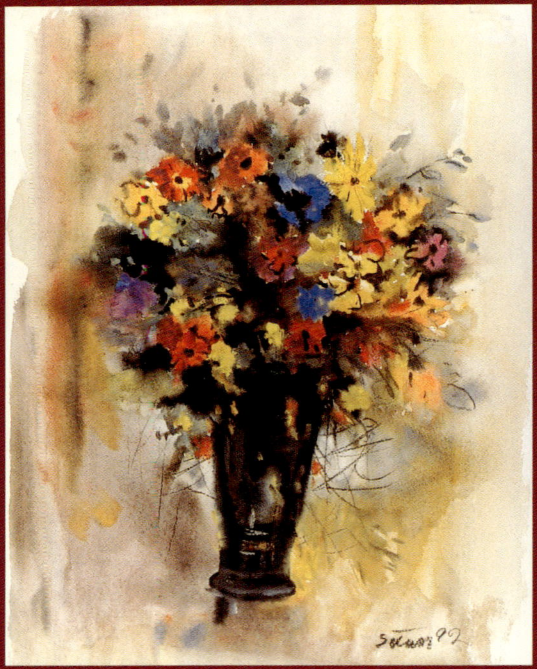 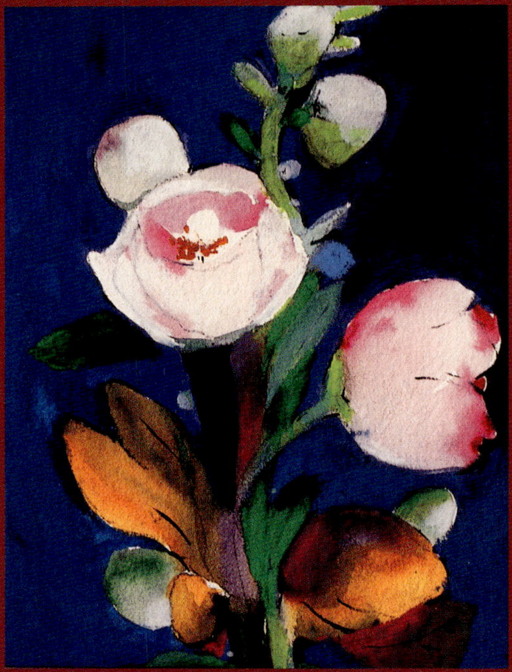 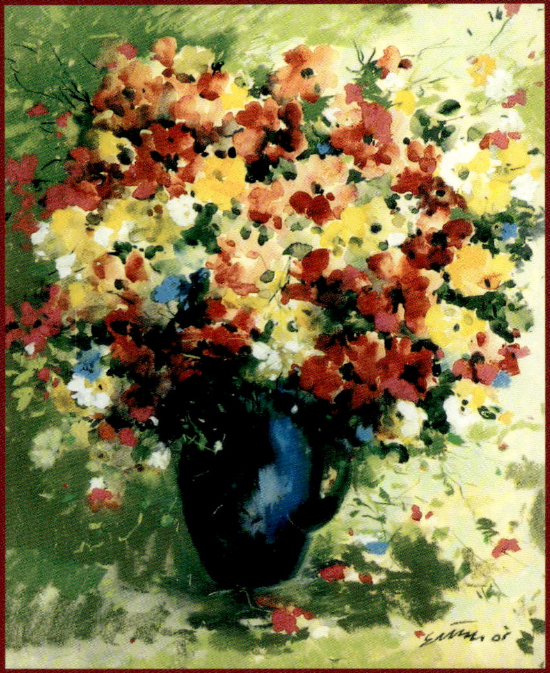

Satish feels that the beauty of flowers is a means used by Nature to awaken the inner self of human beings. "The best way to open ourselves to the influence of flowers is to love them," says Satish. He feels that flowers share their beauty and perfume with one and all, without reserve or restriction. Tender, sweet, so close to us and so loving, always cheerful and happy, their presence fills the heart with joy.

"Be like a flower!" says Satish.

Watercolour on paper,
from left to right: 1992; 2003; 2001.
Facing page: Watercolour on paper, 2003.
Following pages 76-77: Oil on canvas, 2002.

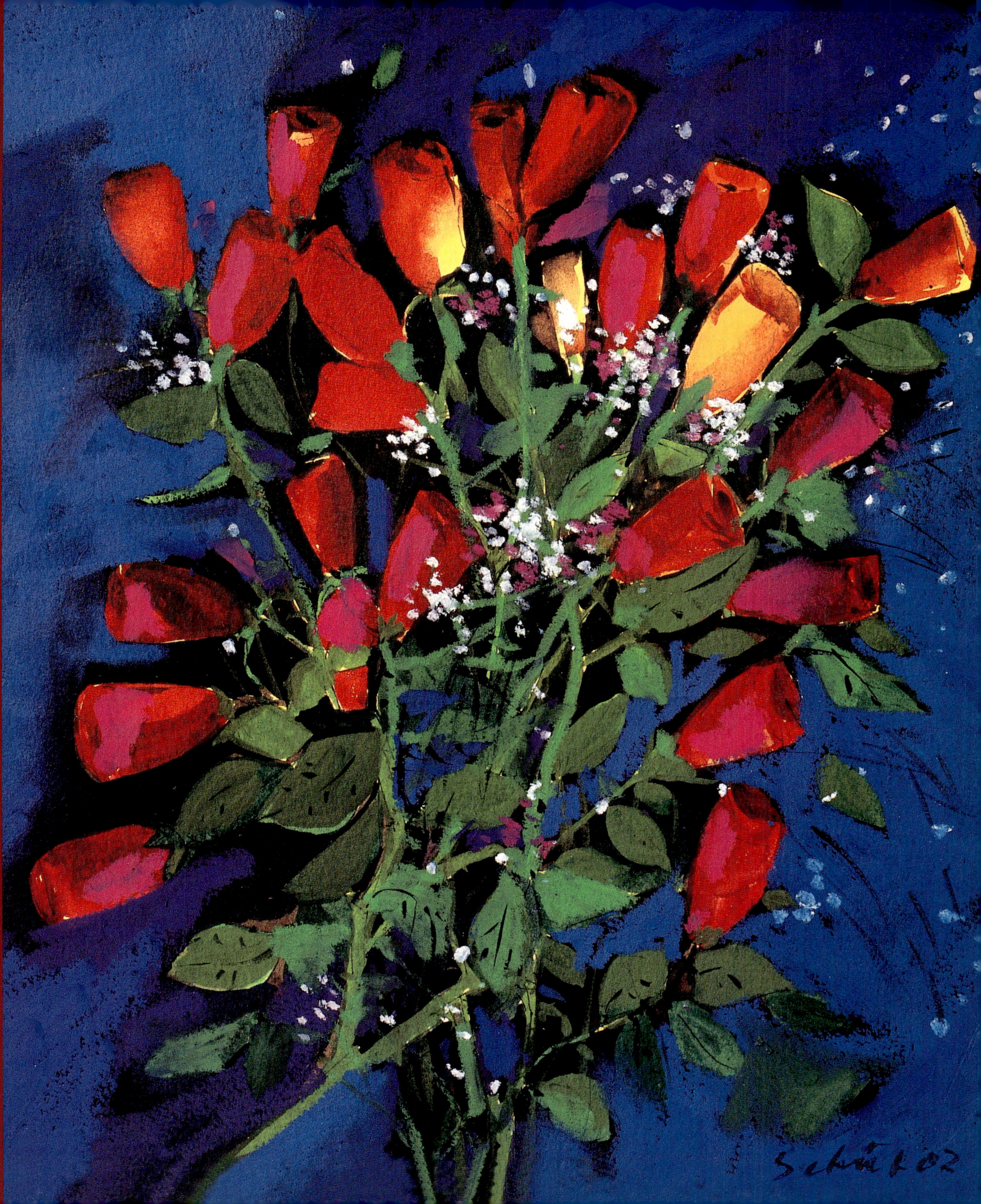

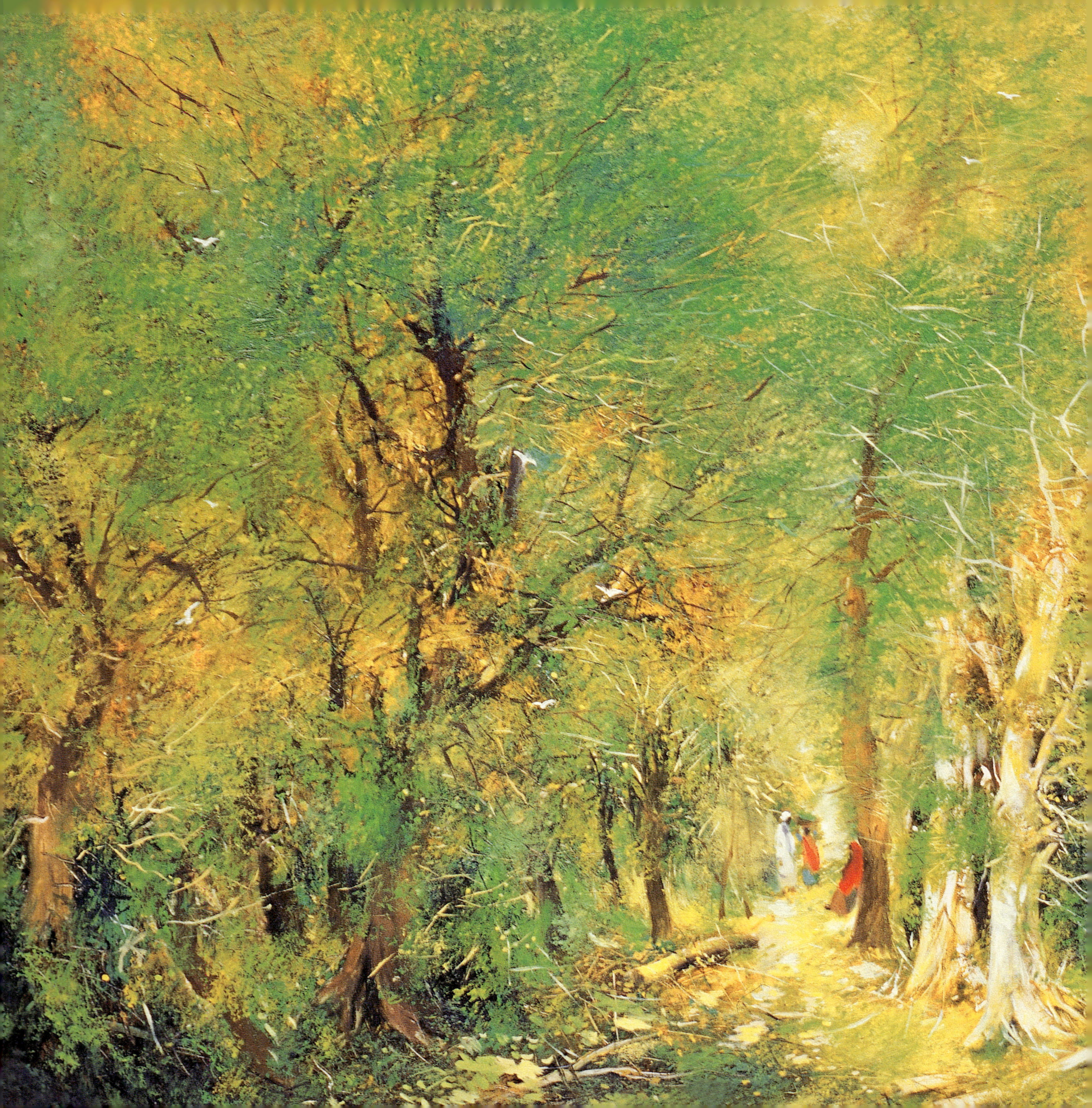

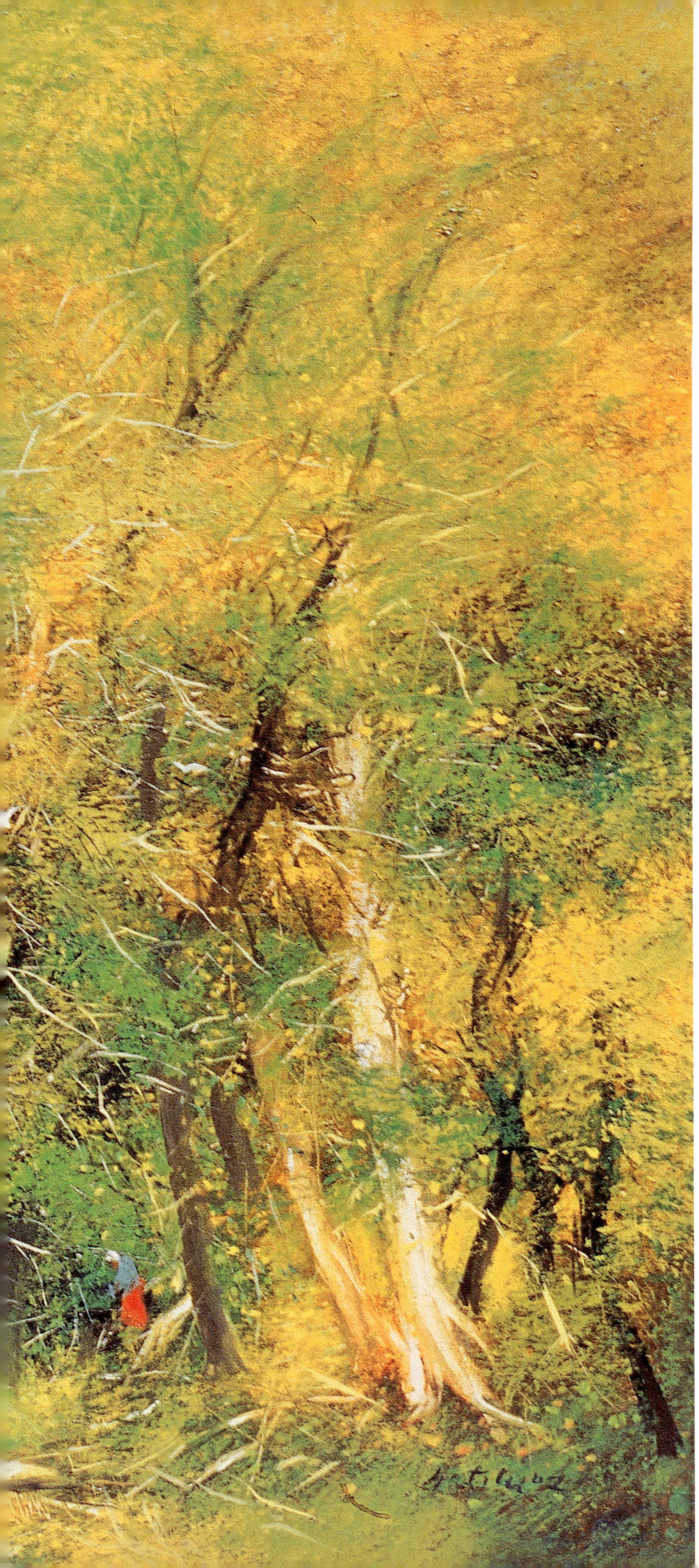

Nature is always bright.
I do not find darkness
anywhere in the world.
Darkness comes
from within.

– Satish Chandra

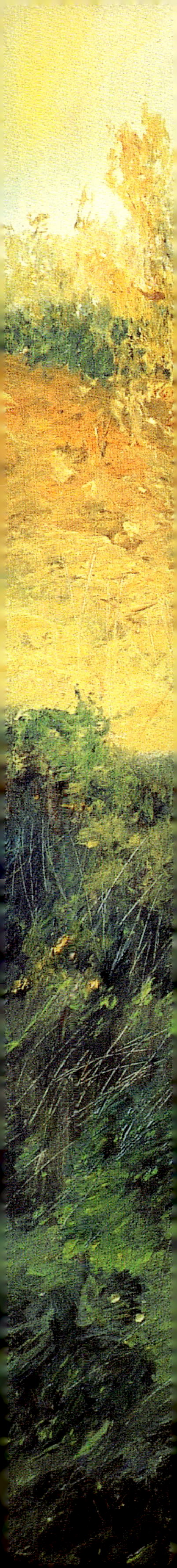

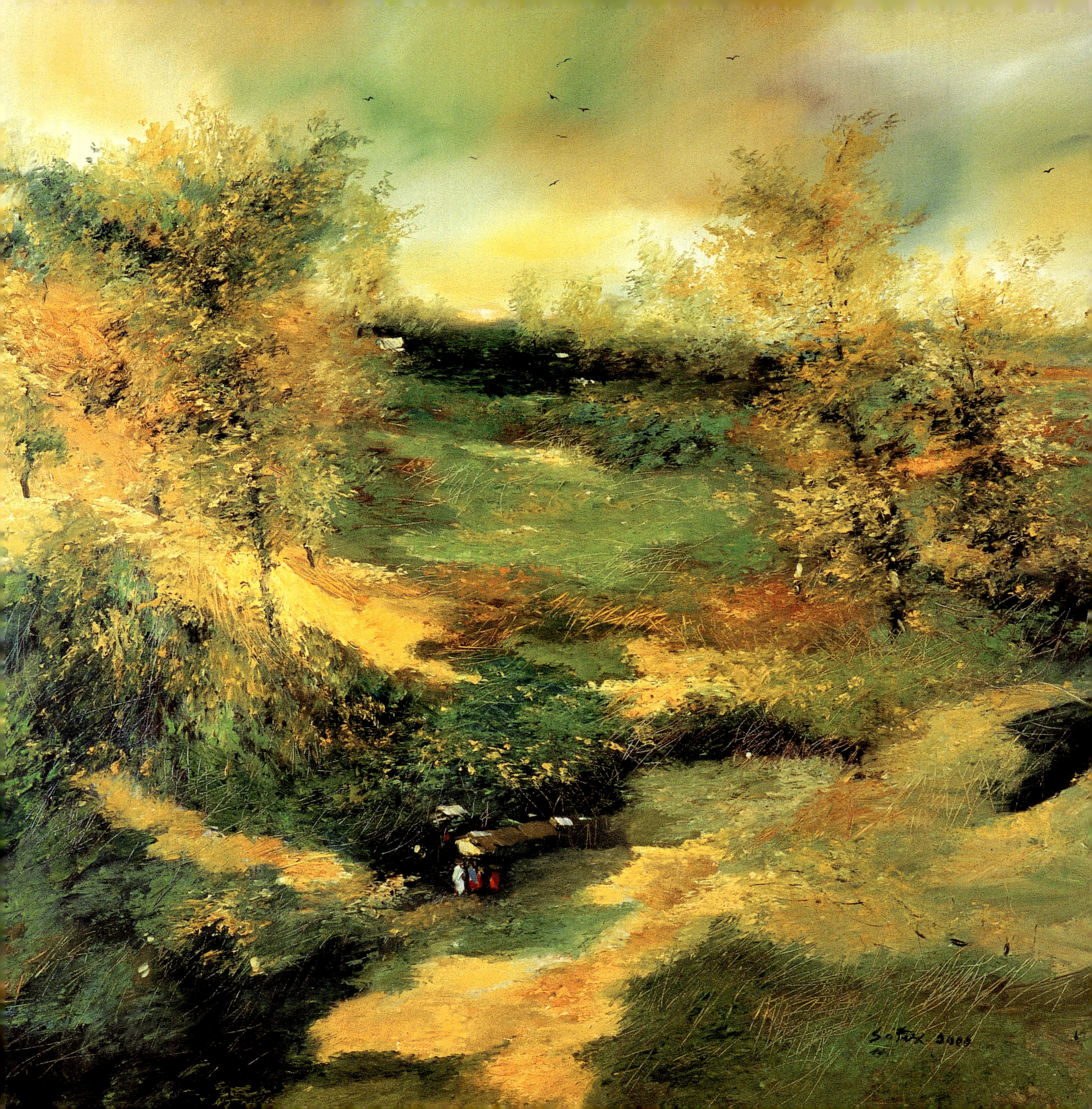

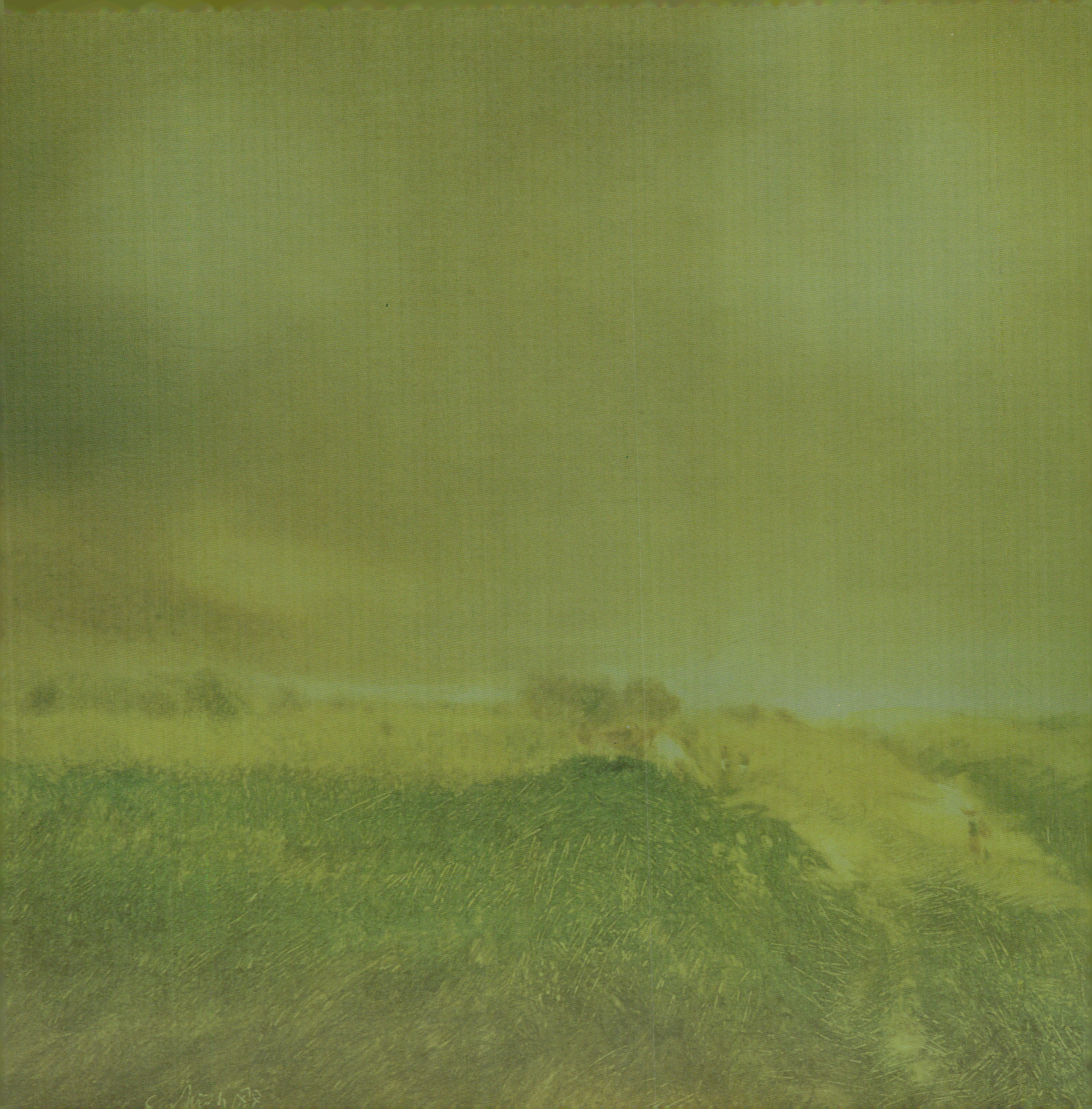

Reaching the Pinnacle

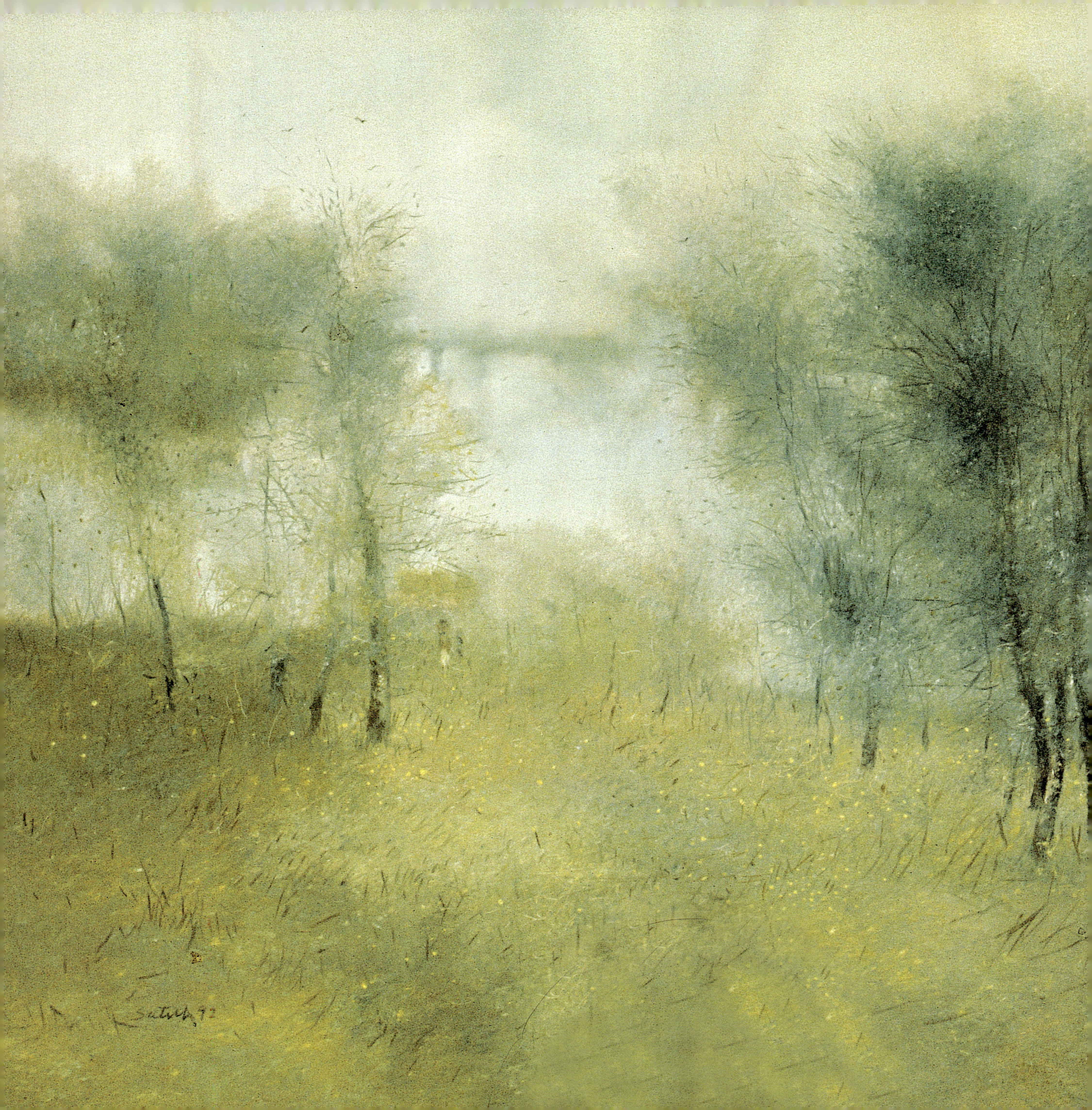

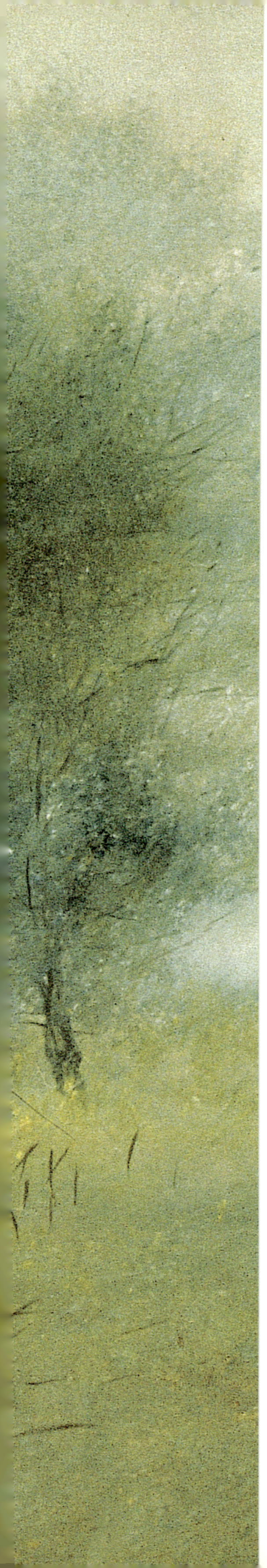

The period that followed our marriage marked the beginning of Satish's success as an artist. Gradually he built up a reputation for creating mysterious and compelling images of remarkable spiritual intensity, for the deeper he plunged into the mystery of colour, the higher became his visionary state. His landscapes were spontaneous representations of his states of mind, thus bringing to mind Wordsworth when he said, "Art is the spontaneous overflow of powerful feelings, from emotions recollected in tranquillity."

In the ensuing years Satish became a celebrated landscape painter on the Indian art scene, patronized by influential leaders, bureaucrats, art connoisseurs and art galleries.

In the years 1964, 1965 and 1967 he was honoured by the UP State Lalit Kala Akademi. In 1968, at the age of twenty-eight, he was awarded the Radha Kamal Mukerjee Gold Medal by the vice chancellor of Lucknow University for his landscape painting.

The years at the College of Arts and Crafts, Lucknow, as lecturer in the department of fine arts were marked by a long and monotonous struggle, for the institution was infested with petty politics. Though Satish steered clear of this campus politics, there was nothing much he could do to protect himself from the overpowering feeling of jealousy and frustration among certain artists against him. For fourteen years he worked 'ad hoc', for in this way they thought they had found a way to break him. Yet, these were the people Satish continued to respect and help whenever they needed help. I would be enraged at the injustice but Satish would calm me down and, in a soothing, soft tone, say: "There is no way that we can escape trials and difficulties in life.

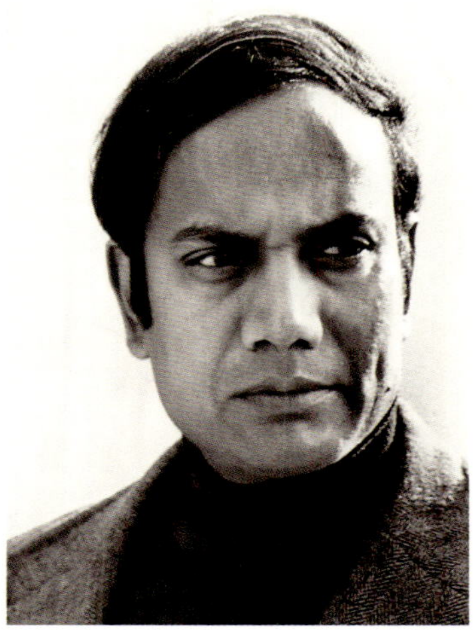

By the time he was thirty, Satish had established himself as a landscape painter par excellence.
Facing page: Oil on canvas, 1992.

The secret to surviving them is our own response to them."

Satish kept himself immersed in his painting and found joy and happiness in his home and among his friends. He did not allow dejection to seep into his soul, nor did he allow those years of strife and opposition to warp his outlook on life and turn vindictive.

He has always been the type of person who, to avoid hurting other people, keeps many things locked inside him. I have often heard Satish softly sing Bulle Shah's famous verse in which he says:

Masjid dhaade, mandir dhaade
Dhaade jo kuchh dhainda
Par kissi da dil na dhain
Rab dilaan vich rehnda.

Break the mosque and
break the temple
But do not break the human heart,
within which God resides.

But I saw the amount of emotional trauma and stress Satish went through. It is not surprising that he developed a heart condition. In the year 1985, Satish was in Bombay, alone, when he suffered a stroke and by the time he was taken to the Bombay Hospital, he collapsed. The doctors' team, headed

Facing page: Oil on canvas, 1999.

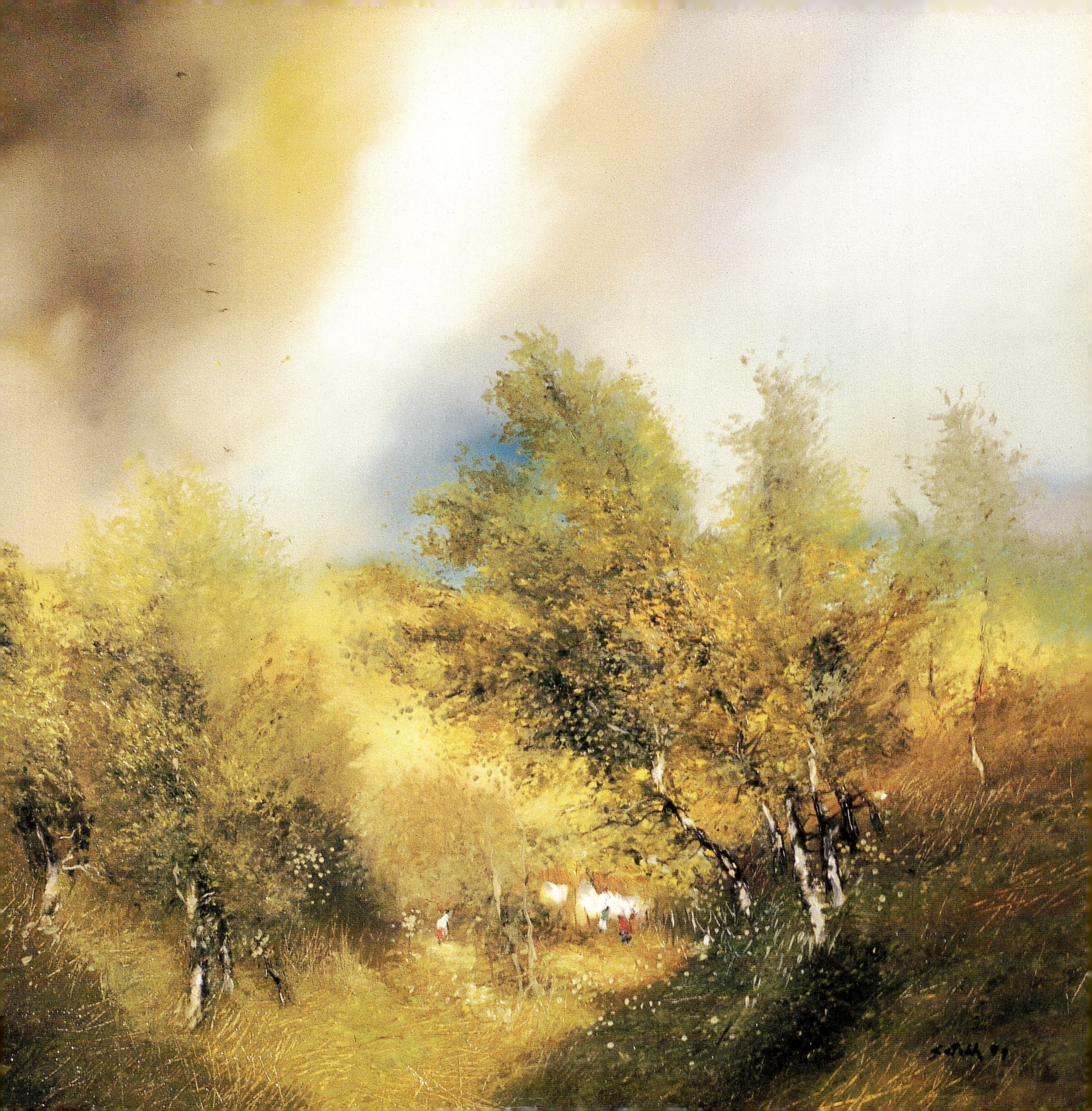

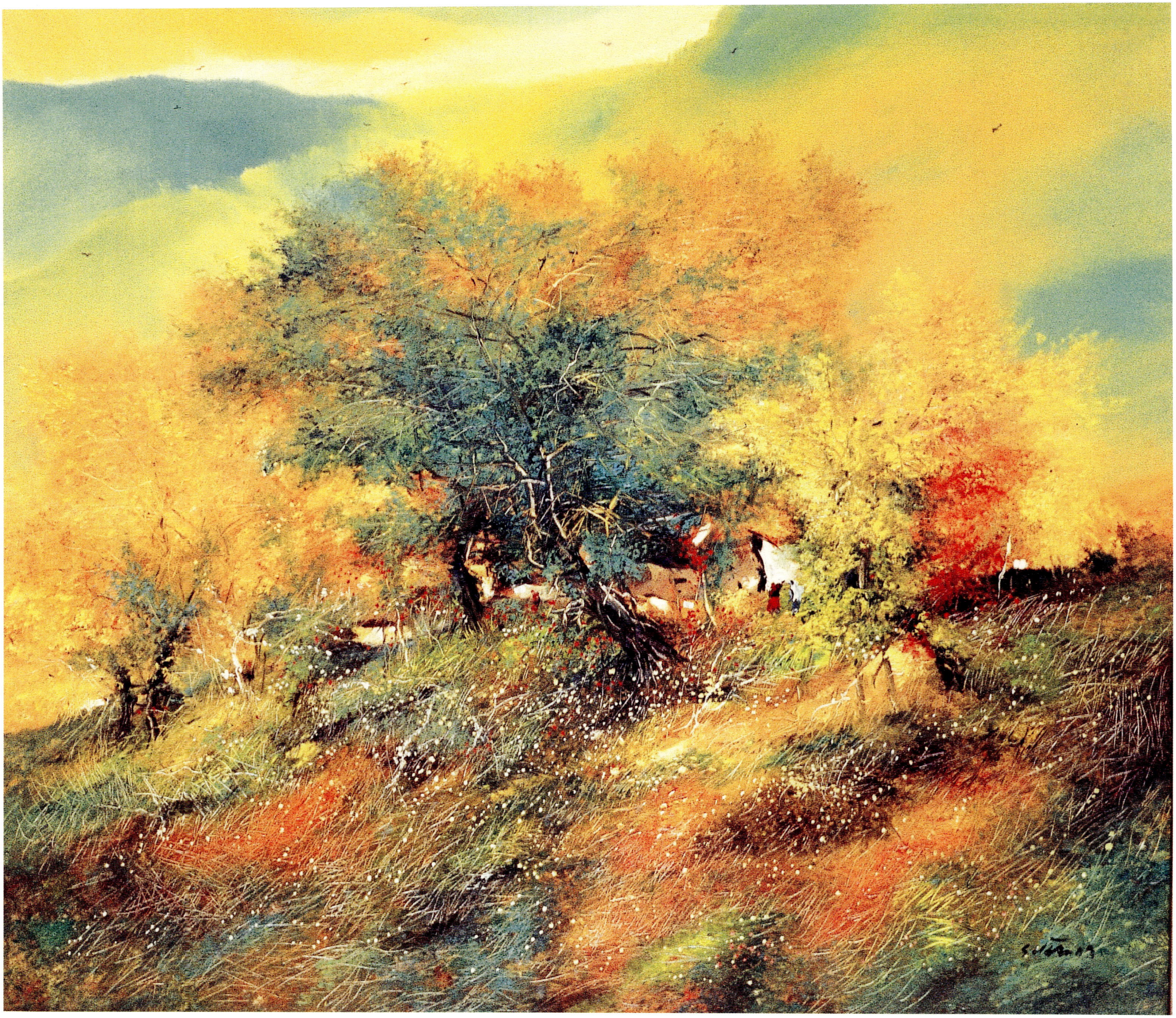

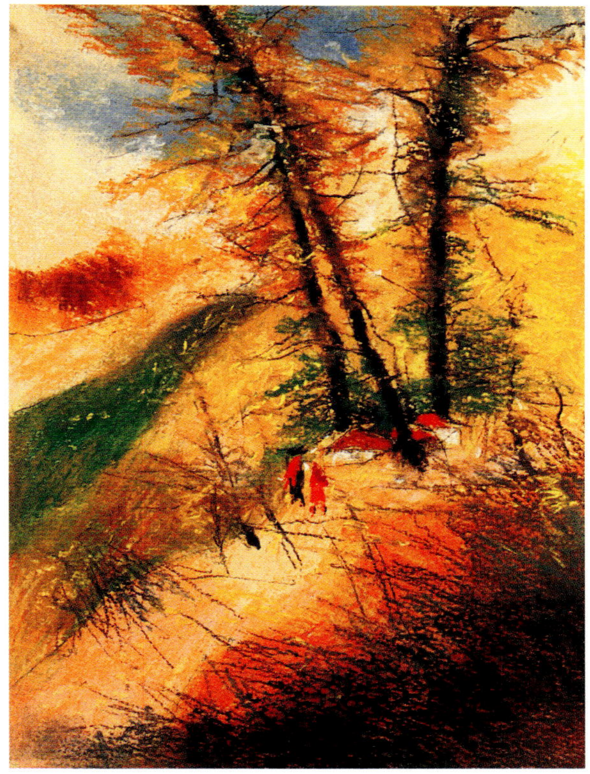

Mixed media on paper.
Facing page: Oil on canvas, 1999.

"My life in landscape painting became a pilgrimage, a sacred path towards the new revelation of my inner being. I understood that my identity as a painter had survived, an identity that no outside force could destroy."

by Dr N.J. Shah, declared him dead and covered him with a sheet. Later, Satish told me about his revelatory experience – "Suddenly my body seemed to disappear and I was out in space, moving upwards at a great speed, towards a very powerful white light that seemed to suffuse me – and then I remembered that my responsibility to my family was my primary duty; a prayer escaped my lips to let me go back, for my son was so very young and so was my wife." The next thing he knew, he had re-entered his body. A sweeper standing there noticed the faint finger movements and called back the team of doctors who had abandoned him for dead. Doctors have not yet understood the nature of this miracle. Satish was just forty-five years old at the time.

This incident transformed Satish's life completely. It marked the beginning of a journey of deep personal and spiritual transformation and it influenced his work as well. Satish tells me, "My life in landscape painting

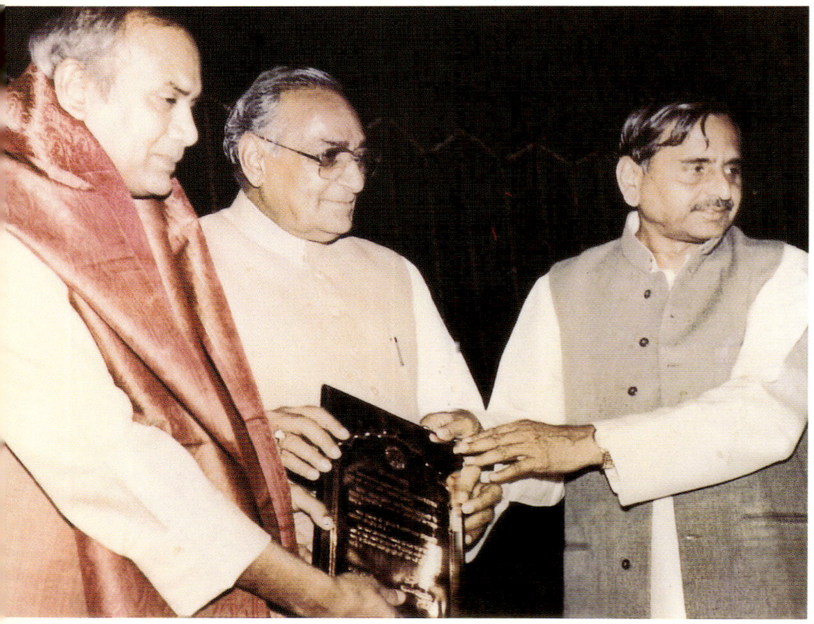

In 1993, Satish received the Yash Bharti Samman from the Uttar Pradesh government as the state's leading artist.

became a pilgrimage, a sacred path towards the new revelation of my inner being. I understood that my identity as a painter had survived, an identity that no outside force could destroy." Intuitively, instinctively, Satish returned to painting.

This stroke of 1985 was followed by other heart attacks. Yet, the period that ensued was one of great artistic achievements. He developed a new sensitivity to colour and many of his finest and most poignant works come from this time. His landscapes came to be distinguished by their powerful mood and atmosphere.

Soon after returning from Bombay, Satish met Dr. Mansoor Hasan, a cardiologist, at a friend's house in Lucknow. Both had heard of each other and they clicked immediately. Dr. Mansoor asked Satish questions about Indian art and religion. Satish felt that Dr Mansoor was a person full of warmth and compassion and was genuinely interested in Satish's views and knowledge. Impressed with each other, they fixed up to meet again. Dr. Mansoor would invite us to his beautiful village home at Garhi Samadabad, built on a cliff along the River Ganga. Over the years, this bond deepened. They met often, and over a cup of coffee and chocolate biscuits, they talked about Indian art and culture, religion and its different aspects, politics, 'shairi', music, and many other things. They inspired each other. Those who were aware of the kind of friendship they shared, called them 'twin souls'.

In 1989, the president of India conferred the National Award on Satish as a leading artist on the Indian art scene, and in 1993 the government of Uttar Pradesh gave him the 'Yash Bharti' award as the state's leading artist. A beautiful park in Modinagar was named after him. He was invited to take part in numerous art exhibitions in India and abroad and held a number of 'one-man' shows. His works found their way into art collections. He was appointed the chairman of the UP State Lalit Kala Akademi in 1994 and continued in that post till 1998.

In 1996, we shifted into a nice little apartment in Gulmohar Enclave on Mall Avenue in Lucknow. And in 2003, a lovely girl named Pooja stepped into our home as our son Siddharth's bride.

In 2001, at the age of sixty-one, Satish was once again seriously ill. This time, it was due to vascular techicardia – his pulse rate went up to 185 beats per minute. He had to be

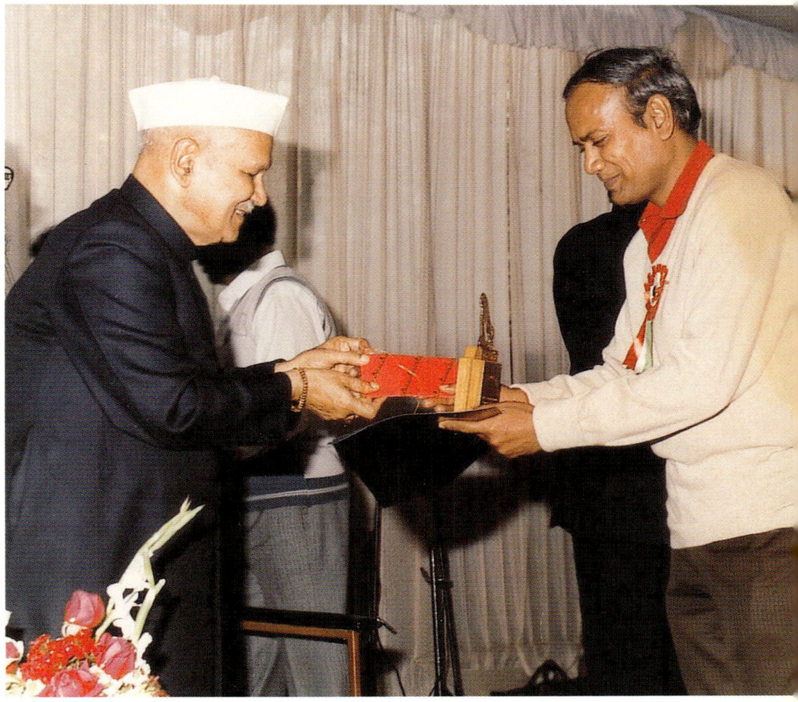

In 1989, Satish received the National Award from the President of India as a leading artist of the country.

rushed to the SGPGI (Sanjay Gandhi Post Graduate Institute of Medical Sciences), Lucknow. Here, he was given multiple electric shocks to bring his pulse back to normal. However, Satish suffered a cardiac arrest in the middle of the night. But once again, he returned – a miracle again? The doctors implanted an ICD (Implantable Cardioverter Defibrillator) in his left shoulder, as a life-saving device.

We returned home with Satish. He looked like a skeleton, on the verge of a nervous breakdown, after the traumatic experience of so many electric shocks given to him in barely one-and-a-half days. However, with the love and compassion of his family and friends, step by step, Satish's body came to life.

Once again, he lit the 'diya', 'agarbatti' and 'dhoop' in his pooja room. His undying faith in God and in meditation gave him the strength to return to normalcy and to his 'first love' – landscape painting. He picked up his brush. Each painting became a prayer offered at His feet. Feelings close to his heart found expression in the writing of Amir Khusro:

Tuan katil ke az - behere tamasha kum
Ke khoon-e-mun reizi
Mana bismil ke zere khanjare khoonbar
me raksham

Facing page: Oil on canvas, 2002.

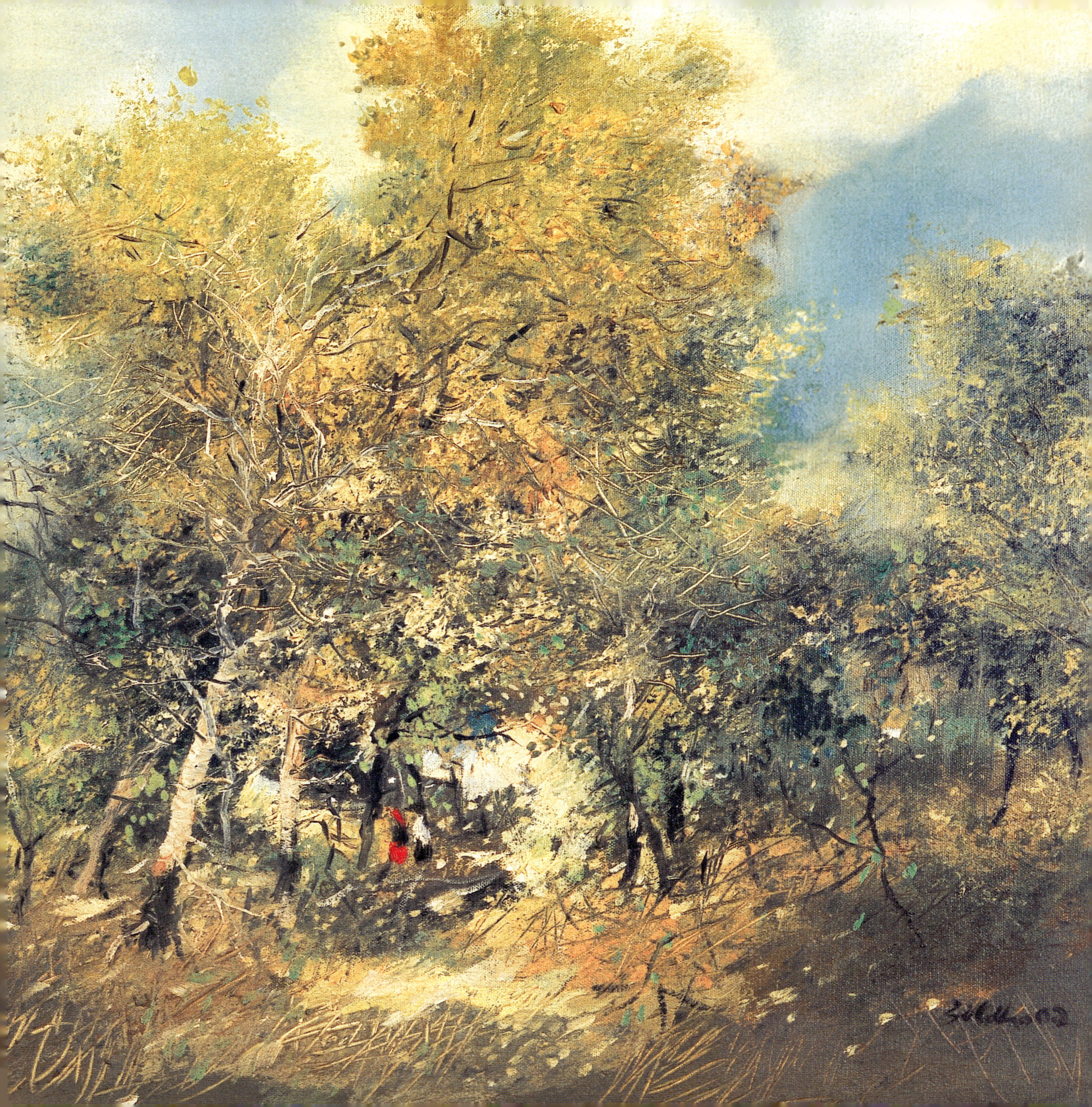

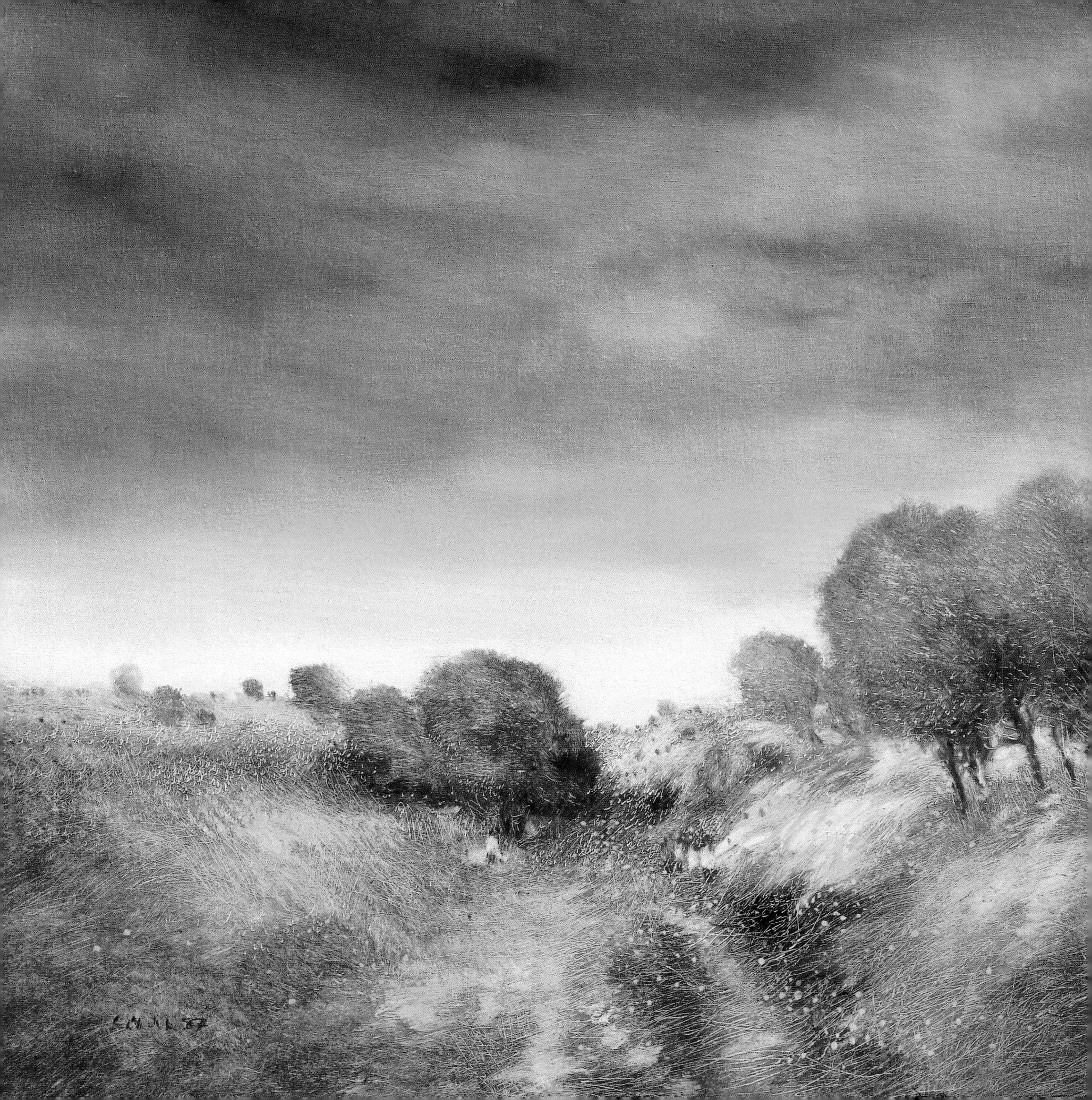

Biya jana ke darambo jabazan
Basad samane ruswai sare bazaar me raksham.

Look at me, in a state of imminent death,
I dance under the dripping blood-stained dagger
Amidst the throng of your devotees I dance
With all the denunciation that I may receive as a madman
I still dance with joy in your love.

Gradually, Nature healed him. As he said, "In the lap of Nature, my internal vision brightens, worldly preoccupations vanish and the sacred dialogue between myself and Nature begins." It was at this time that Satish's paintings gained in intensity and spiritual essence, and the colours glowed on his canvases with the inner glow of his spirit.

Facing page: Oil on canvas, 1987.
Following pages 94-95: Oil on canvas, 1983.

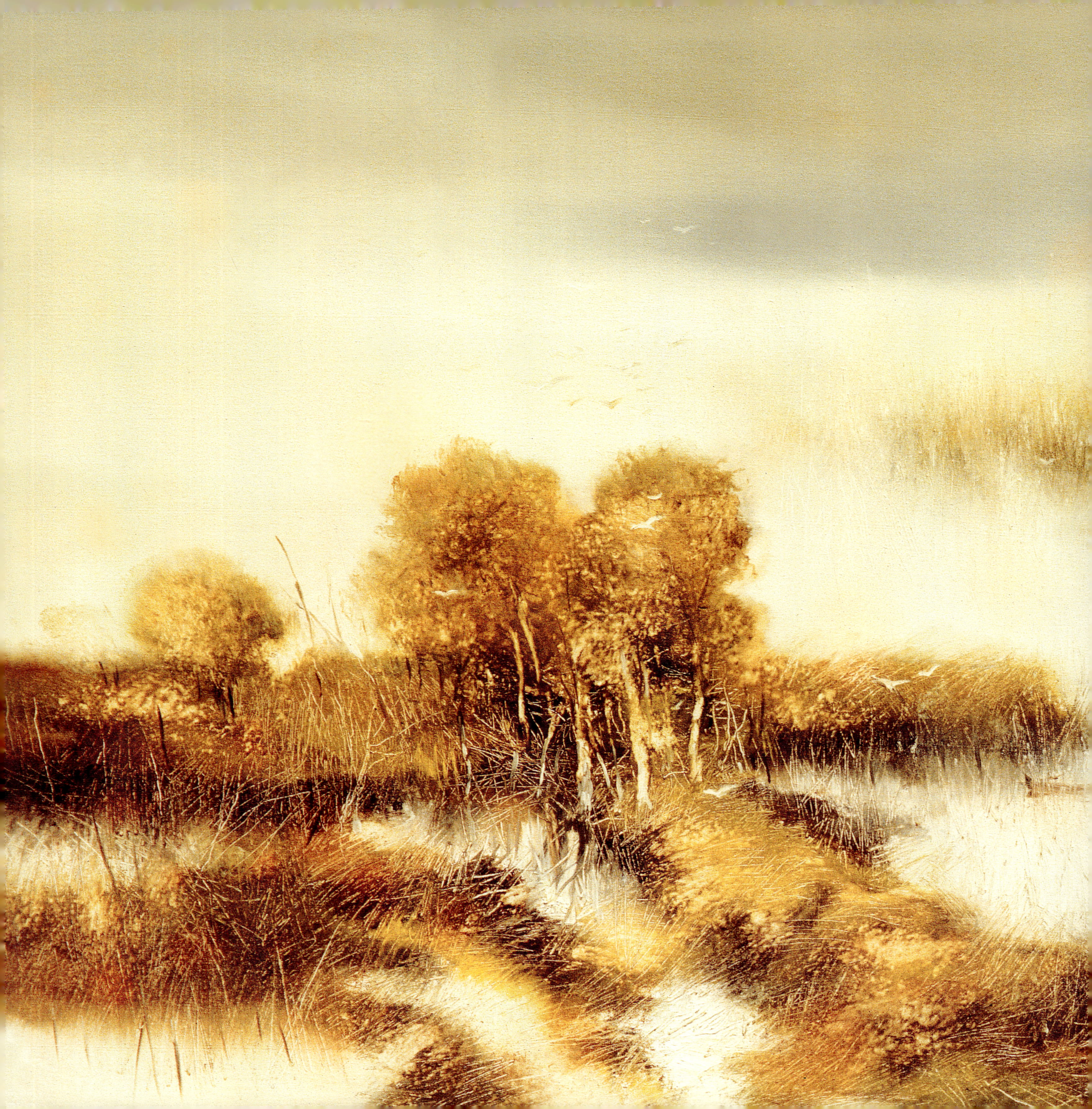

In the lap of Nature my internal vision brightens, worldly preoccupations vanish and the sacred dialogue between myself and Nature begins.

– Satish Chandra

A Touch of Magic

"... There is a touch of magic in his paintings, that inexplicable extra quality that sets apart a work of art. ..."

– The Afternoon Despatch & Courier

Facing page: Mixed media on paper, 1999.

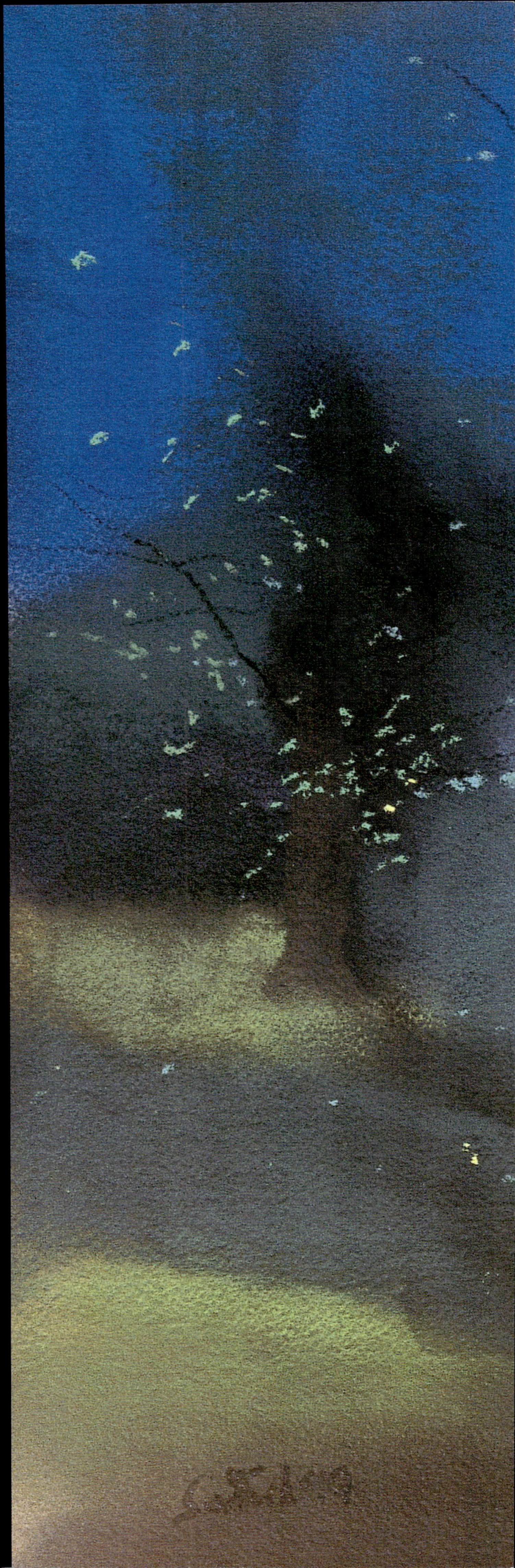

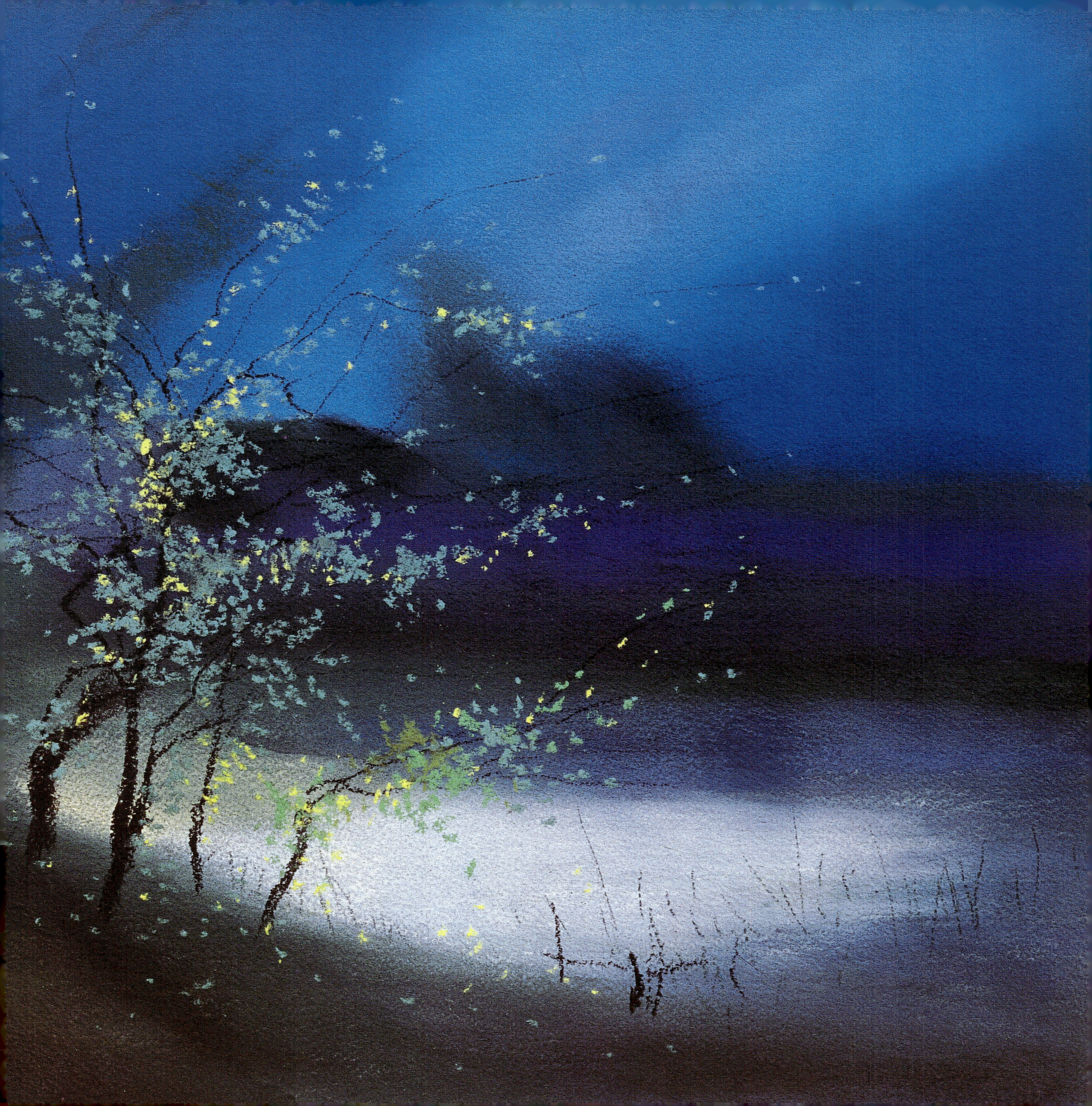

Understanding the Artist

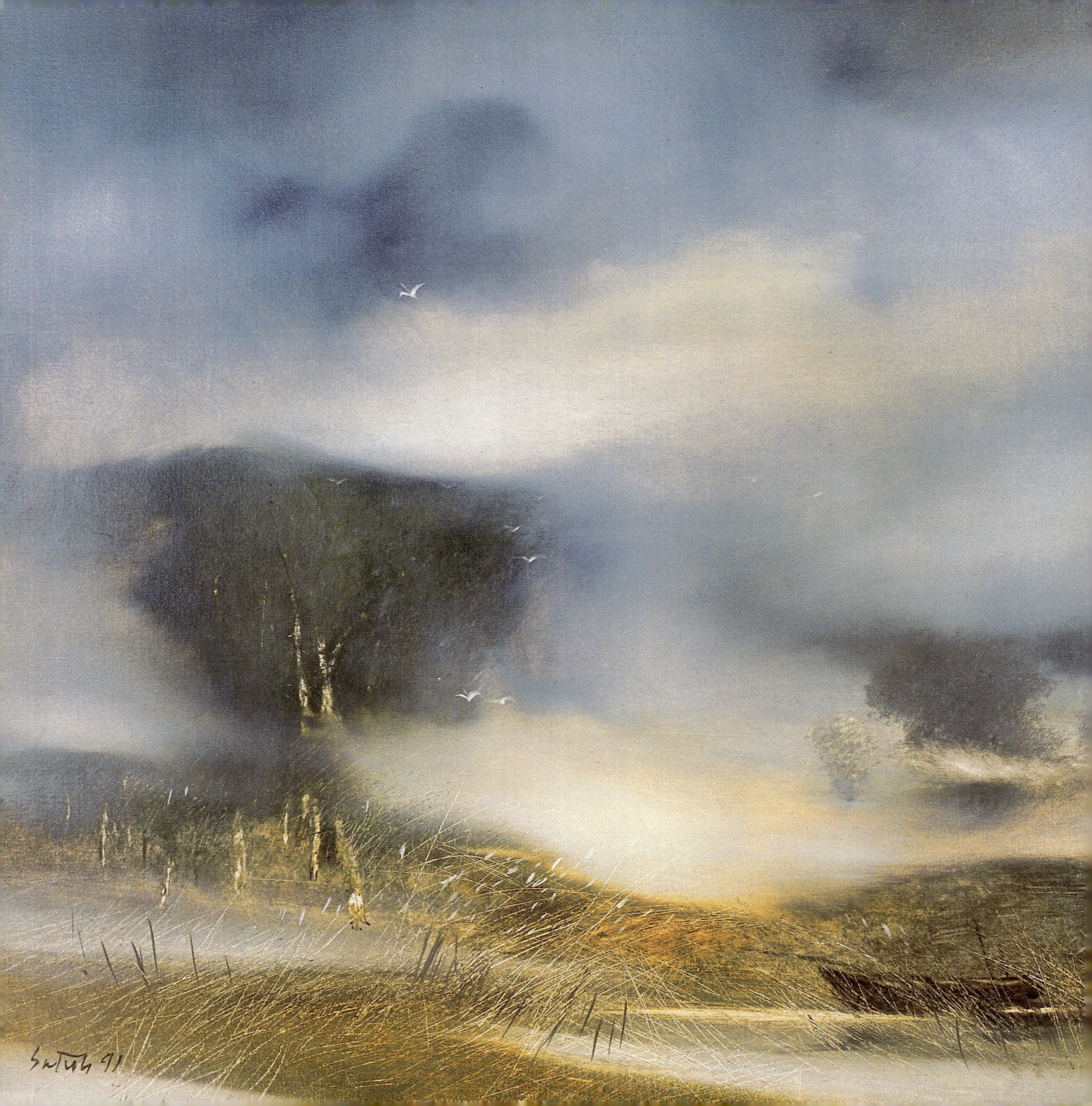

Acquaintance with an artist has to be nurtured. It does not mean knowing his name and age, or nodding to him when one comes across him in the street or even spending hours in conversation with him. It means knowing his work well enough to be able to spot it immediately.

In an age when abstract and figurative paintings dominate the art scene, it is a pleasant surprise to come across an artist devoted solely to landscape painting. Although Satish has passed through the alleys of abstraction in his early years, landscapes are and have been his first love.

Often ignored as a cliched genre, landscape painting has a small but dedicated group of artists in India such as Gopal Ghosh, Ram Kumar, Paramjit Singh, Joshi and Dhond. Satish continues in this illustrious tradition. What makes his treatment different from that of his peers is the ability to imbue the ordinary in Nature with a distinctive vision, characteristic of his art, that commands attention and contemplation.

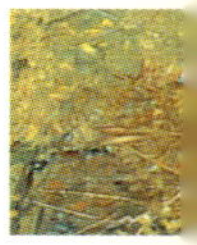

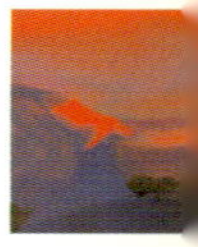

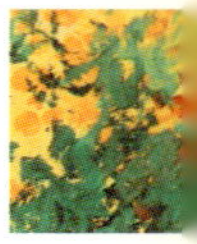

Wisely, Satish does not go after self-conscious experimentation in landscape. "Isms appear to me to be a conscious striving after originality. True originality should be a direct and unconscious revelation of personality," says Satish.

Satish would disdain painting a picture in which several pretty and colourful objects are assembled. He would probably say, why not have a colour photograph? Human art as distinct from mechanical art is eternal, founded on some ineradicable instinct that is part of the human psyche. A fine painting is a personal achievement and as much a part of the creator as his own heart and mind. Behind the hand that paints is a mind, not merely the tradition of a craft. The mind sets itself rather difficult problems: to make a picture yet not an illustration of a beautiful place, scene or assembly of objects. The effort is to be creative rather than descriptive. Many virtues enter into it – the most important of which are love and reverence. It is an arrival, after blundering through a tortuous alley of avoiding

Facing page: Oil on canvas, 1991.

"The moment we start listening to this voice (deep within), a higher level of consciousness is activated and we realize that all that truly matters – inner peace, love, joy, beauty, creativity – arises from beyond the mind. This realization awakens us to a new dimension of life, a spiritual dimension."

cliches and repetition and yet being sufficiently and strikingly communicative. In this situation, being communicative means being recognizably individual, or, in other words, to have a style of one's own.

To a layman, a natural landscape is more or less a monolithic phenomenon. But to an artist who has a keener sensibility, Nature is not a dead but a living thing with its moods and shades – sometimes agitated and wrathful, and sometimes serene, pensive and thoughtful. To the artist it is a subtle and exquisite combination of diverse elements – symphony, colour, music, beauty, harmony and so much more. To capture the different moods of Nature and to depict the natural beauty of a landscape by enhancing its component elements is a task which needs great discerning power. Therefore, to be able to enjoy and interpret a painting we not only need our vision but also our intellect.

Satish does not agree with the assumption that the public does not understand art and is incapable of learning. He wants to break this barrier erected between the artist and the layman. Says he, "Painters are not a race apart and they are really quite human! The idea that they are

Facing page: Mixed media on paper, 2001.

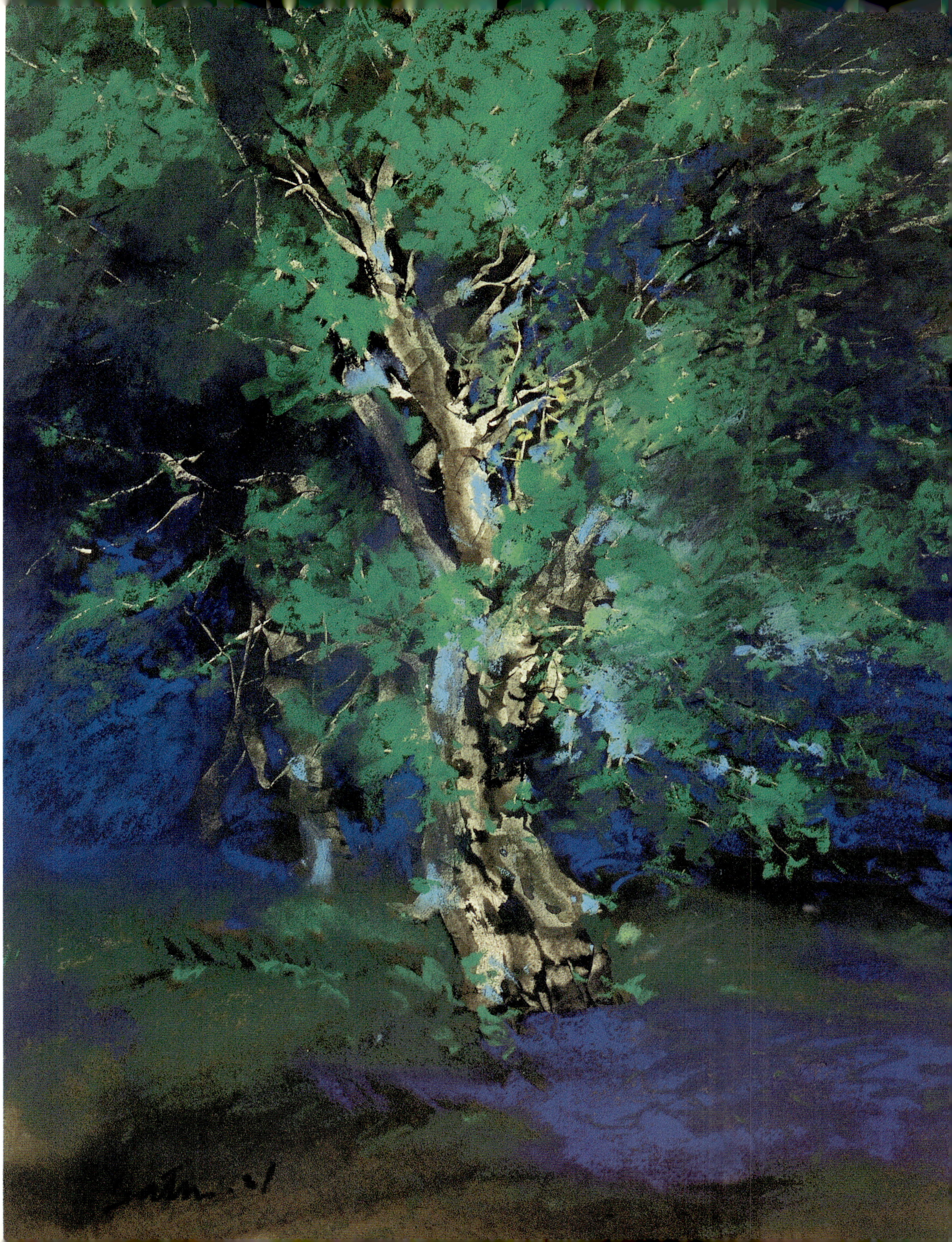

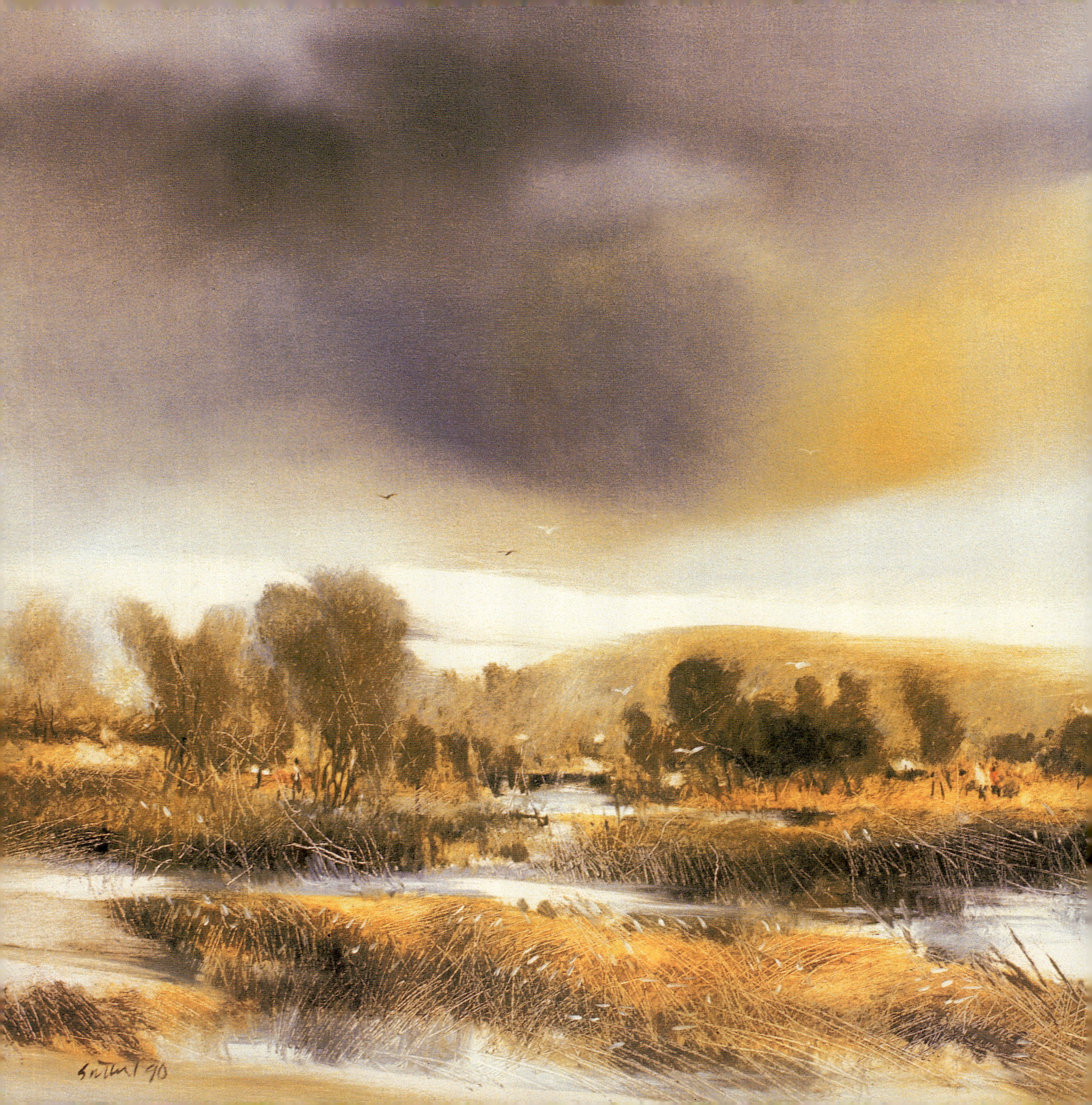

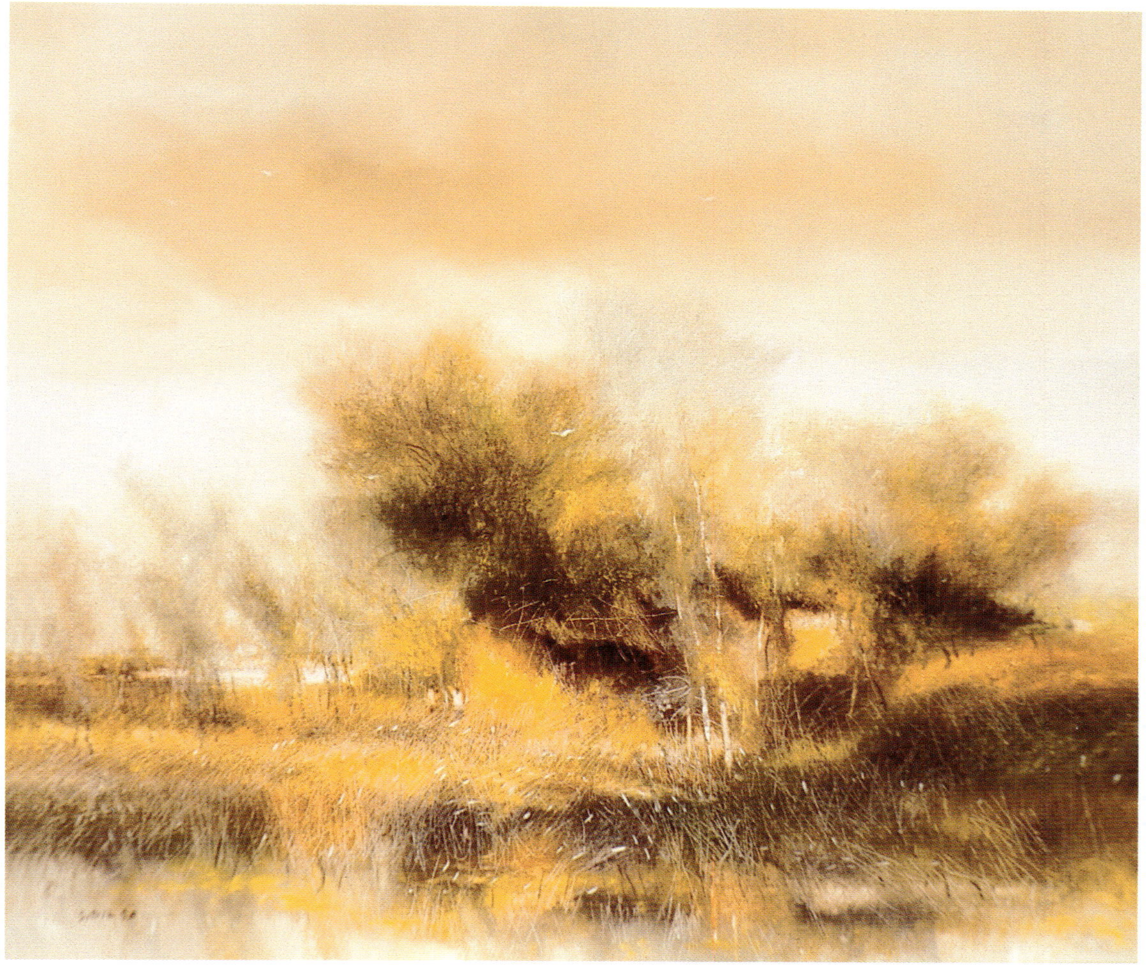

Oil on canvas, 1990. *Facing page:* Oil on canvas, 1990.

eccentric and wild, hopelessly impractical, and that they live in cuckoo land is not true!"

As for an artist's 'moods', Satish is of the view that all intelligent people with feeling suffer from these, more so the artist – it is the very driving force behind any creative activity. It is the power to see further and to feel more deeply than those not similarly blessed.

Satish wants the viewers to look at his paintings not through the artist's eyes but through their own. He wants the viewer to enter his mind by dissolving himself into the painting. He wants the viewer to savour the beauty of Nature in the space within – the sanctuary of the 'self'.

Satish does not title his paintings because he does not want his words,

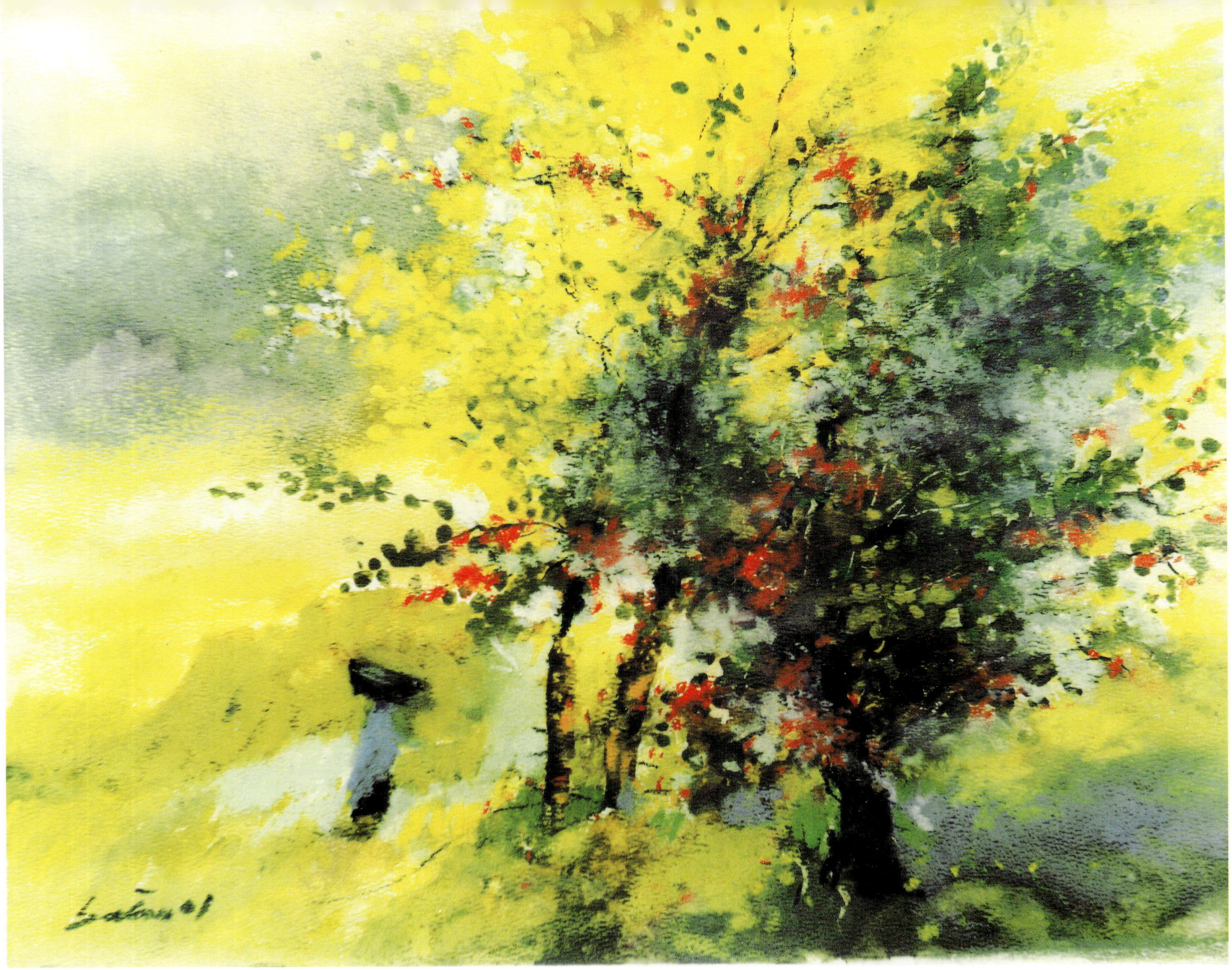

Mixed media on paper, 2001.

labels or judgments to influence the viewer. Satish wants the viewer to start listening to the voice deep within. "The moment we start listening to this voice, a higher level of consciousness is activated and we realize that all that truly matters – inner peace, love, joy, beauty, creativity – arises from beyond the mind. This realization awakens us to a new dimension of life, a spiritual dimension," says Satish with great conviction.

An artist's powers of perception and interpretation increase with time and experience. After many failures and years of practice, there is always some new way of expressing old truths and the power of interpretation is fresher each time. A fine painting is a result of intense concentration. Satish believes that good work must eventually find its place so that it can bring joy to humanity. "All passes, art alone endures."

Satish has not been swept away by academism but has kept intact a creative fervour distinct from mere pedagogy. He understands the demands that art makes on landscapists and at the same time is aware of what the landscape can offer to art.

Says Satish, "Of course, there can never be an identical reproduction of Nature and we should not want that. I feel that when a scene leaves its impact on me, it sets in motion a series of emotions and feelings. These go into the background – like a memory that fades – but I can recall that memory at a later date and it finds a powerful expression on my canvases."

Mixed media on paper, 2001.
Following pages 108-109: Watercolour on paper, 1993.

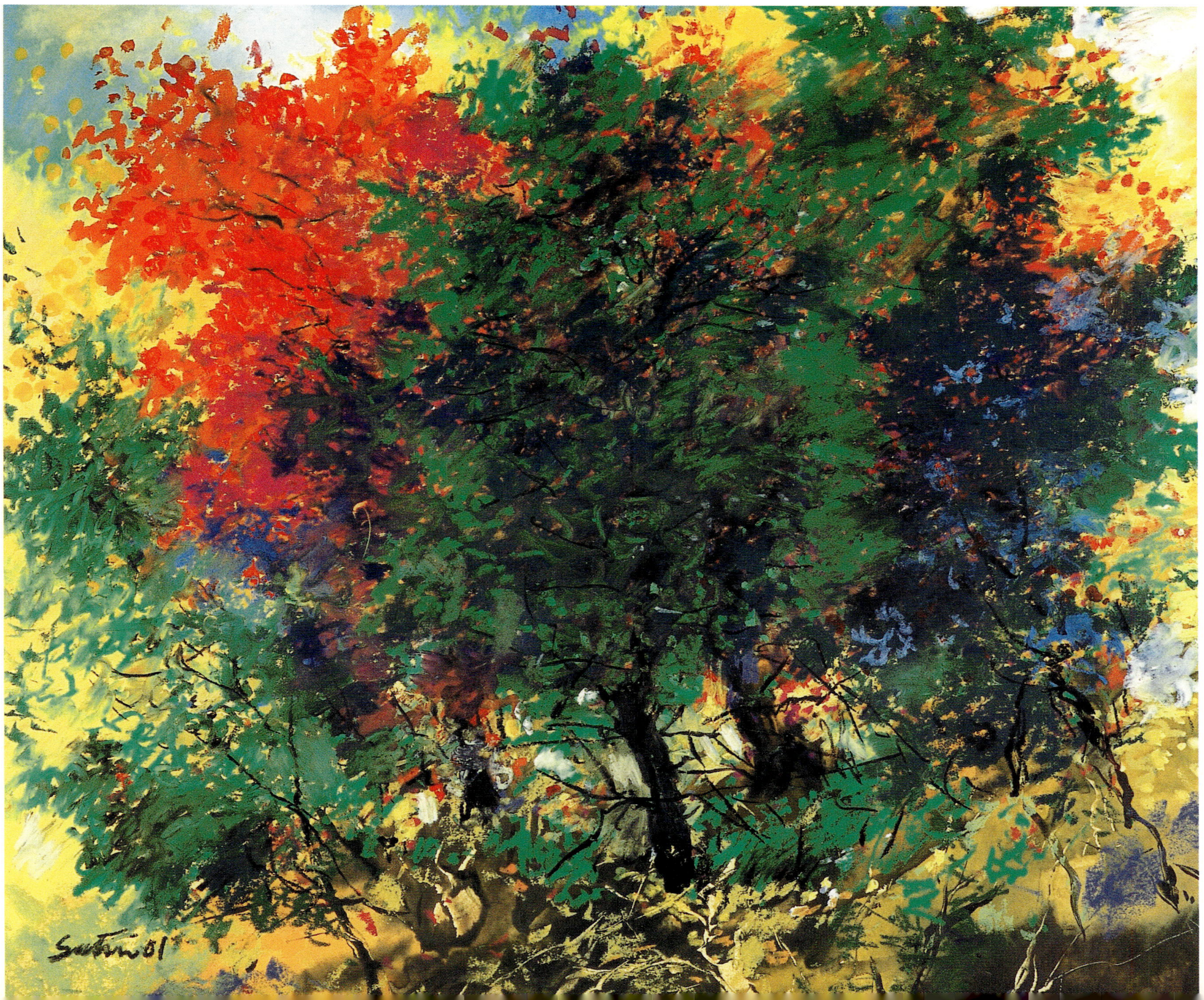

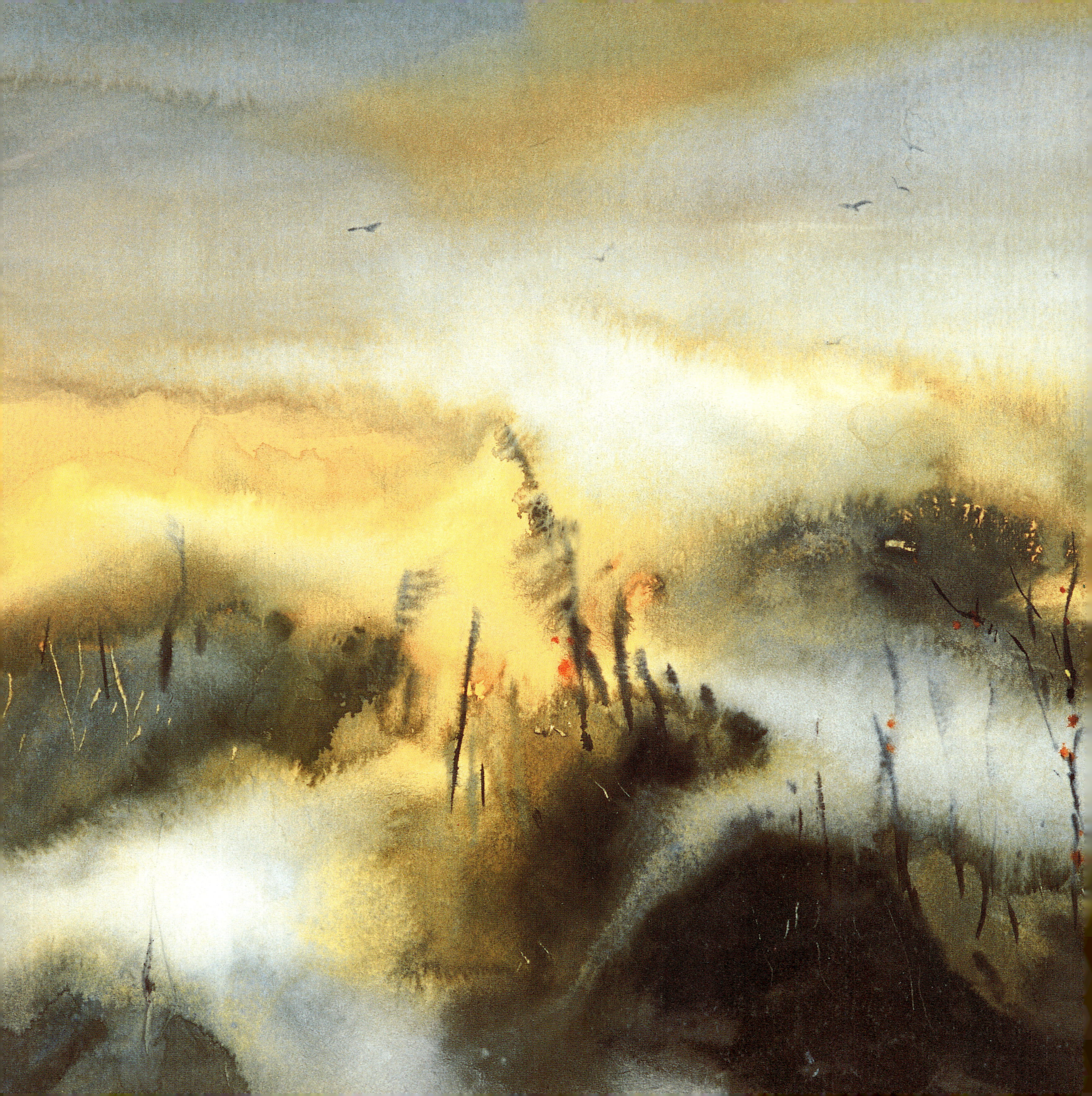

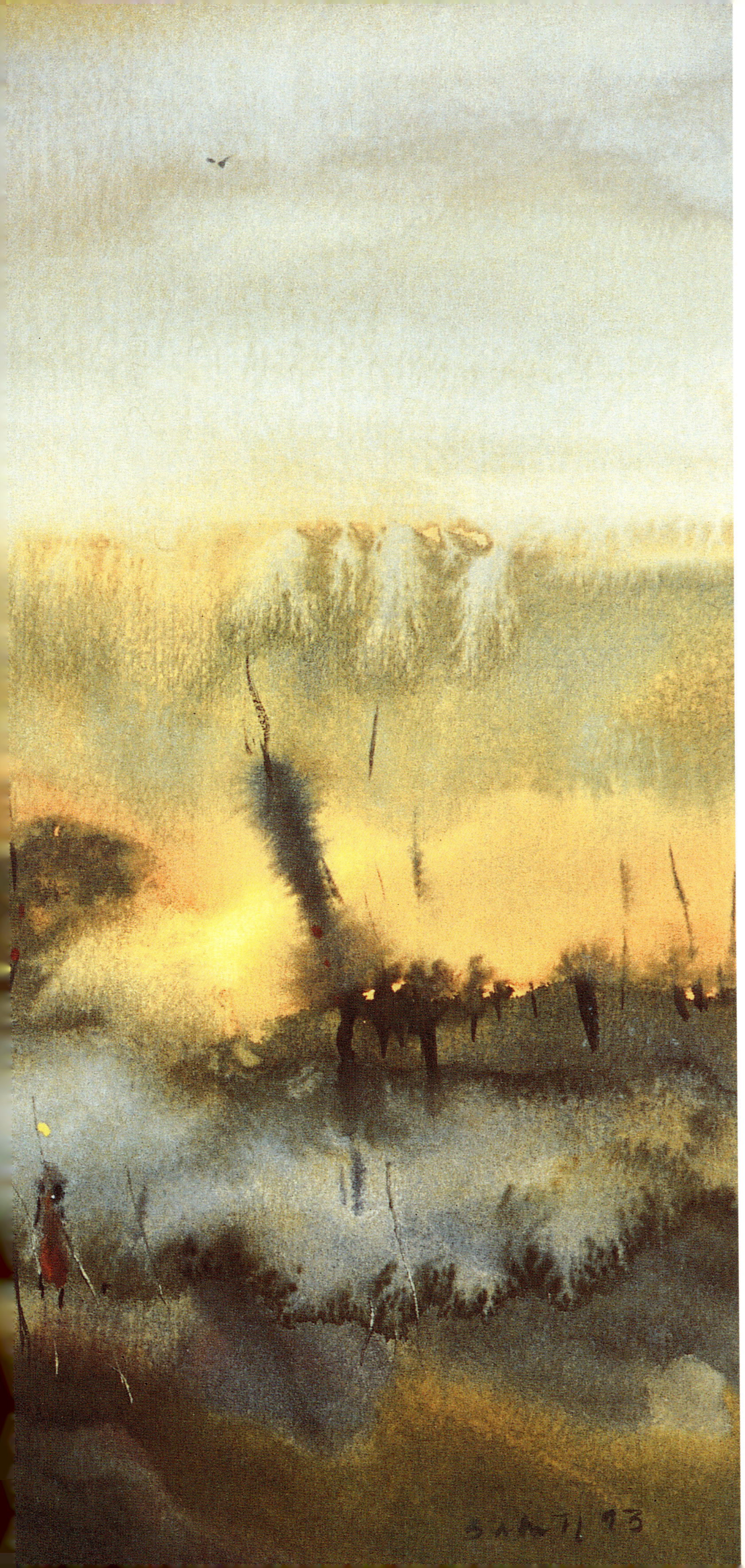

Isms appear to me to be a
conscious striving after originality.
True originality should be a direct
and unconscious revelation
of personality.

– Satish Chandra

A Rippling, Waif-like Energy

"... His depictions are dainty and pleasant, with a fineness of texture that lends it a filigreed look...

... Neither the sky nor the foliage is completely realistic. For example, one does not get to see a turquoise sky. But it is a perfect foil for the landscape below, and that is his triumph. With more realistic treatment, the effect would never be quite as sensational.

The dramatic effect of the sky with its exaggerated colours demystifies the shadows under the trees.

The surface is activated by the broken lines of its finely textured foliage, such as grass blowing in the breeze. Yet it is a rippling, waif like energy, not a violent one."

Aruna Bhowmick
The Statesman, New Delhi
15 December 2000

Facing page: Mixed media on paper, 2002.

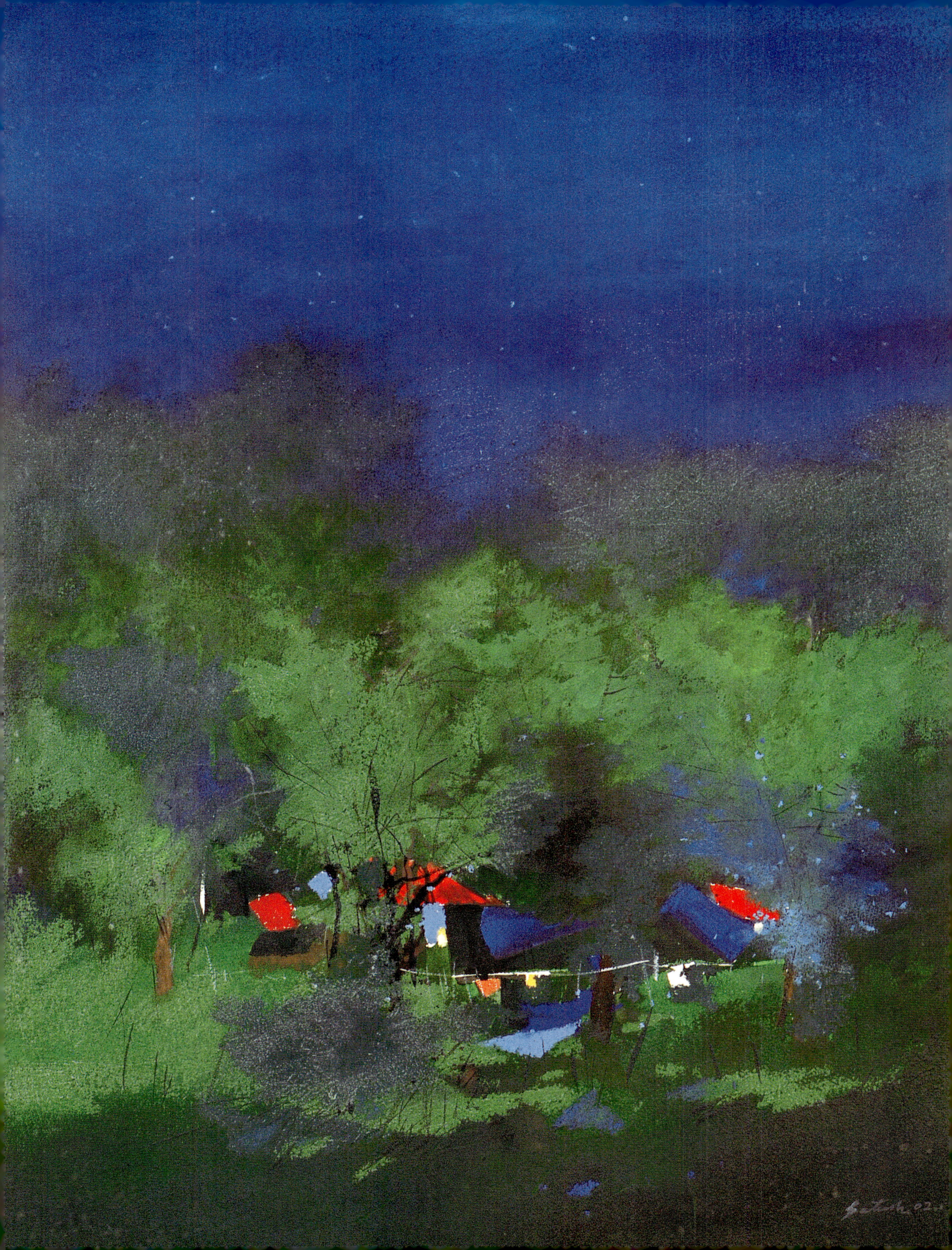

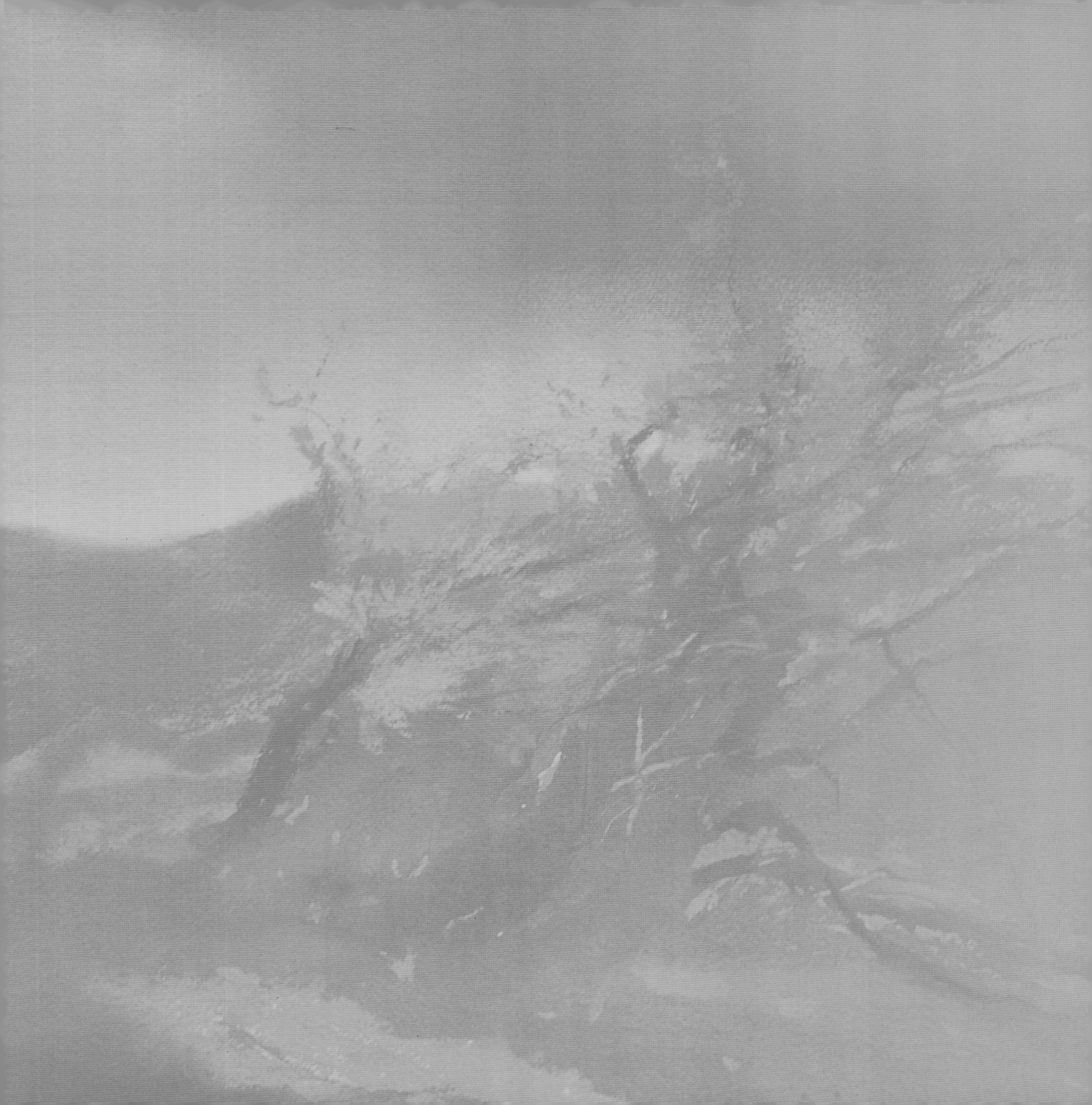

Method and Style

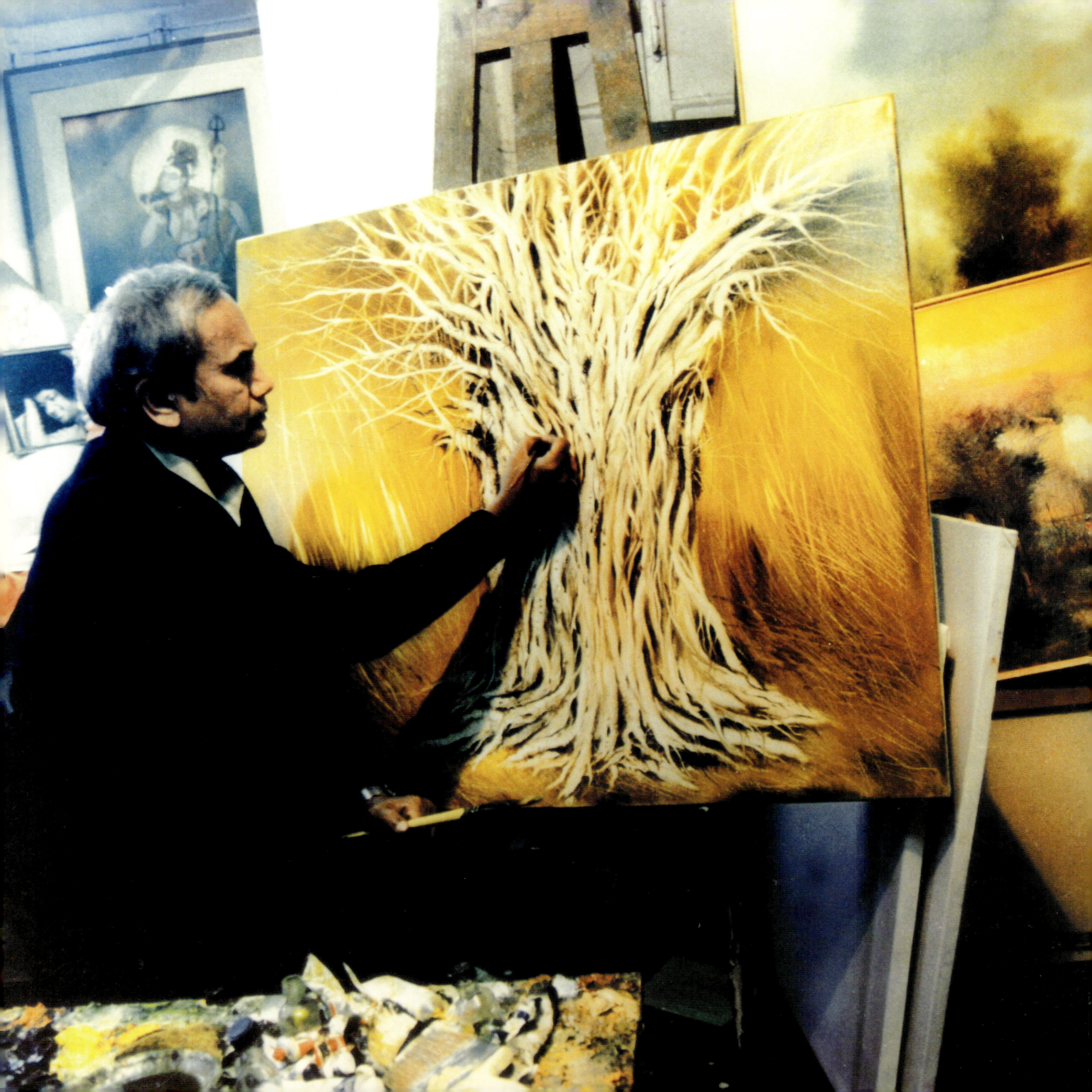

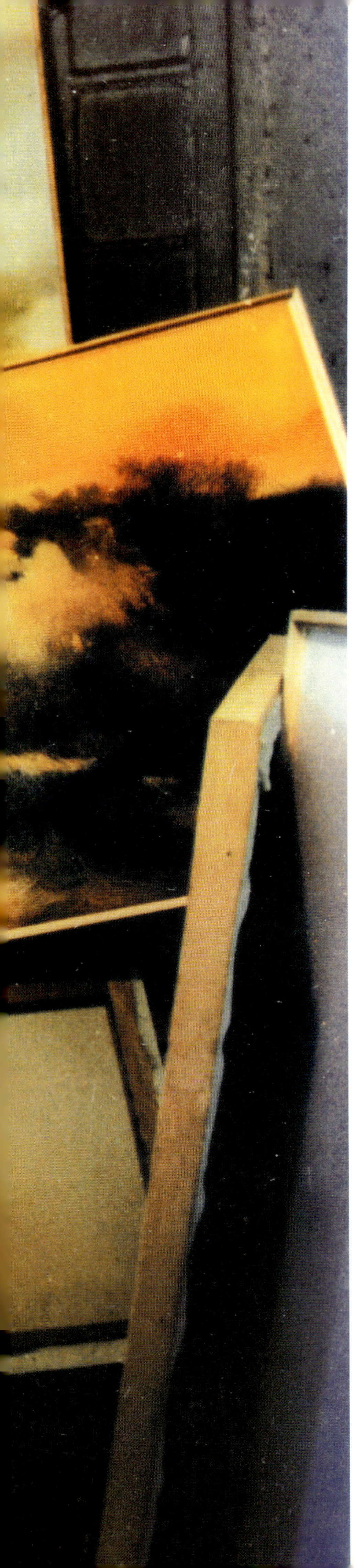

Quietly, I watch him as he works like a child, his grey hair dishevelled, his countenance suffused in an ethereal glow. He senses my presence. His eyes look up – soft and mild – and his lips quiver into an innocent smile as though he hadn't created anything... But the flowing colours grow and diffuse under his hand and moods take shape. Known forms emerge as he creates a world of his own: a world that draws the beholder back to Nature and experience the ecstacy of an inspired mind...

In his studio, Satish has nothing but the bare essentials around him – his easel, canvas, palette, paint and brushes. He sits there in deep meditation until the image of a picture stands life-like before his soul. He then sketches it on the blank canvas in thin outline and proceeds directly to the painting. The brush moves swiftly, easily, spontaneously. The colours flow naturally, as if from the depths of his soul, on to the canvas. This reliance on the mental image emphasizes the visionary nature of Satish's work. Viewers are struck by its haunting, enigmatic quality and many have searched his paintings for hidden meanings.

In his landscapes Satish not only depicts what is immediately visible, but also captures the underlying mood – the essence, the soul – of Nature. His work has a freshness and a spontaneity that springs from his impression of a scene. The subtle luminosity, the reflections and shadows, the casual passers-by and the very movement of the trees and birds are accurately depicted.

An optimist, Satish combines realism and impressionism aesthetically so as to assume newer and fresher dimensions – mixing the two in a way unlike any in recent times.

Satish's art is marked by a strong sense of individuality. Says he: "What I paint are my impressions of Nature and 'impressions' are what lie between stark reality and fantastic imagination. My landscapes are not faithful reproductions of

Facing page: In his studio, Satish had nothing but the bare essentials around him.

Nature as seen by the naked eye. They are representative of the mood a particular sight of Nature evokes in me."

The mystic and the philosopher

Satish has an extraordinary ability to create not just a three-dimensional effect but a fourth one – of the presence of a 'beyond' – giving the canvas a sense of endless expanse. The countryside rolls away into the distance and the eye drifts towards the far horizon – the land recedes gradually from the foreground – and this impression is enhanced by the sky lightening and finally dipping into a thin strip of white. Yet the viewer remains transfixed, holding his breath, wondering what lies beyond this thin strip of white betwixt him and the unknown. These paintings highlight the vastness of Nature, its tranquillity, and yet, bring on a feeling of yearning, of wistfulness.

The mystic Satish, in his soul-searching efforts, moves beyond man

Facing page: Oil on canvas, 1987.

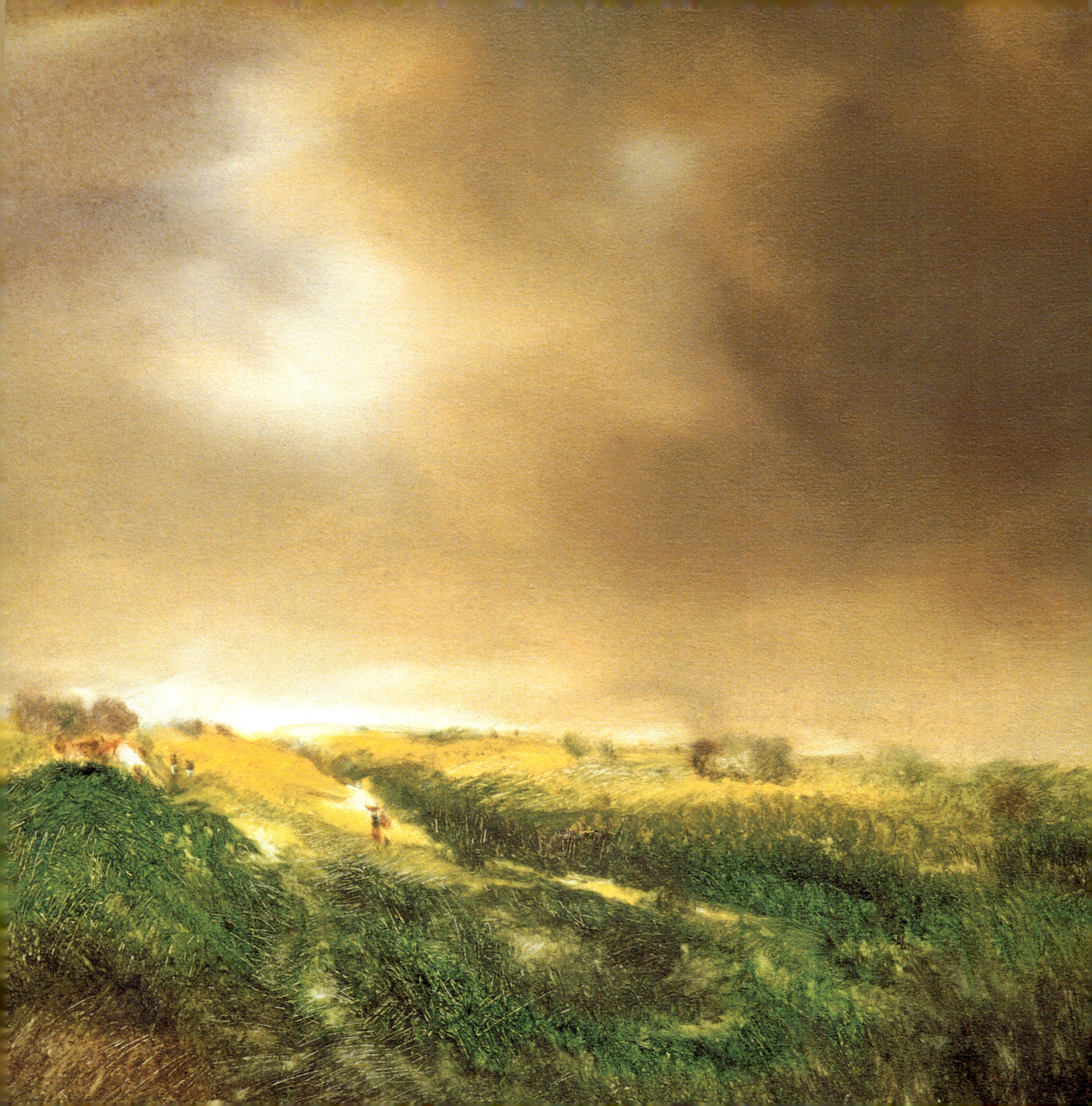

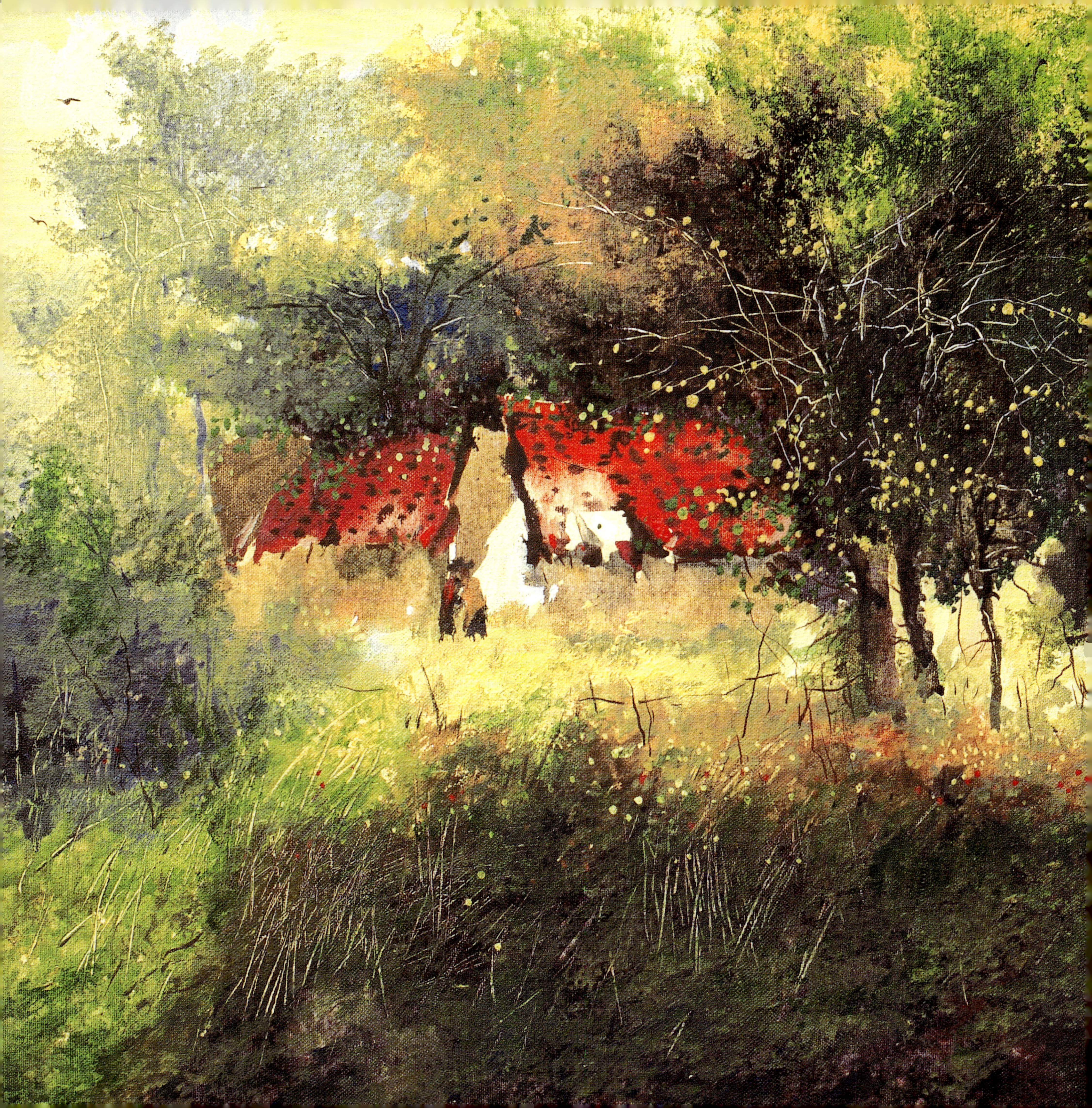

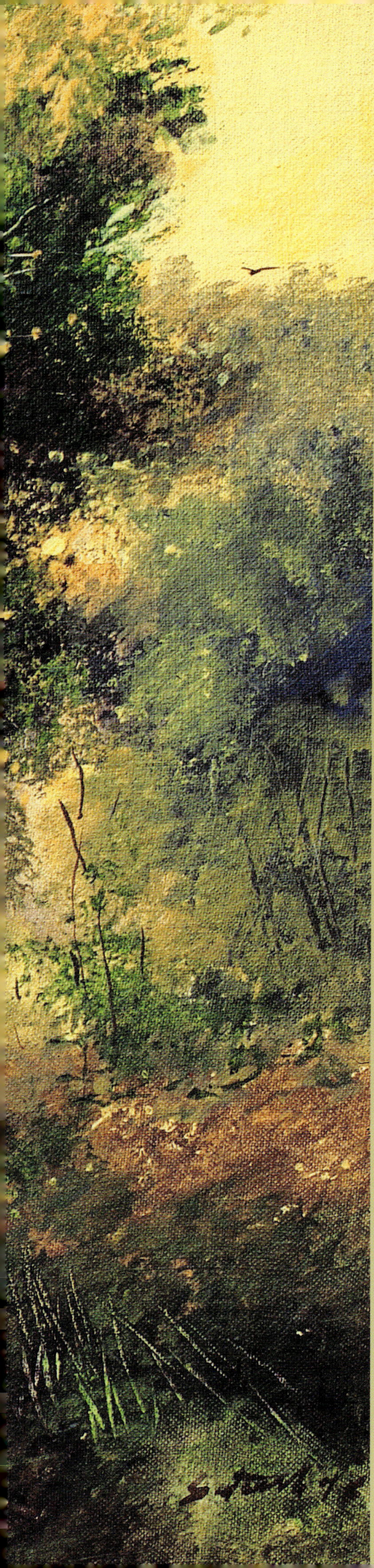

and Nature towards a silence so profound that he touches the glory of a greater truth, and realizes the oneness of God and man.

Using the same implements available to the academics – those of light and shade of external and tonal range – Satish fashions 'inspired' portrayals of Nature, which, in oils, possess all the delicacy of an aquarelle. There is a touch of magic, mystery and enchantment in Satish's paintings – that inexplicable extra quality that sets apart a work of art.

Satish emphasizes the delicacy of colour patterns and the simplicity of composition. The pigments are so thinly laid, often so diluted, that they flow freely, giving his landscapes the elusive, luminous transparency of watercolours. There is an immensity and vastness allied to his work that gives it subtle and engaging depth.

A maestro colourist

It is through colour and admirably textured tones that Satish turns a prosaic vista into a slender poetic vision. He uses warm colours like earthy browns, warm yellows and flaming oranges, placing them alongside blacks, blues, greens and whites. He invests the whole view with a shimmering light – the overall effect gives birth to a feeling of calmness and tranquillity, wiping out restlessness. A flutter of fine brush strokes marks the texture of his oils. The poetic impulse is given free play. Romantic elements find their way into the brush strokes.

"I seek forms through colour and find a peculiar fascination for grey, green, yellow, red and orange, which have a great range and depth of

Facing page: Oil on canvas, 1978.

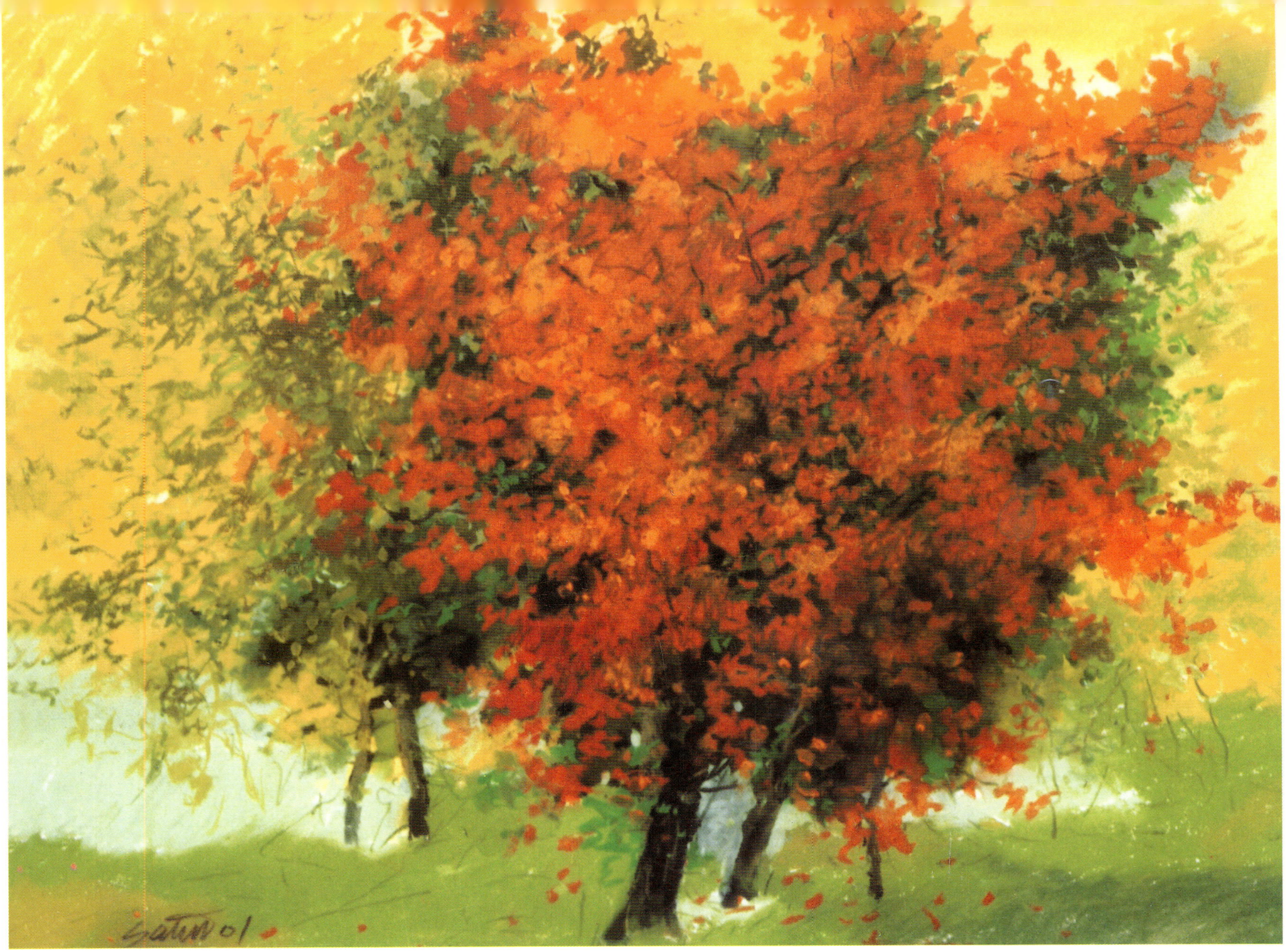

Mixed media on paper, 2001.

feeling. I like to maintain the character and transparency of colours in order to give freshness, softness and intensity to my painting. Often, I use only one colour in my painting and find it effective in capturing the aura of a scene," says Satish.

By his careful and skilled use of colour and brush he suggests movement. His canvases contain views of grasslands, rolling fields, trees and open skies; of forests, mountains and rivulets – each vibrating to the play of light. Apart from technical manipulations, Satish varies his colour scheme and always arrives at the required rhythm of harmony, sometimes concentrating on the horizontal sweep and, at other times, visualizing the composition as leading inwards. The various shades of green, bronze and ochre are applied with a gentle, sensitive hand. The landscapes are inventive in detail and succeed in creating a mood.

A master of atmospherics

Satish lures the sleeping earth into springing up in fire – smouldering orange soil sears into autumn bushes, which themselves spread into tree bursts, the viridian tinged with bronze where the autumn light catches it.

A slight shift in the viewer's position effects magical changes in the landscape – a marsh and a tree exchange colours; tracks which, from one angle, seemed to be leading out of a copse, begin to point fiercely into it.

He paints trees that live, breathe and sway in the breeze. They show a season, a mood, a state of things. We see a storm, a bare autumn, monsoon and winter. Sometimes they burst into the magic of spring with a myriad colourful flowers smiling in the showers of light that filters through the

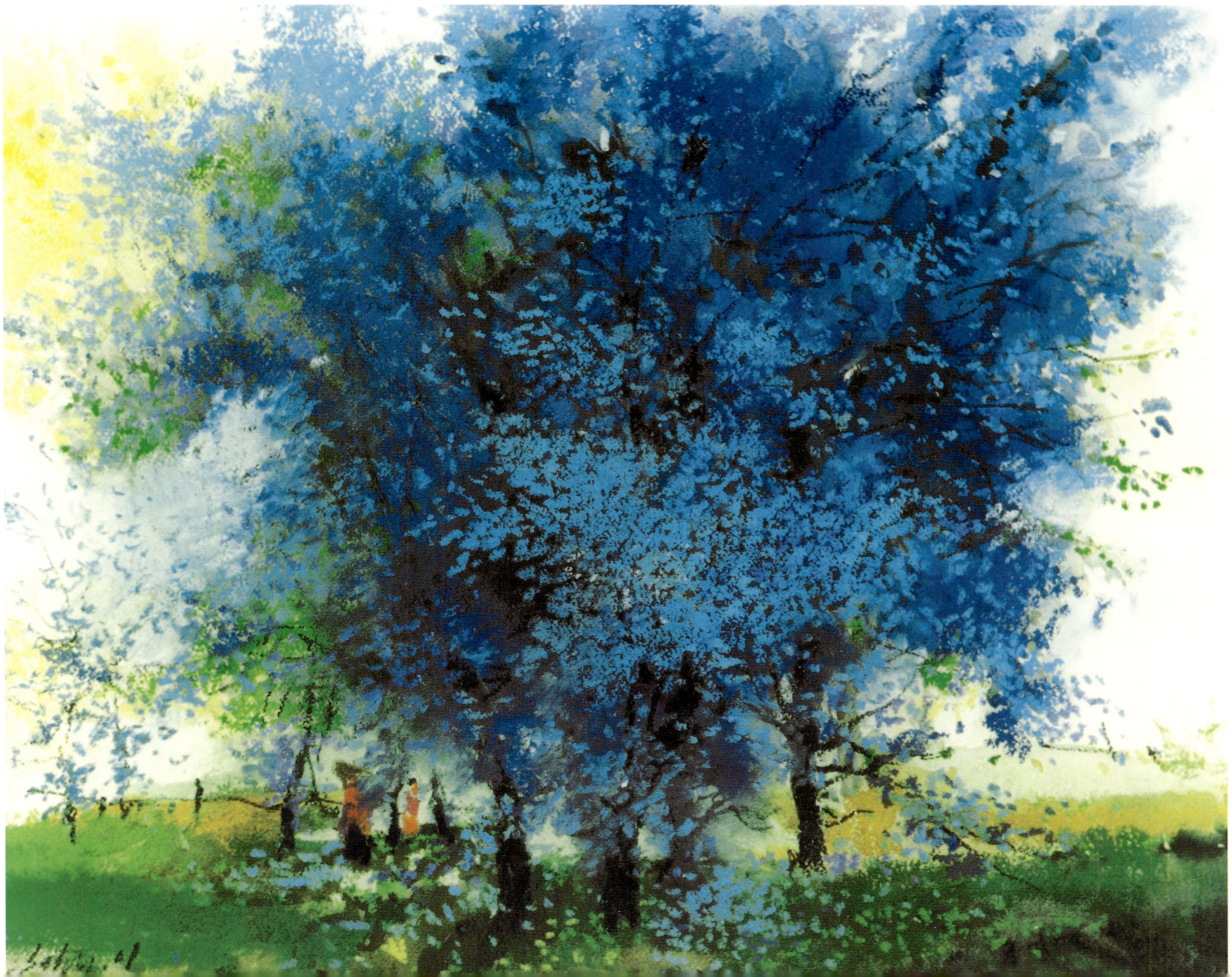

Mixed media on paper, 2001.

clouds, filling us with joy, giving rise to doses of delicate feelings and intense passion. A group of feathery trees sweeps towards an arc of tantalizing blue, and the white of light gives depth to a grove. Or then, the leaves, russet and flame-orange, leap upwards like flames. Then again, the trees puff upwards like clouds of smoke into a misty sky – the upward lift is like a steeple, a 'shikhar' or a 'minar', associated with worship.

The vertical lines of trees seem to connect the earth below to the heaven above – the viewer's eye is led to the wide space between these two planes wherein atmosphere is created to depict a certain mood. This space also adds a dimension of time and distance to the painting.

Then the nail brush is used effectively to scrape the colour, yielding a vast ground, allowing the play of wind amid the tall trees, grass or standing crops. But above all, and even more than the clusters of trees in yellow, ochre and brown, it is the sensuous handling of undulating grass and of burgeoning growth – with a startling splash of colour in the tiny flowers and weeds strewn across a slope – which makes Satish's paintings distinctive. It typifies his ability to create a languorous mood.

In his paintings, water flows in crystal streams and rivulets that meander through meadows along green banks. Serene, tranquil, they reflect the

Mixed media on paper, 1998.

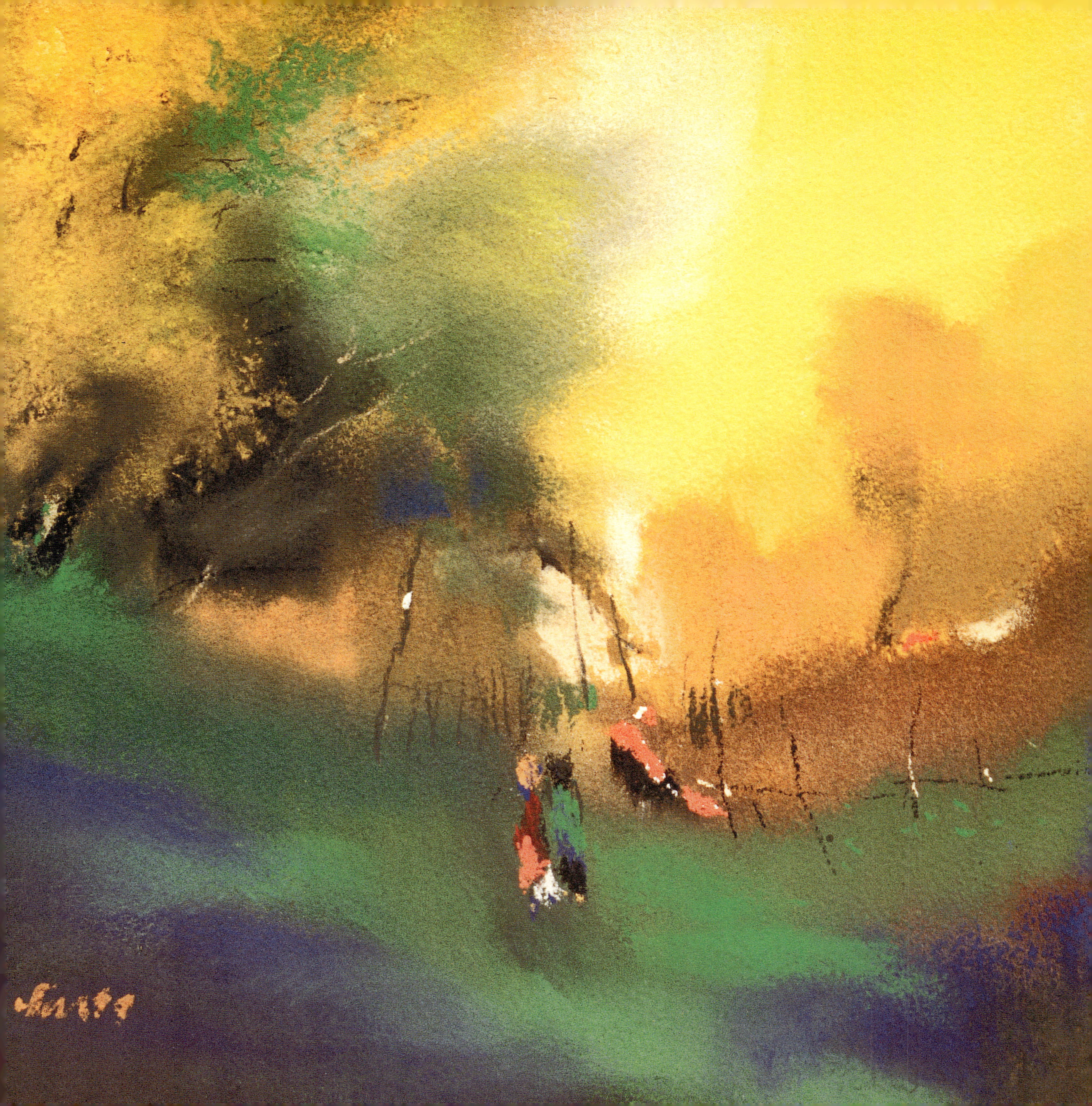

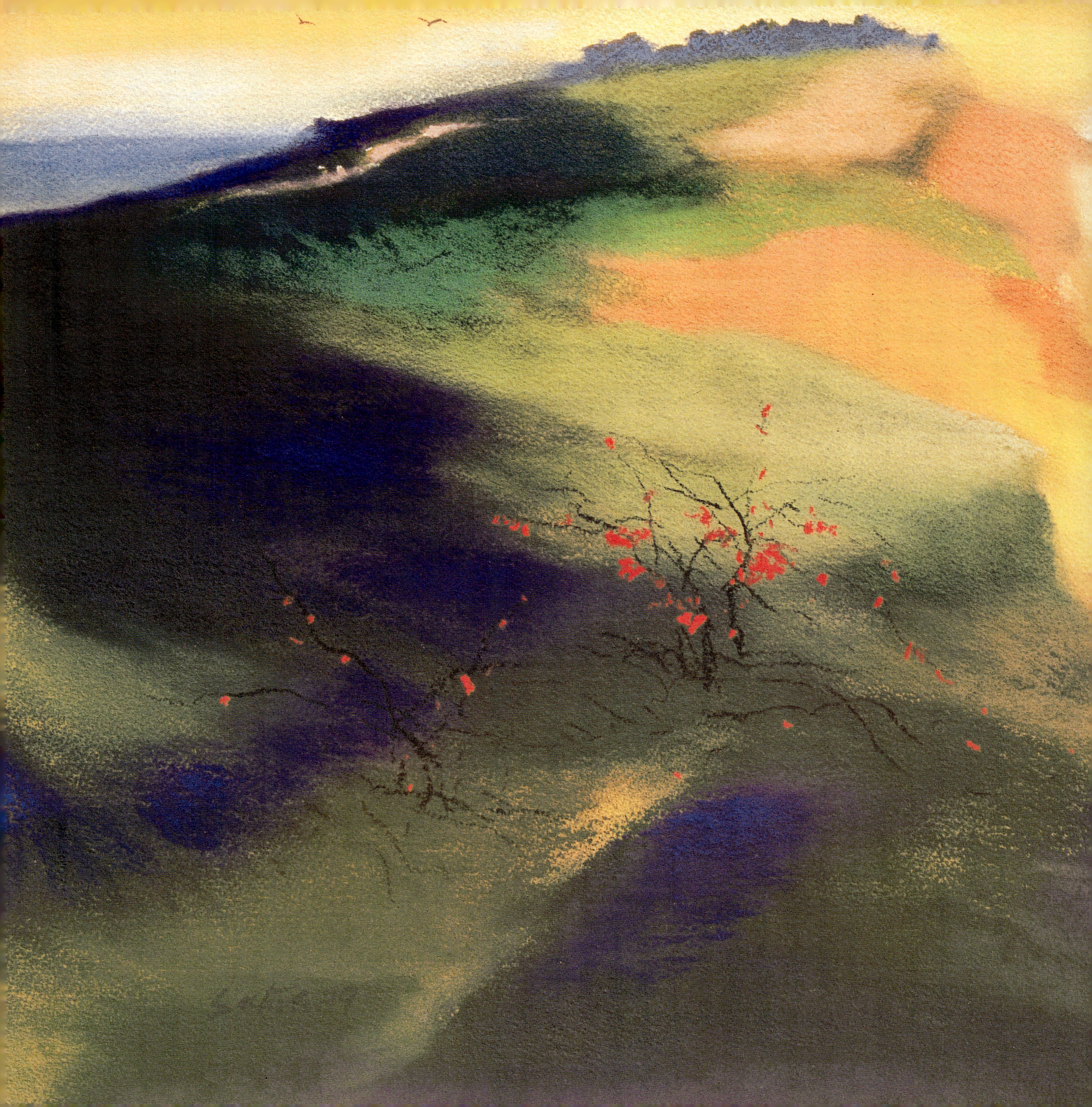

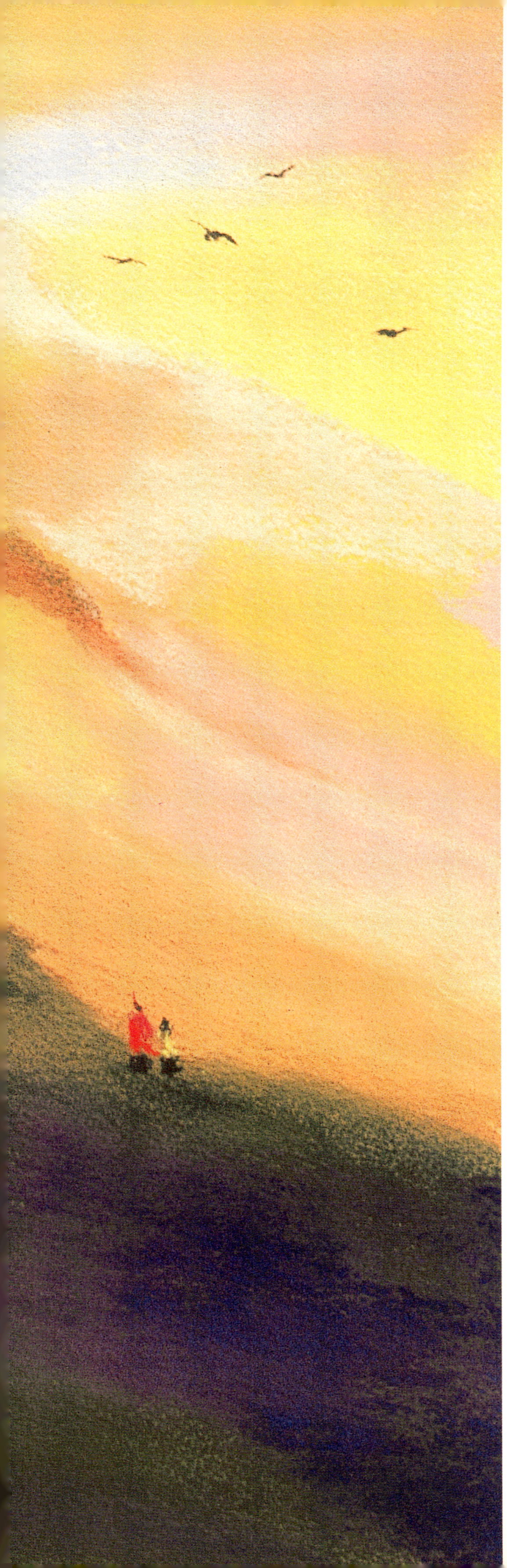

mood of the sky above. The weeds and reed-like stems jutting out of the side of a lake are reflected in the water as it shimmers in the light. The breeze caresses and plays with the ripples in the water. A solitary lakeside village is seen in the tranquil spread of the morning. Sometimes cartwheel marks can be seen in the freshly sodden earth.

Satish's forests are an ensemble of deftly scuffed foliage, scumbled undergrowth, brambles and long grass that the knife has scratched across the canvas. At times, the large twisted trunks of trees with their roots penetrating deep into the bosom of the earth, and twigs hanging from the branches, give rise to a mysterious and haunting atmosphere, bringing on a feeling of loneliness. The foliage merges with the background of the sky or, in the case of the trees, with space. In open fields, the standing crops wave into a pattern to reach the humble huts.

Facing page: Mixed media on paper, 1989.

Human beings (which most landscapists use as a counter-point to Nature) appear occasionally, losing their way in the shrubbery, or moving in the wind like tiny specks. Almost insignificant, they are usually absorbed in some activity – sitting down, bending over, working or even with their backs to the viewer. These figures are tiny in relation to Nature, perhaps to show that man is helpless against natural forces. "I feel that man is miniscule compared to Nature – no matter what progress man makes, he can never totally alienate himself from Nature; he was, is and will always be only a part of Nature – this is why in my landscapes, man, though important, occupies a secondary position," says Satish.

The motif of wings, to mark the migration of birds, indicates animal life in this otherwise unchallenged realm of the arboreal.

The mountain ranges Satish paints, often depicting a temple roof fading into the sky, suggest a higher spiritual level of consciousness. In a very visual way, for the viewer, it is now much more than a physical journey: it is the journey of a searching soul. The viewer first travels up the mountain ranges to reach the temple – and then the mind's eye reaches up towards the mountain peaks, into the brightness of the clouds at the summit beyond which his eyes cannot penetrate.
Yet he yearns to go beyond the clouds – and his quest for immortality begins.

In Satish's paintings, the very sky seems to move with the moving clouds

Facing page: Oil on canvas, 2000.

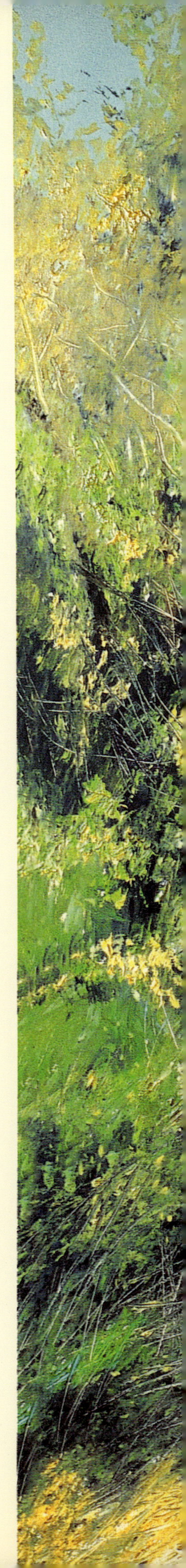

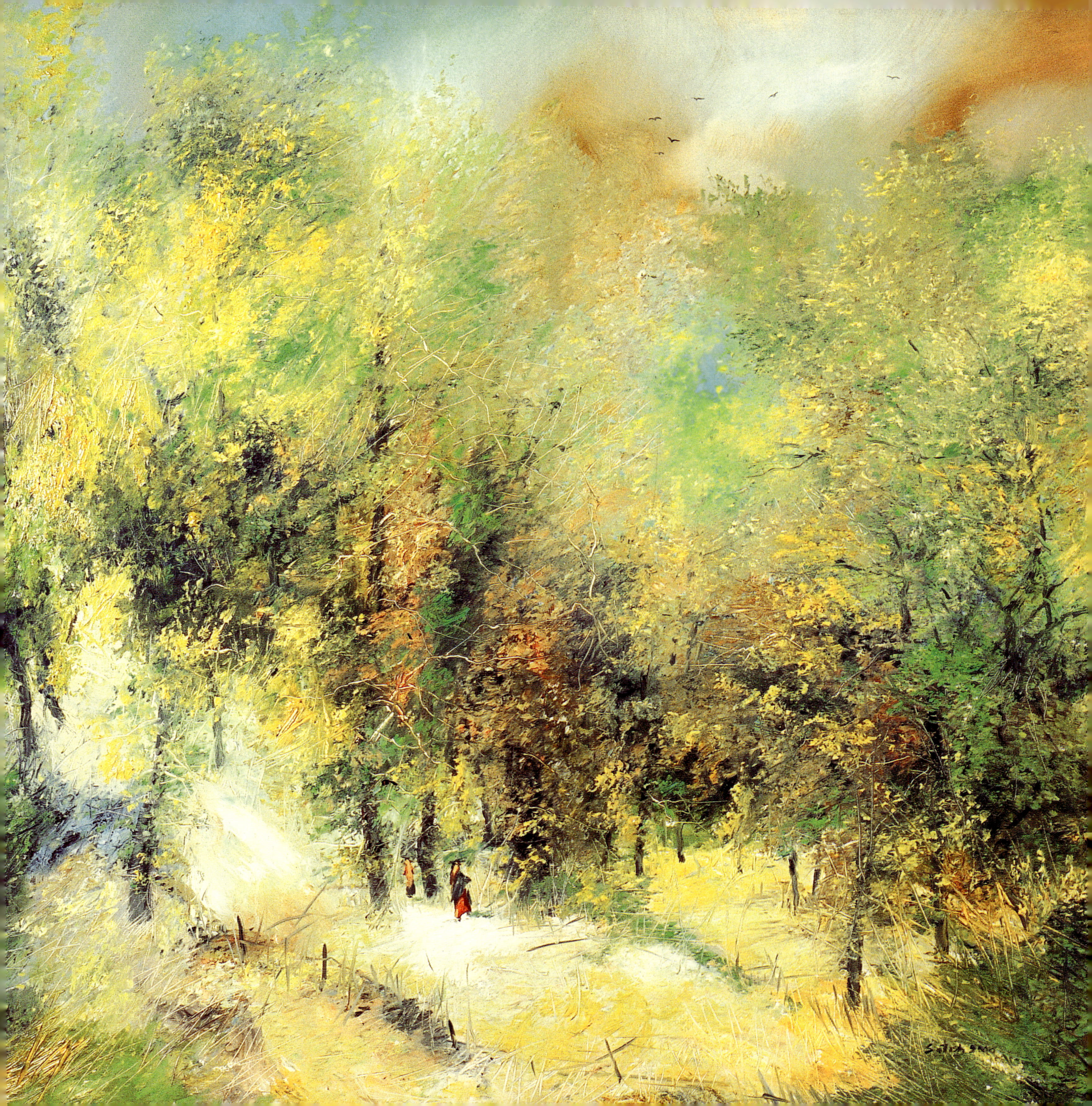

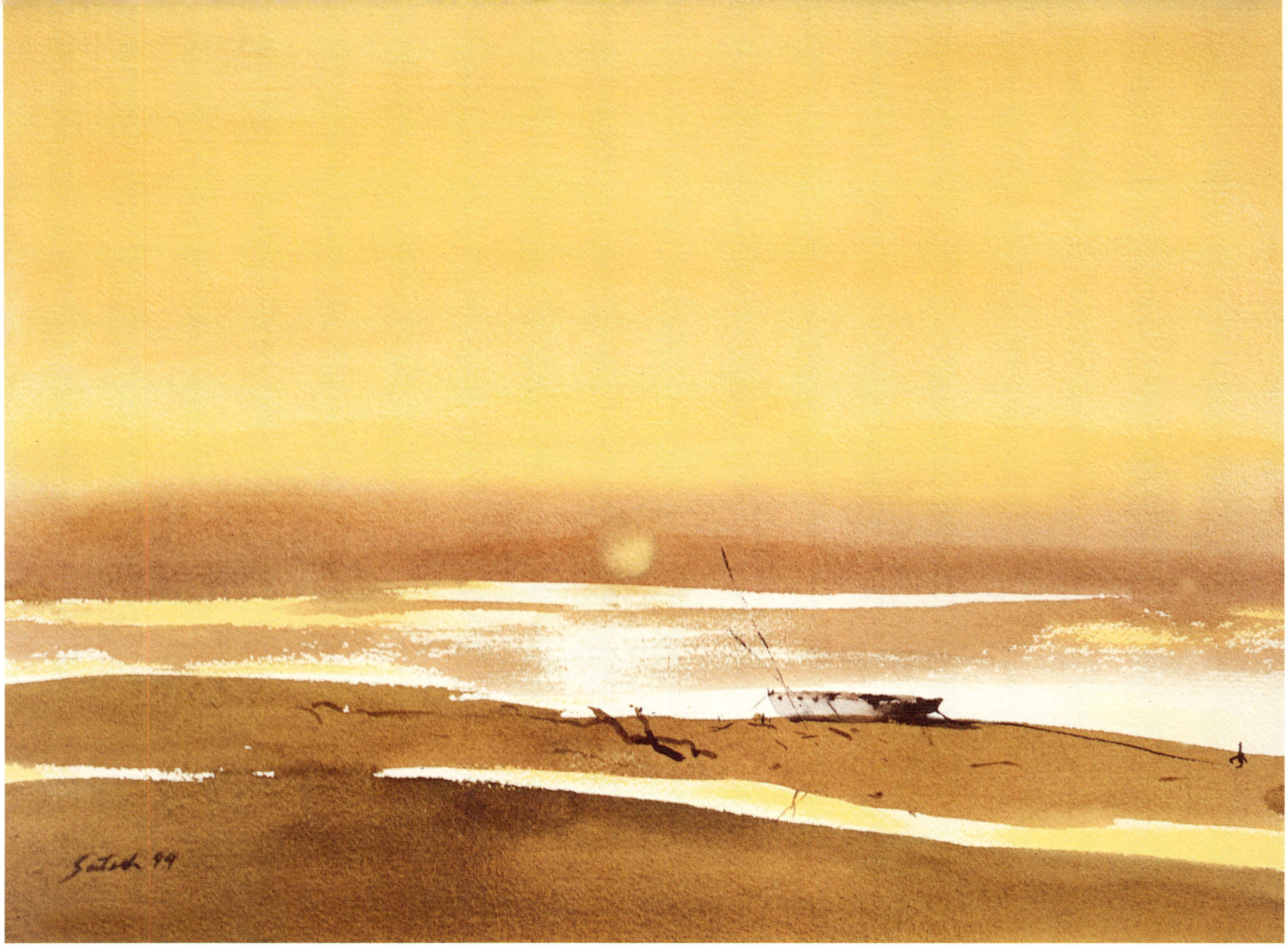

Watercolour on paper, 1999.

as they flit across, the sun playing hide-and-seek with them. Sometimes, the clouds are bare shadows and at other times, they are luminous, filled with light. At times they are bursting with raindrops. Or then, they look like the softly drooping transparent wings of fairies in mauve, blue-grey and white, catching, ever so softly, the light of the sun in shades of pink, purple, orange and gold. Satish paints mist and clouds as they cling to the hillocks, huts, trees and plants, making a sea of glowing colours rising up in spirals.

The ever-changing sky is a source of great fascination for Satish. "The sky is the source of light in Nature and governs everything. The quality of light in the sky has a direct influence on the atmosphere and mood in my paintings," says he.

His interest lies in the rendering of a certain quality of light in the invocation of a fleeting mood or moment in time. In his work he captures the magical light of sunset, light on the trunks of trees and penetrating the dark undergrowth, light filtered through the foliage of trees, reflected off the surface of water or muted by the clouds in the sky. Hutments are glimpsed between the trunks of trees, light is diffused and interrupted, shadows are cast. Or then, sunlight filters through foliage of a cluster of trees and is reflected by the river in a superbly tranquil scene. It is not a dull universal daylight that falls on a landscape, but a breathing, animated, exulting light – glowing or flashing or scintillating, according to what it touches; or perishing and passing away, entangled in drifting mist. It is light which sleeps but never dies.

Original, creative, throught-provoking and soul-searching, each canvas throbs with the artist's pulse, the gamut of his emotions – and one sees the world as the artist sees it.

Watercolour on paper, 1999.

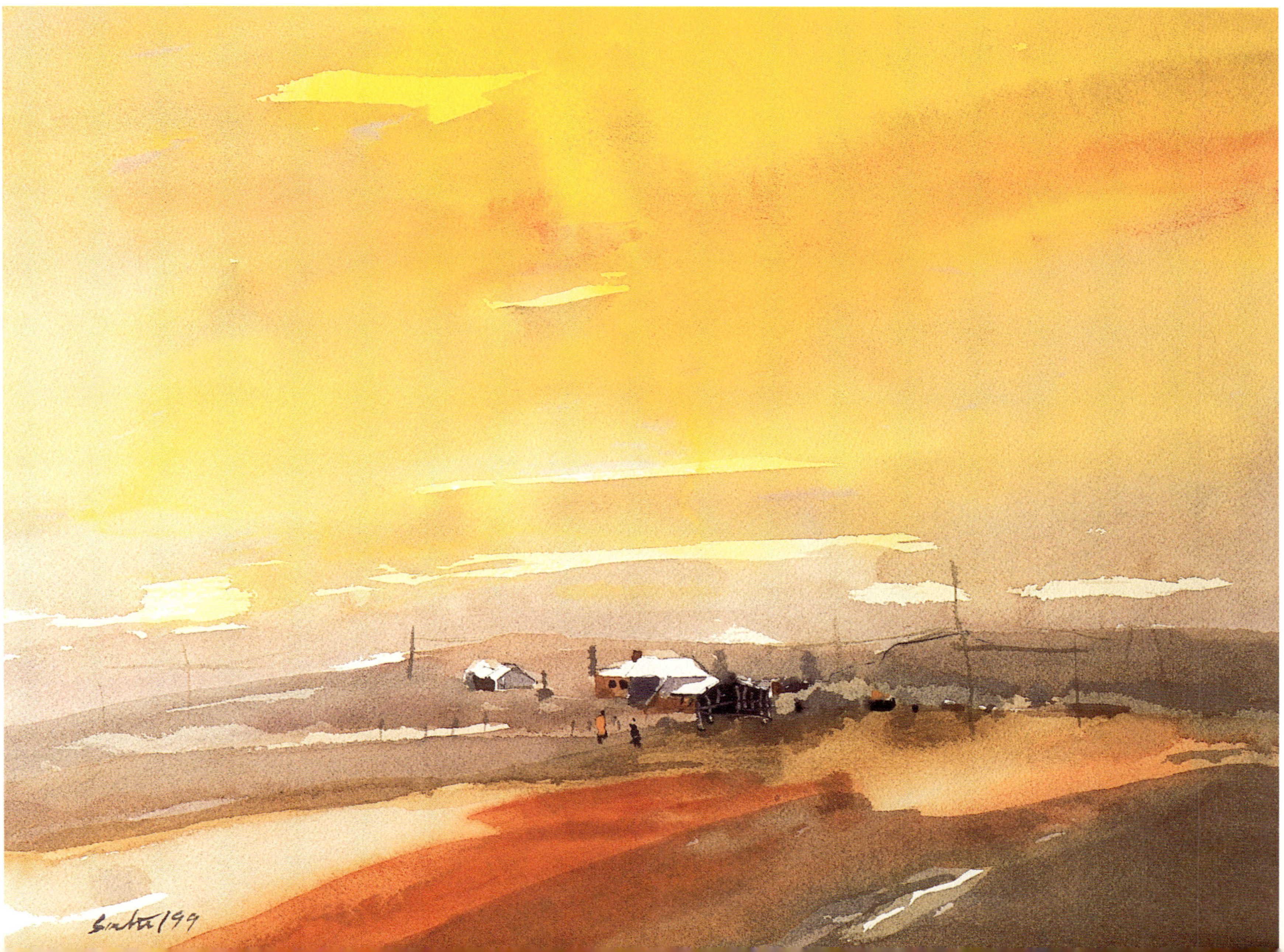

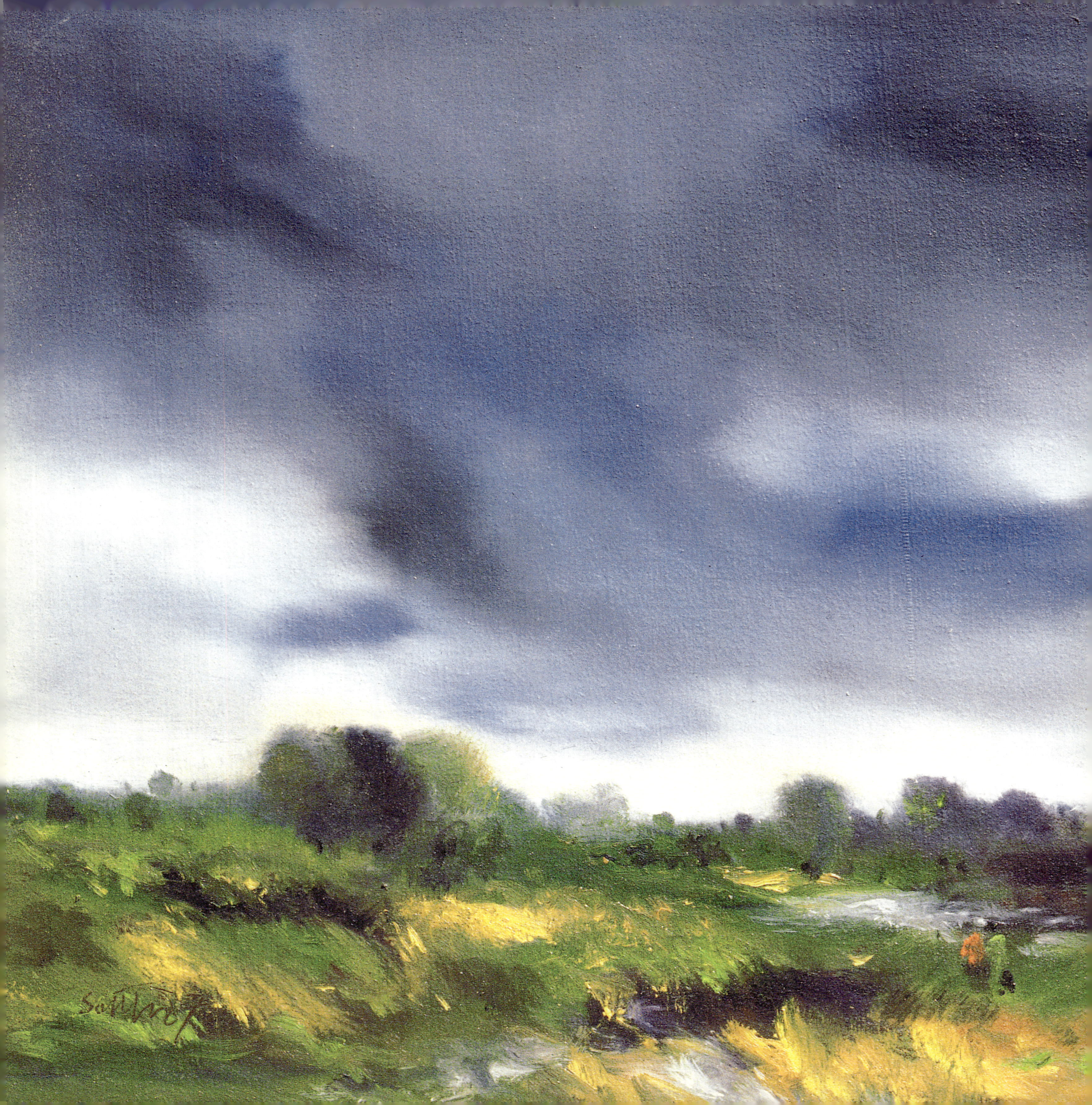

"The sky is the source of light in Nature and governs everything. The quality of light in the sky has a direct influence on the atmosphere and mood in my paintings."

Be it a sojourn through jungles, mountains, fields, village lanes or along riverbanks or along the sea coast – the traveller in Satish's paintings is alone. Yet, the vivid green of the trees, and the glowing flame of a campfire or lantern is company in itself, mingling the stranger's desires with the natural beauty surrounding him.

There are times one can walk into a painting – when Satish follows the course of a path to take us into the interior. It requires the active participation of the viewer, who decides at which pace he will travel through the painting – a participation that is physical as well as mental. At other times, the landscape forbids us entry and only offers its vastness for appreciation. The landscape remains

Facing page: Oil on canvas, 2001.

aloof, however much we may claim to be well-acquainted with it. Very often he succeeds in creating an introspective mood – the dark clouded sky enveloping the space of the canvas, with a mere strip of the beach or land presenting a hut or a boat. The blue in its darkness strikes an overwhelming pitch and a strange, strong silence ensues.

Eventually, the silence in a painting is far more eloquent than all the wail and thunder of expressionism. Muses Satish, "Silence can help us get in touch with the innermost essence of our being and we align with the power that manifests everything in the universe." Satish wants to reconnect us to the wellspring of calm that may be dormant within the 'self', that sits there quietly awaiting our arrival.

 Facing page: Watercolour on paper, 2003.

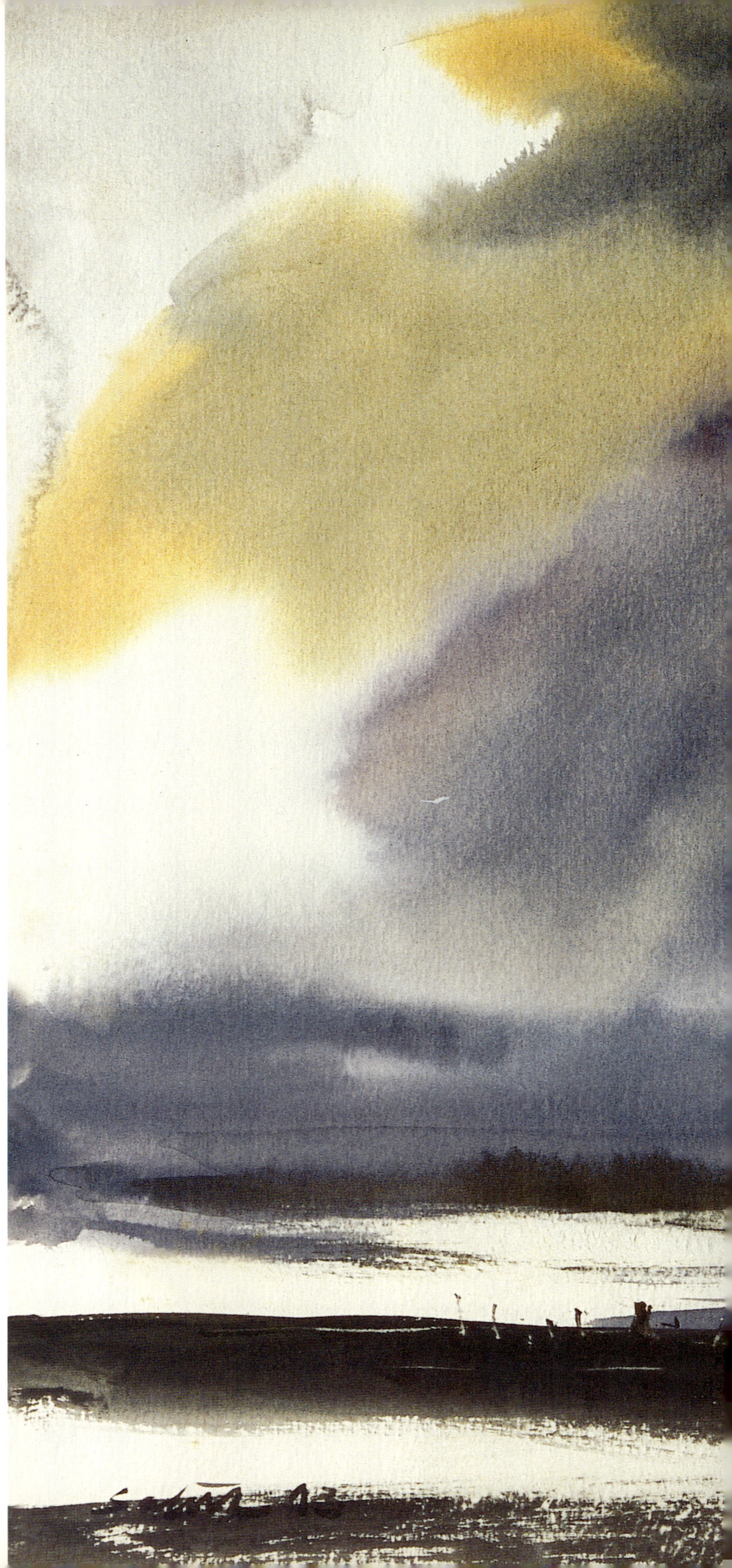

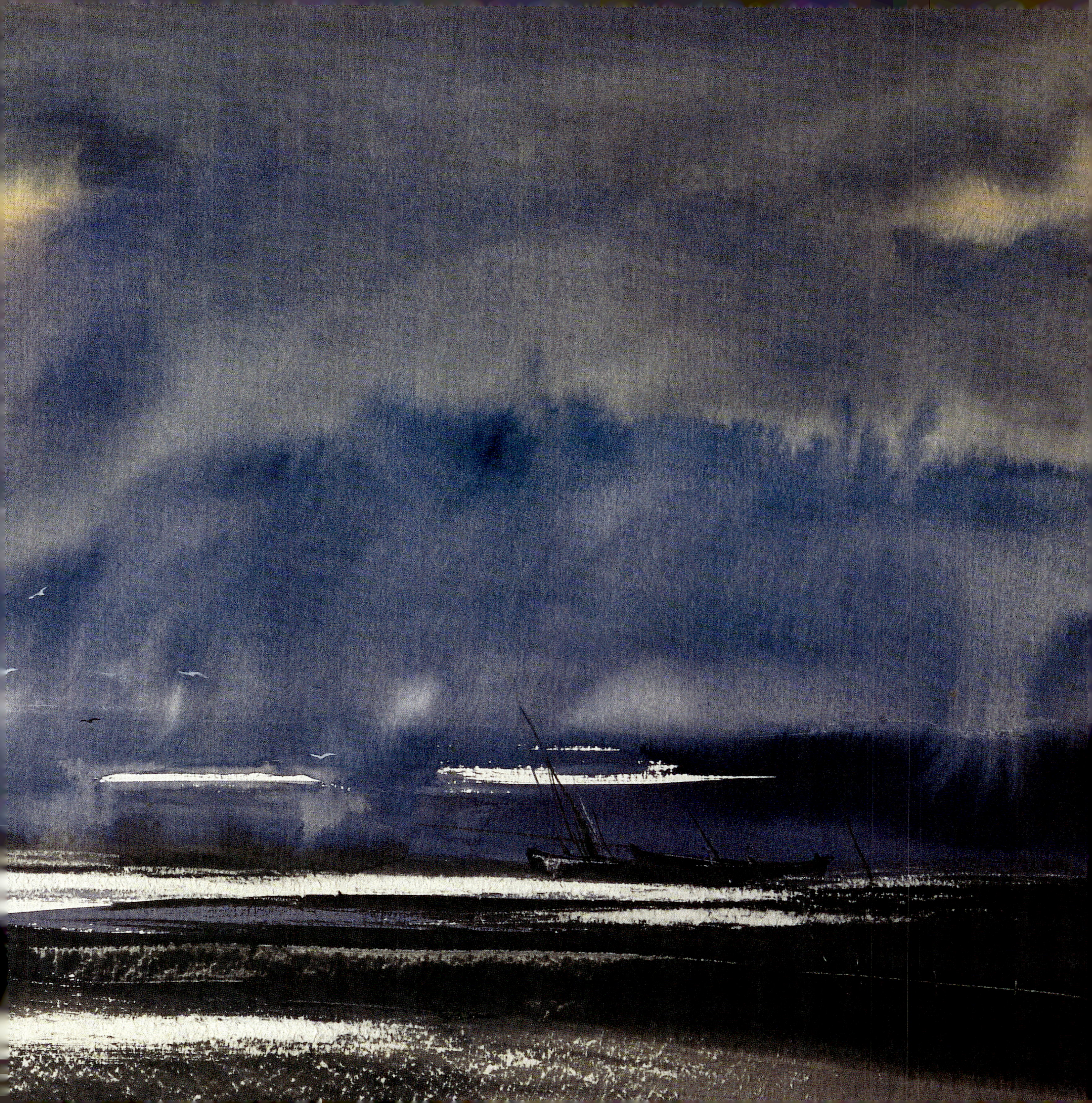

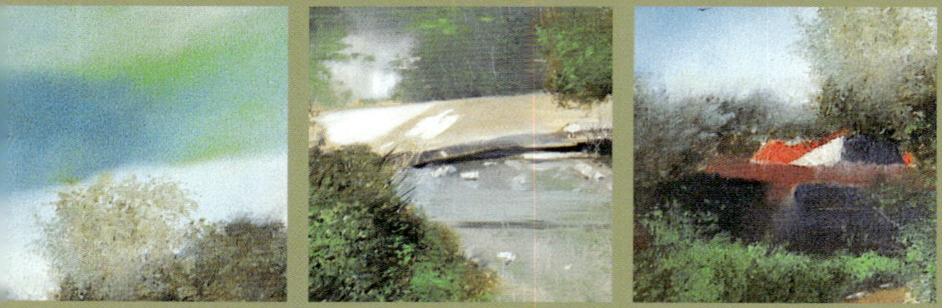

Satish's compositions are visualized from these approachable and unapproachable ends, and this is what gives his paintings a distinct touch.

Most obviously in his images of a desolate moorland – such as that of a blizzard riding down a slate grey horizon – and more subtly in the muffled explosions that bathe the meadows in mustard, one senses the cultivation of a distance between the scenes and the viewer. The cumulative impression of Satish's landscapes is one of splendid isolation. We are not allowed to participate in the rites of spring and autumn; we are held apart, remote from a roar and a swish that we cannot hear, that are stilled by a sobering touch of grey. And when we see this, our exile from the scenes of sylvan glory, we know that we are not presented with a facile, theatrical encapsulation of Nature for urban consumption, but a deeply poignant knowledge of what we have lost.

Facing page: Oil on canvas, 2000.
Following pages 136-137: Oil on canvas, 1991.

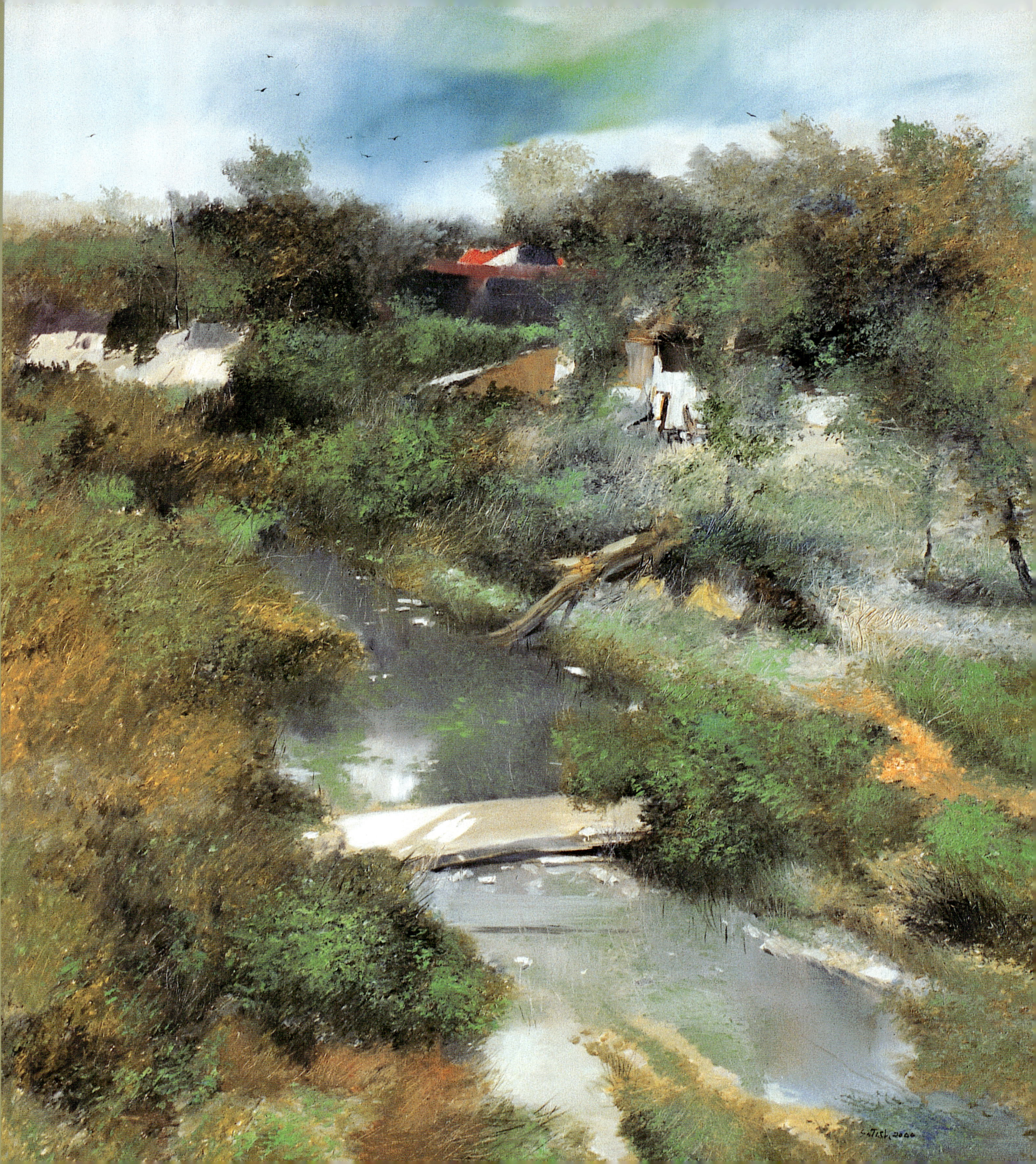
SaTish, 2000

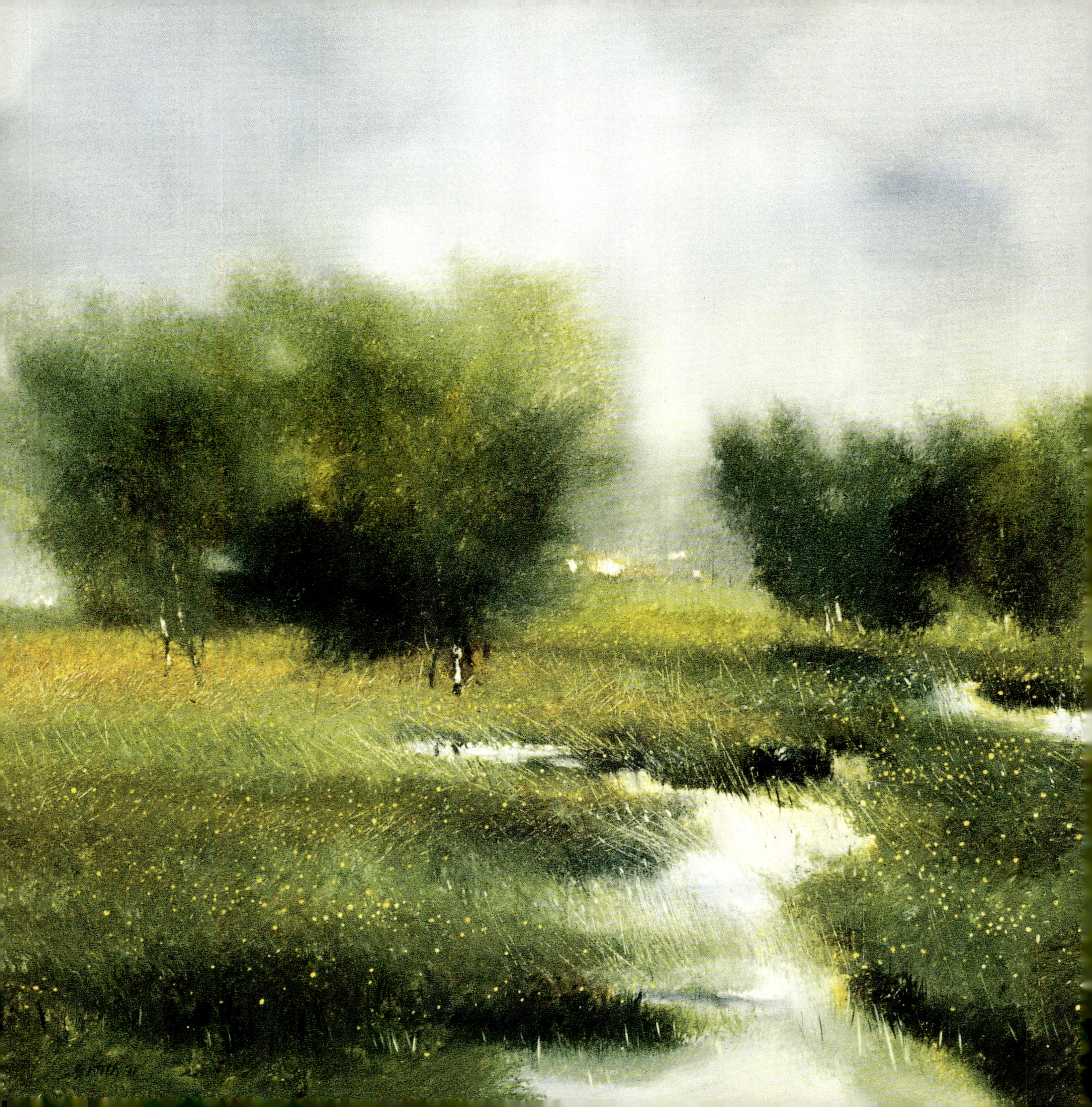

Silence can help us get in touch with the innermost essence of our being and we align with the power that manifests everything in the universe.

– Satish Chandra

Windswept Look

"In his paintings the artist has given an impressive windswept look to the landscapes, and by scraping his paintings with a scalpel or blunt knife, he has given a unique depth and added a dimensional feel...

Thus you can see billowing wind, dancing trees, chirping birds, human figures caught amidst wind currents, struggling to find their way, drifting clouds and their flight, (favourably compared with the artist's flight of imagination), conflicting emotions of the sea with its different moods – a quiet sea shore with a multi-hued sky, the peace and tranquillity of an early morning on the sea shore...."

– Seema Javed
Express Newsline,
Lucknow
22 May 2002

Facing page: Oil on canvas, 2001.

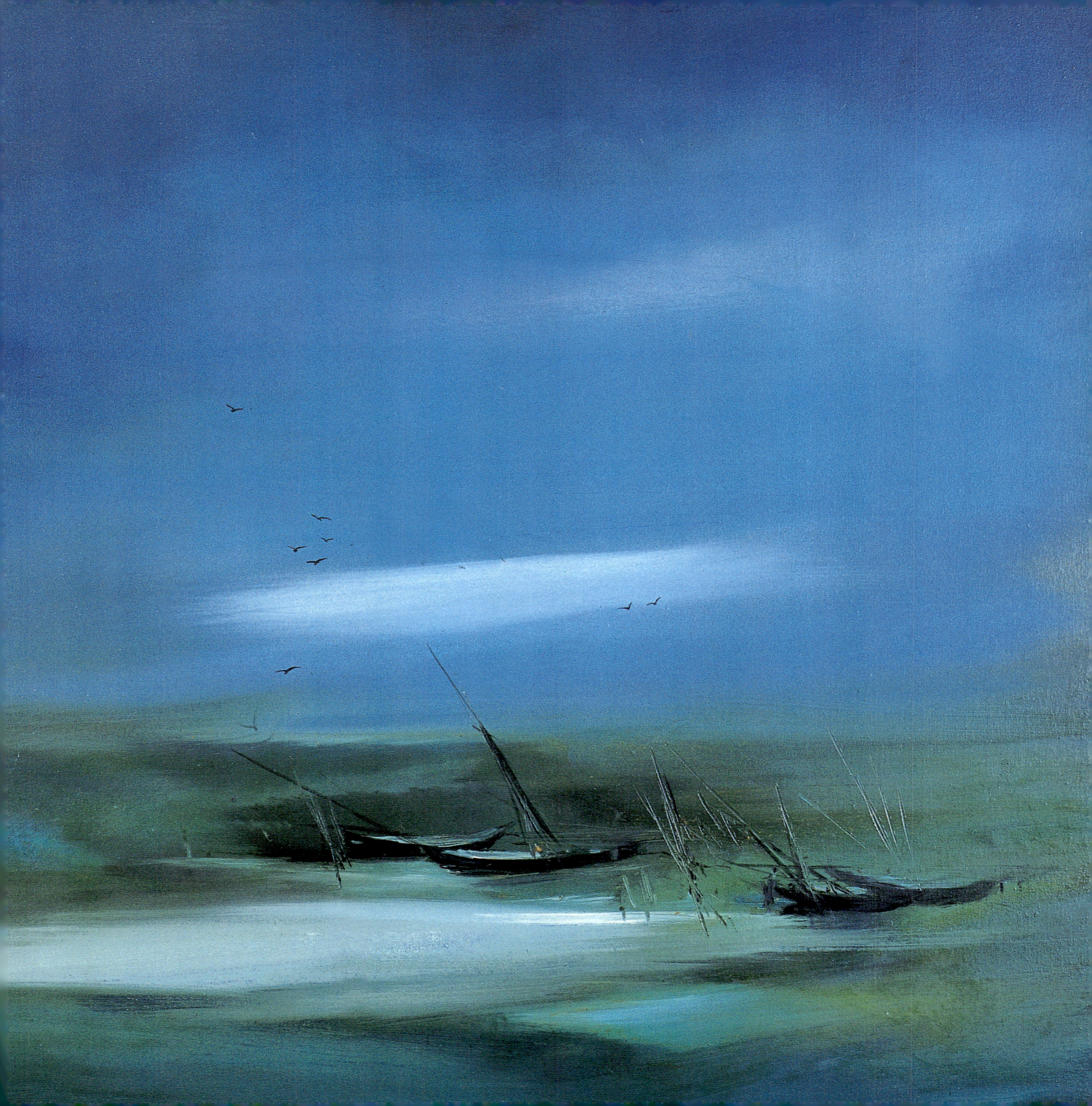

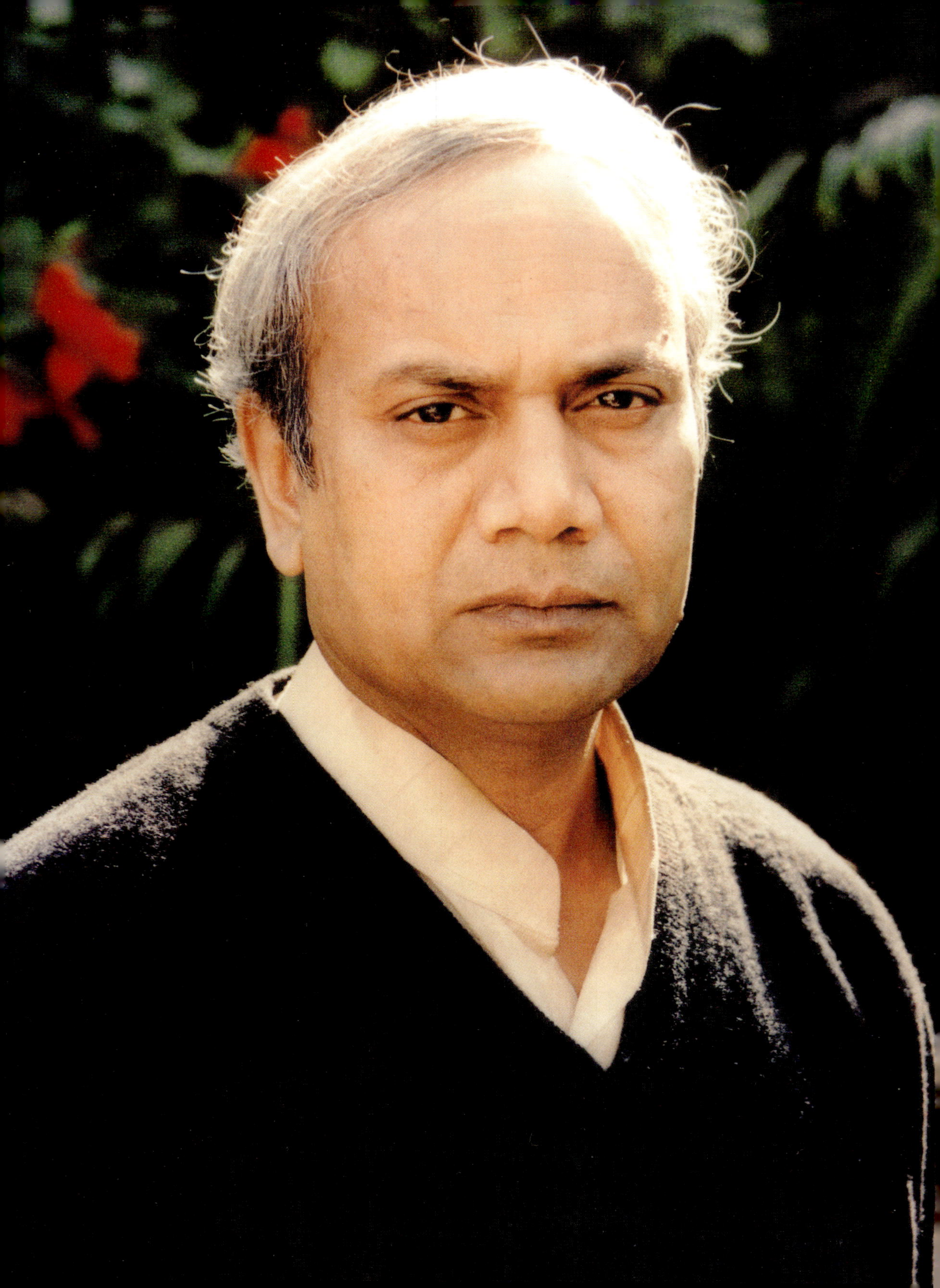

The Last Journey

Nature has treated Satish as the 'Blessed One' whenever he has picked up the brush. Ever since I have known Satish, painting has been his life force. For over eighteen years, he battled illness. I was by his bedside, my own breath ebbing and flowing with his. My husband felt he could breathe easy as long as he was with his brush and colours. His life itself was a communion with Nature that gave him the tenacity to face anything – absolutely anything – and return to his canvases every single time.

Today Satish Chandra's studio, the womb that gave birth to his creations, lies silent and cold. On 21 November 2004, at the age of sixty-four, Satish left for his heavenly abode after battling brain cancer for a year in Delhi.

Even during this period, his bond with Lucknow, and the need to paint, tugged at his heart more than any pain could. But destiny would have it otherwise. The wing of darkness touched him, and Satish passed away in his sleep with a soft smile on his lips. It was his last journey, from this world to the one beyond. At last his 'tapasya' of a lifetime was over, for he had himself attained what he had striven to explain through his paintings – that ultimate truth, the oneness of God and man.

Remembering Satish

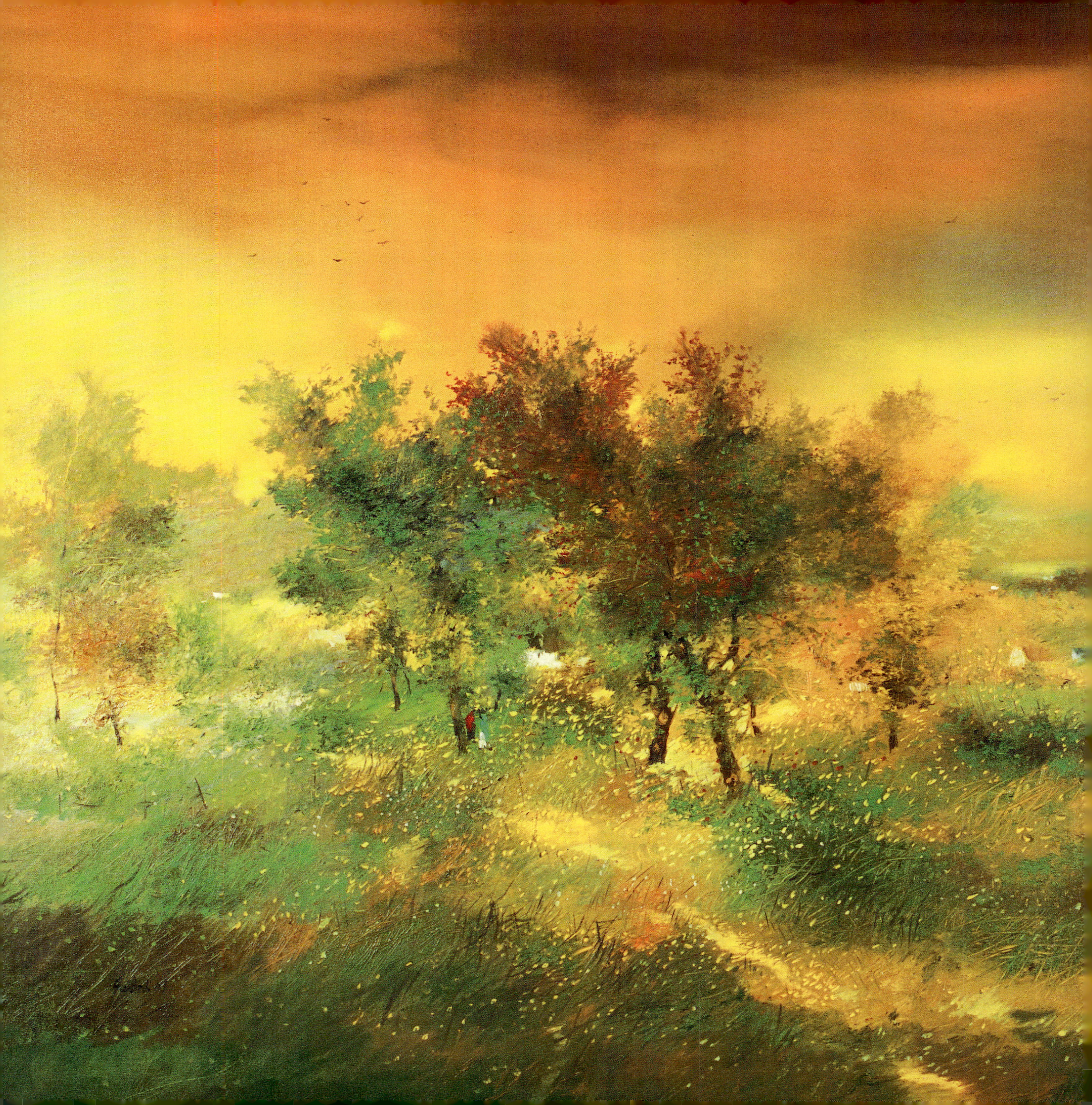

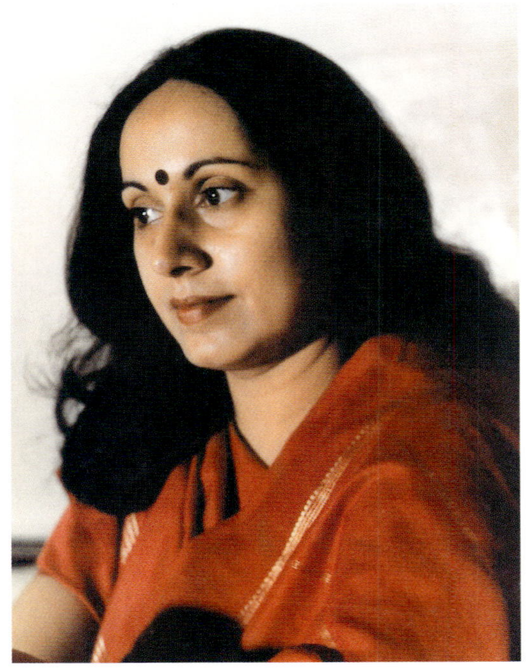

The Blessed One

Meenakshi Chandra
Wife

In the turquoise sky
A splash of colours,
As if to the Painter's stroke.
Covered with flowers,
Frozen and still
As if under the gaze of God
Slept Satish, in deep slumber.
The year 2004, it was 21 November,
A white sheet covered his body.
For one year he had battled brain
    cancer in Delhi,

Oil on canvas, 2001.

Away from home, Lucknow, his
beloved city.
Even in that one year
The urge to paint tugged at his heart
strings
More than any pain could,
But Destiny would have it otherwise.
The wing of darkness touched him,
Hesitatingly too –
He passed away in his sleep
Into another world.
A soft smile was on his lips,
No pain. No fear.
A countenance so expressive –
Beaming with the light of true
achievement.
His hands joined in oblation,
His worldly duties he had performed,
Had lived pure amid life's temptations,
Preparing himself for departure from
this world of illusions.
Nothing could lure him back to stay at
home,
No shackles could bind him now

From embarking on this last journey
Into eternity.
While alive, he wanted to paint
Something closer to his heart,
Something he had evolved from,
Something that resolved his being.
He had lofty goals,
High as the peaks,
He remained open and adaptive
Like the flowing streams, never
stagnant.
Never hesitant to change,
A Nature lover and explorer,
Close to Nature and of deep aesthetic
sense
He painted Nature in all its
magnificence.
He pondered
The truth of Nature,
The nature of truth,
Nature and God.
In Nature he saw God's manifestation,
In Nature he saw, to the Supreme, its
sublimation

Nature enshrines spiritual light,
The light he saw in meditation.
Each canvas throbbed with the gamut
of his emotions,
Each canvas a prostration before the
Lord,
He had attained sagely humility,
Was inspired, and enhanced the
spiritual.
Heightening the sense of devotion for
the Almighty
He attained spiritual heights,
His roots deep in the soil,
His spirit soaring high in the skies.
Full of love, hope and faith,
The 'roohani noor' of this Sufi,
Radiated in his personality,
Reflected on his face.
Satiating the environment
With soft words and serenity,
With his spiritual fragrance,
His whole existence

Facing page: Oil on canvas, 1998.

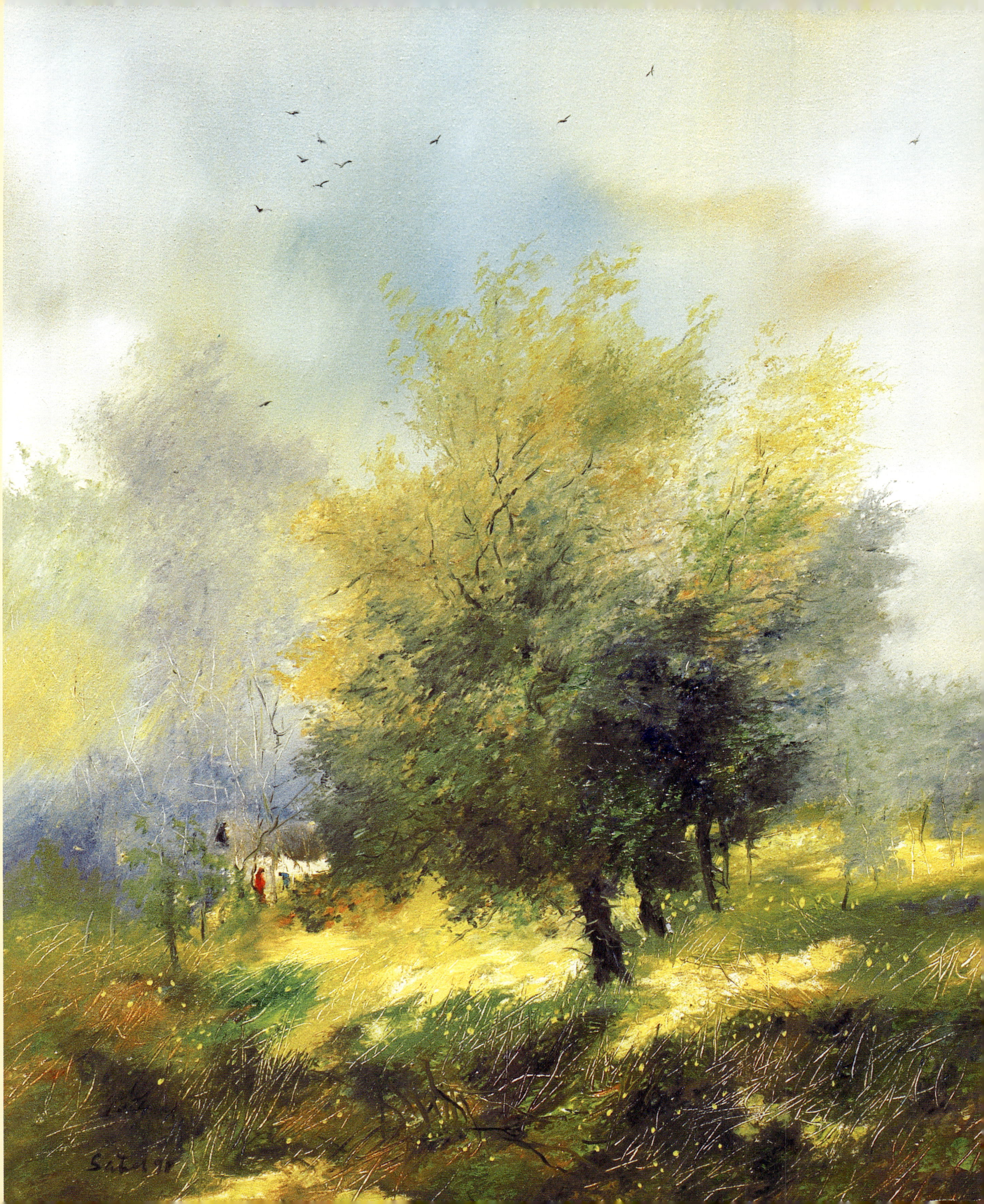

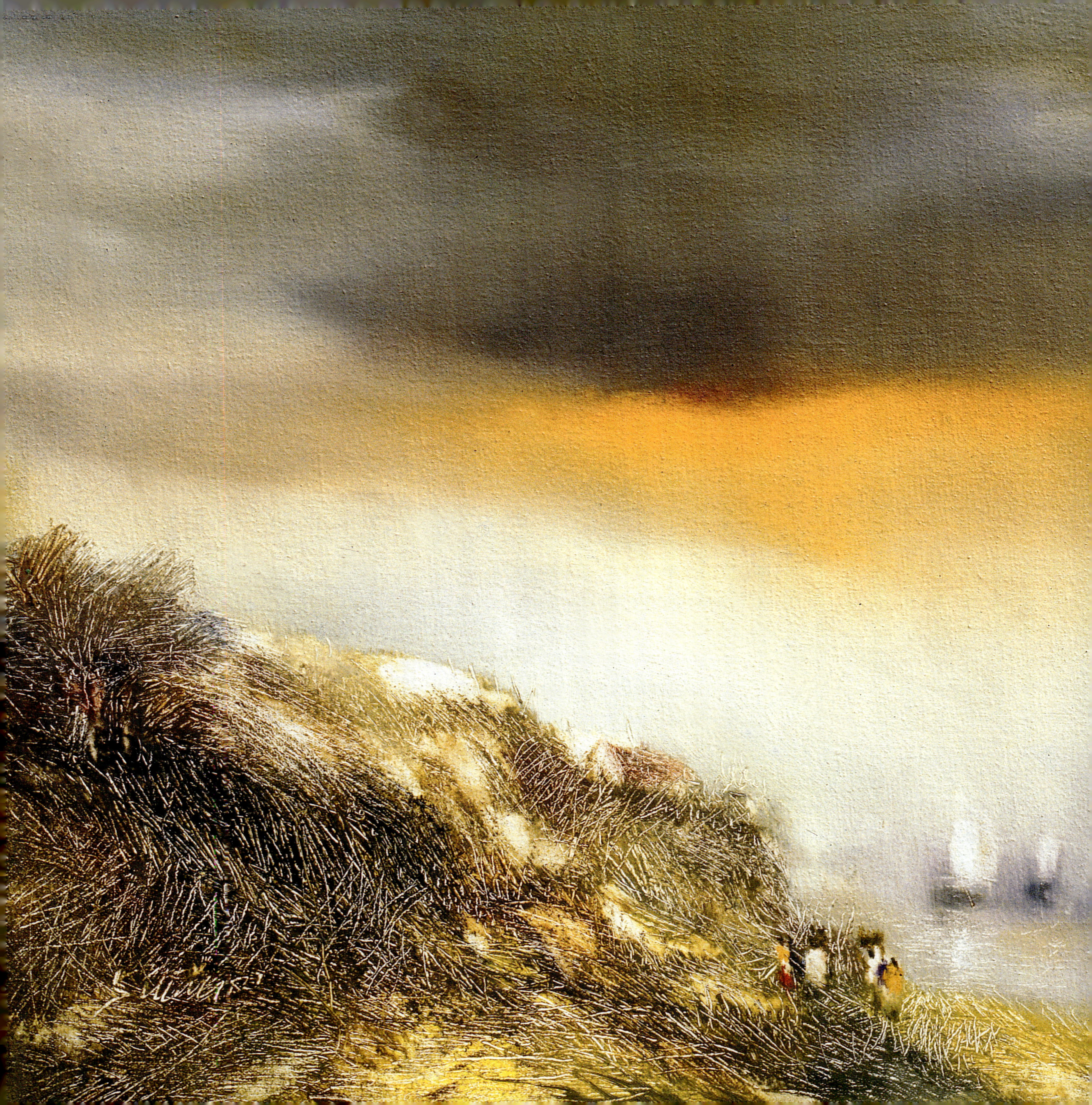

Dissolved within the Divine Unity
Until he arrived
At the junction of nonexistence
Within the Divine Existence.
And when the smoke arose
From the pyre to the Heaven,
With the devout chanting shlokas,
Giving up the earthly body,
Unfettering the soul,
A spiritual ascent
Uniting the Soul with the Supreme –
A surrender to limitless space, a timeless regime,
It seized the hearts of one and all,
Relatives and friends,
Gathered to bid good-bye to him,
A tender last farewell.
For some it was too much to bear,
There had been so much to share.
Too young still, just 64 years,
The thought brought each one to tears.
Even as the flames consumed your body,
I watched helplessly
My soul-mate, Satish,
You stood there in my mind's view
Reminding me that life is God's gift
And pure love, its anchor.
Bringing me to tears afresh,
Washing me anew.
In your studio, sitting alone,
Surrounded by your paintings,
I remember you. Again and again,
My mind flits through the passage of time –
Filled with the perfume of memories both painful and sweet,
My crystal heart is illuminated
By the Light of the Divine
In which I see clearly
Reflections of you.
Nature treated you as the 'Blessed One'
Every time you picked up the brush,
In your work you live for posterity,
Immortalized forever.
Many oyster-shells exist in the ocean deep,
But very few hold a rare pearl like you, Satish.

Facing page: Oil on canvas, 1982.

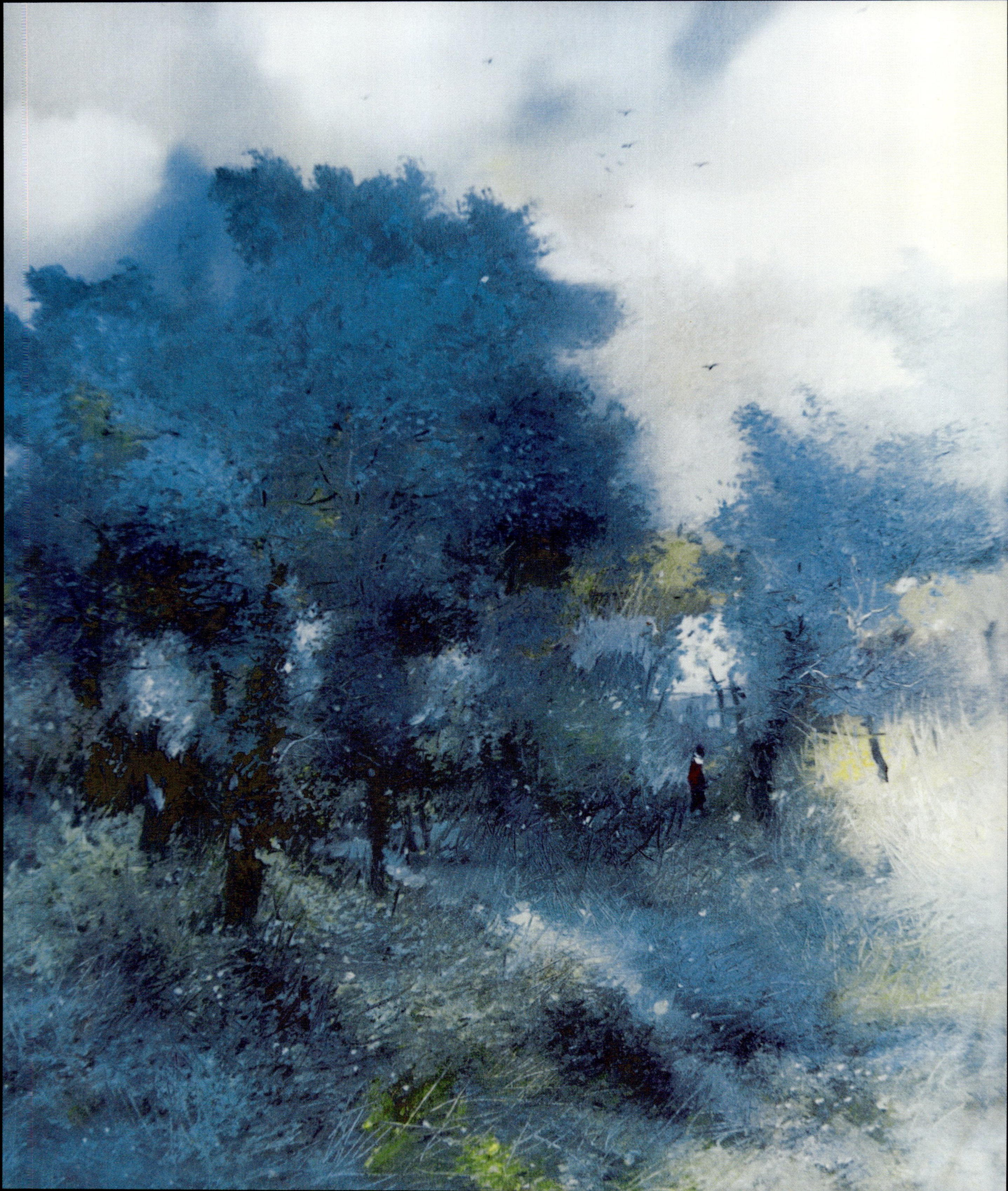

Oil on canvas, 2001.

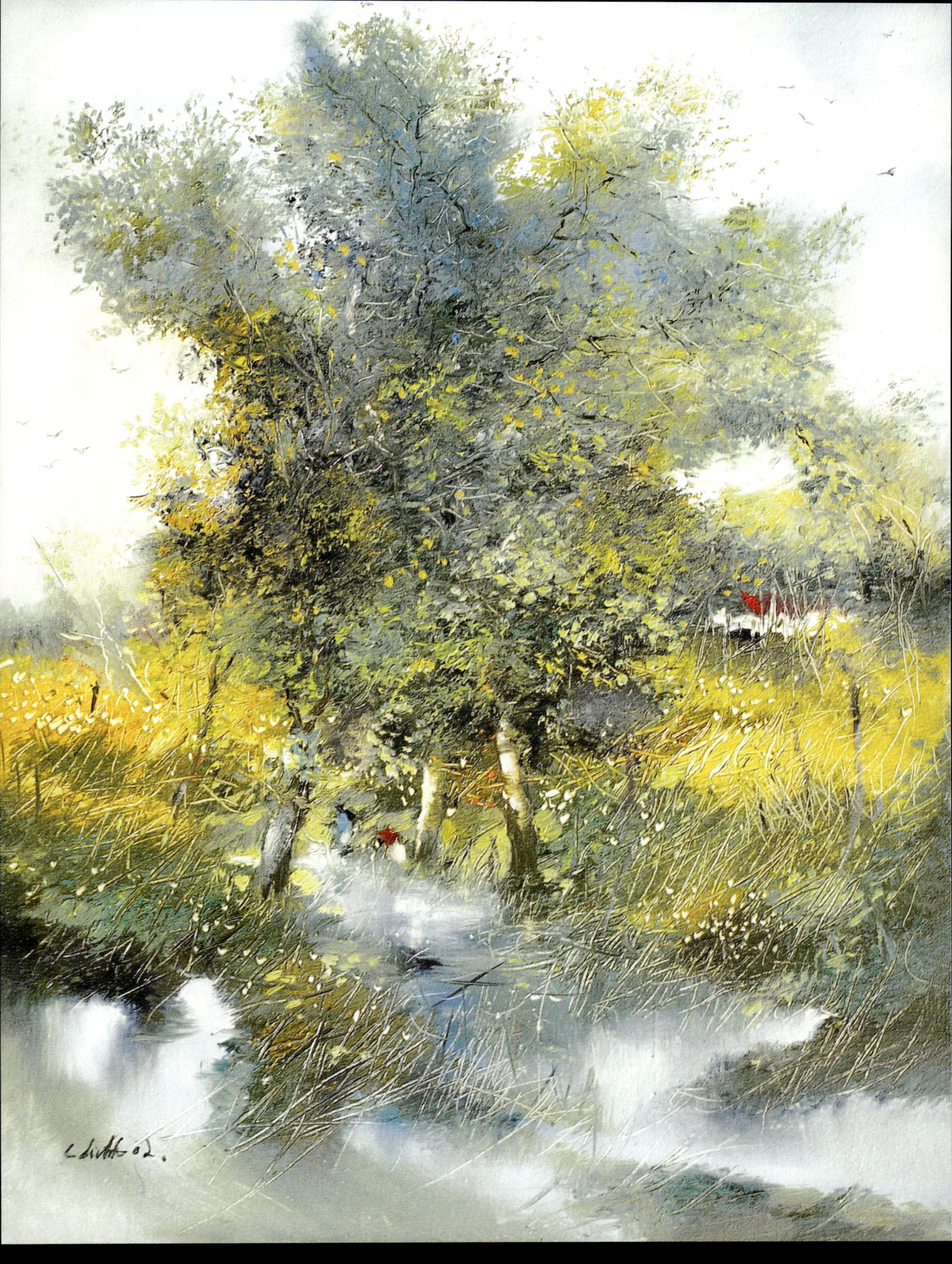

Oil on canvas, 2002

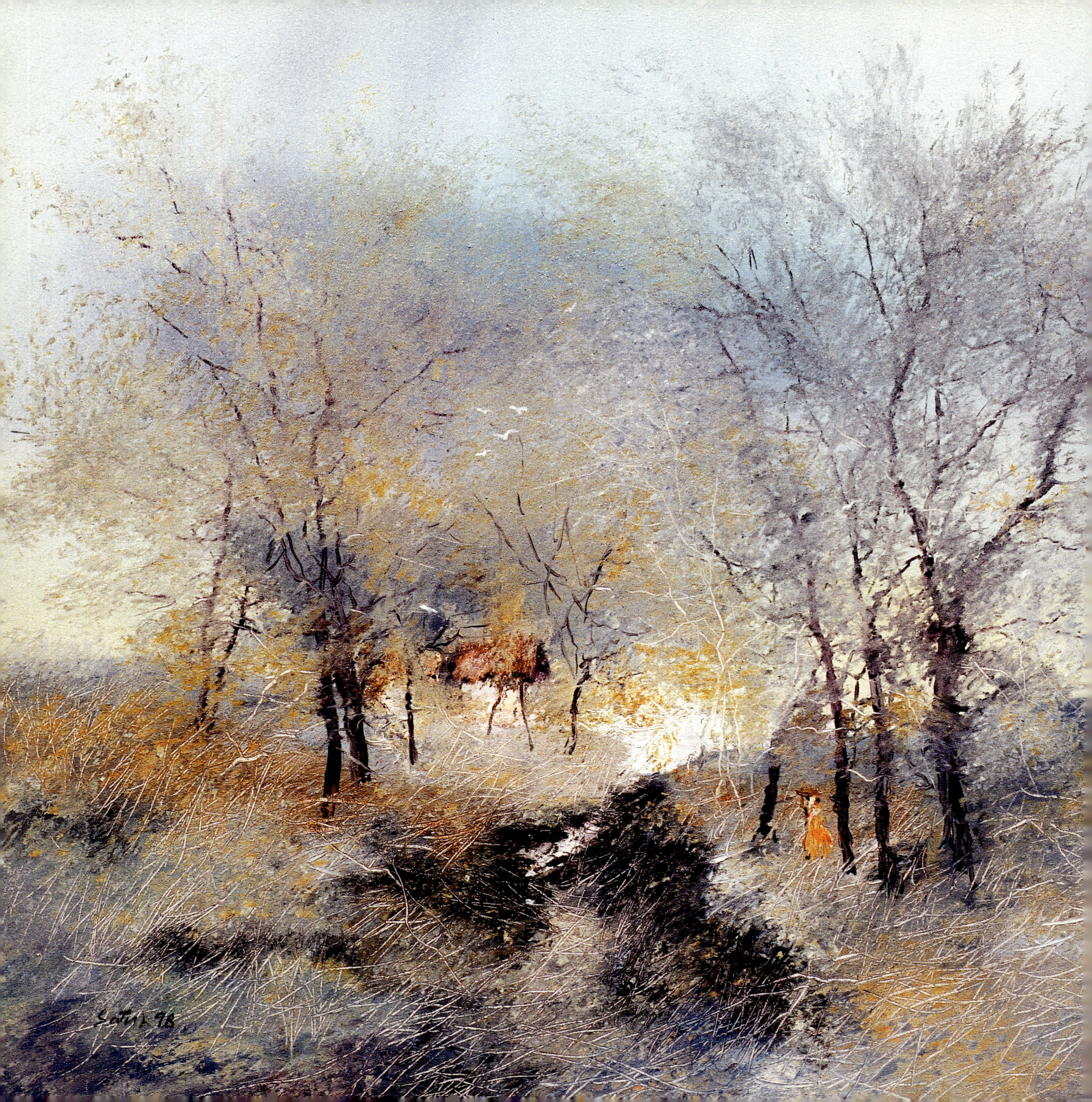

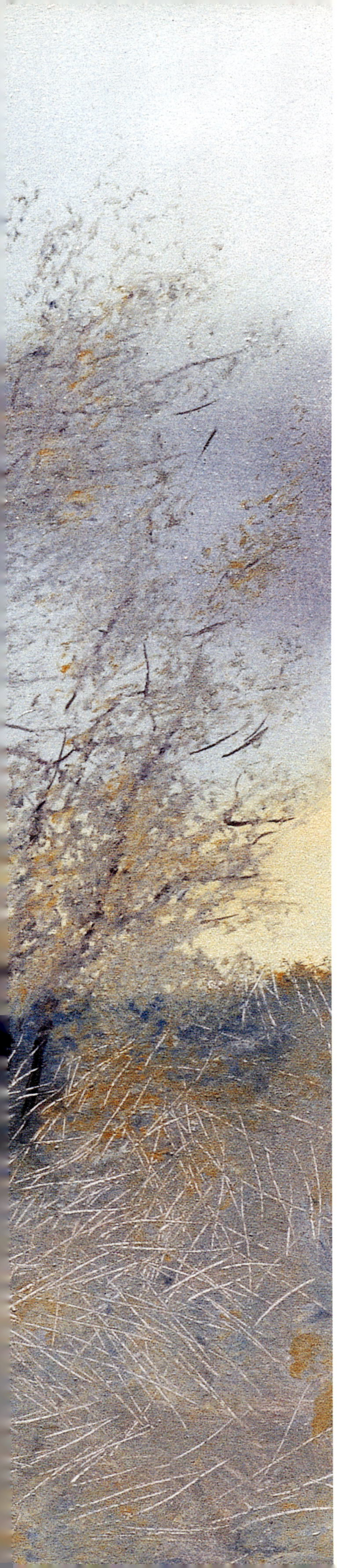

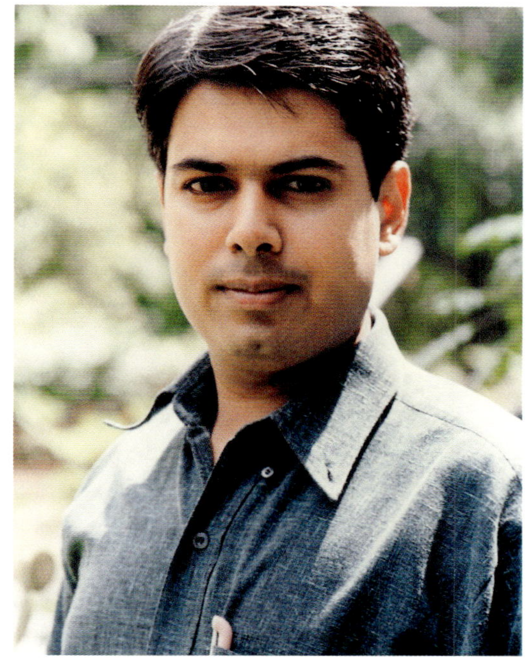

Miracle Man

Siddharth Chandra
Son

'Papaji', for me, is a very special word. Woven from the notes of a melody, even today it twinkles and shines at me.

To translate all those moments I shared with Papa would not be possible here – after all, it takes a lifetime to explain a bond with a person who showered all his love on Amma (my mother) and me.

It took me some time to develop an understanding of Papa's thought process when he painted his canvas –

Facing page: Oil on canvas, 1998.

the urge to become one with Nature and God is what I could see in each and every stroke of his brush.

Every summer vacation of mine was spent with Amma and Papa in a hill-station, more often than not Nainital. I still remember the days when Papa would pick up his pad and start painting as clouds entered our room through the open windows. I would be out the whole day and when I returned to the room, I would be greeted with a string of water-colour paintings, a sight that would delight me, making me feel one with Nature.

Papa used to pamper me so much so that a simple cut on my finger would bring tears to his eyes. No matter what I decided to do, my parents would not only encourage me but also help me find the means to reach the goal. This confidence they reposed in me made me feel even

Facing page: Watercolour on paper, 1998.

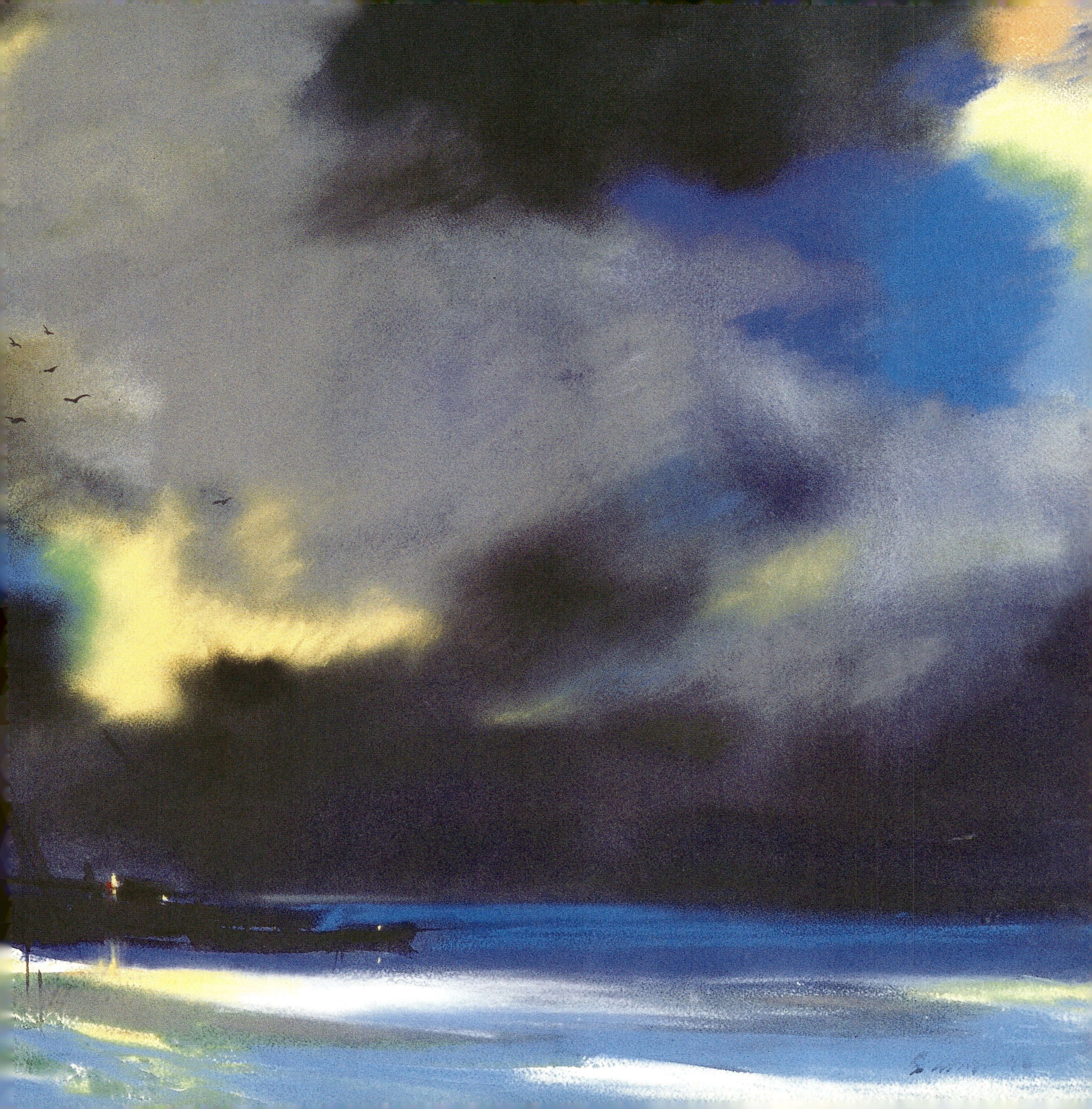

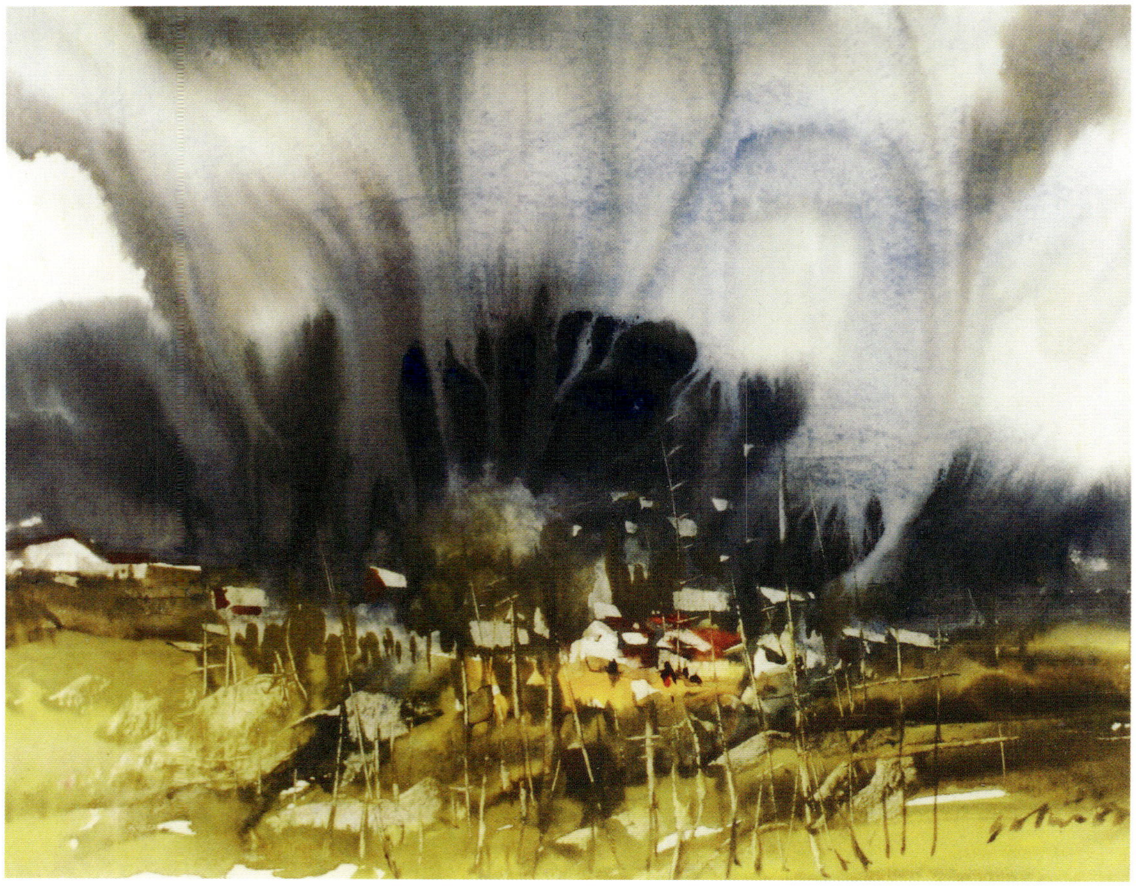

Watercolour on paper.

more responsible for every action I took.

I was one of those lucky children who are given full freedom to choose their careers – I was always curious to know how electrical stuff worked and was later interested in making my career in the IT world. Today my ambition is fulfilled not so much because I wanted to do it but because Papa and Amma always told me, "beta yadi tum sochte ho ki ye theek hai to man laga ke karo." ('If you think this is right, then do it with all your heart.')

With Papa being an artist, Amma in the teaching profession and myself in the IT world, we always had lots of interesting stuff to share with one another. But nothing good lasts forever.... 2003-2004 brought with it the moment I had always dreaded.... Papa was found to have a brain tumour. It had gone undiagnosed for a couple of months and had turned life-threatening. No medicine could stop the cancer which, day by day, was taking Papa further away from me.

During this time I saw my wife Pooja and Amma struggle all alone with the cancer and what took us through this rough time was the serenity and peace on Papa's face even though his pain and suffering was extreme.

I would return from office, lie down beside him and he would stroke my hair and say, "beta main bilkul theek ho jaoonga". I would go off to sleep nuzzled against him as if everything was perfect and suddenly wake up to see my Papa's condition.... panic-stricken, I would be on the net searching for a cure that would be available in some part of the world.

Papa suffered too much – his entire left side paralysed due to the cancer in his brain. This not only shook his willpower but also took away from him his greatest sustenance – his ability to paint. He craved to paint but found it more and more difficult to do so. What remained close to his heart was prayer and love for all those around him. I think it was during this time that Papaji learned to transcend his body. In this last one year of his life, he slowly but surely let go of all worldly attachments.

Days went by, months melted away, and after a year, on 21 November

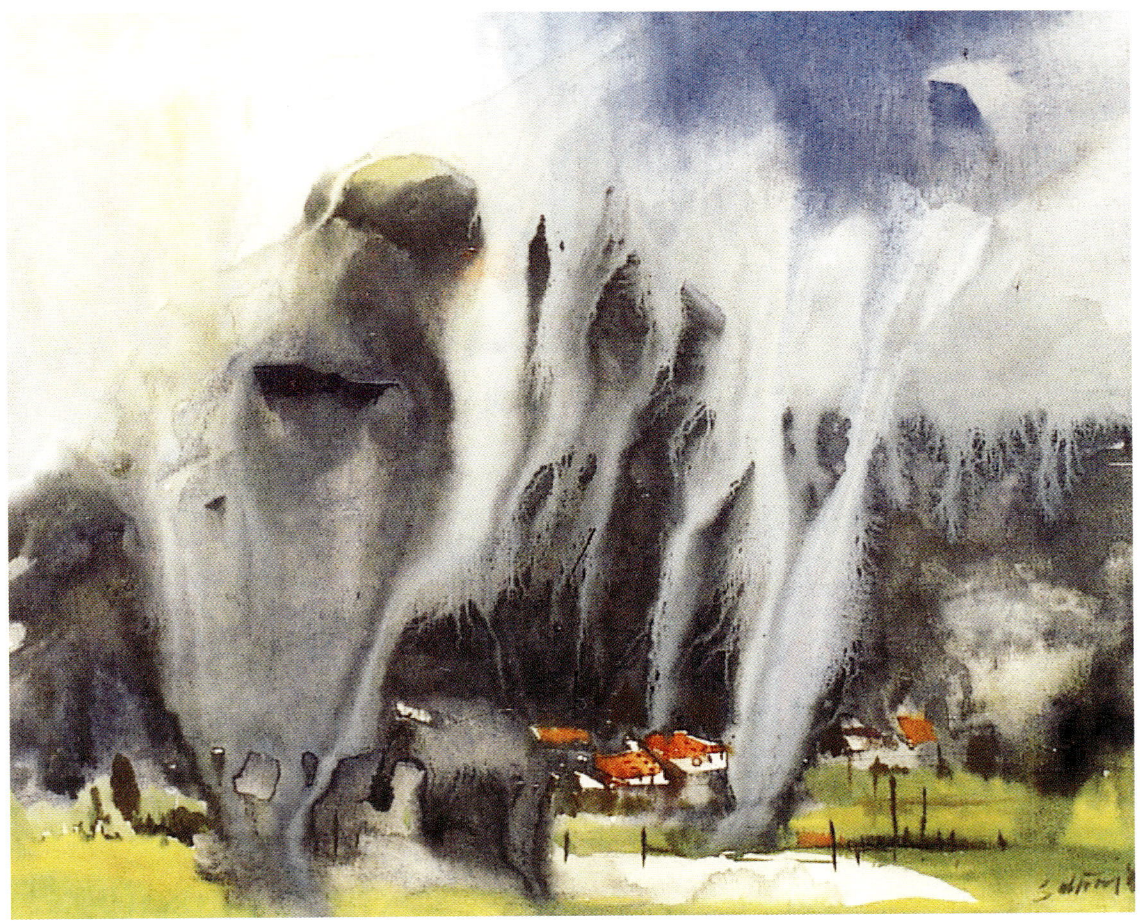

Watercolour on paper.

2004, the battle between God and Papa ended. I realized that I had to control my emotions but could not. Amma, Pooja and I massaged Papa's feet and palms for a few hours, thinking our action might just get him back to us. Doctors had given up but we did not. After all, in 1985, Papa had suffered a massive heart attack and was given up for dead for over ten minutes – it was a miracle that he had come back to us. But this time, Papa did not return.

I know that I will never stop missing Papa but I always feel his presence in the smallest of things. I know that he and Amma will always be there by our side whenever Pooja and I need them. I still feel his tender touch and I still feel loved by him from wherever he is. If there is life after death, I would pray to God to let me have Papa, Amma and Pooja in every lifetime of mine.

Facing page: Oil on canvas.

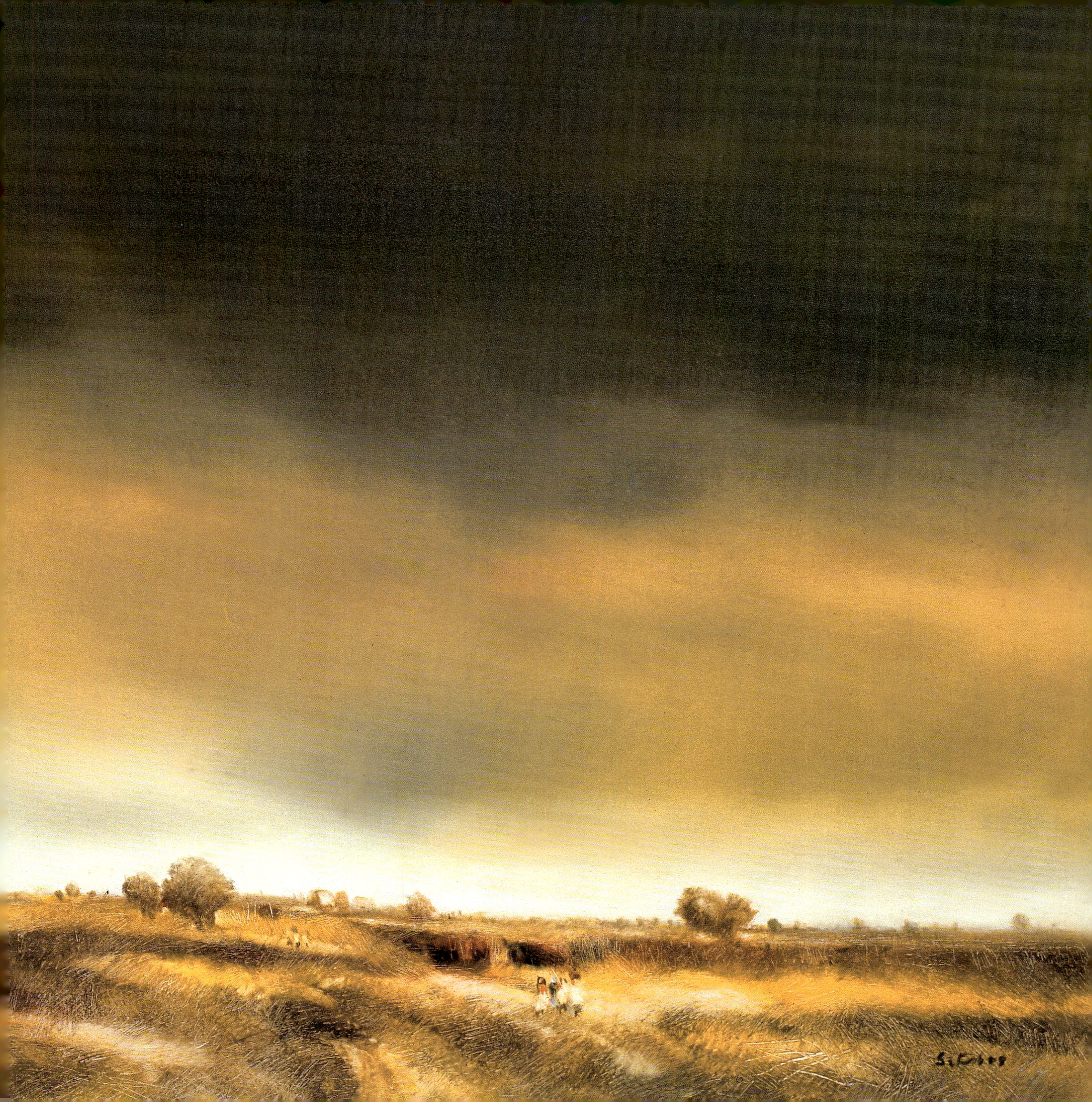

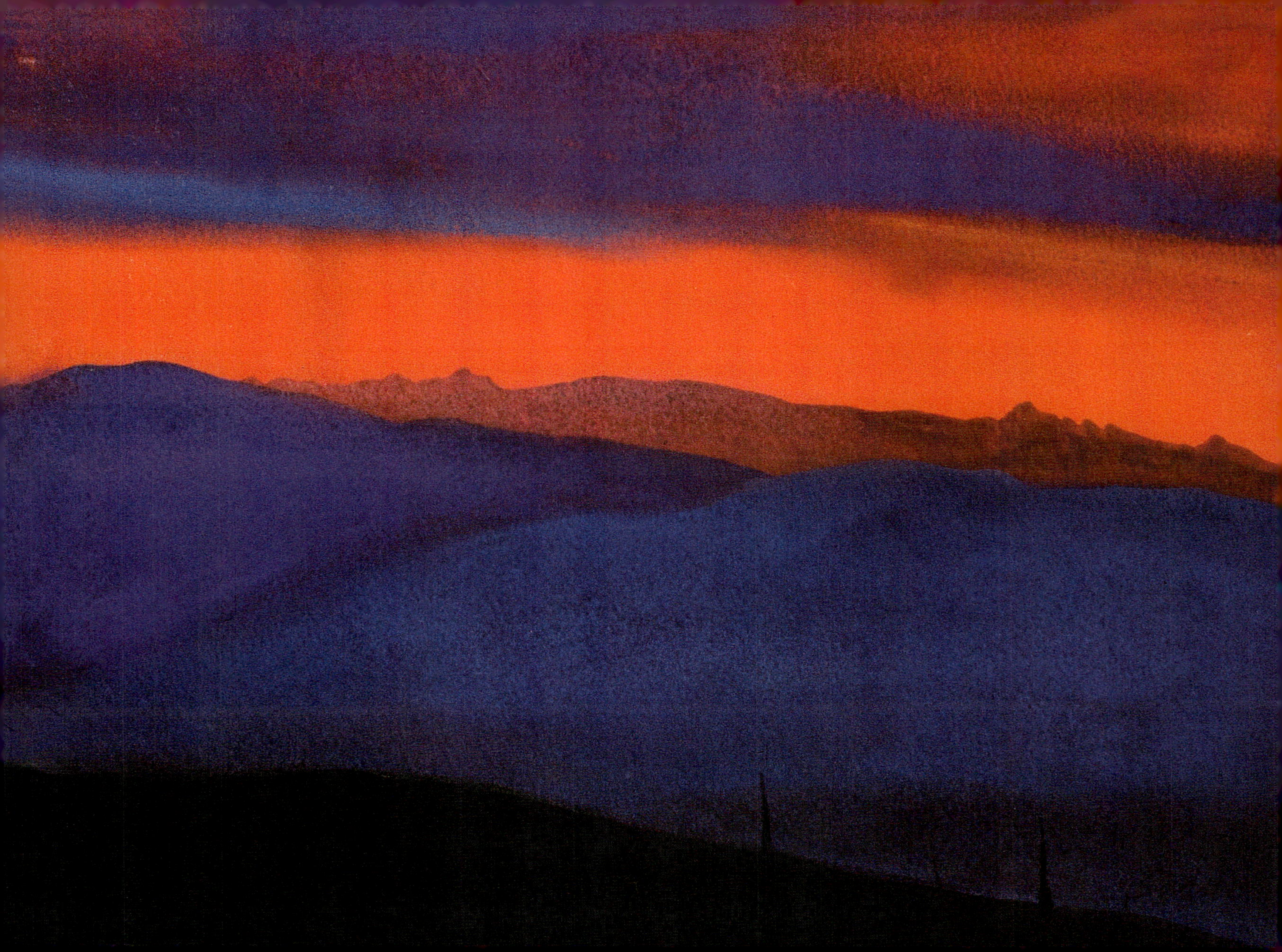

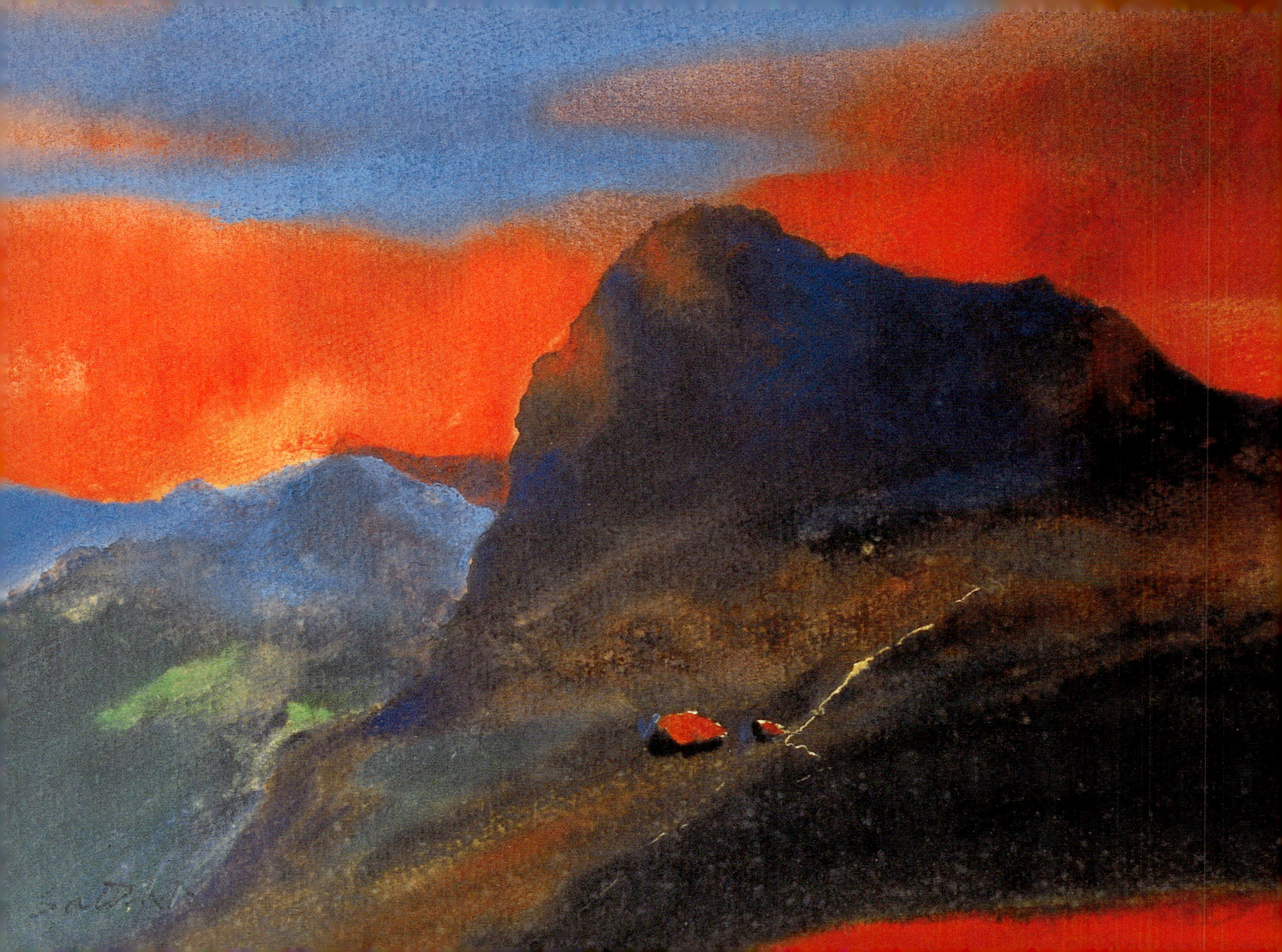

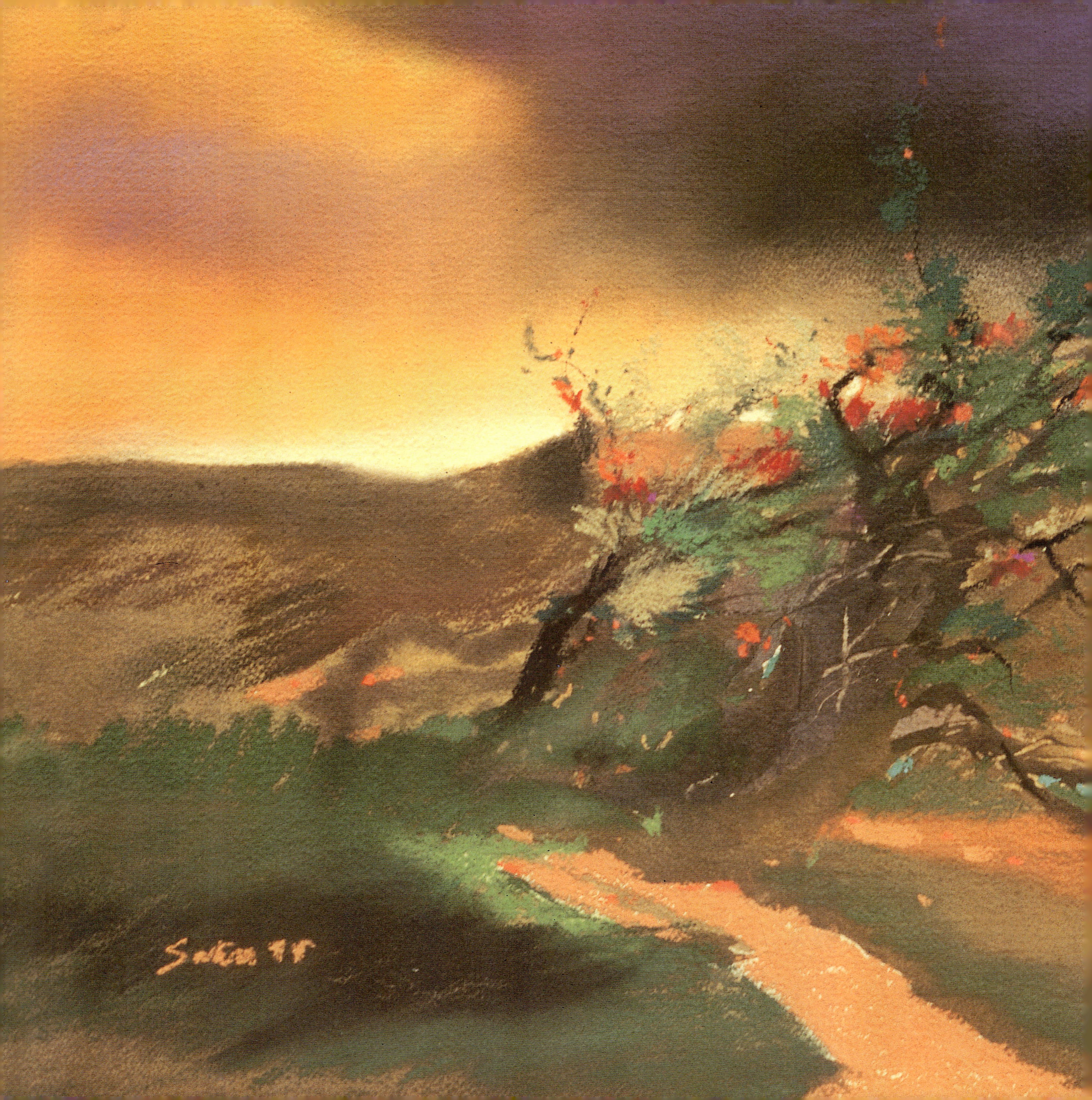

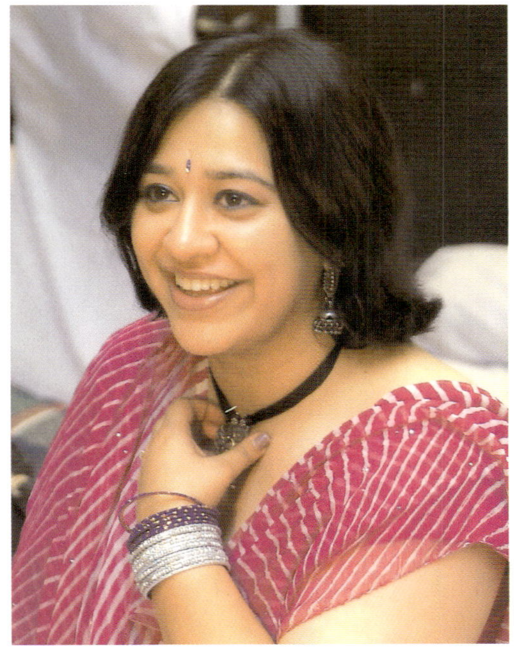

A Saintly Soul

Pooja Chandra
Daughter-in-Law

It is believed in all religions that if a soul suffers but still maintains faith in God and Nature, then it possesses saintly dimensions.

My father-in-law (Papaji) was such a man. During the last year of his life, God chose to inflict immense physical and mental suffering on him. In a matter of months, he lost his ability to walk, work and above all, paint. Still, through the haze of the pain created by the golf ball-sized cancerous

Facing page: Mixed media on paper.

tumour in his brain, he always had a kind word and a smile for everybody.

Above all, he had a sustained faith in God. To him God was not a vague, all-knowing, all-powerful obscure presence but a vibrant living entity which manifested itself in every tree, in every colour of the sky, in every drop of rain – it just had to be felt to be seen.

He paid homage to God through his art. To him work was really worship. He was time and again called a "Sufi" by his friends and contemporaries as his work possessed the same divine quality.

He had mastery over his technique and exquisite control over his brush and palette but, in these times of figurative and abstract art, he only painted Nature. He said that it was not about what sells but about passion and conviction.

From the perspective of a layperson like me who has had no exposure to art, he was a wonderful person and artist to discover it all with. No tree, shrub or blade of grass on his canvas ever seems ordinary.

He also happened to be a wonderful father-in-law. For a girl who was leaving the security of her own home and stepping into a whole new life, he was a kind and gentle mentor who made the entire transition effortless. He welcomed me as a father embraces his first-born – with the same enthusiasm and wonder. He told me that the love and bonding he felt was inevitable. This feeling of belonging is a gift that I will always cherish.

It is still hard to believe that he is no longer with us, but we do feel him spiritually within and around us. In every swish of a tree, in the first shower of the monsoons, in the molten colours of the sunset – he is finally one with Nature and with God.

Facing page: Watercolour on paper, 1982.

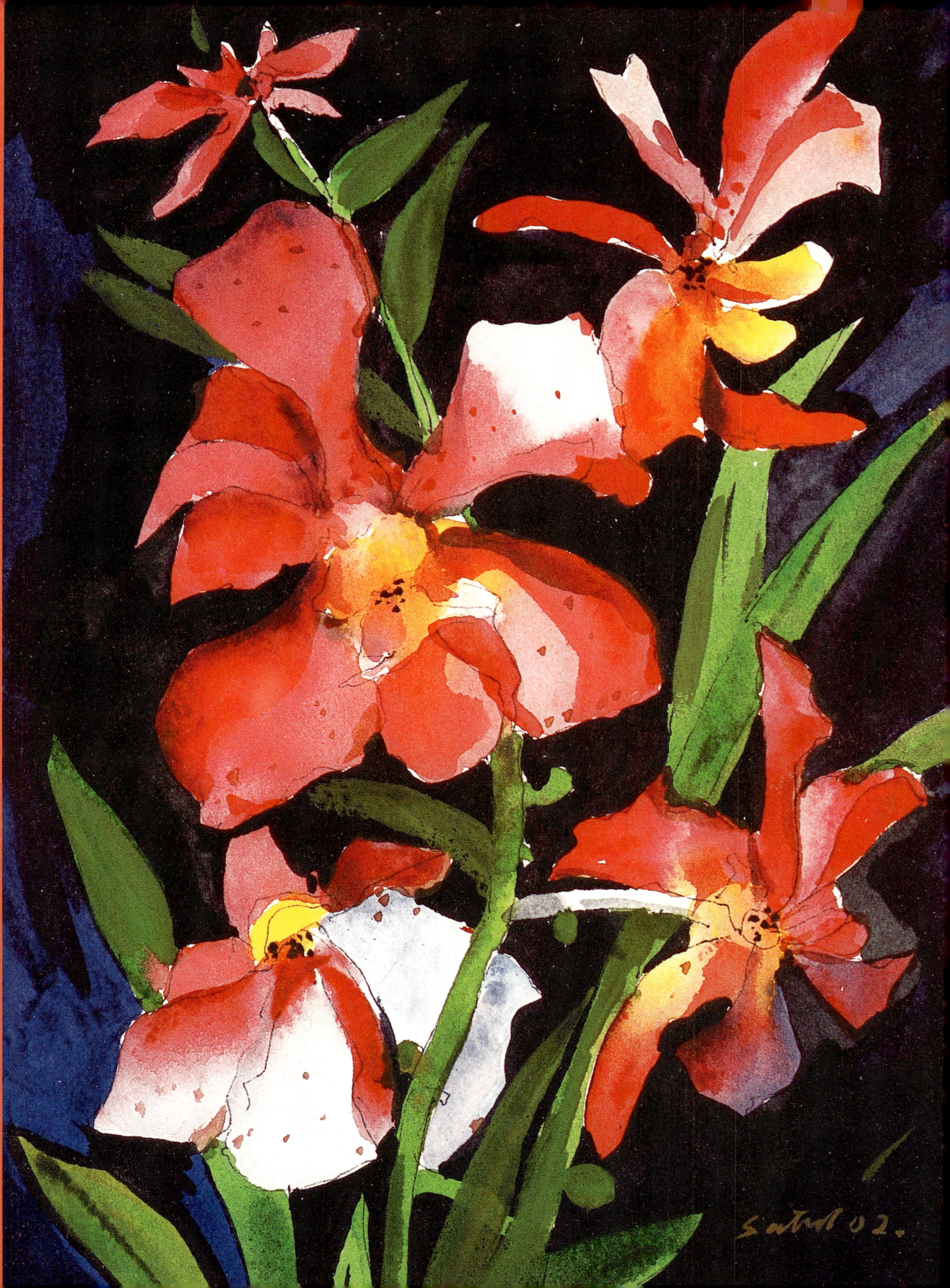

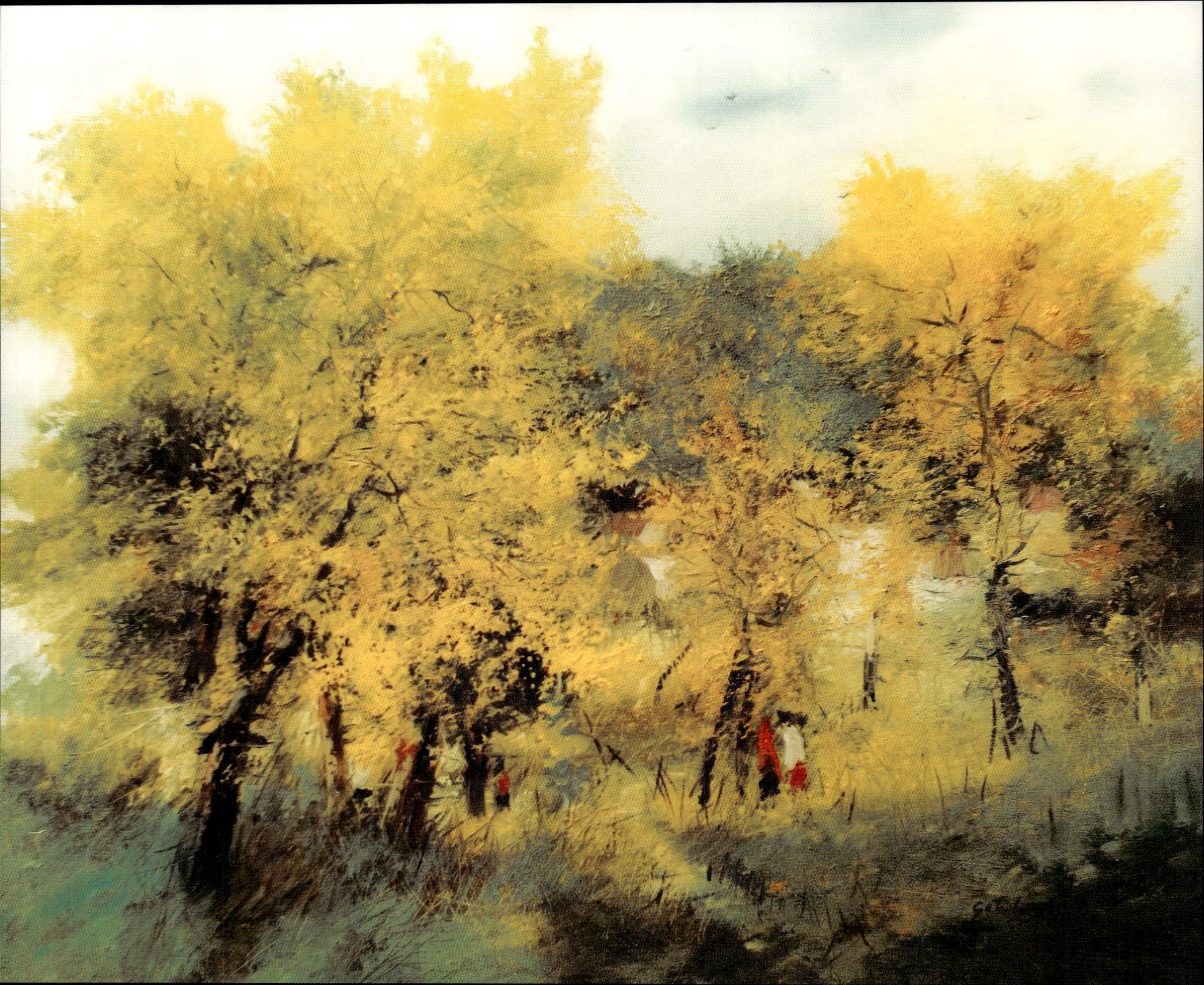

Oil on canvas, 2001.

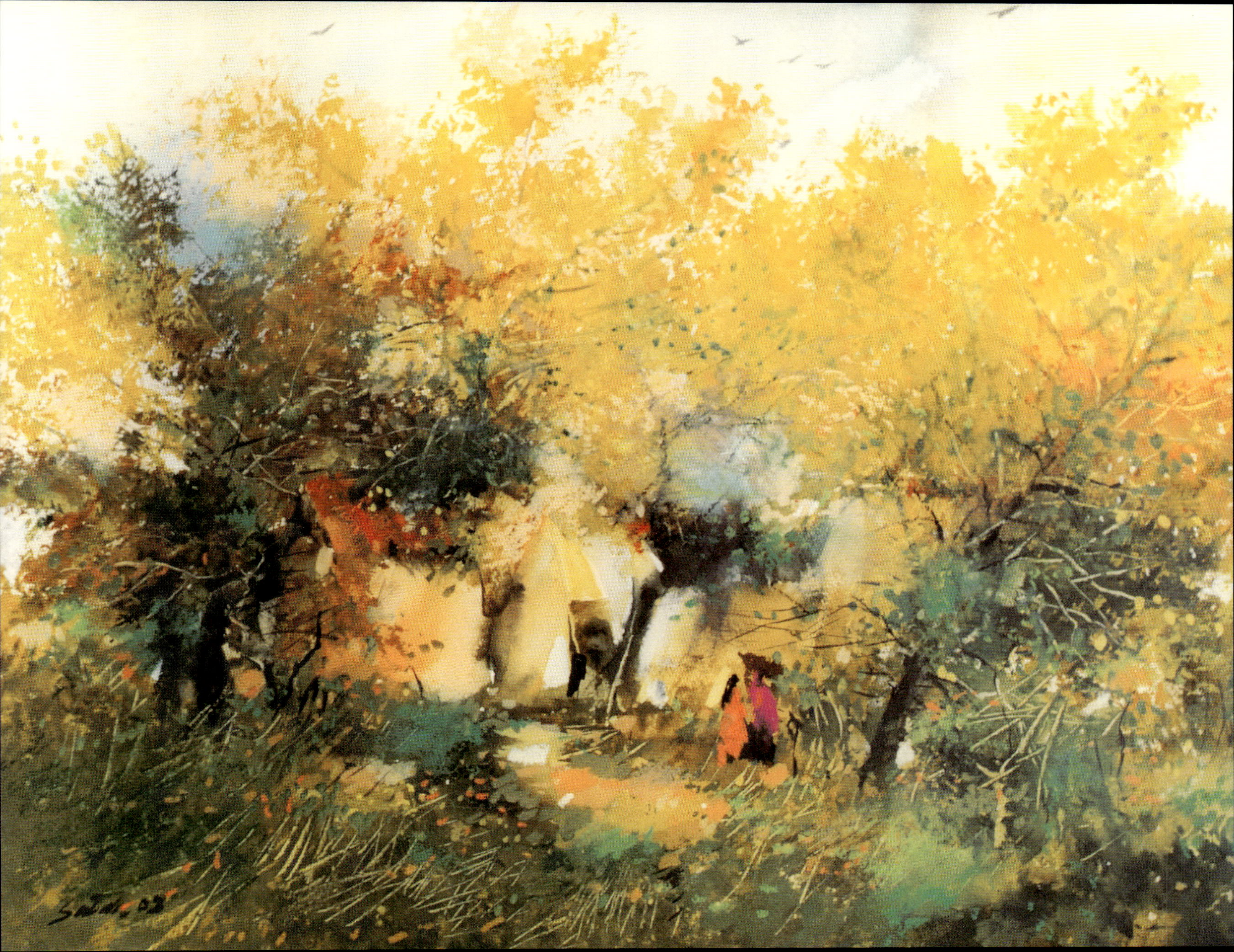

Mixed media on paper, 2002.

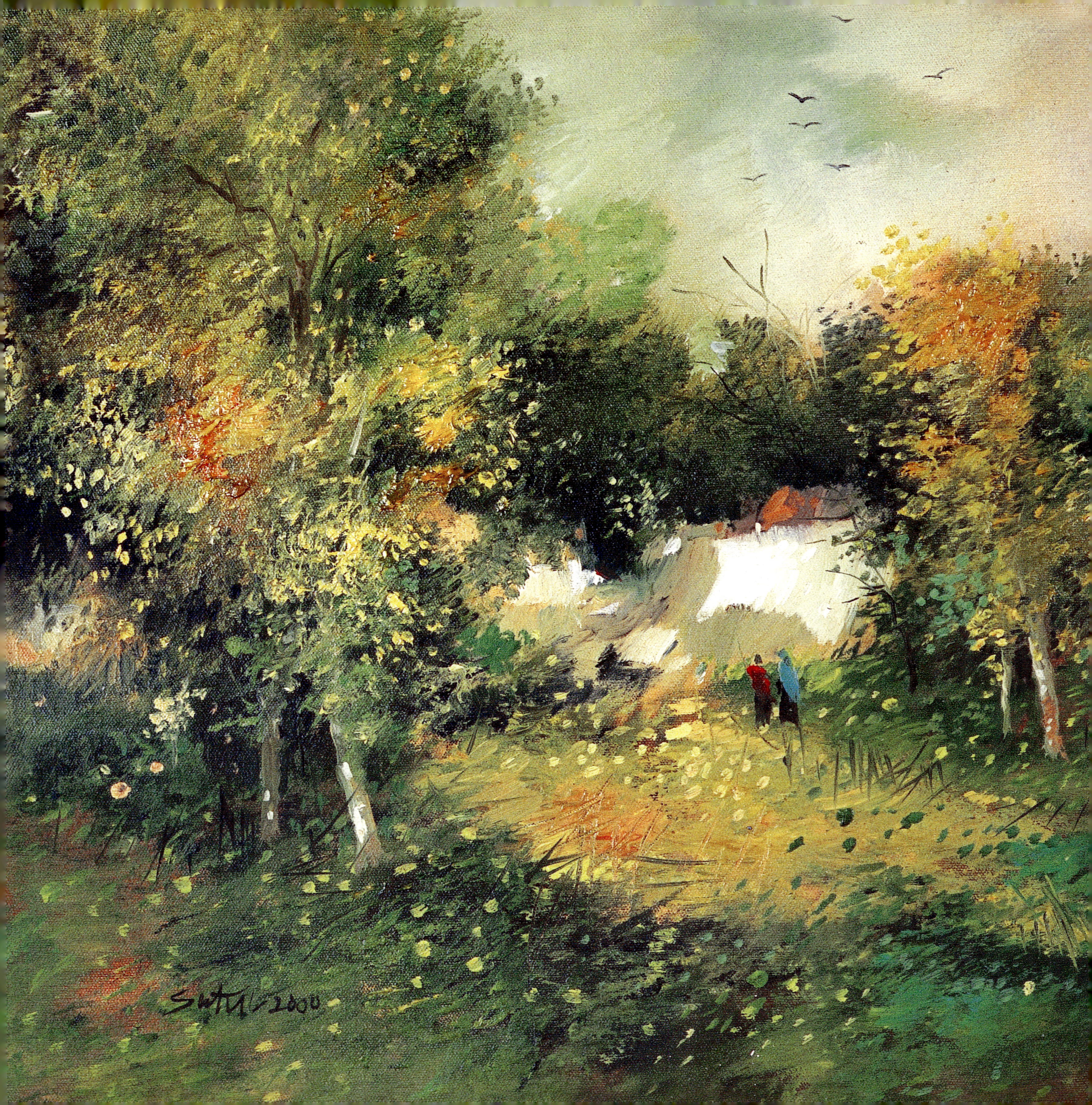

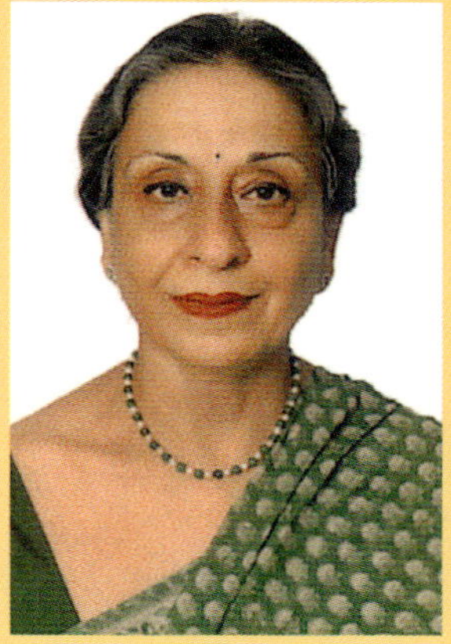

Pristine Painter

Shobha Bhatia
Owner, Gallerie Ganesha

Artists tend to have a keen perception and imagination, an observing eye and a sensitive nature – some more so than others.

Satish was one such sensitive human being, an exceptionally talented artist who focused on creating beautiful landscapes even as some of his other contemporaries moved on to other genres.

For Satish, communion with Nature in its pristine form – capturing the atmosphere, 'the moment', 'the light'– through his landscapes was of supreme importance and he was able to do so with great skill and ease. His paintings have the capacity of transporting the viewer to ecstacy or providing a sense of tranquillity and feeling of oneness with Nature.

My first encounter with Satish Chandra's work was in the early 1990s when I saw an award-winning painting of his at the National Exhibition of Art organized by the Lalit Kala Akademi in Delhi. The impact was so great that I started a search for him and finally contacted him in Lucknow. From that point onwards we began to represent his work at our gallery and have held a series of very successful solo shows of his exotic landscapes.

Besides being a capable and skilled artist, Satish Chandra was a man with

Facing page: Oil on canvas, 2000.

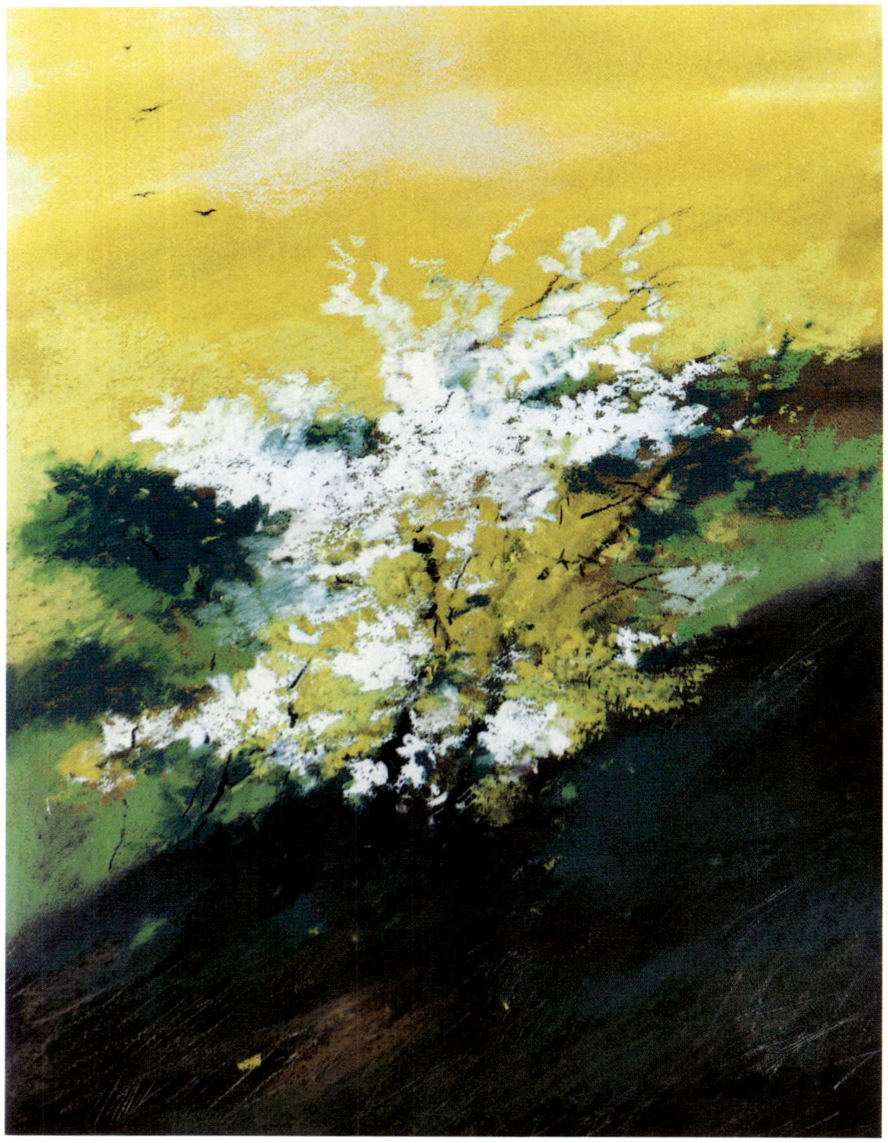

Mixed media on paper, 2001. *Facing page:* Oil on canvas.

great human qualities. Needless to say, he and his wife Meenakshi had become friends of ours and visited us whenever they came to Delhi.

A few years ago, he happened to be visiting the gallery when, during the course of our conversation, he learnt that it was my husband's birthday. Generous that he was, he immediately took one large painting out of the ones he had brought for our gallery and handed it to my husband as a birthday gift. That was the kind of human being he was.

One will always regret the fact that his life was cut short and that there will be no more landscapes from him capturing the "ephemeral aspects of a changing moment".

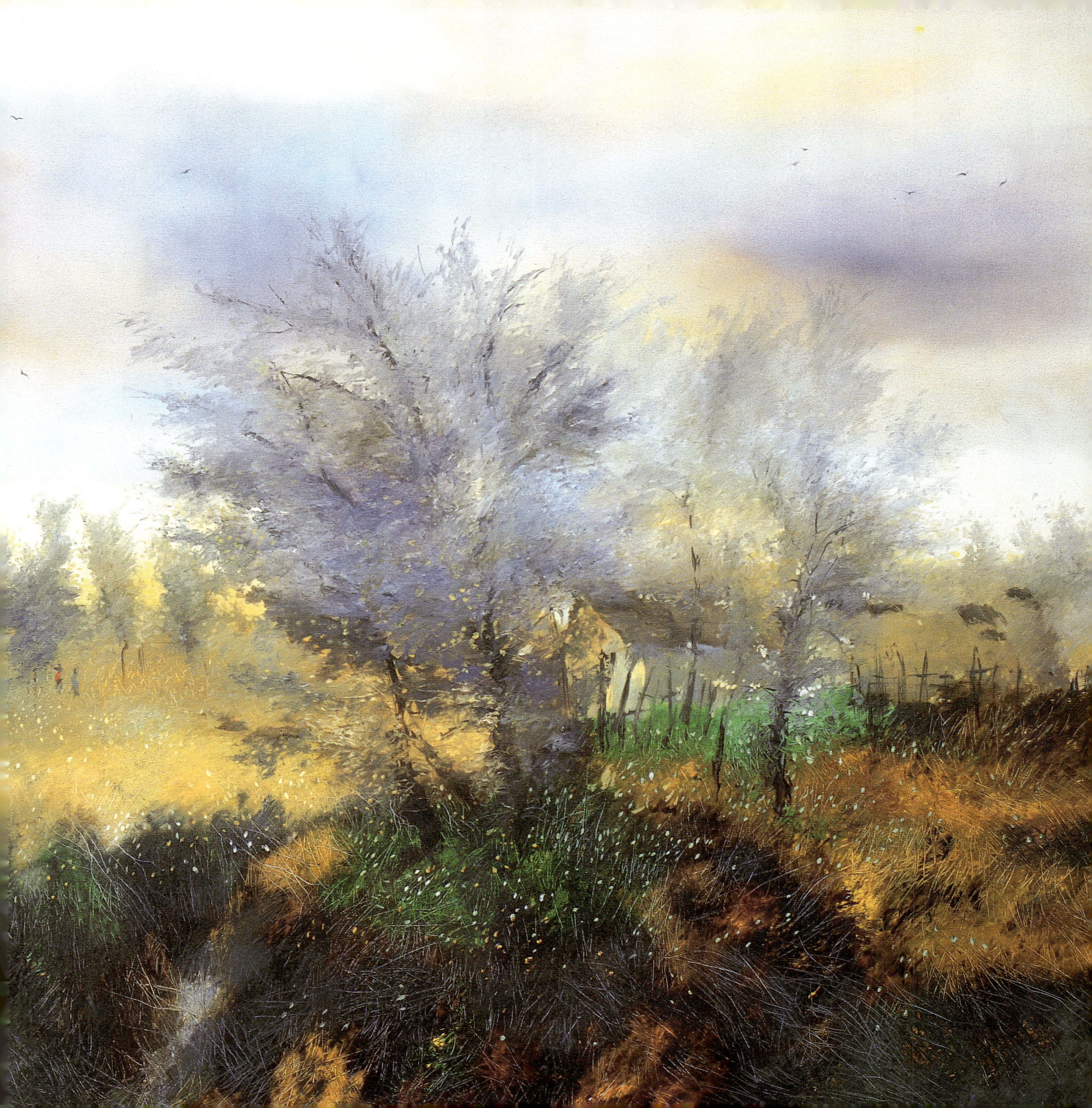

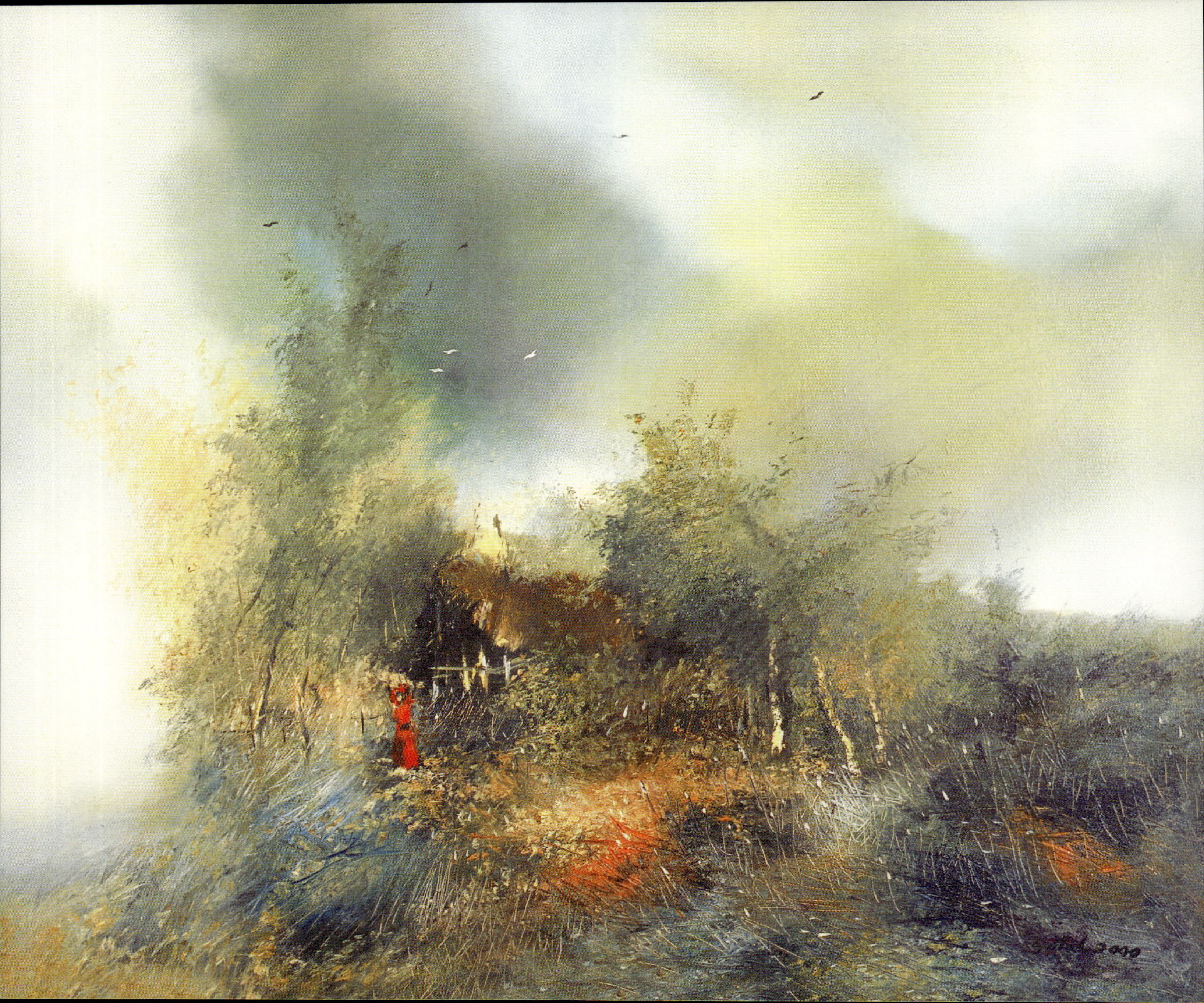

Oil on canvas, 2000.

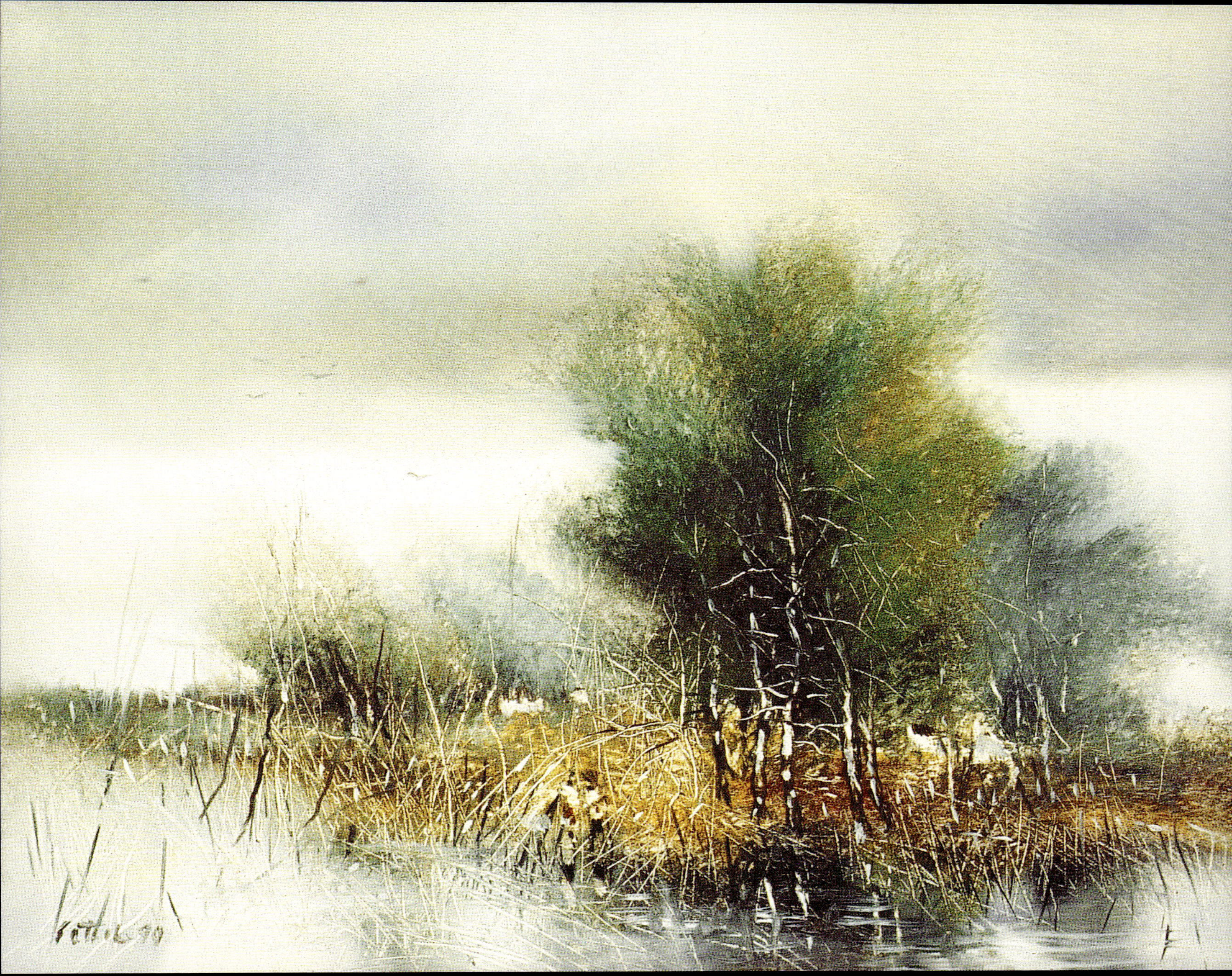

Oil on canvas, 1999

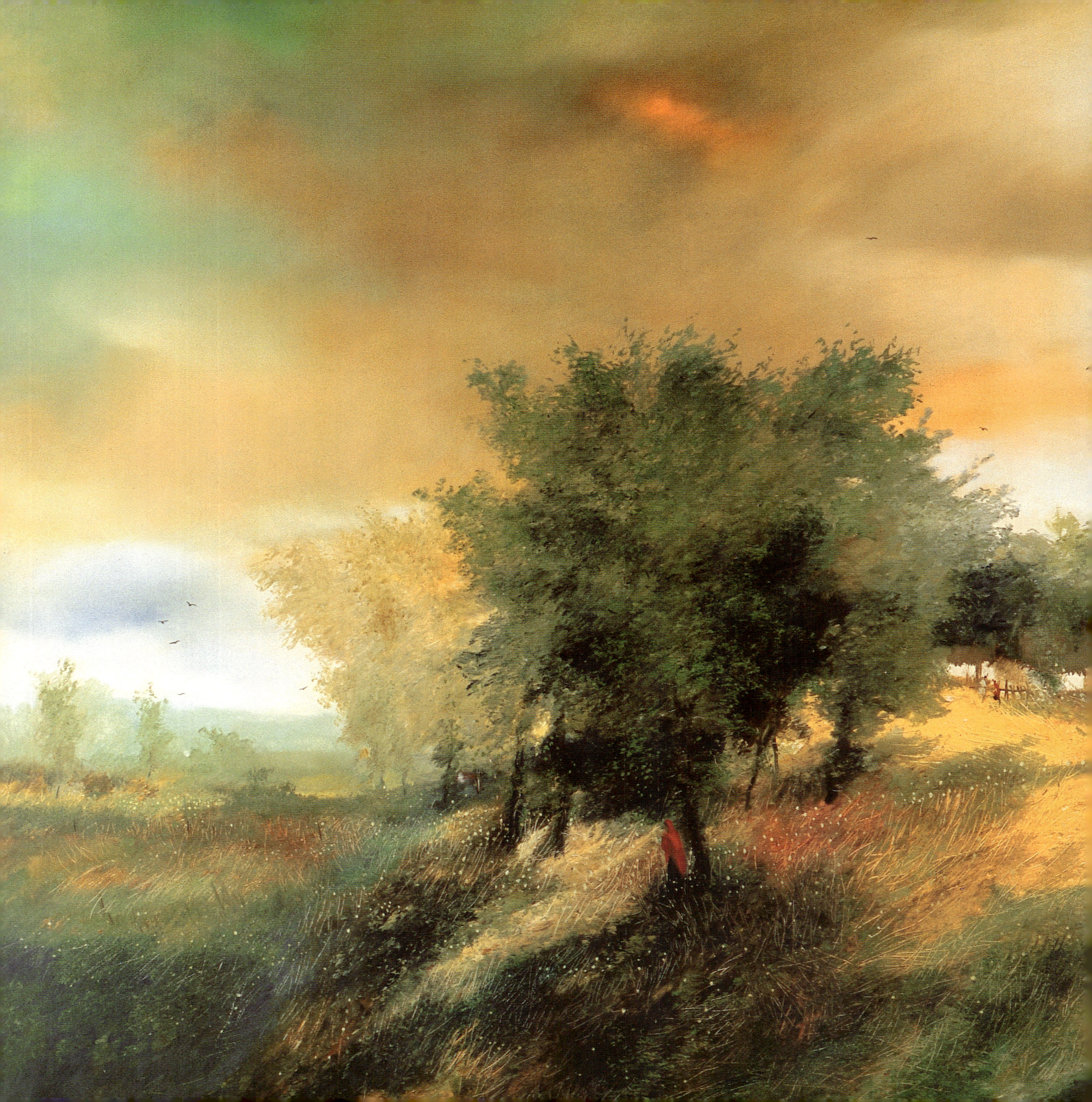

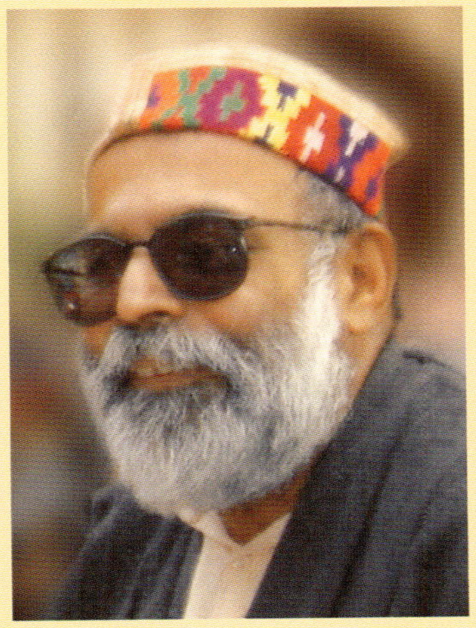

The Art of Felt Truth

Suneet Chopra
Art Critic

Satish Chandra was an artist of a very special mould. He was unassuming, firm and resilient as very few can be. Indeed, it was this quality of perseverance that found a special place in his art. He painted landscapes that showed towering mountains and the profusion of growth of all kinds: of tall trees, shrubs and undergrowth. All of nature found a place in his expression, nothing was overlooked.

This profusion formed the lower half of his canvases, reminding one that one cannot prevent processes close to the ground from taking over the space they have claimed as theirs by right. These areas of his canvases always remind

Facing page: Oil on canvas, 2000.

me of that refrain of the heady movements of the 1960s in asserting the rights of the exploited, the oppressed and the underdog: "We shall overcome!"

The top half of his canvases reflect another part of his being, a lofty idealism that allowed him to overlook the petty barbs and irritations of daily life with remarkable equanimity. This high-thinking of his is reflected in his treatment of the sky in his landscapes, which shows a remarkable depth as well as variations of colour and cloud formations. It is an idealism like that of a poet whose deep knowledge of the thorny undergrowth of the woods allows him to rise above it and fly free like the speck-like birds of his landscapes. This optimism of his in the cycle of creation being able to right all wrongs of daily life gives his art its resilience and his landscapes their spiritual flavour.

It was characteristic of him that he never allowed his sentiments to become mere slogans. They permeated his very

Facing page: Watercolour on paper, 2003.

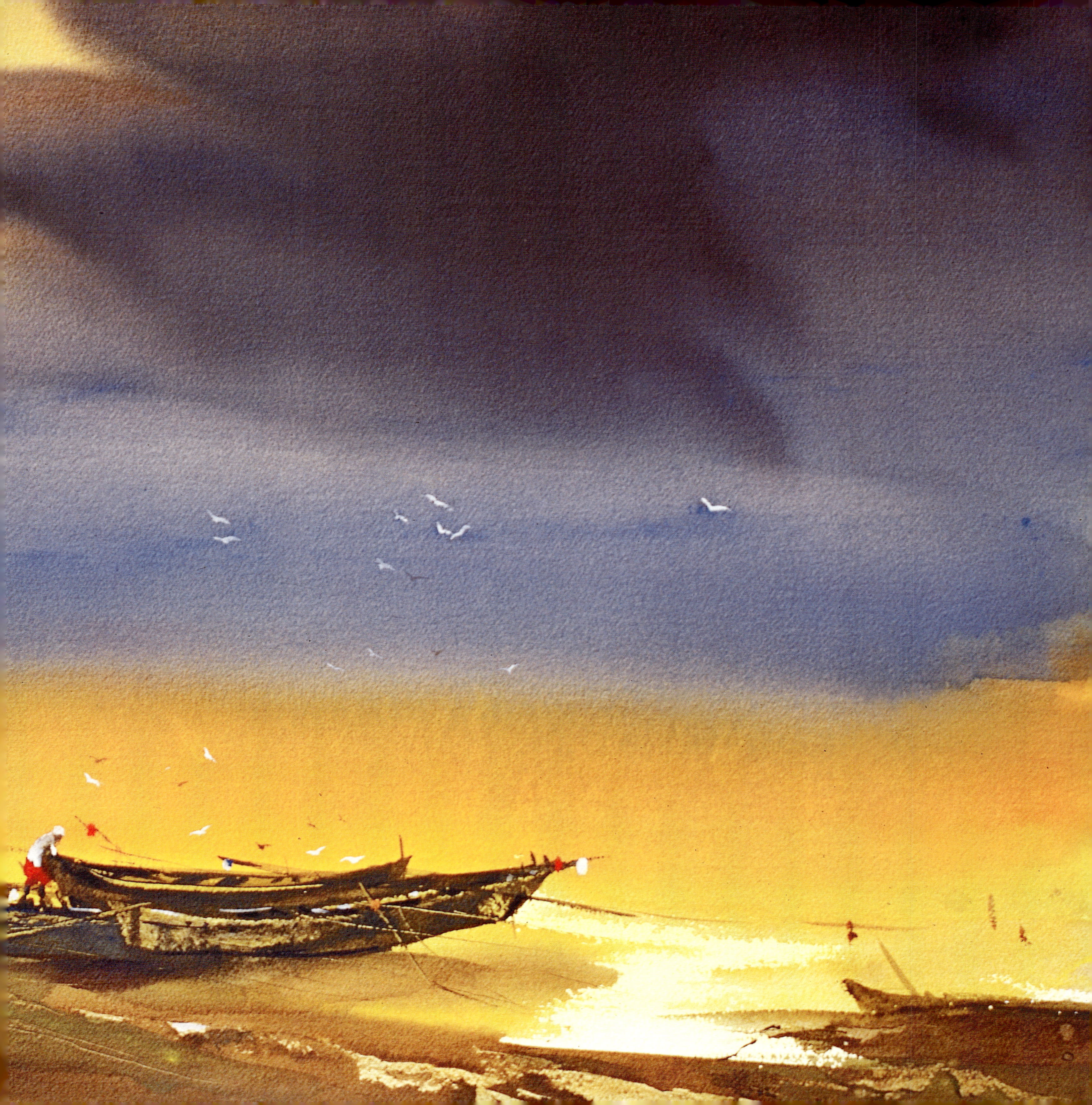

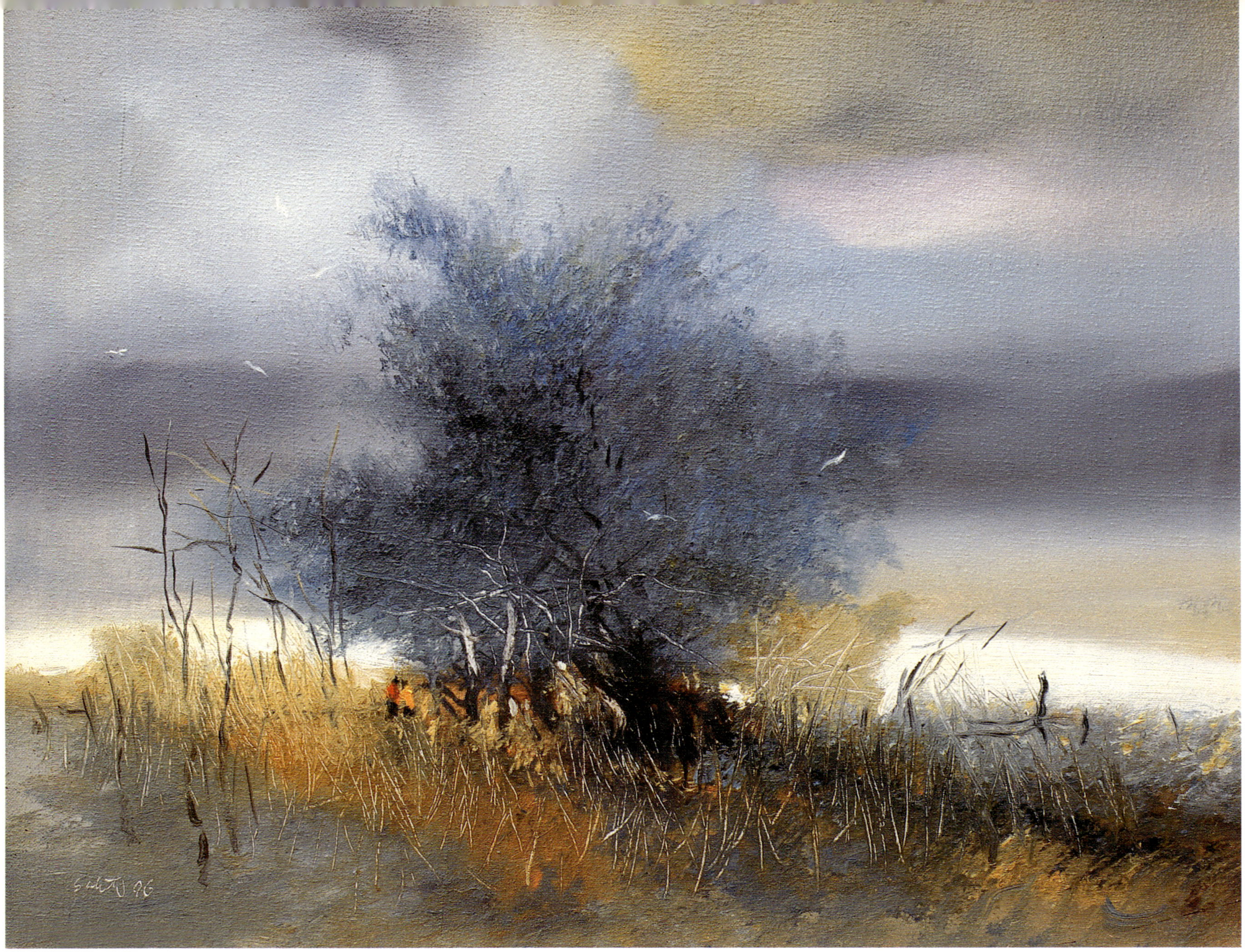

Oil on canvas, 1996.

being and then found expression in the movement of his hand. Like every good artist, he let his hands express visual realities as words could never have done. And indeed, it was this quality of his being able to express the depth of his feelings in a generalized way that drew people to the spirit of his work without having to exercise their minds excessively.

In my view, he is the true artist of India's northern plains, of fields and thorn bushes, of yellow skies and biting dust storms or of the heavy grey cloud cover of the monsoons, of cooling showers that bred a new abundance in the ground below. The landscape of central Uttar Pradesh became his vision of the disappointments of day-to-day life and the open sky his vechile of transcending them and making them irrelevant to his onward progress as a creative human being.

I fondly remember an incident which was characteristic of him. As chairman of the state Lalit Kala Akademi, he had invited me to deliver the Radha Kamal Mukherjee memorial lectures in Lucknow, and I brought a number of original works from my collection that underlined the basic radicalism of our contemporary artistic tradition. The lectures and the exhibition of works, going back over a hundred years, were sufficient proof of the propriety of the theme and the path of logic taken to present it, so I did not think anything untoward would happen.

It did, however. A number of petty individuals with no standing in the

Oil on canvas, 1995.

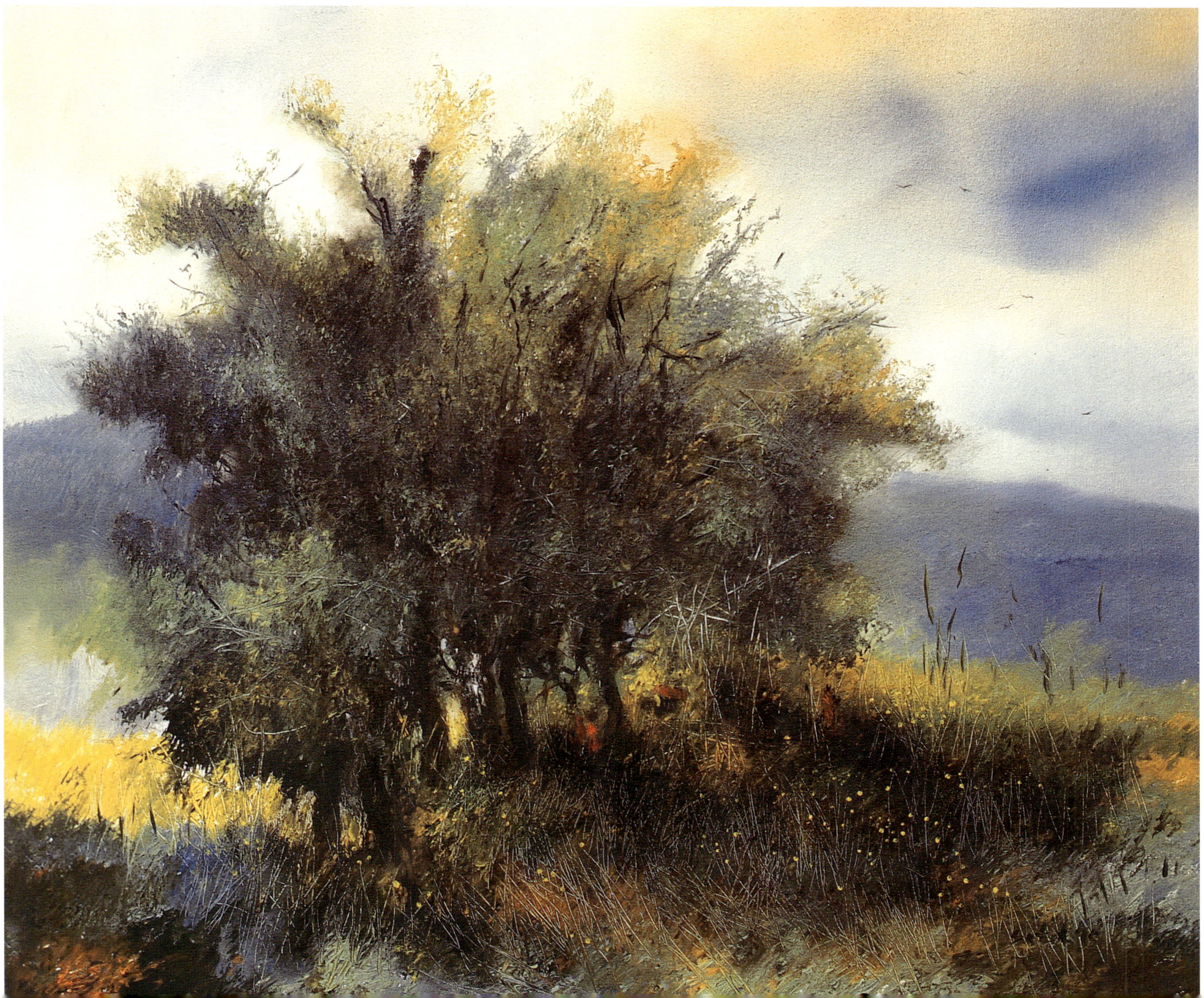

world of art raised a hue and cry and had him removed from the chairmanship. I only found this out some weeks later from newspaper clippings a friend sent me. But it was typical of him that he neither contacted me about the matter nor asked me to intervene in it. His graceful exit and the mess that followed are more than ample proof of the correctness and dignity with which he handled all problems in life. Eventually his detractors found themselves discredited and were themselves summarily removed by popular demand. This sort of retribution did not concern him unduly. His knowledge of his own correct behaviour in the matter was sufficient for him. He needed no external confirmation of it. The artist in him knew that his inner truth, that had evolved over the years through his perception of the reality around him, was of far greater relevance in the external world than the spurious truths manufactured by vested interests for petty personal gain.

This confidence allowed him to

Facing page: Oil on canvas, 1991.

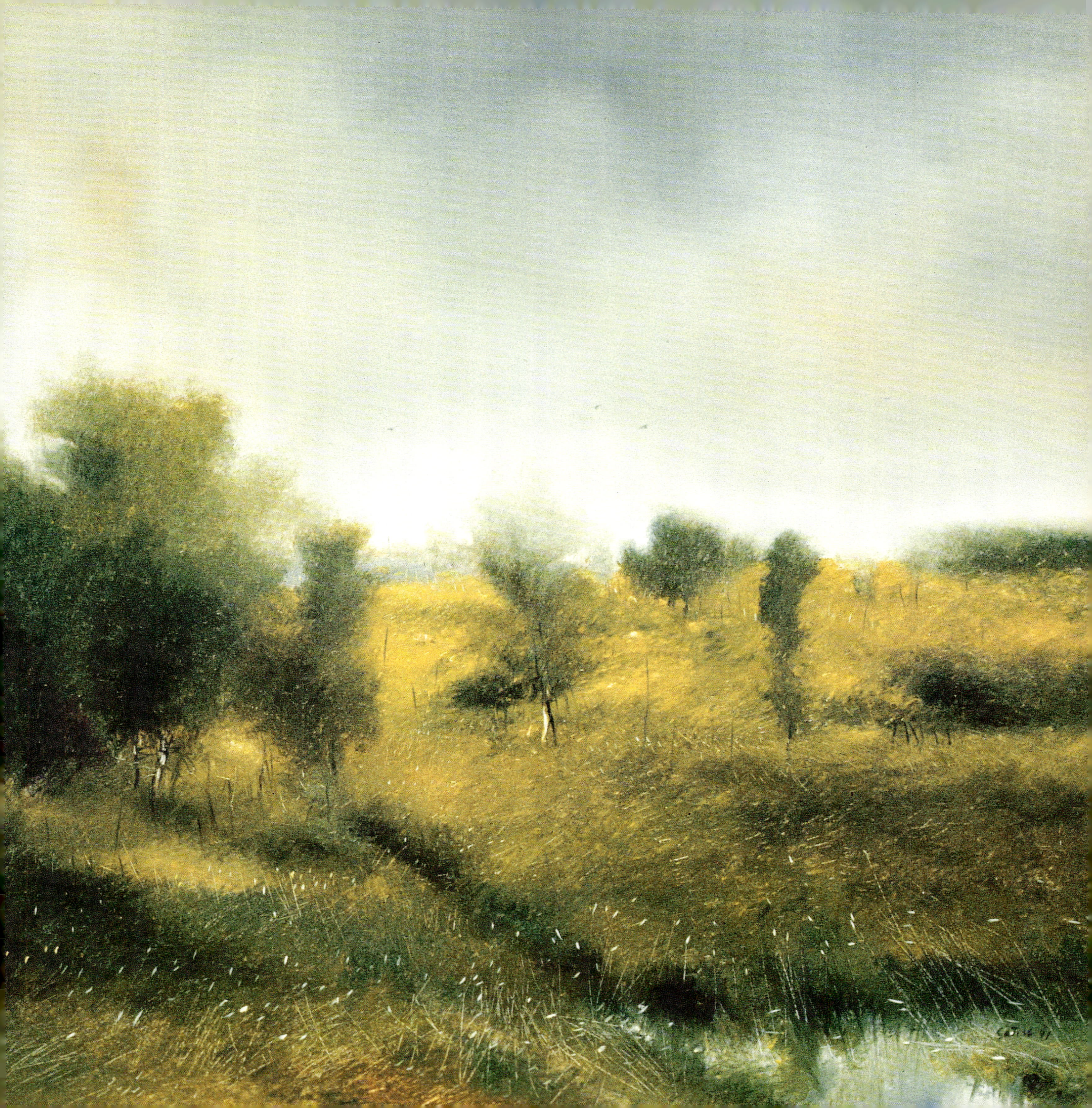

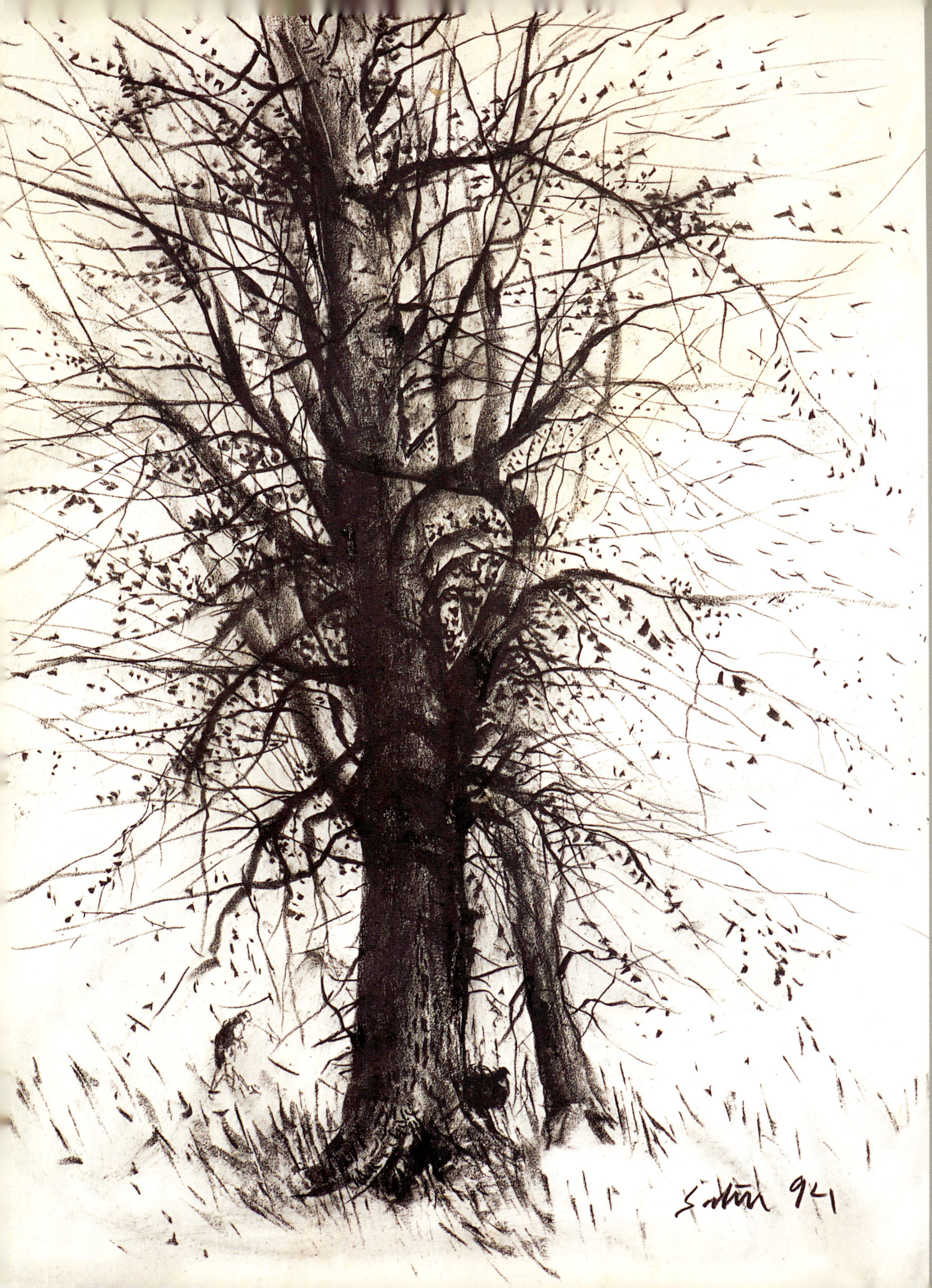

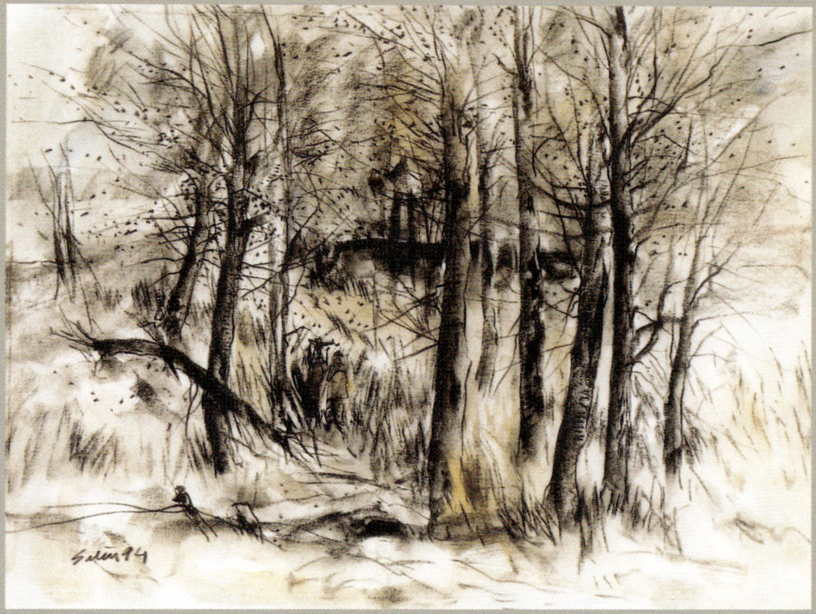

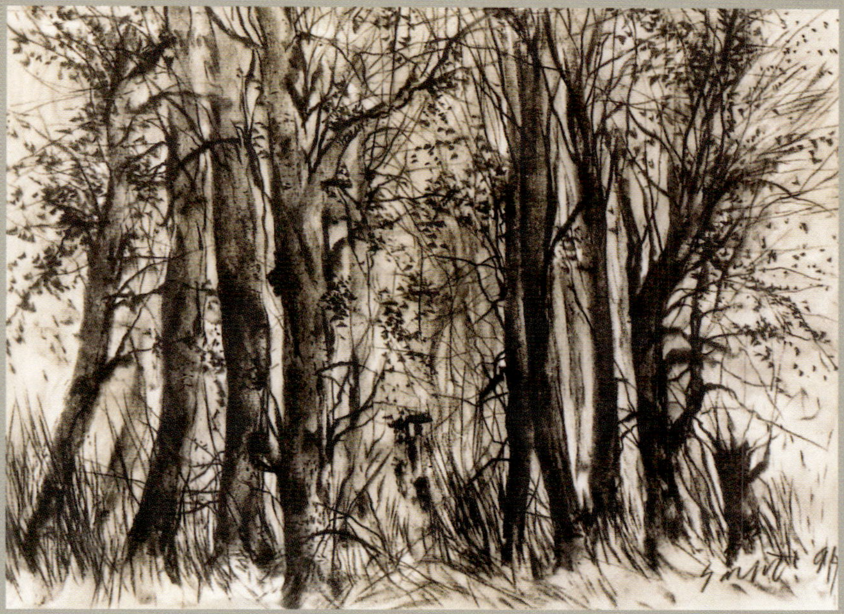

Charcoal on paper, 1994. Charcoal on paper, 1994.
Facing page: Charcoal on paper, 1994.

spend years on an unfashionable theme like the landscape, from an unfashionable region like central Uttar Pradesh, with very little that was controversial in it, and yet acquire a reputation that is no less than that of artists resorting to every gimmick in the book. His passing away has not dulled the demand for his work, as was obvious from his posthumous exhibition held by the Gallerie Ganesha at the India Habitat Centre in the capital. His art reflects a very valid solution to very real problems we face in our daily lives today. The dignity and virtuosity with which he presents this solution to the viewer is refreshing in an age of hype, self-promotion and overstatement. And it is this that will ensure his art will not be forgotten.

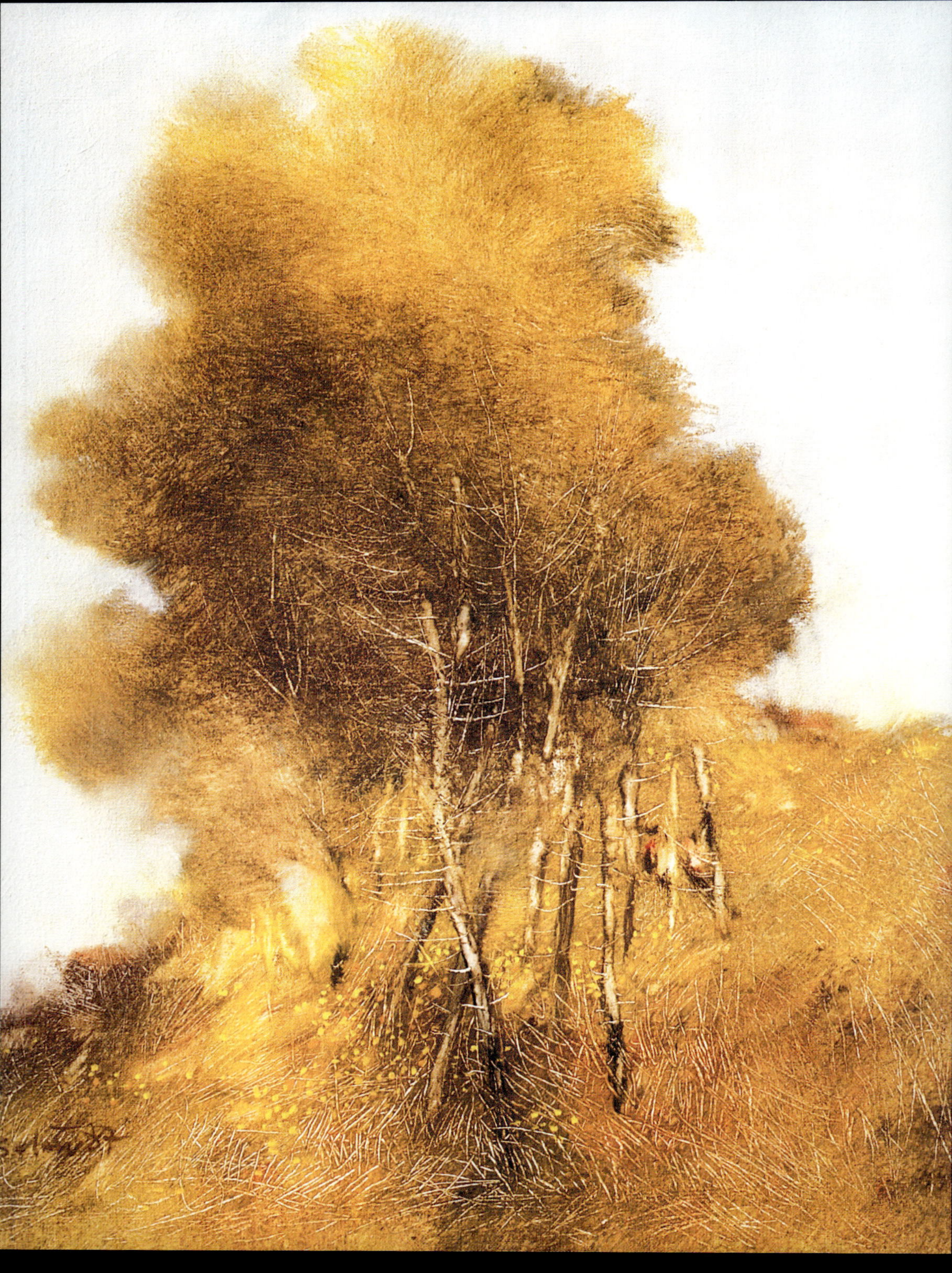

Oil on canvas, 1987.

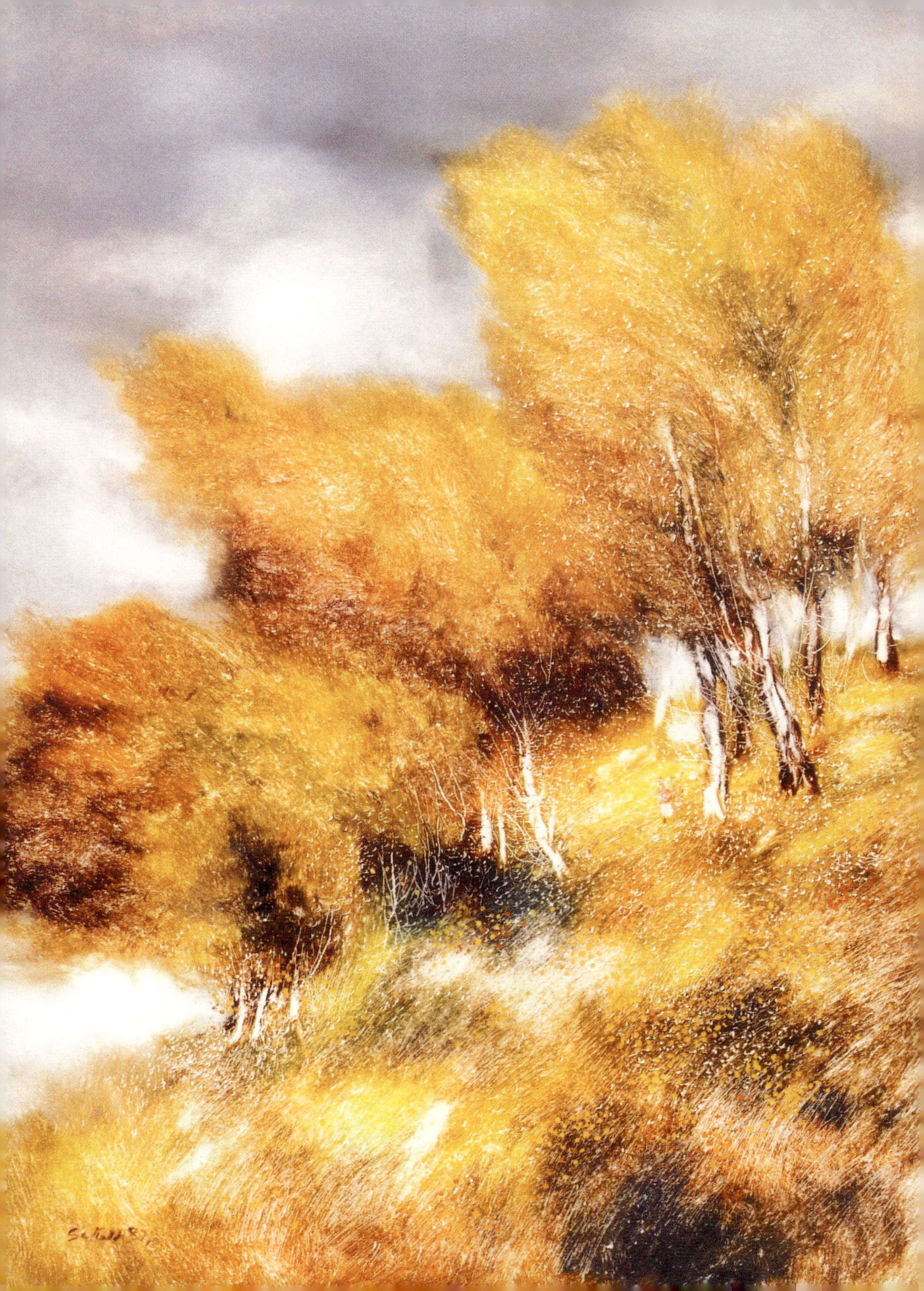

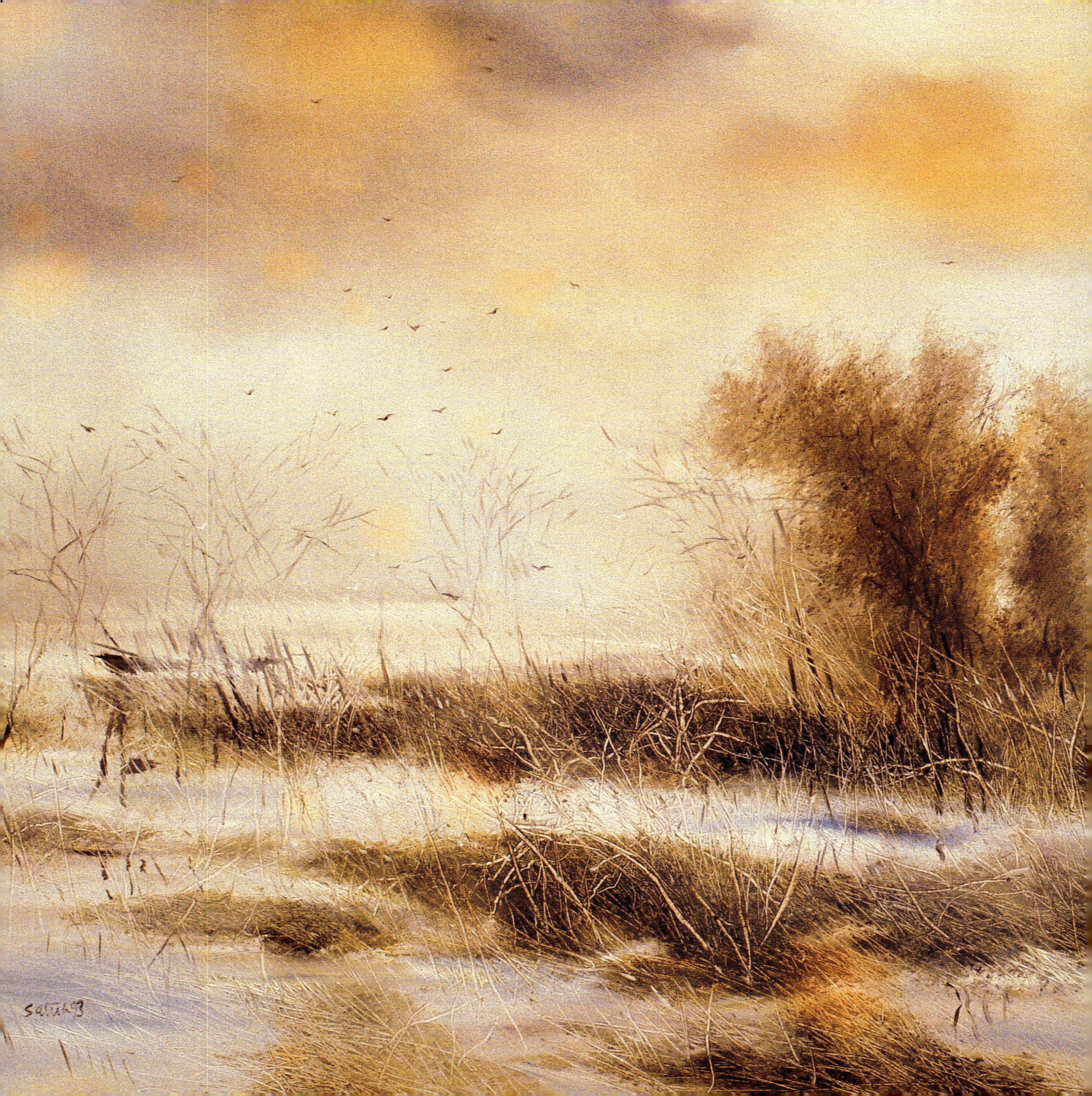

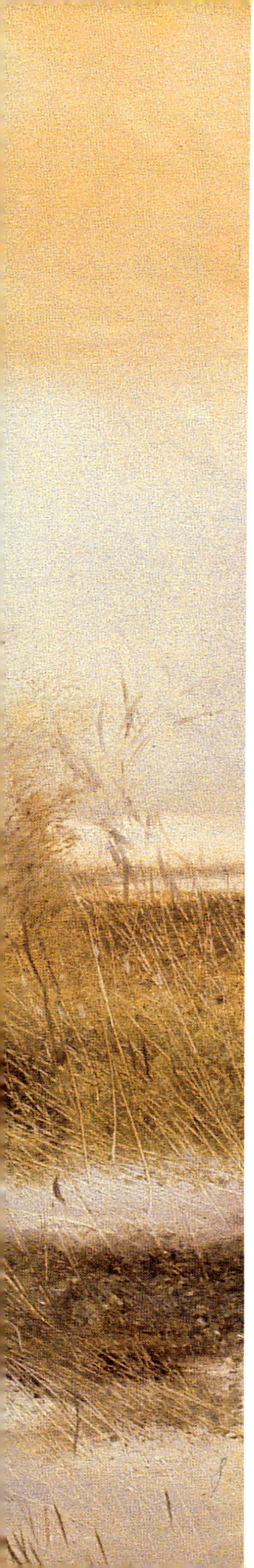

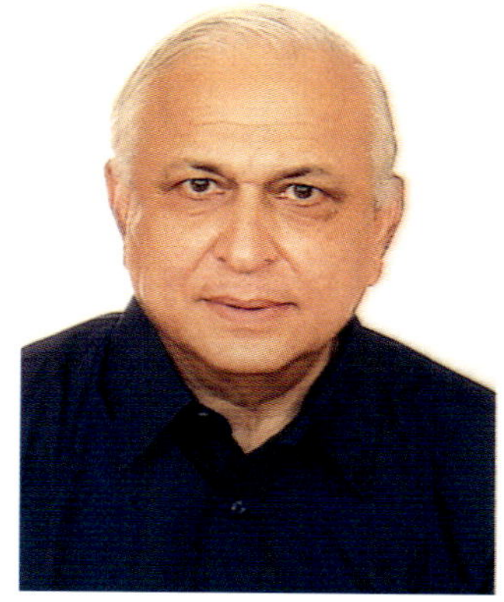

One From the Heart

Dr Mansoor Hasan
Friend

Ghazal usne chheri mujhey saaz dena
Zara umre rafta ko awaaz dena.

Behold, someone sings a ghazal, let me
play the chords,
Oh mate, recall the moments, the
beautiful past gone by.

The couplet echoed again and again in my mind. Meenakshi had asked me to write something on my friend Satish – some events, some anecdotes, some memories I hold close to my heart.

It was 1966. As I walked past the Mayfair theatre in Hazratganj, I bumped into Surendra Chaturvedi, a family friend, poet, journalist and humourist. He called out to me, "Hello, Mansoor Bhai! Meet my friend Satish... he is a great artist, you know!" I found myself shaking hands with a smiling young man, warm, polite. "I know you are the 'heart doctor'... welcome to Lucknow!" he said, walking a few paces with me.

I met Satish off and on but it was not until he married Meenakshi, whose parents were my parents' very dear friends, that I really came to know him.

I remember Satish and Meenakshi celebrating their son's third birthday. It was a memorable evening. Siddharth was the apple of everyone's eyes. I also remember an exhibition of Satish's early works at Clarks Avadh Hotel. He stood

Facing page: Oil on canvas, 1993.

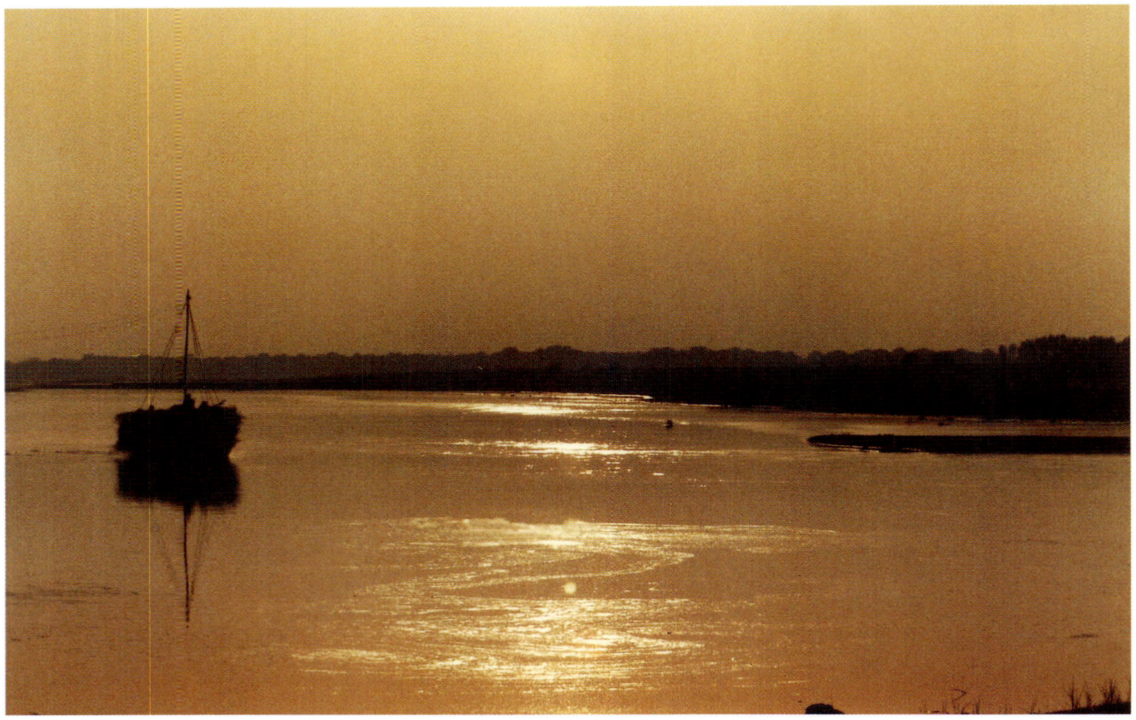

A photograph of the River Ganga at Garhi Samadabad. Satish and his friend Dr Mansoor Hasan used to sail down the river, with Satish painting the play of light on the water.
Facing page: Watercolour on paper, 2003.

outside the gallery as I entered, "Come and see my paintings, Mansoor Bhai!" "Since when have you become a modernist?" I asked Satish. He laughed and said these were just experiments in his journey. "Don't worry, I will be back to my landscapes soon!"

Over the years, we met often. He went ahead as a landscapist, on his way to fame and recognition. For hours on end we would talk about many varied topics connected with life. I would recite Sufi poetry to him and he would talk to me about his painting and the art world.

I would invite Satish to my village home at Garhi Samadabad, built on a cliff along the River Ganga. We would arrange for a boat and sail down the river as Satish painted it at various times of the day, observing the play of light on the water, capturing the silvery noon light that played upon the foamy ripples on a windy day. The sunset was mesmerizing. Suddenly the river would become quiet, placid, as if the water had stopped flowing – it would turn a pink-red as the day and night met in the embrace of the sunset, like two lovers who cannot part for a moment. Satish would sit in absolute silence, speechless, taking in this scene. An inner calm swept over us. Perhaps, it was an awareness of God, something

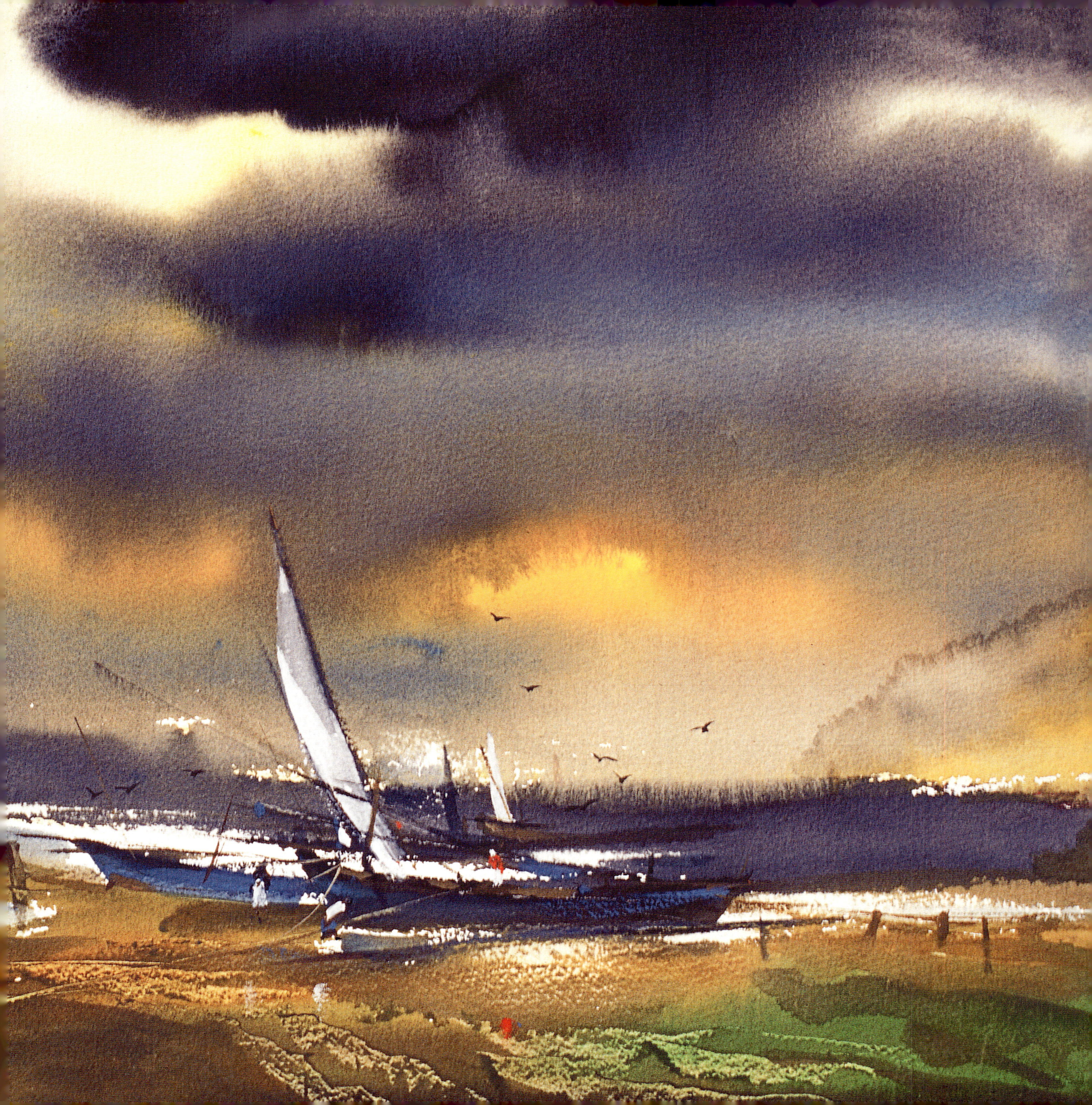

over and above this physical life. Soon, darkness would set in and the dim, shimmery lights from the Manikpur Fort, a little upstream, would be seen. We would then walk back to the farmhouse to enjoy a delicious meal which included Satish's favourite 'shami kebabs' and 'biryani'.

After dinner we would listen to 'qawwalis', under the canopy of twinkling stars. Satish would be ecstatic, listening to the Sufi music and the 'kalaam' of Amir Khusro, Rumi and other mystics.

Over the years, Satish evolved into a highly sensitive and mature artist and a quest for spiritual grace engulfed him. The colours he used grew bolder and brighter, taking on a spiritual tone. In Nature, Satish saw the divine.

His depiction of light and shadow in Nature was masterly. Satish often pointed out to me that colour depended on the light in which it was viewed. No work could be really commented upon unless seen in different shades of light and shadow. Under the trees in the jungles and in the countryside, Satish would paint a glow of yellow light streaming through the green canopies, playing on the

Facing page: Watercolour on paper, 1993.

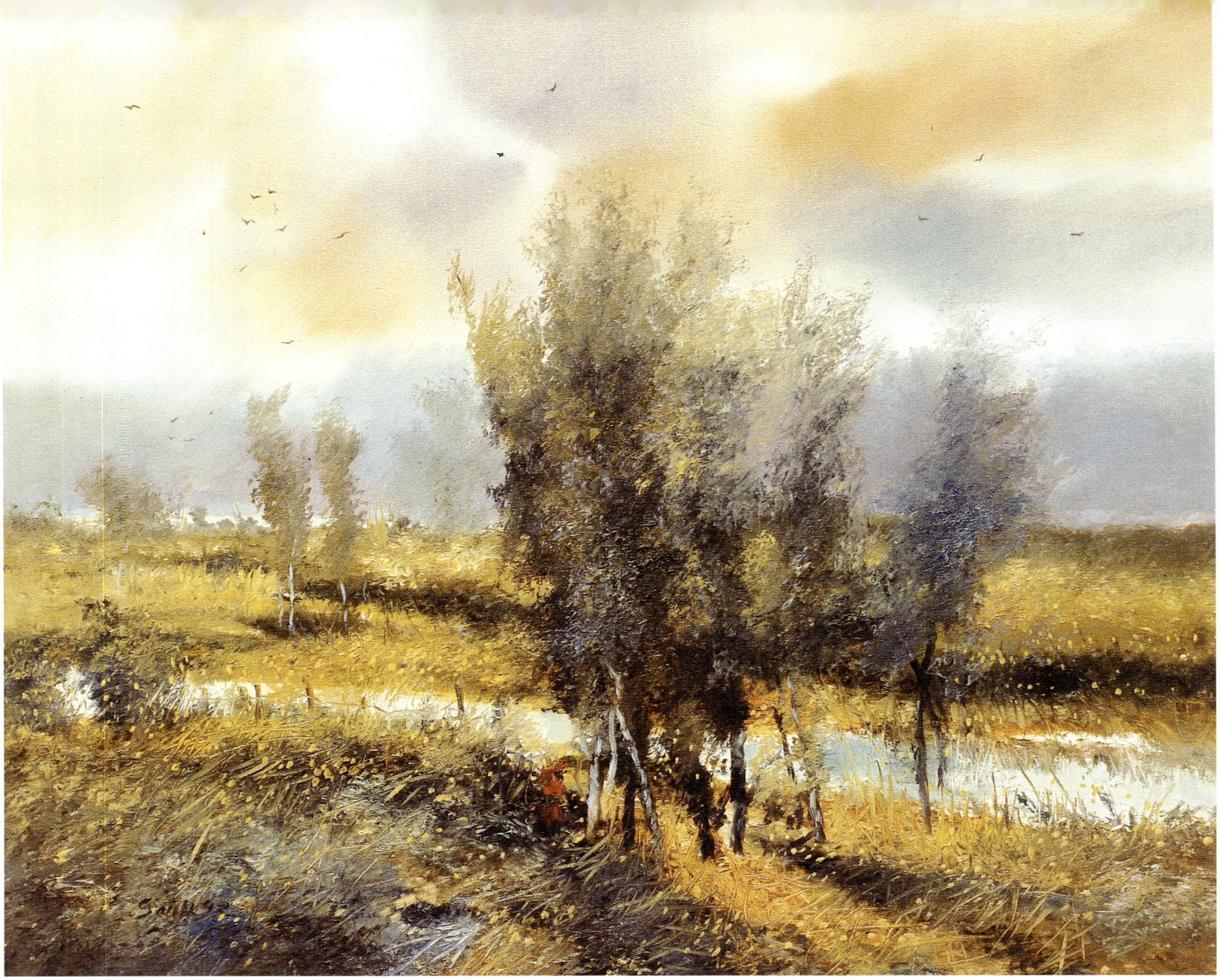

Oil on canvas, 1992.

weeds, around the tree trunks and on the watery muddy furrows of the freshly ploughed fields. Such touches of observation were his signature in his landscapes.

He would refuse to paint a landscape on order. He refused to copy or reproduce his own work. 'Cloning' was not his business, however lucrative it might have been. Each painting was exclusive and in a way sacred, like a prayer. The colours he used were of a mystic, indescribable beauty. I am fortunate to have a collection of some of his most beautiful paintings in my home.

Besides Sufi music and poetry, Satish enjoyed romantic Urdu poetry. He spoke of his visits to Sufi shrines of Hazrat Bal (Srinagar), Nizamuddin Aulia (Delhi), Khwaja Sahab (Ajmer) and Deva Sharif (Barabanki).

Satish's own perception of love was tender, forgiving and inclusive. He looked upon love as a healing remedy. One of his favourite Persian couplets, which gives an insight into his being, is:

Mun tu shudam tu mun shudi
Mun tun shudam tu jan shudi
Takas na mi goyam baad azin
Mund di garam tu di gari

Let me be you and you be me
Let me be body and you be the soul
So none may say when we are gone
That you were you and I was I.

This loss of duality takes place when the soul merges with the ultimate reality.

In 2003 Satish's son Siddharth got married to Pooja. I was one of the

Facing page: Oil on canvas, 1998.

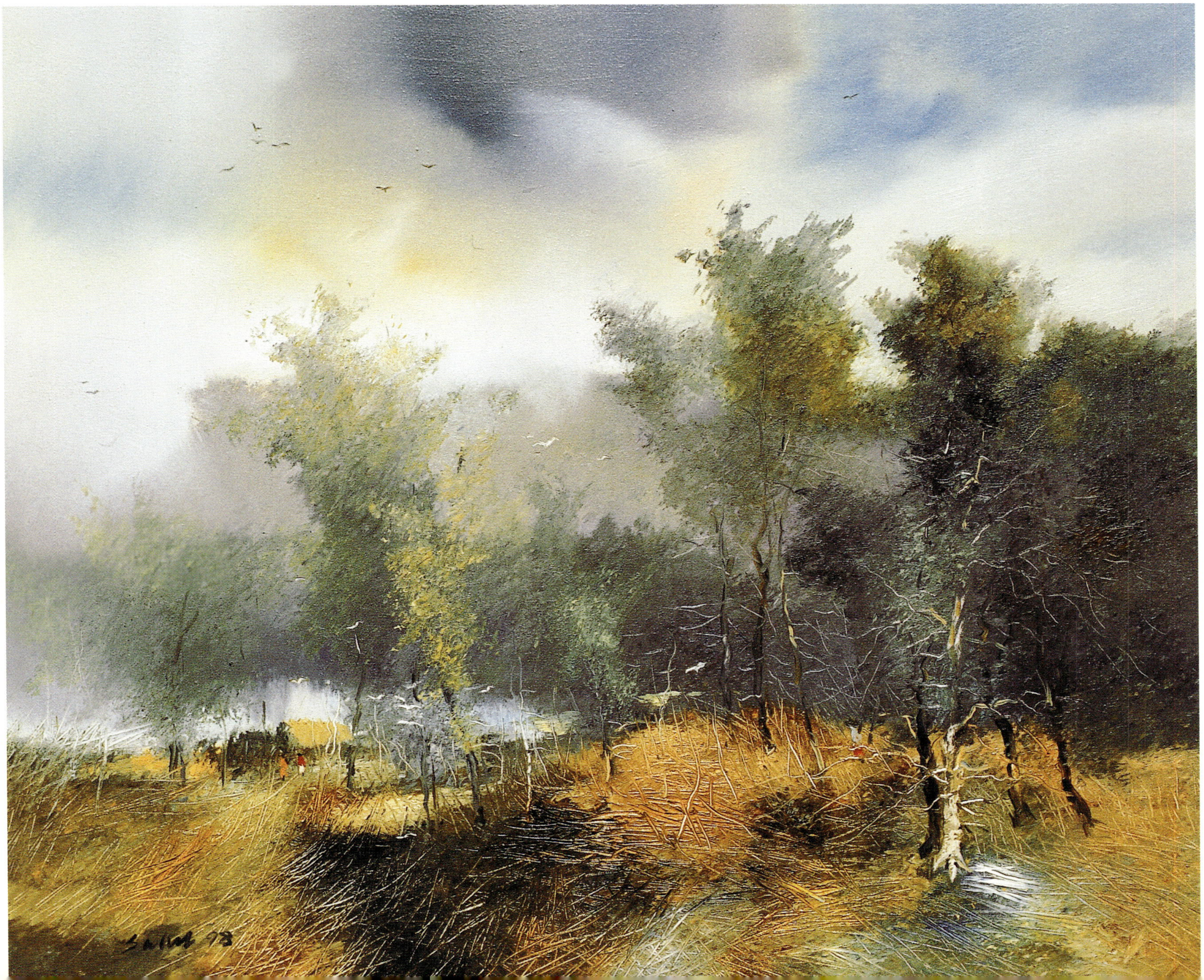

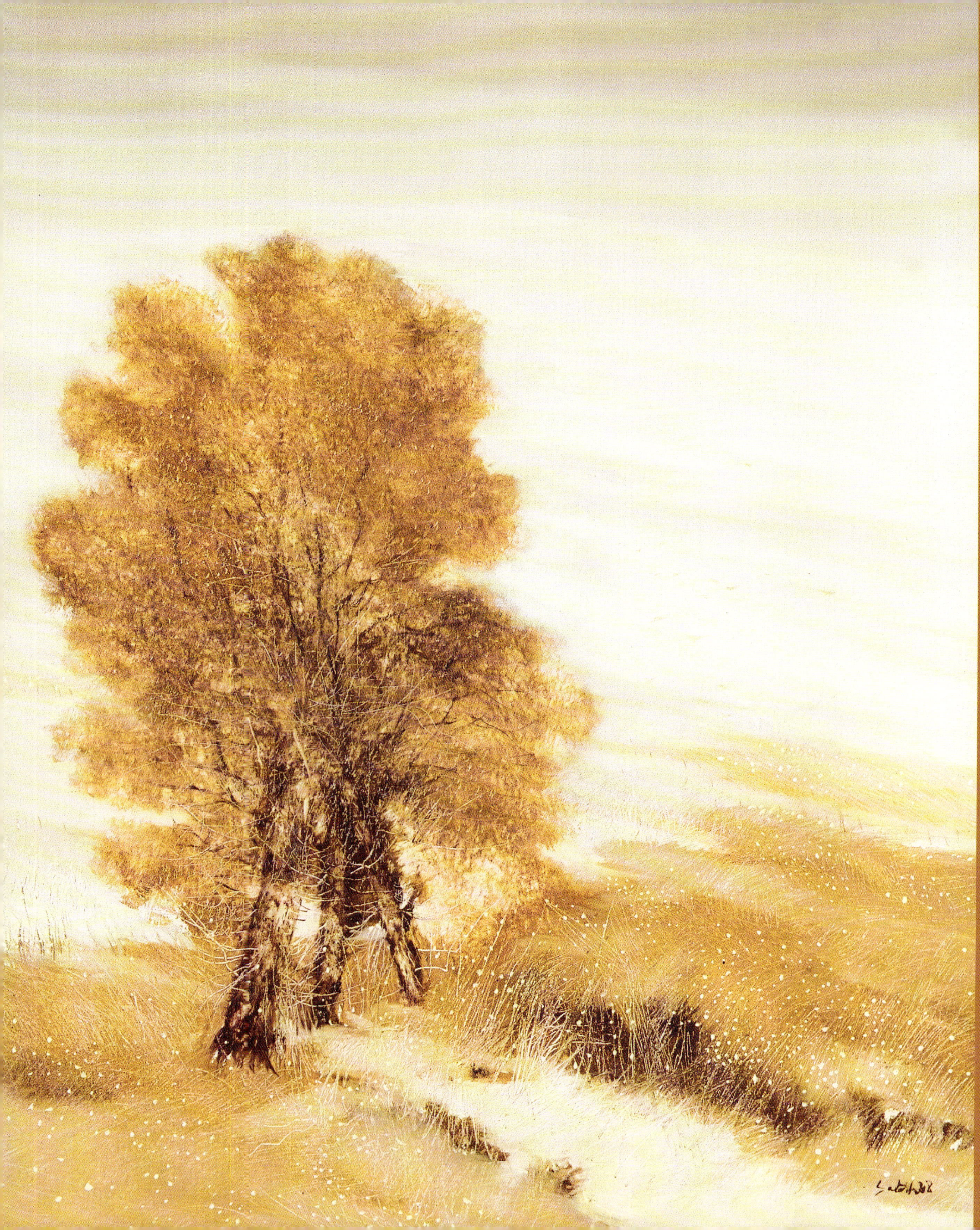

'baraatis' at the marriage held in Delhi. Satish and Meenakshi were very happy to get a daughter-in-law like Pooja.

But happy days never last forever. The end came, as it had to. Satish's friends will not forget his last journey from Delhi to Lucknow. Siddharth would again and again touch his father's feet and put his hands to his eyes. For me this scene is etched in my mind forever – a loving son's last tribute to his beloved father.

Tears came to my eyes. One trickled down and mingled with the earth; the other went into my heart where it turned into a shining crystal – in it remains the 'tasveer' of my friend Satish. So long as I live that crystal will shine with his image, quiet and yet always there.

If there is another life after this, if there is a Heavenly Abode of the souls – I am sure he would be waiting for me. And when I go, I will surely reach for my friend and clasp his hands in joy; for both of us believed that friendship is thicker than blood.

In these moments, I recall the words of Faiz :

Saba ke haath mein narmi hai unke haathon ki
Woh haath dhoond rahe hain bisaat-e-mehfil mein
Ke dil ke daag kidhar hain nashiste dard kahan.

The early morning wind touches the heart
Like the soft hands of my beloved,
Searching for the pain of suffering and loneliness,
And they bring me solace as no one can.

Meenakshi is the real soul-mate of Satish. She is the embodiment of grace, culture, patience and courage. She was his 'Rafique-e-Hayat', in the real sense. The holy Koran mentions the wife as a friend and companion for life – the essence is friendship.

In Meenakshi and Siddharth live both the shadow and the reality of my friend Satish.

Facing page: Oil on canvas, 1988.

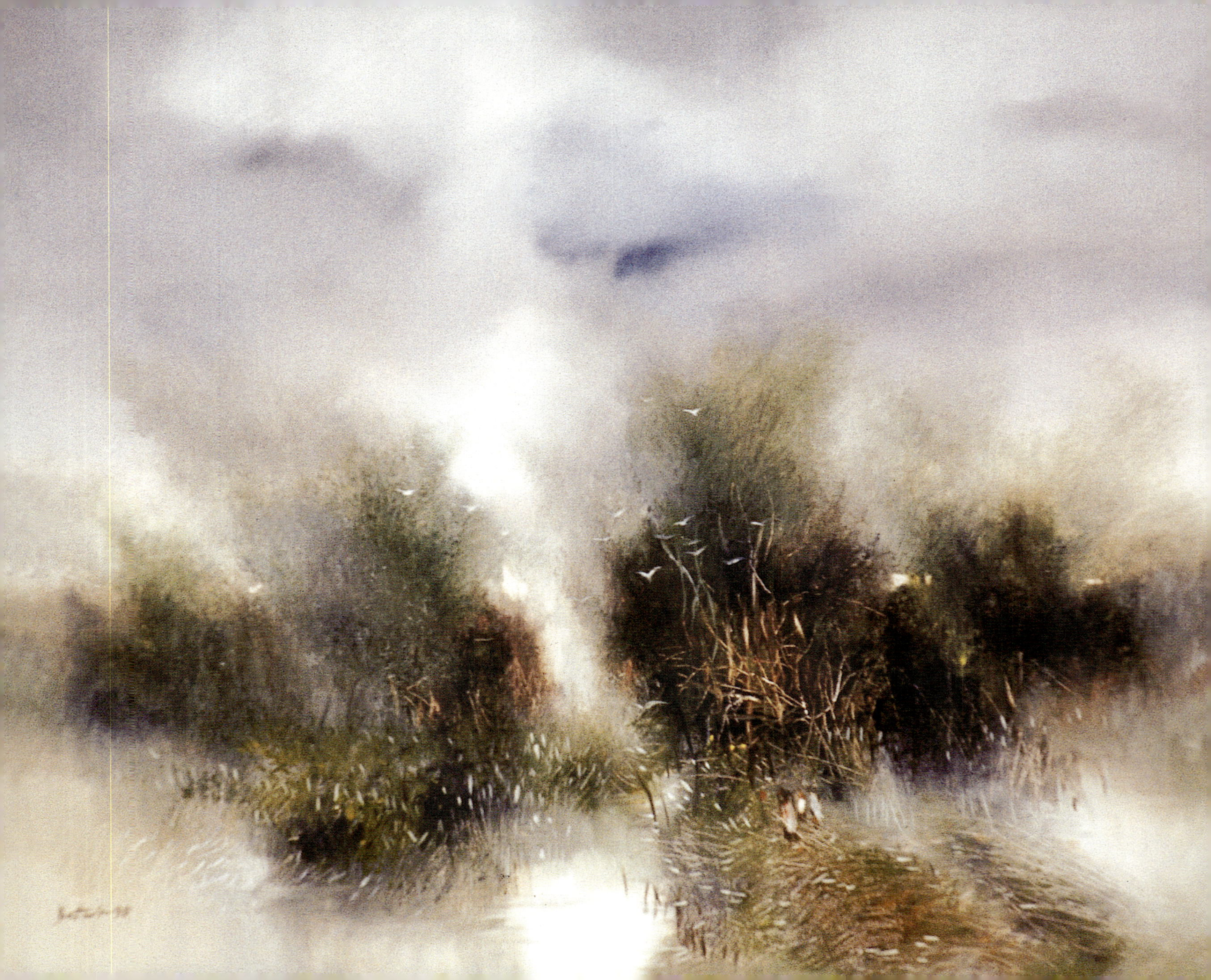

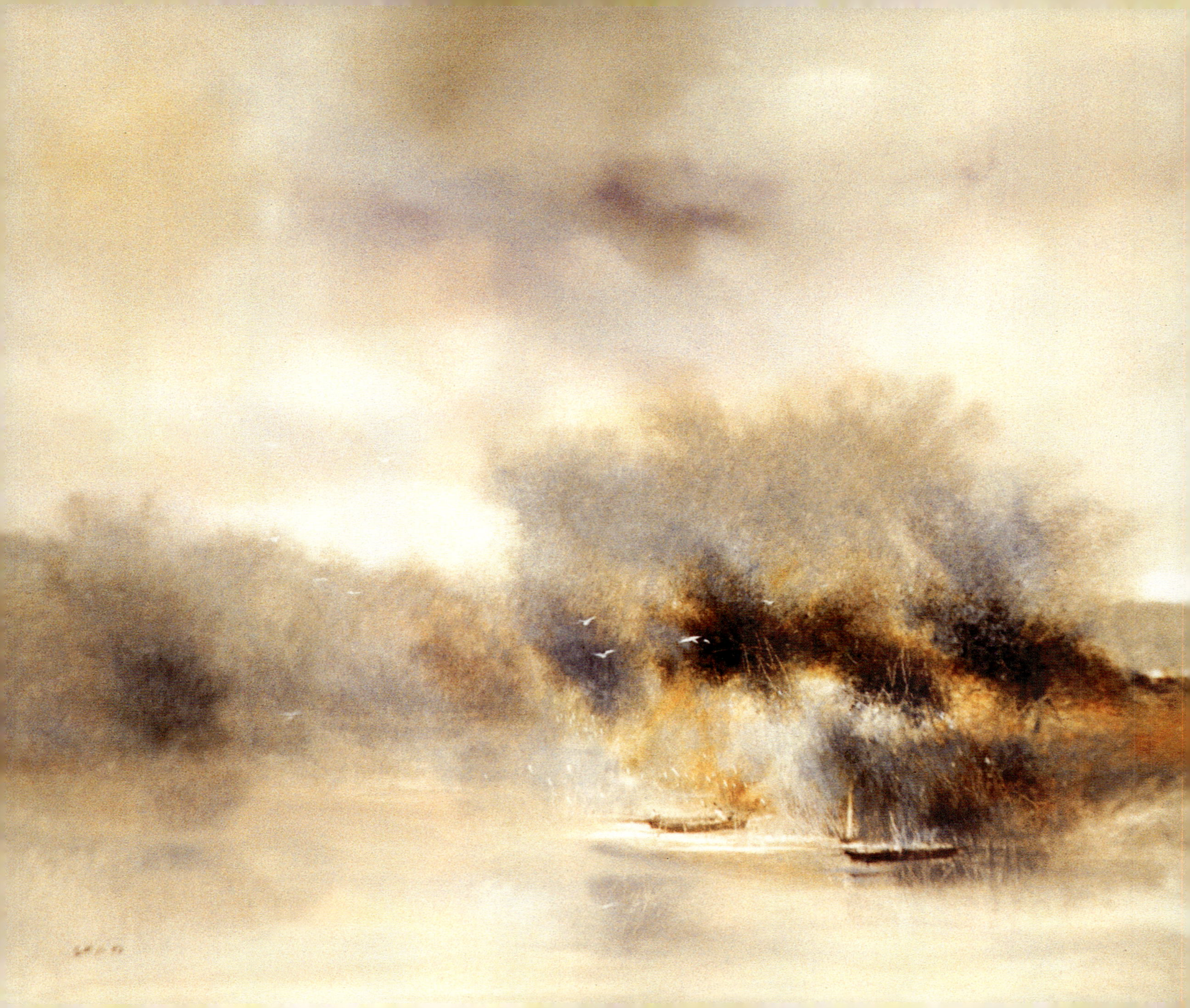

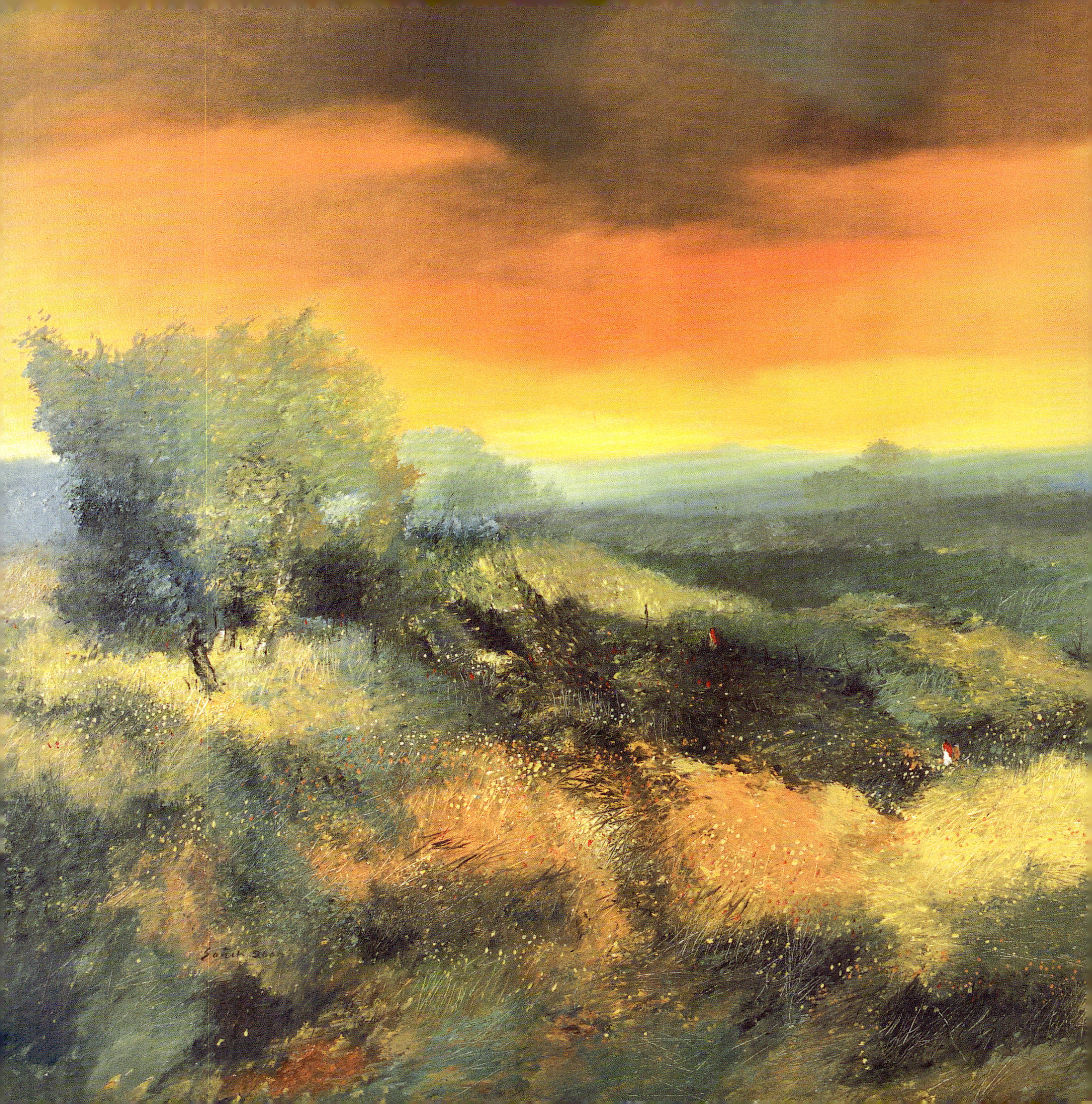

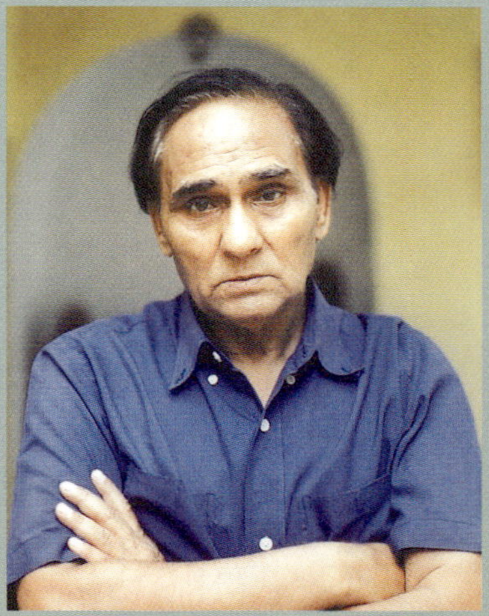

A Popular Personality

N. Khanna
Friend

It was on 21 November 2004 that Satish Chandra merged into the colours on the horizon – the same colours that had been his life.

Satish was possibly the most popular painter even during his student days and the only one who was felicitated by the state government with the Yash Bharati award in 1994, one of many in his career.

Initially, Satish was deeply interested in the wash technique and also experimented with pastels. He believed that while the artist no doubt had to explore realism, somewhere that should lead to an exploration of the

Facing page: Oil on canvas, 2000

Oil on canvas, 1992.

subconscious. Satish's canvas was not a mere statement but a search. His art is a reflection of his fine technique arrived at after hard labour and an in-depth study of the property of colours. He used to work in an extremely organized manner and had the unique ability to focus on the entire canvas.

Satish himself saw two important turning points in his life. The first was right after completing his post-graduation, when he went on a trip across Punjab and Himachal Pradesh. Up in the mountains, at an altitude of 14,500 feet, it was a journey of the heart for Satish.The colours on his palette grew richer. The other turning point came on 31 January 1972, when he married his muse Meenakshi, who proved to be an inspiration for Satish at

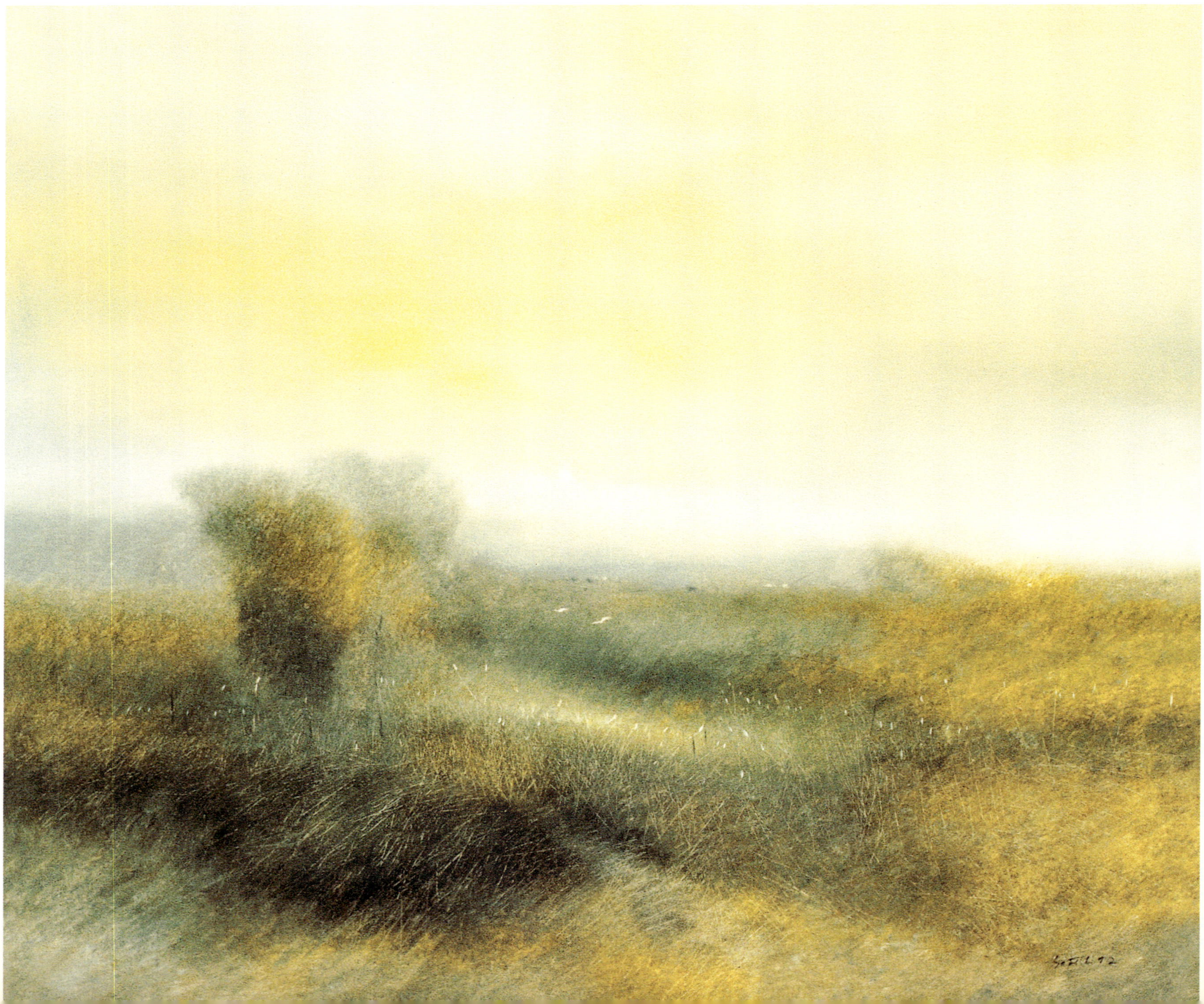

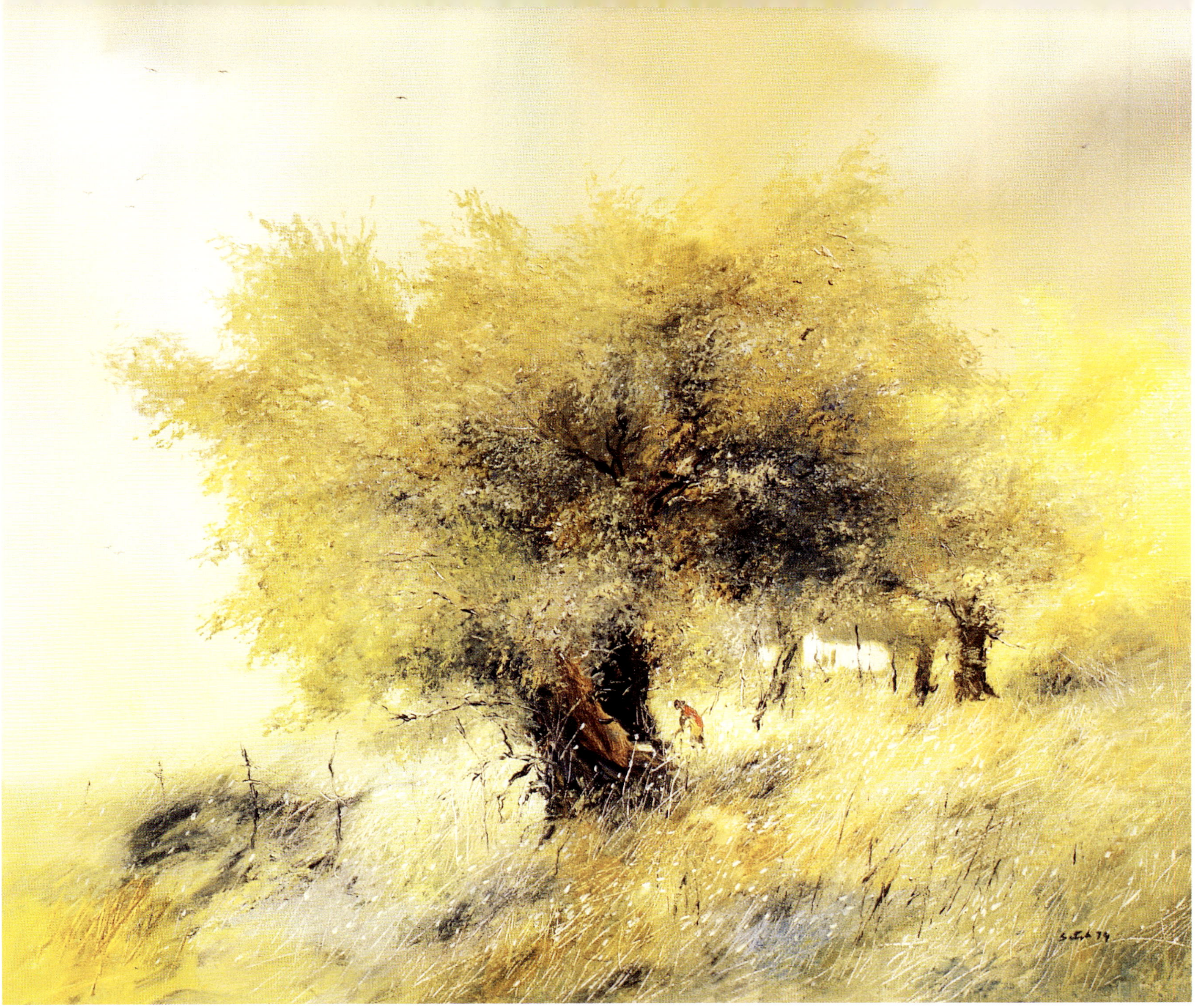

every step. Even today, when Satish is no more, she continues to 'nourish his art'.

Satish was a friend with whom I shared so much for almost forty-five years. He studied fine arts while I studied commercial art in the same institution. We stayed in the hostel together. Satish had, since his student days, an interest in various creative activities. He was a good hockey player and an excellent coach as well. Debates on various topics were a part of our daily routine. He was sophisticated, reserved and witty, though that side of him was seen only by his close friends. Hypnotized by Nature, he spoke of scaling new heights. God bestowed His grace upon him and for that, Satish was forever grateful to Him.

Oil on canvas, 1974.

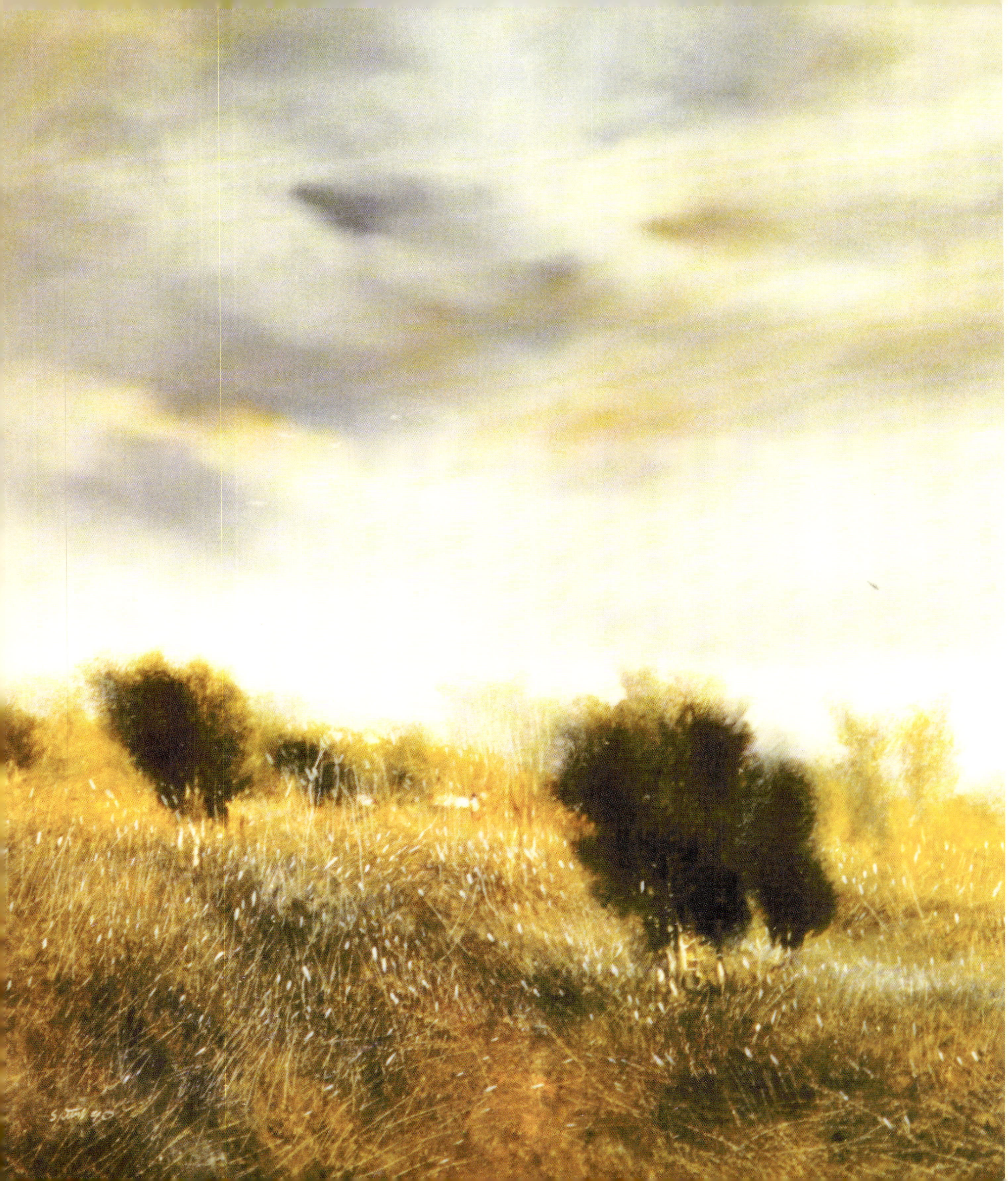

As our friendship grew, I understood that he had the potential and the ability to achieve what he desired. One day, Satish told me that he wanted to paint clouds like the British painter Constable. Indeed on his many tours, he studied clouds – and his clouds 'move' in his paintings!

In his hostel room, he had placed a painting of an imaginary girl with a softly expressive face. He told me that one day he would marry an innocent girl like the one in the painting. In Meenakshi, he met the girl of his dreams.

It was in 1963 that he dedicated himself to landscape painting. First he used watercolours but then moved on to oil, pastels, pencil and crayons. He was extremely sensitive to the inherent powers of each medium. Art became life itself and his art percolated into every aspect of his daily living too. For the last nineteen years of his life he suffered from a heart problem but never felt tired when it came to art. Doctors had forbidden him to stand in front of the easel but he returned to his paint and brush each time. He used to tell me he was a traveller and "would not like any pause in my art as long as I am alive." Illness was not able to break him or his dedication to his art.

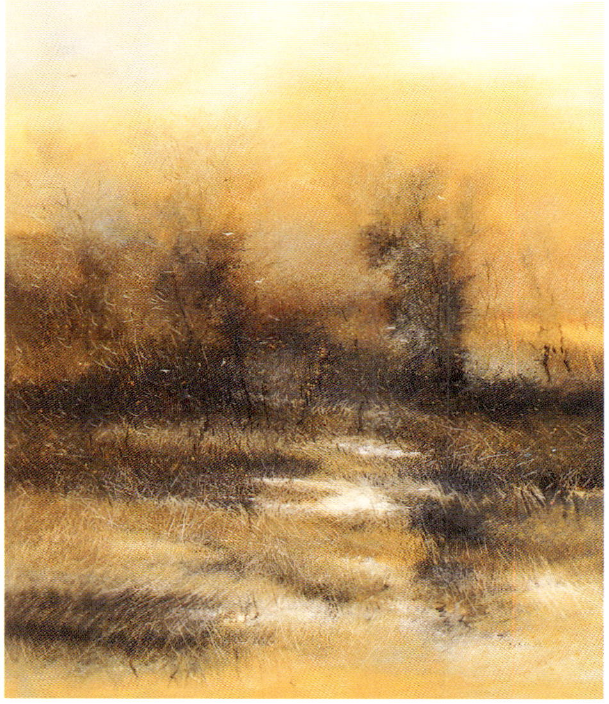

Oil on canvas, 1990.
Facing page: Oil on canvas, 1990.

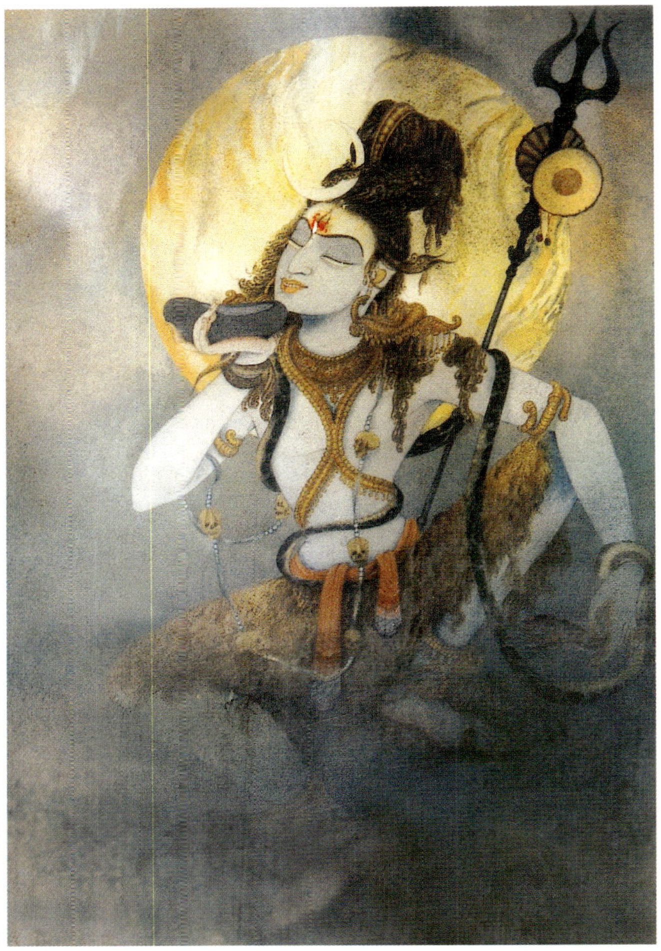

Painting of Lord Shiva in the wash technique, 1962.
Facing page: Oil on canvas, 1990.

Satish was a popular teacher too. Even after he retired from the College of Arts and Crafts, Lucknow University, his expertise continued to be sought by students, specially those who were writing a thesis on him, as well as by the Lucknow University and other institutions and committees of which he was a member.

I can clearly recall a day in 1962. I saw him make a painting of Lord Shiva in the wash technique, in which he

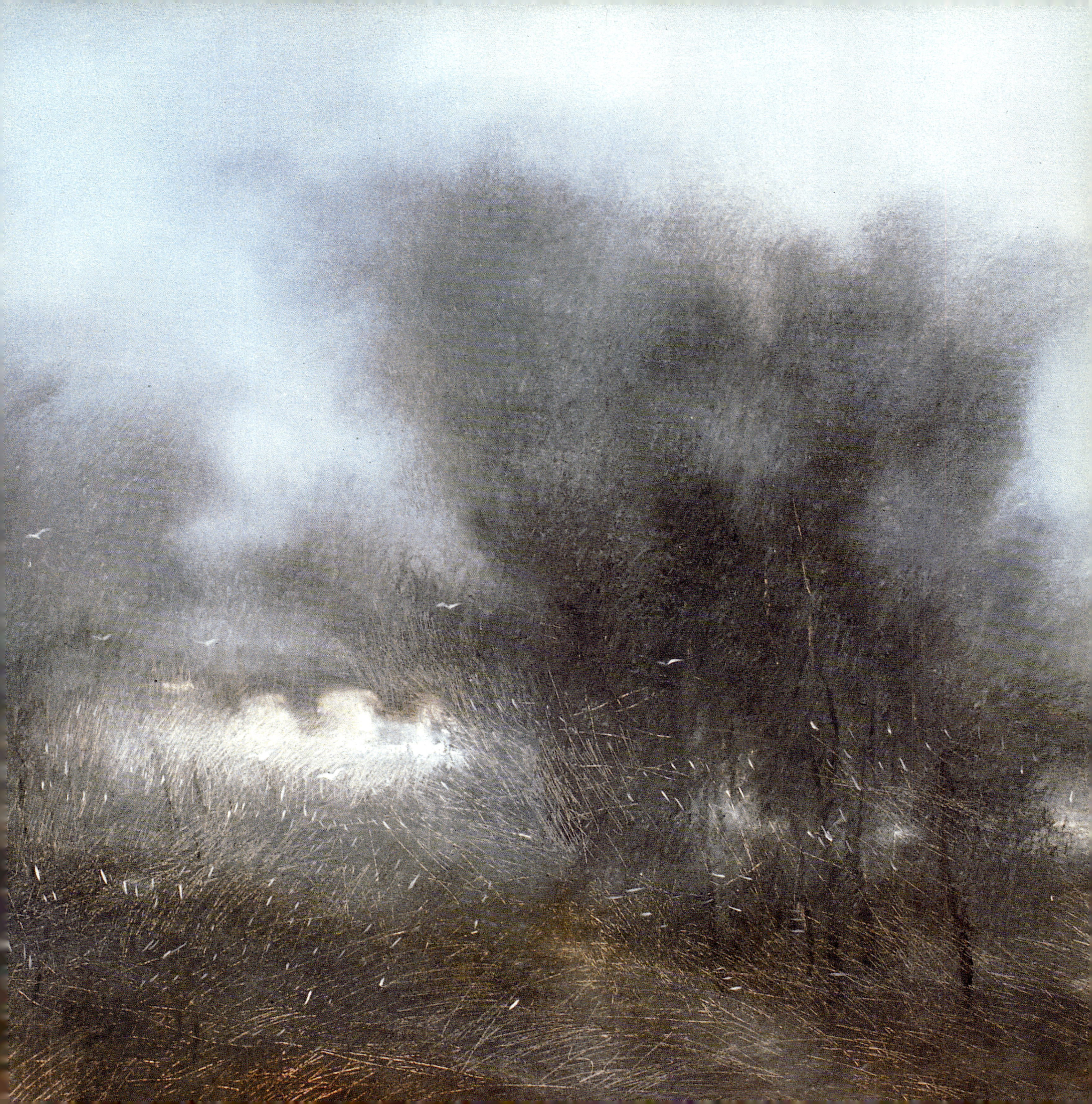

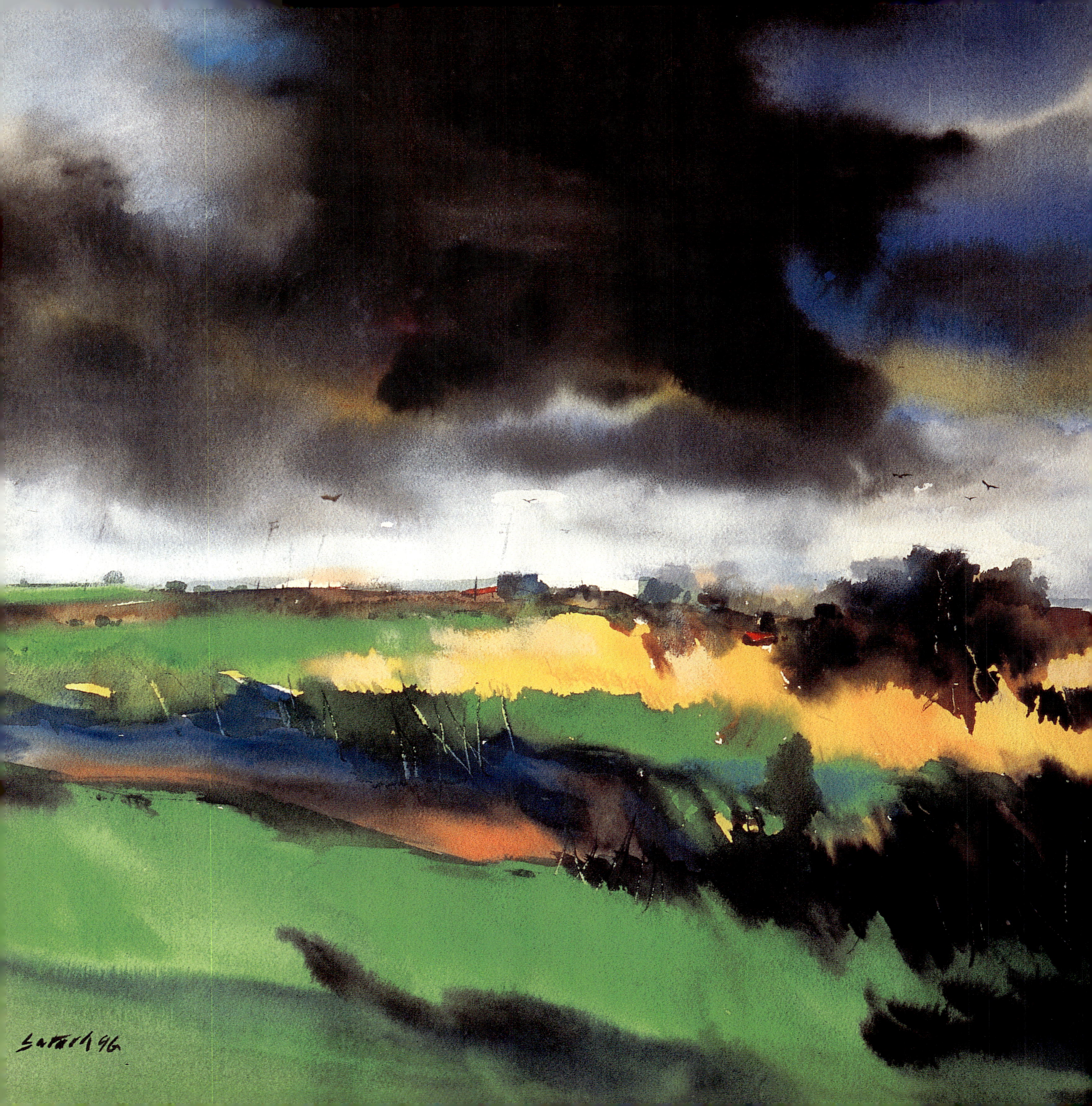

excelled. I advised him to make more such paintings, and he answered that his path led him towards Nature. This particular painting was made so that he could pay his obeisance to 'Shivji' every morning in his room. As destiny would have it, after Satish passed away, this very painting stood beside Satish's photograph during the 'Shantipath'. The sight brought tears to my eyes.

Today, Satish Chandra's canvases occupy a central place in private and public galleries across the world. He remains immortalized through his canvases.

Facing page: Watercolour on paper, 1996.

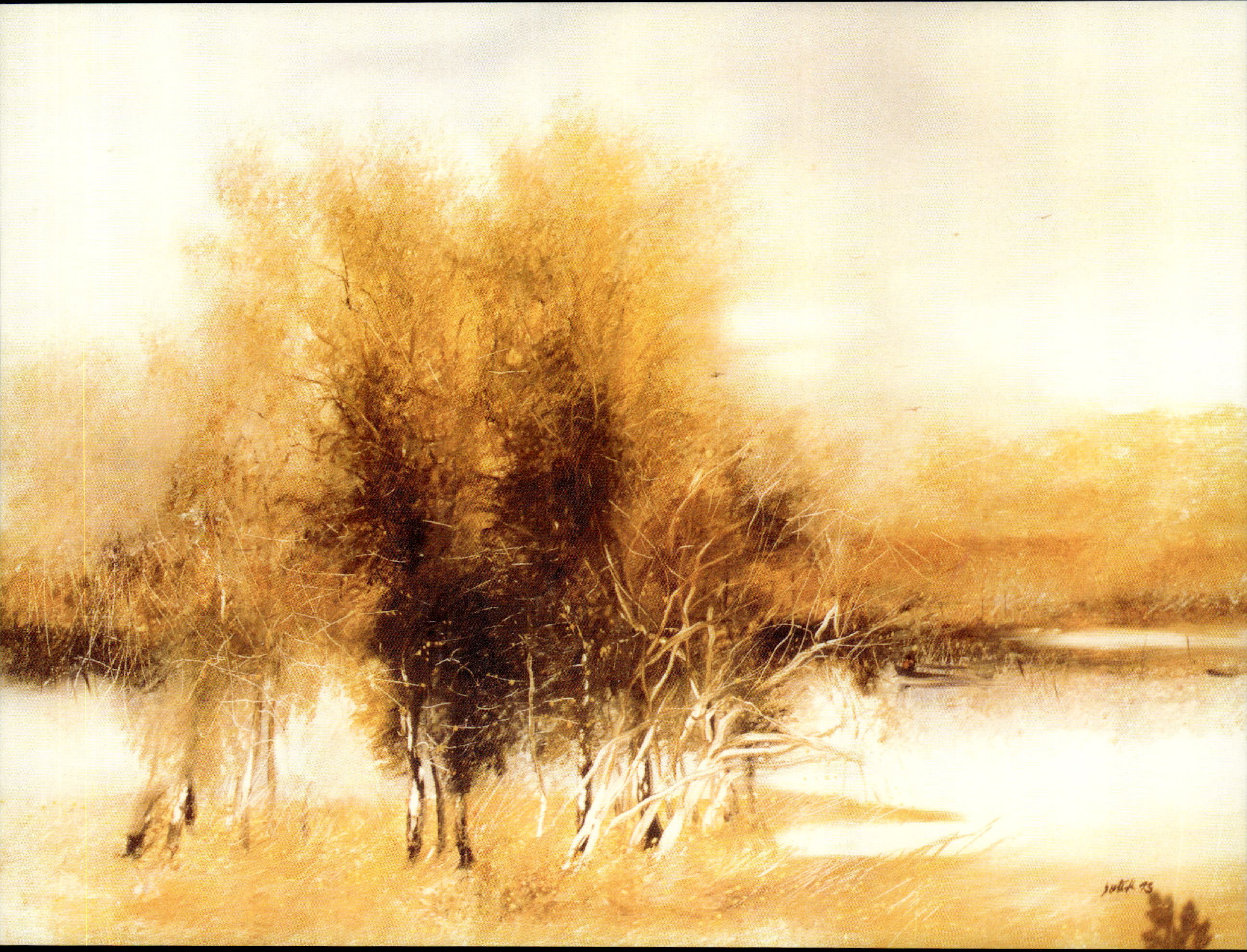

Oil on canvas, 1993.

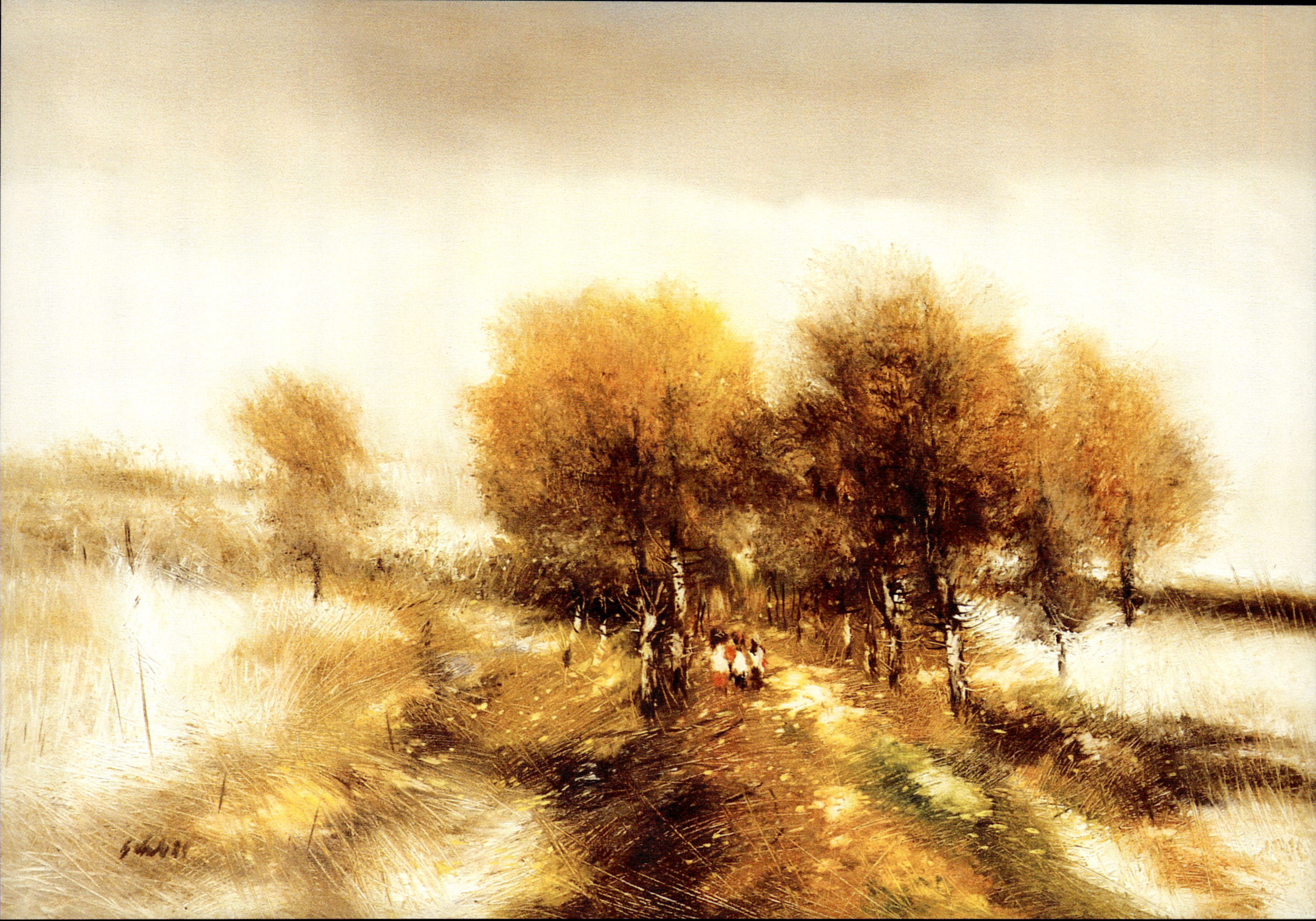

Oil on canvas, 1989.

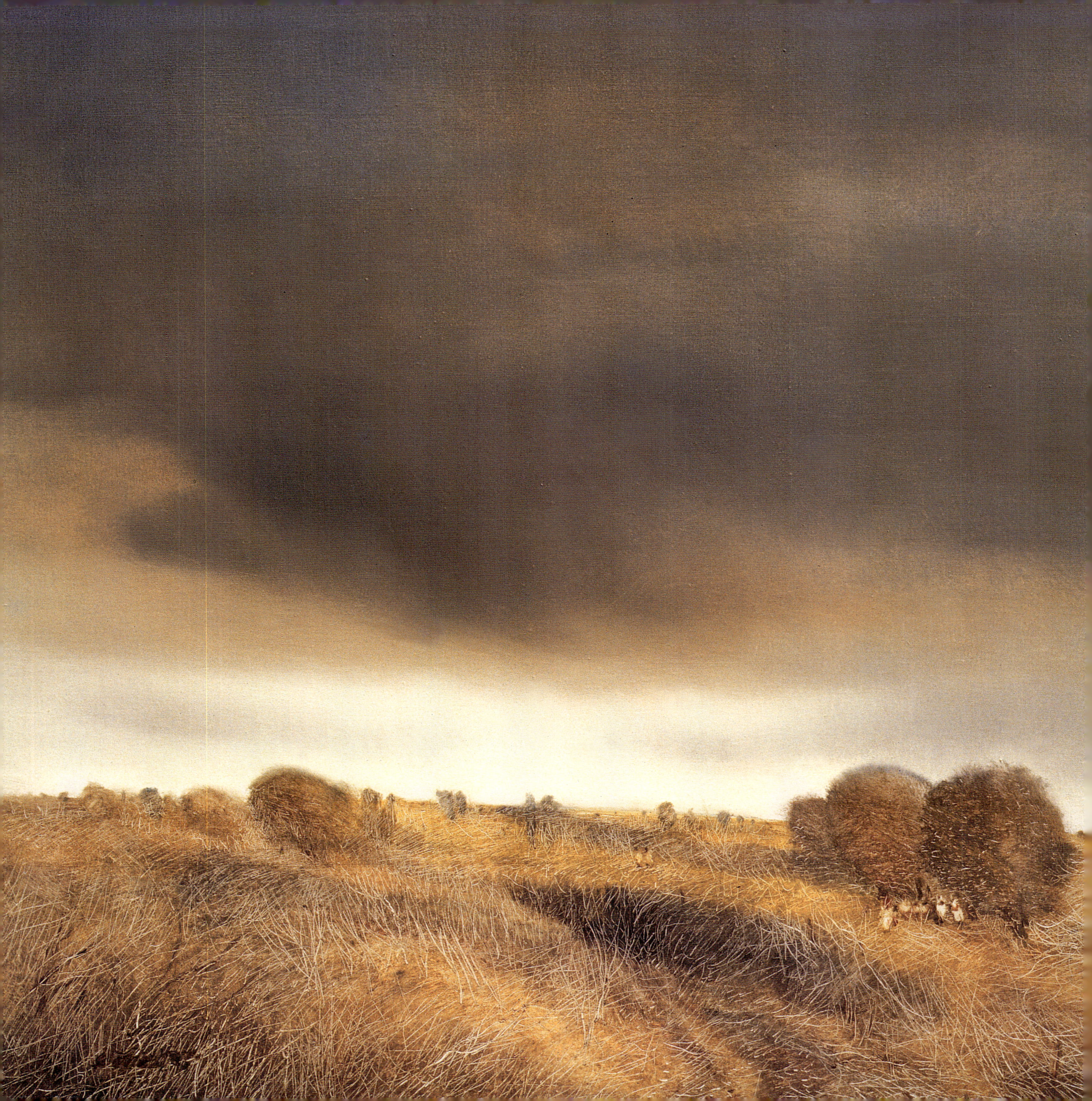

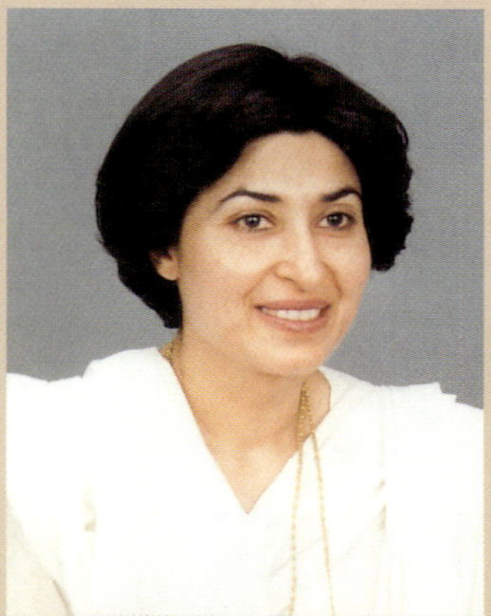

An Indulgent Brother

Suniti Ghai
Friend

"The only real voyage of discovery consists not in seeking new landscapes but in having new eyes." Marcel Proust wrote this line, but Satish lived it. Of course I know this in hindsight, from the vantage point of forty years later.

When I first met Satish I was all of ten and I accepted his inclusion in our family as a matter of course. My father, a managing director at the Carlton Hotel, liked him from the moment they were introduced by the principal of Arts College, Lucknow. An exhibition had been organized at the Arts College, and my father spotted Satish's watercolour of the Chowk's

Facing page: Oil on canvas, 1987.

Rumi Darwaza straightaway. The ruined majesty of the Rumi Darwaza and all the commercial activity going on apace around it had been captured brilliantly by Satish's brush. My father was very impressed. Satish wanted eighty rupees for it and my father gave him one hundred. A mutual love and respect was born that day. My father invited him home for a visit and we never looked back. He just became a part of the family. He would come and go as he pleased, and was always welcomed lovingly. There was something very endearing about Satish. We were all drawn to him for different reasons. My mother says today that it was a certain quality of sweetness and humility that drew her to Satish, and as for me I saw him as an indulgent older brother, who, very confusingly, called my father 'bhai saheb' and my mother 'bhabhi'. My father, an intensely discerning man, was drawn to him for qualities that were not obvious to the rest of us at that time. He could see that Satish, although still maturing as an artist, had a wealth of talent, and persistence to go with it. He often told us, "Tum dekh lena, yeh ladka bahut door jayega." And so it turned out.

Satish brought an uncompromising passion to his art and my father was quick to see that. I think Satish was equally drawn to my father because of his belief in him.

When I look back I see him as a slim young man walking in the Carlton Hotel corridors, in a kurta pyjama and rubber chappals. He had a pleasant, smiling face, and discerning eyes. I didn't see Satish as a great artist, I just saw him as someone who always had time for me, even though he was so busy studying and painting. Whenever he could get away from the college he would come and visit us and I would latch onto him. I remember many

Facing page: Oil on canvas, 2000.

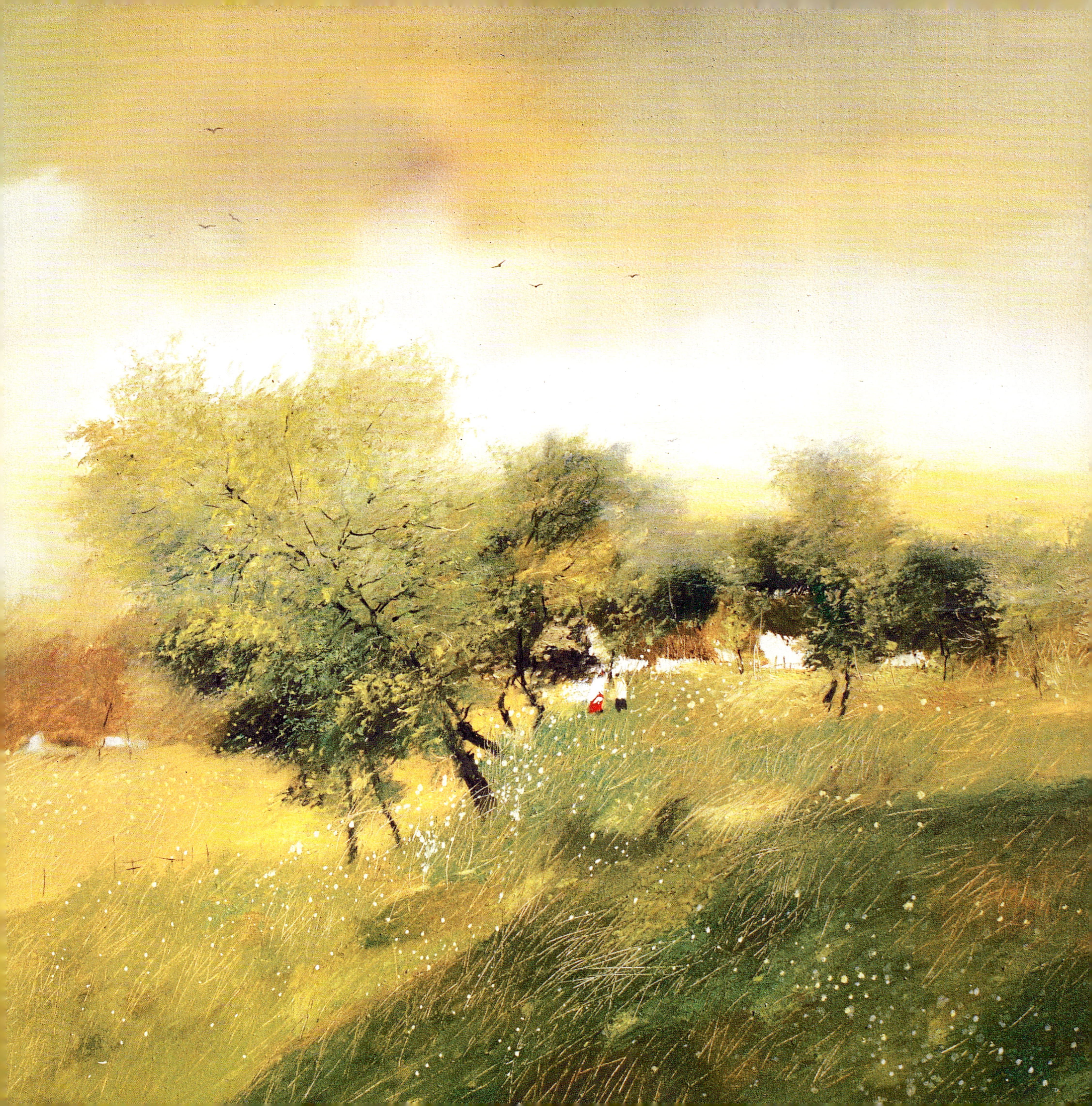

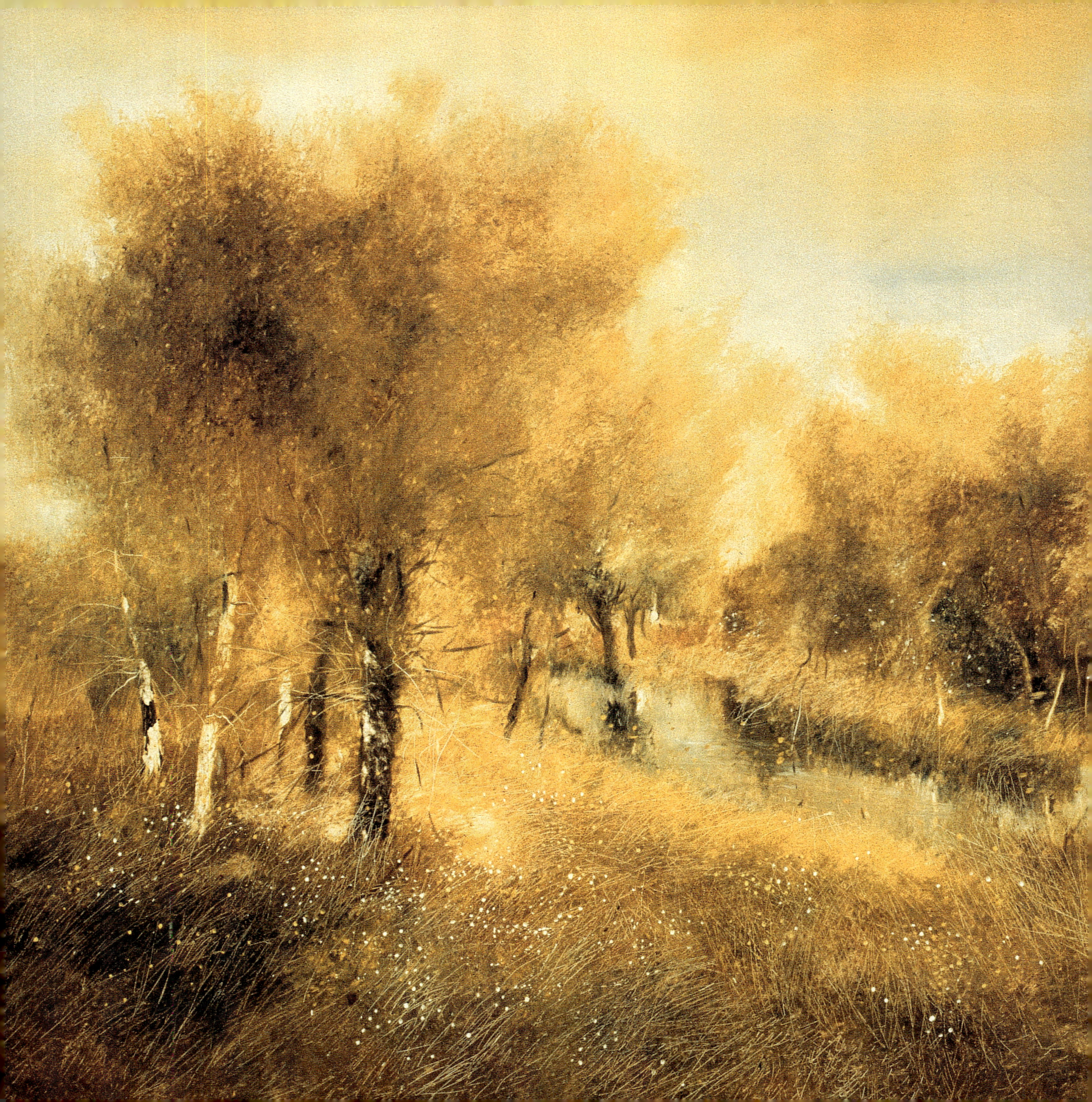

walks with him in the Carlton gardens, with my dogs at my heels. He wasn't too fond of dogs but he tolerated mine – mostly because I made sure they didn't get too close to him!

At that time Carlton was in its heyday with my father, Satendrajit Singh (Sunny), and my uncle, Yogendrajit Singh (Yogi), at the helm. The building and gardens were incredibly beautiful, and he came to drink in the beauty and spend time with my father. They would sit together and talk in the lawns of the hotel. My father, who always thought he could do anything he put his mind to, would try to teach the artist how to practise his art. Satish was never fazed by these lecturers. He would listen with a smile and a nod, only very rarely protesting.

Satish was teaching at the Arts College by the time I finished school. During the holidays I decided I had a burning desire to be an artist like Satish. I had seen him working – he would just sort of wave his brush and the most amazing watercolour paintings would emerge. It looked

Facing page: Oil on canvas, 1992.

deceptively simple. Satish agreed immediately to teach me. He worked so hard with me. I tried waving my brush around in imitation and only succeeded in wounding Satish's sensibilities. Poor Satish! How he suffered! I hadn't one particle of talent but he wouldn't give up on me. When he saw I couldn't even manage the most basic of things, he told me to make any geometric patterns that appealed to me and he would have them transferred to cloth, and maybe, if it was good enough, it would make a nice wall hanging for my father. But I was a miserable failure at that too. Eventually he gave up trying to teach me, but it was a wonderful month of my life. I just hung around his studio in the college, or walked with him in the grounds, feeling quite proud to be escorted by so popular a professor.

Satish had the most delightful little cottage in the grounds of the college. It was small, but what struck one most were the colours inside and out. With unerring taste he collected exquisite objects d'art and later, when he married Meenakshi, the cottage became even more beautiful. My mother tells me there was a regular riot and rumpus when Satish and Meenakshi wanted to get married. As always, marrying for love was not condoned. My parents, of course, were in Satish's corner. They felt that Meenakshi was just the right girl for him. She was very talented, and her tranquil beauty captured all our hearts. Satish looked happier than he had ever done and we were really thrilled for him.

My father was Satish's sternest critic when he went through his abstract art phase. He used to tell Satish that his forte was the realism in his paintings. But I thought that the colours in his abstract art were amazing. However, it was just a phase,

Facing page: Oil on canvas, 1987.

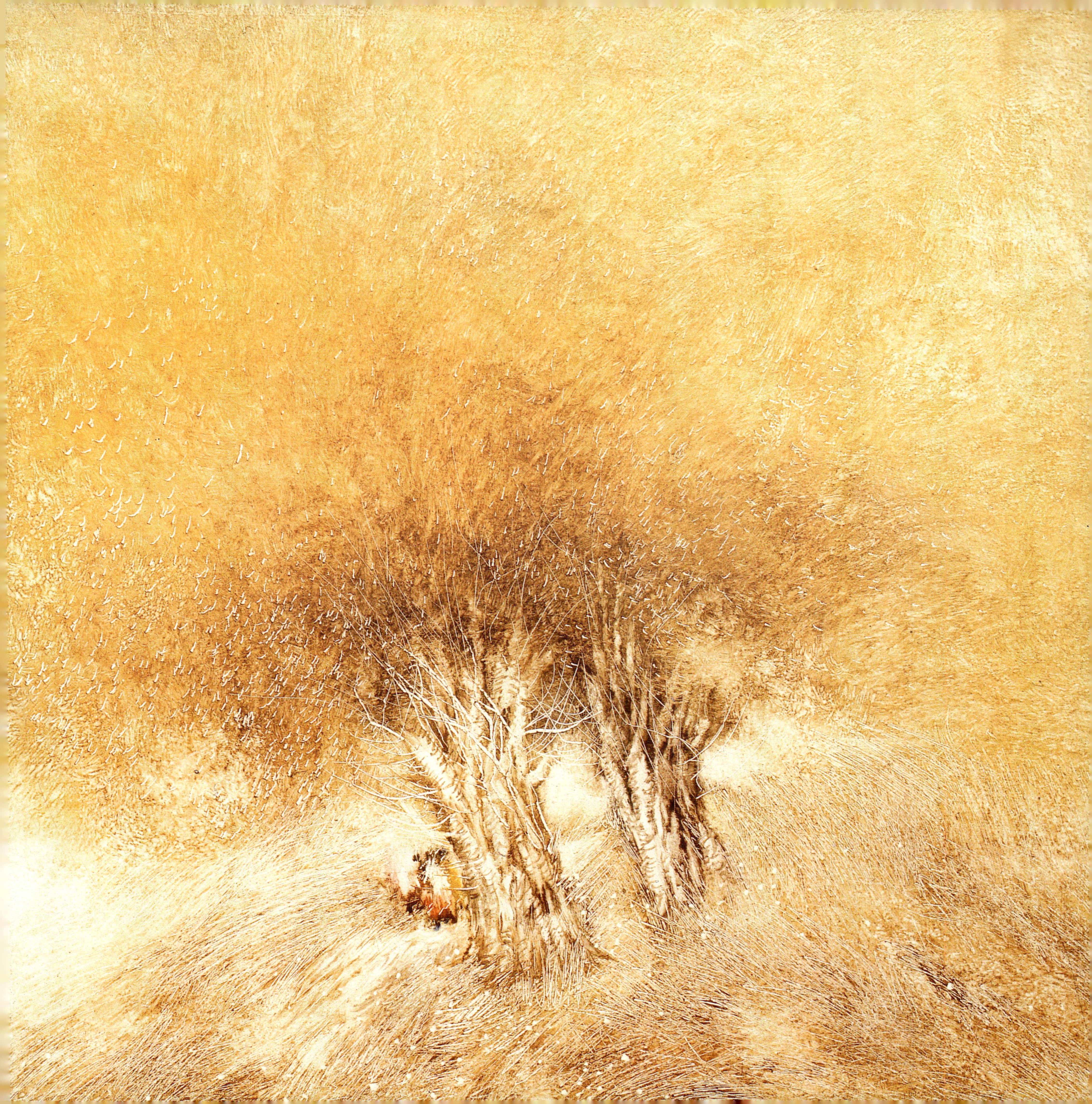

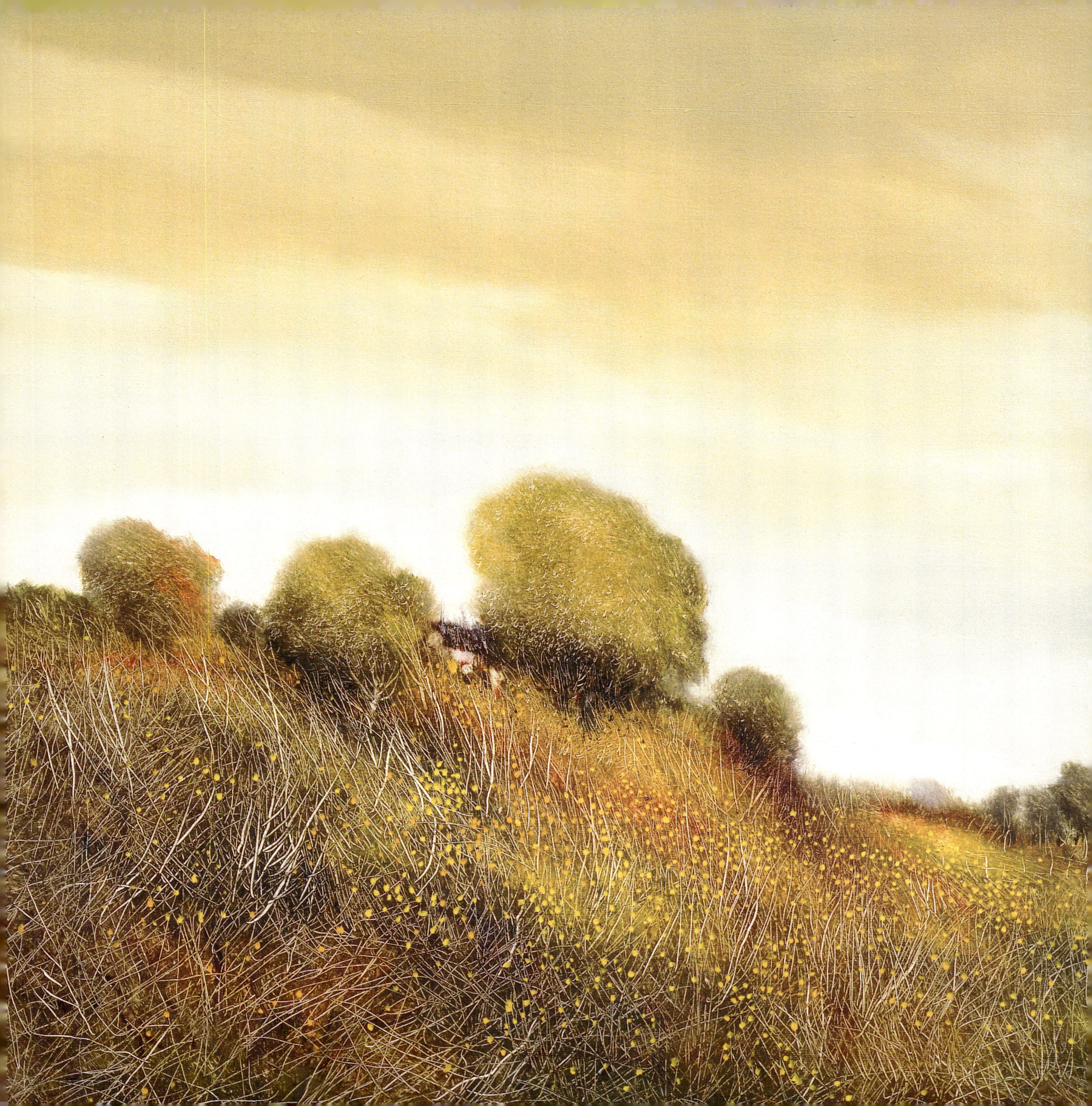

much to my father's relief, because Satish soon reverted to his own unique style, with Nature as his primary content. I know very little about art and have never done an art appreciation course, much to my distress, but I know how I feel about Satish's paintings. The horizon seems limitless and one can just drown in its beauty. Not a description that would impress an art critic, but it is very true for me.

My account of our family's relationship with Satish would not be complete without the narration of this one incident in which he proved himself to be a real hero. It was my sister's wedding and all of Carlton had been lit up. It looked like a fairy land. Unfortunately, fairyland had a major flaw – the people who had put up the lights had left some live wires on the ground. There were scores of people milling around and children were playing everywhere, blissfully unaware of these live wires. It was my five year old cousin who ended up stepping on a live wire. I suddenly heard this huge commotion and a couple of screams but I couldn't actually see anything. I was told later that Avantika, my little

Facing page: Oil on canvas.

cousin, had stepped on one of the live wires, became stuck to it and went into convulsions. A lot of people were just standing around wringing their hands and looking at her helplessly, when Satish, hearing the commotion, went running up. With typical artistic license he had come to the wedding in his usual footwear – rubber-soled shoes. He took in the situation at a glance and didn't waste a moment. He stepped on the wire and sustained a shock as well, but he pulled with all his might and yanked Avantika away and hurried off to the house, carrying her. She had fainted and Satish was feeling a little shaky too. Doctors were sent for but Avantika was alright,

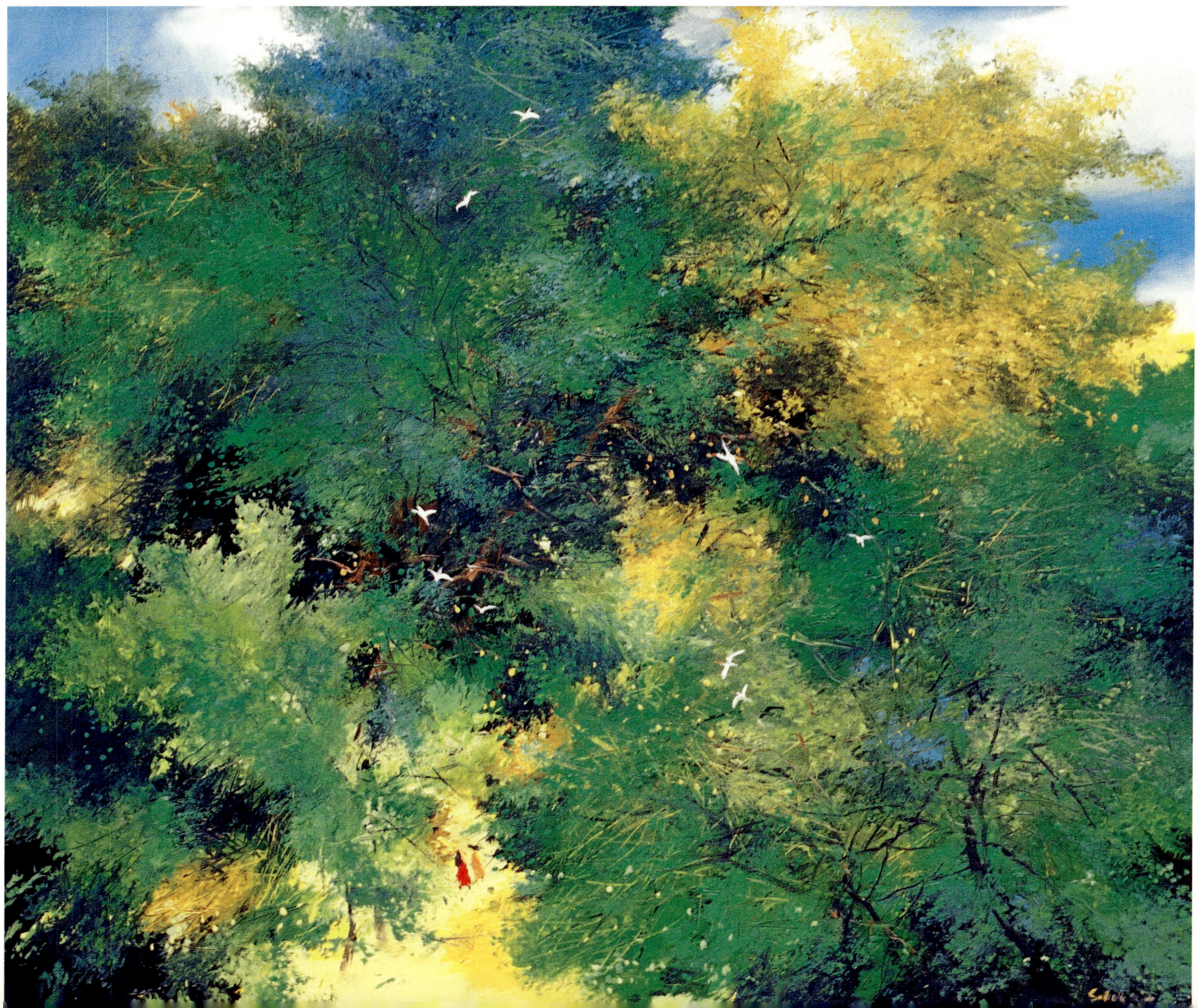

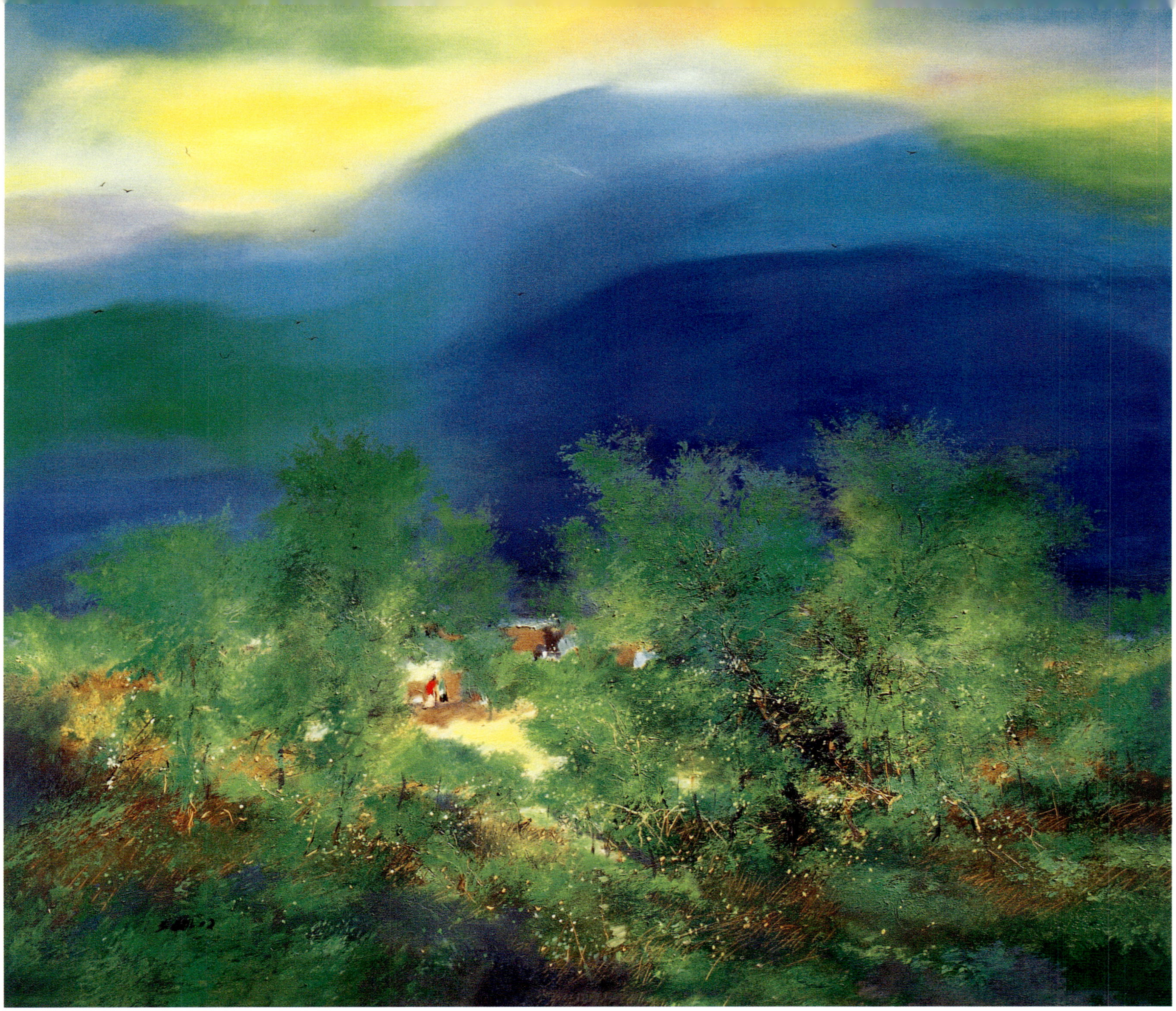

thanks to Satish's timely action. Satish shrugged off any suggestion that he was a hero but we knew better. He said it was an ordinary thing he had done, but heroes are just ordinary people who do extraordinary things.

I know Satish became a very well-known artist later on, holding exhibitions and one-man shows all over India and in the States, and that he held important posts, but for my parents he stayed the simple small-town lad he had always been, and as for me, I will cherish my memories of him as long as I live.

Oil on canvas, 2002. *Facing page:* Oil on canvas, 2002.

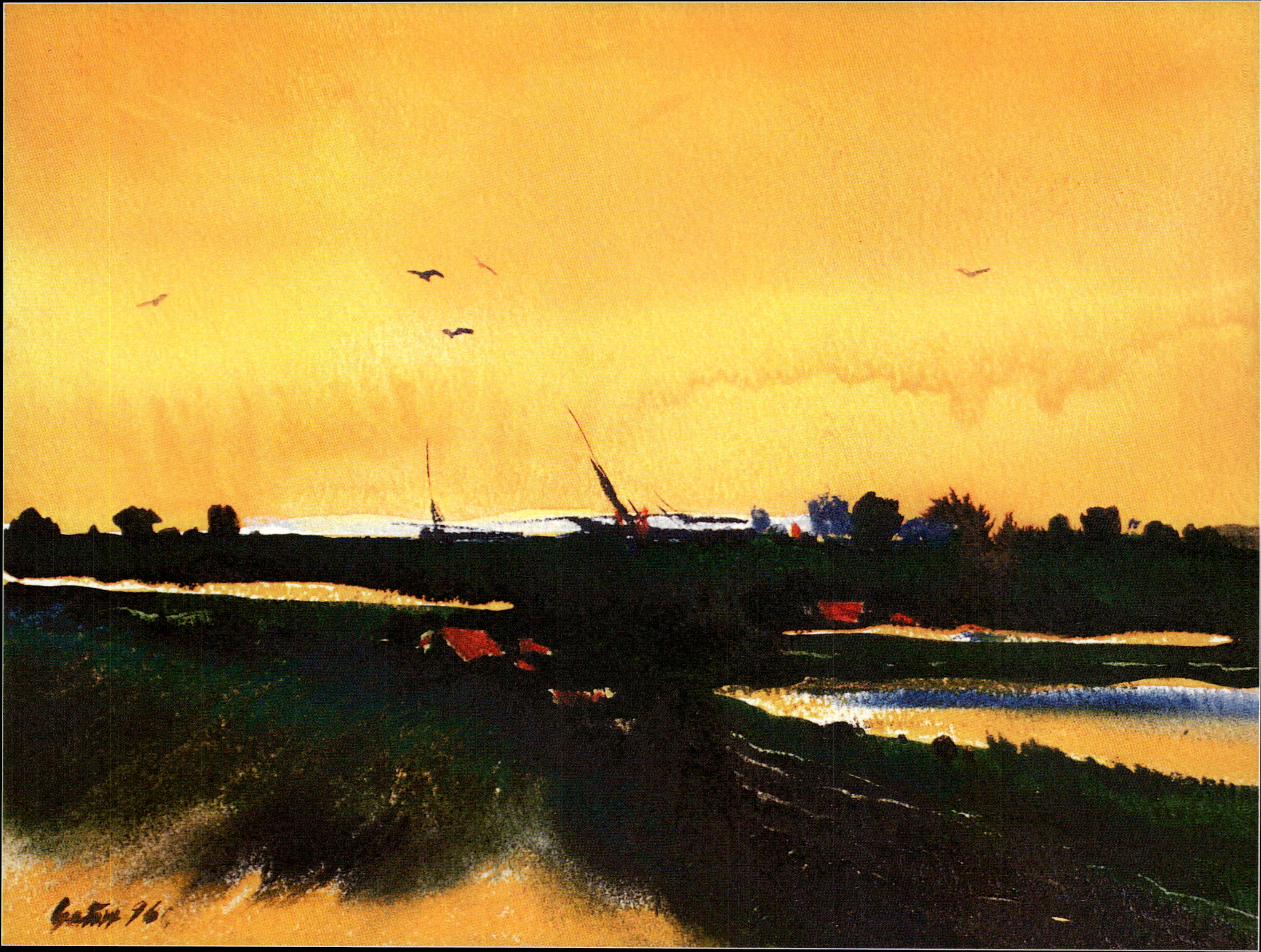

Watercolour on paper, 1996.

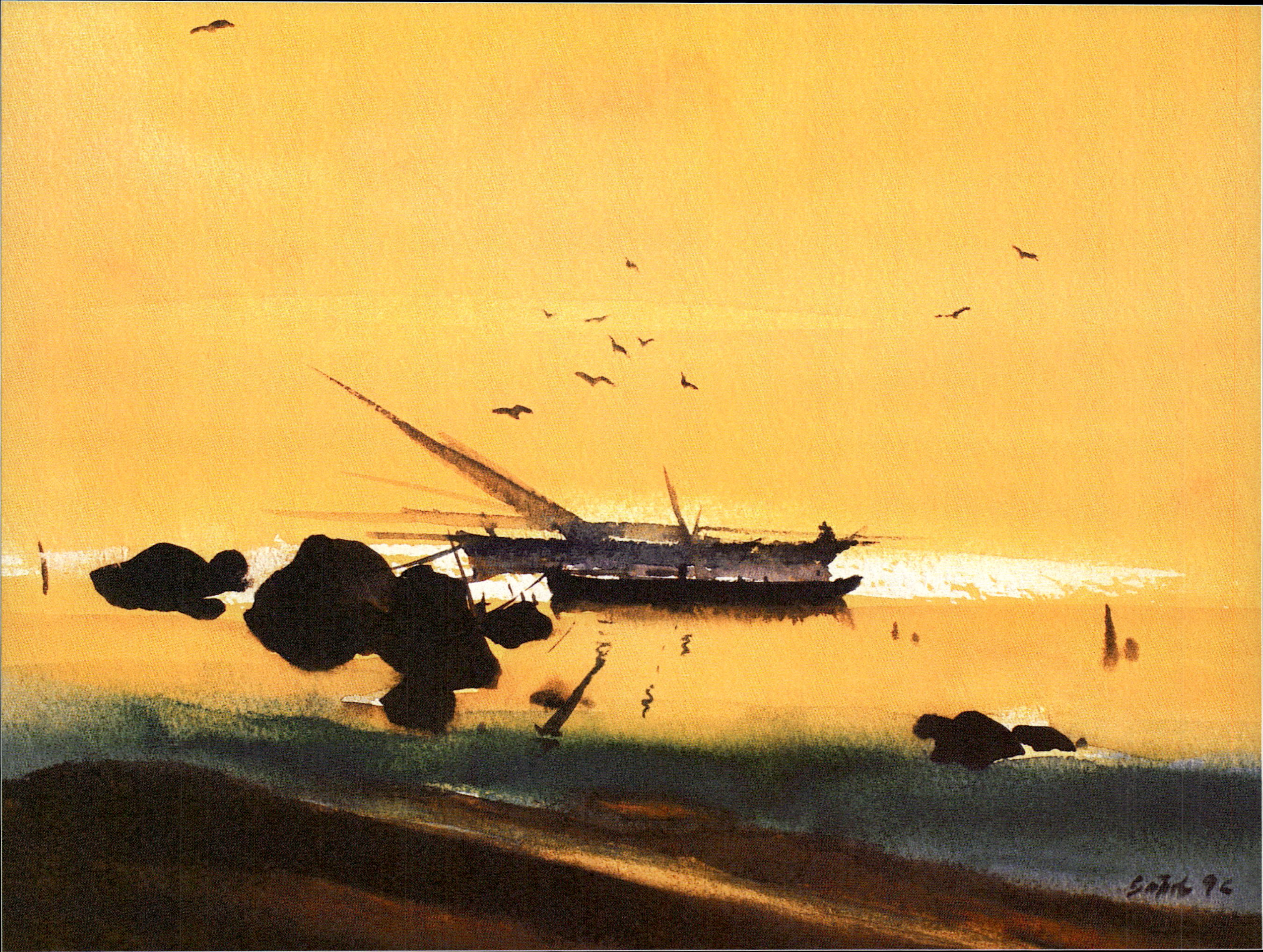

Watercolour on paper, 1996

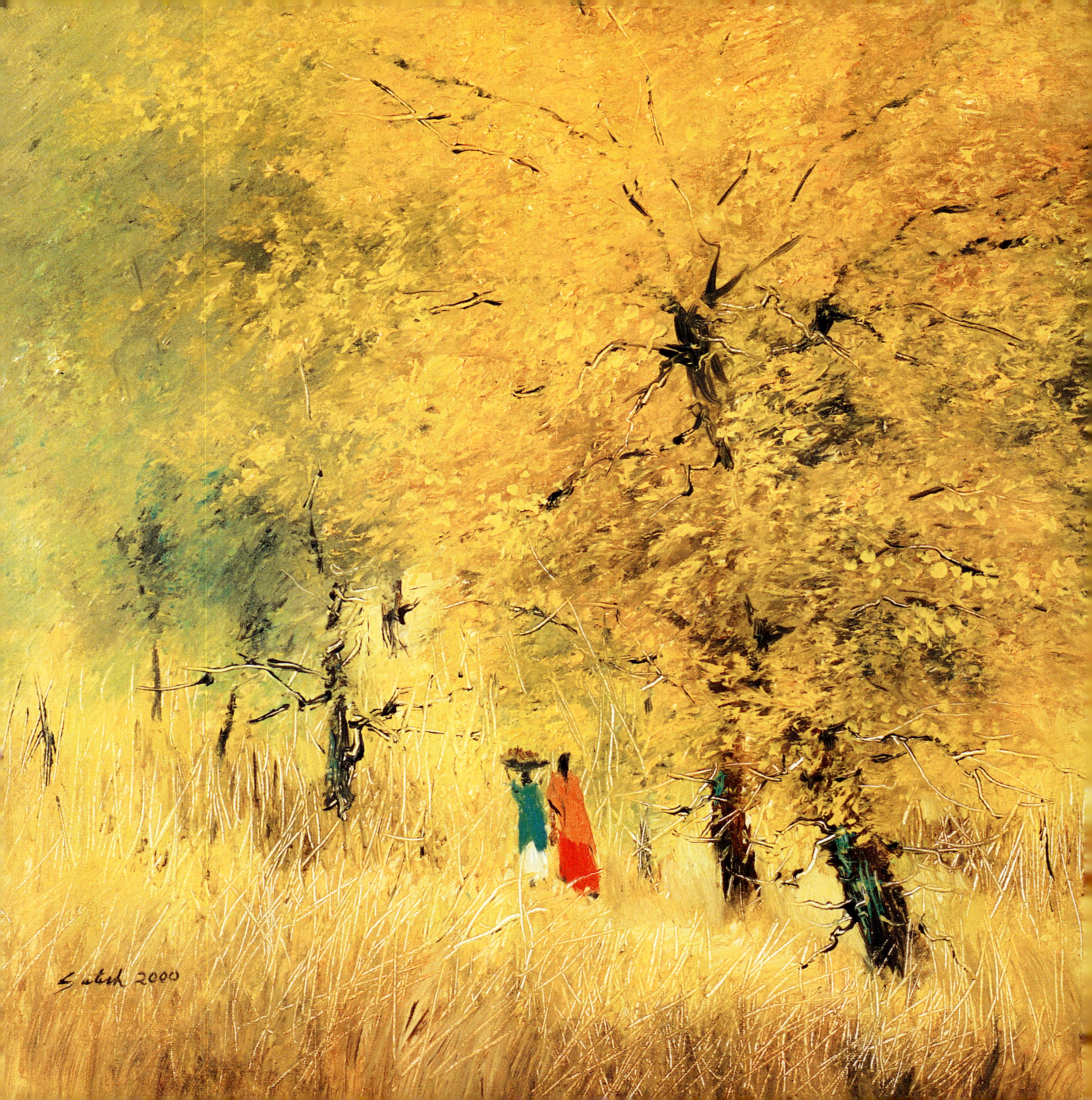
Satish 2000

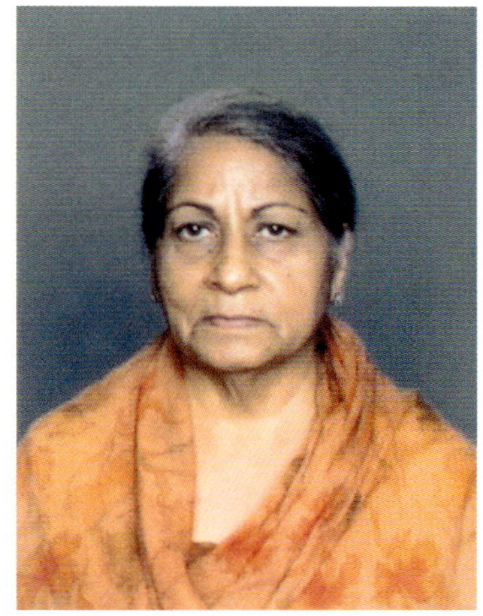

A Spiritual Connection

Usha Kumar
Mother-in-Law

It was February 1971. My daughter Meenakshi rolled onto my bed one afternoon and said, 'Mama, there is a boy whom I like. I want you to meet him and to get to know him.' That's when I realized that my daughter had grown up!

Satish was with us the very next day. He was a good-looking boy. There was something about him which caught my attention and I found him looking at me as if reassured of a mother's love. He was sincere, understanding and compassionate. A lover of Nature and of beauty – he endeared himself to all. I never knew him to raise his voice or lose his temper.

Facing page: Oil on canvas, 2000.

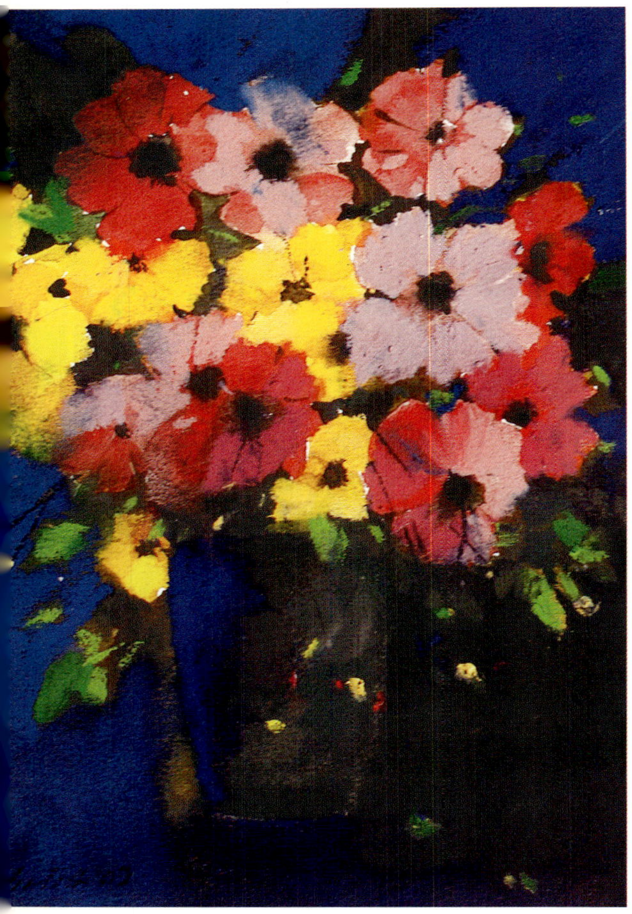

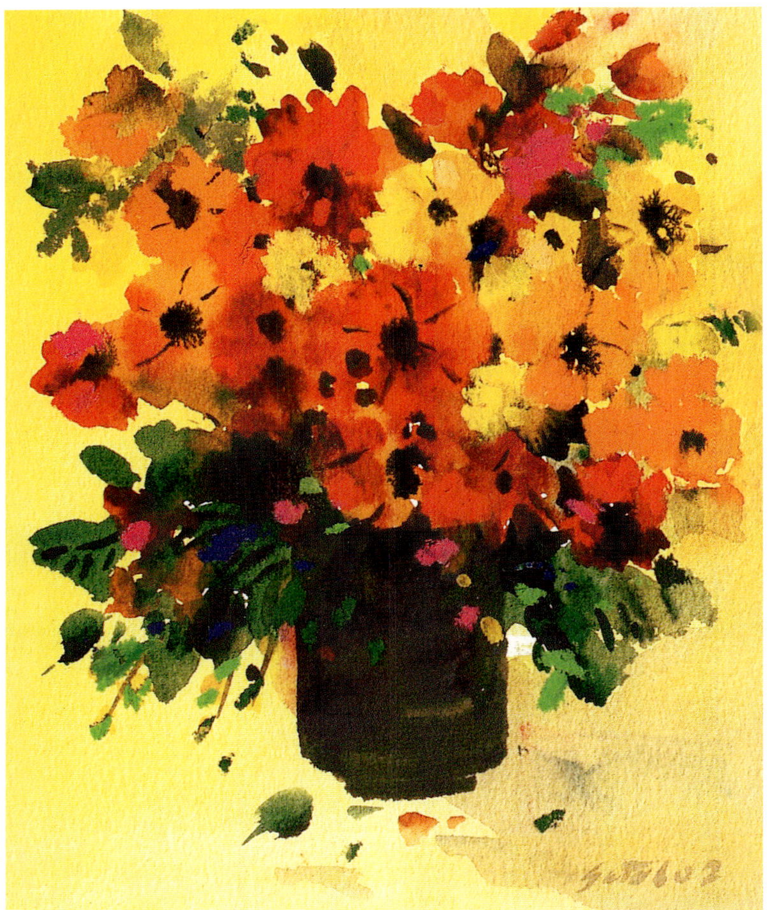

His circle of friends was wide and it widened as he rose to fame. For Satish there was never an evening when he did not have friends with him.

When he fell ill in 2003 – with his left side paralyzed and which was later diagnosed to be due to brain cancer, I made several trips to be with him. He liked me to be around and to recite 'shabdas' (prayer verses). All through his illness his one and only question was – would he be able to paint again?

Siddharth left no stone unturned to restore his papa back to health. God's will was otherwise. He passed away leaving a vacuum never to be filled.

Left: Mixed media on paper, 2002.
Right: Mixed media on paper, 2002.
Facing page: Mixed media on paper, 2002.

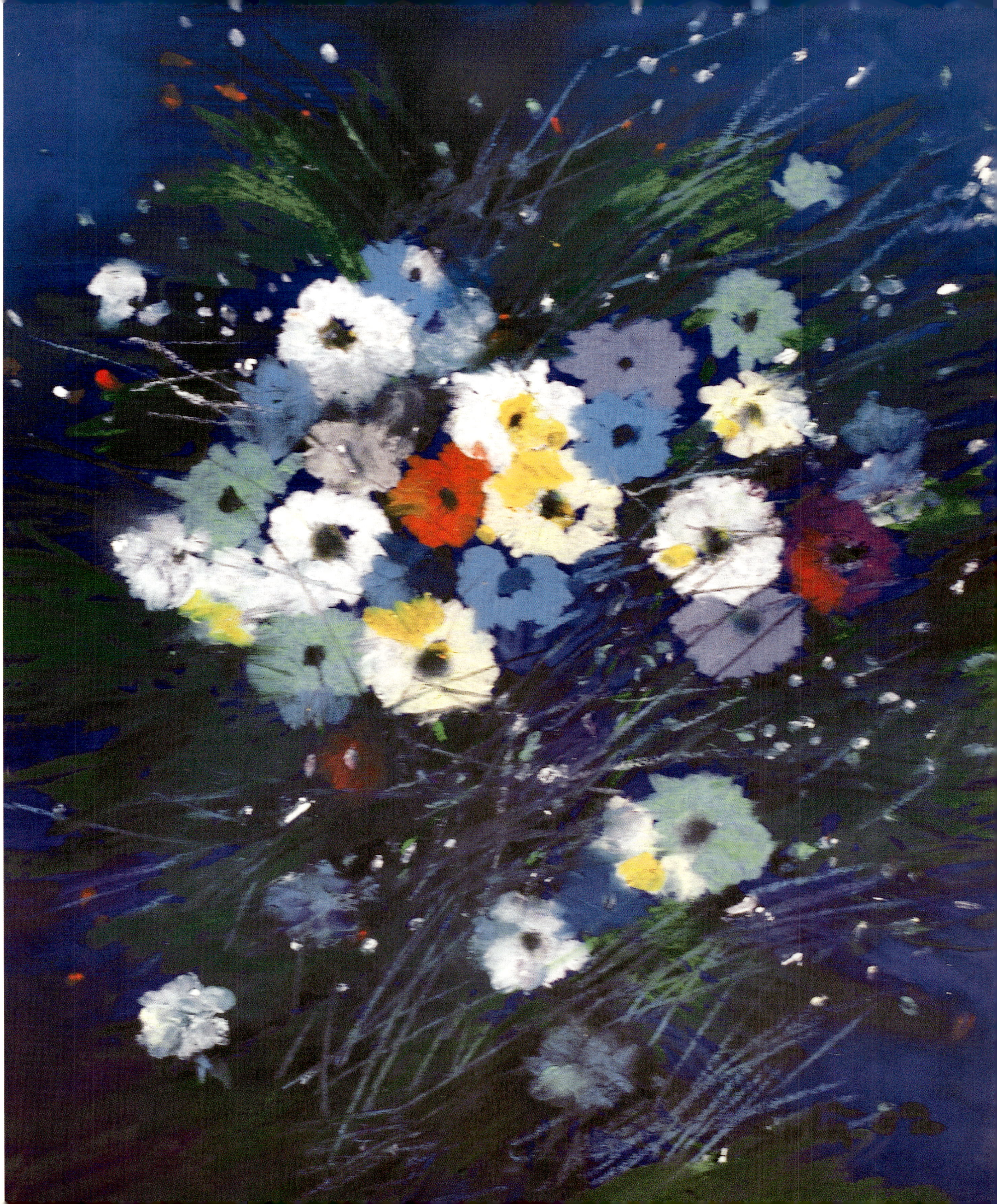

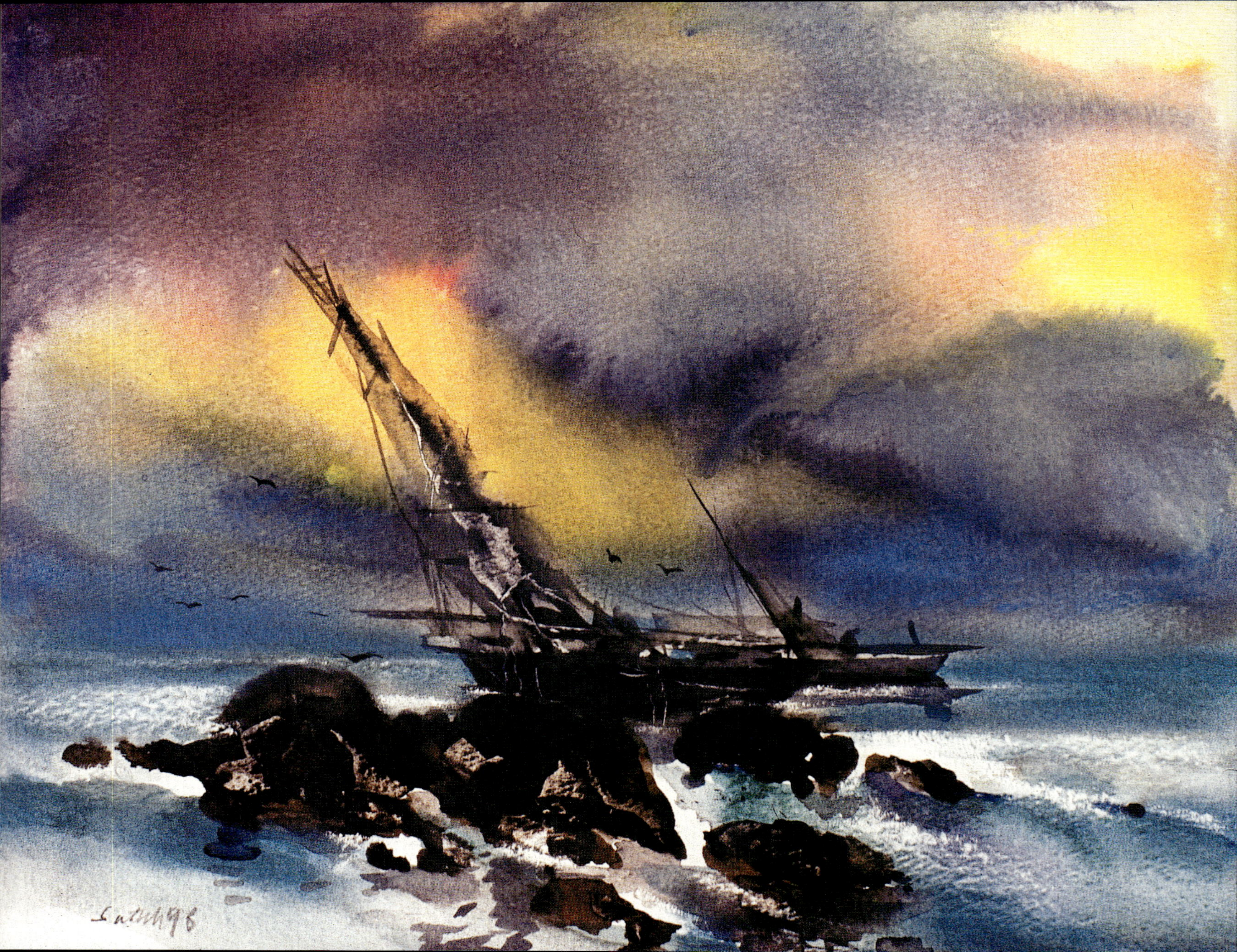

Watercolour on paper, 1996.

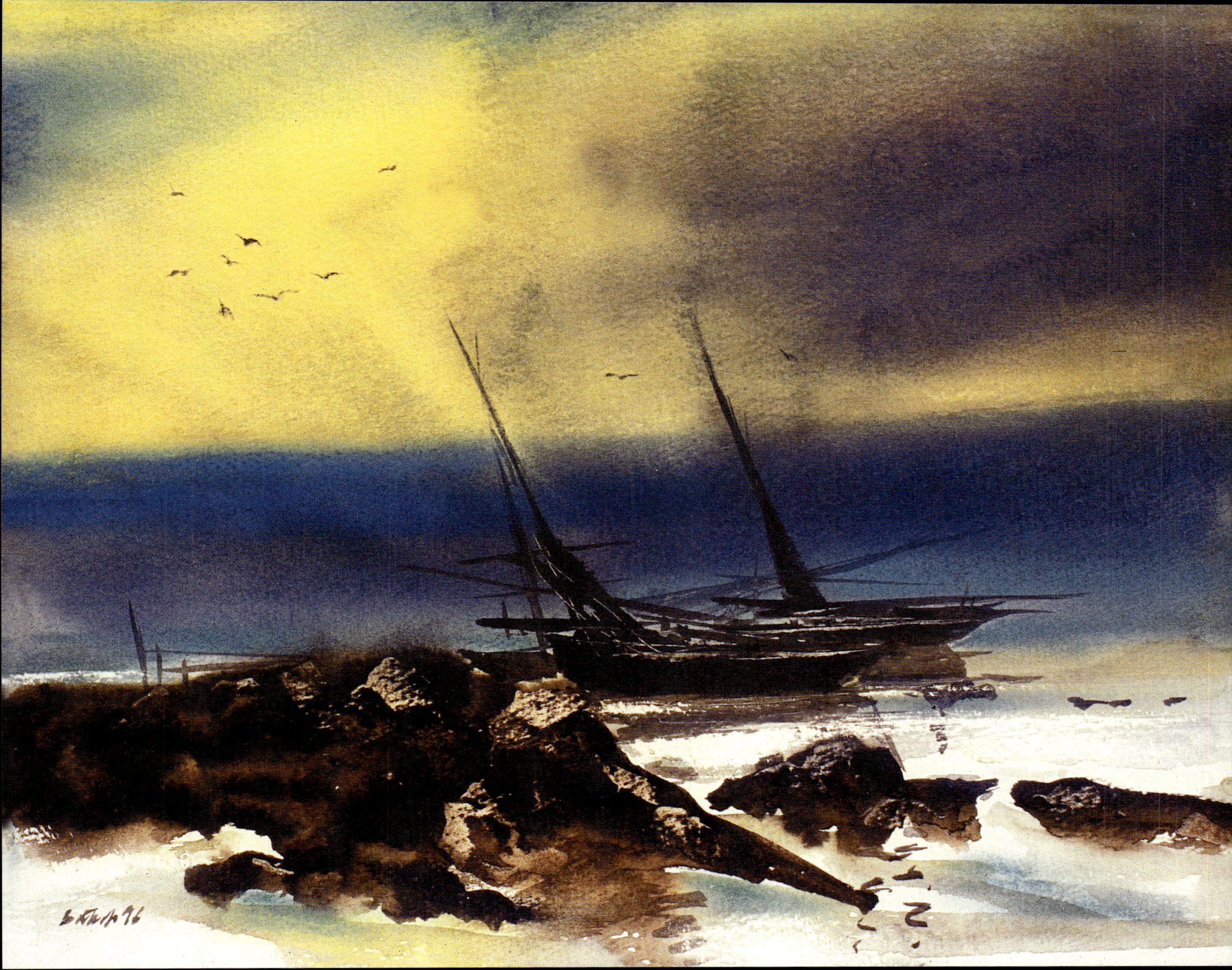

Watercolour on paper, 1996

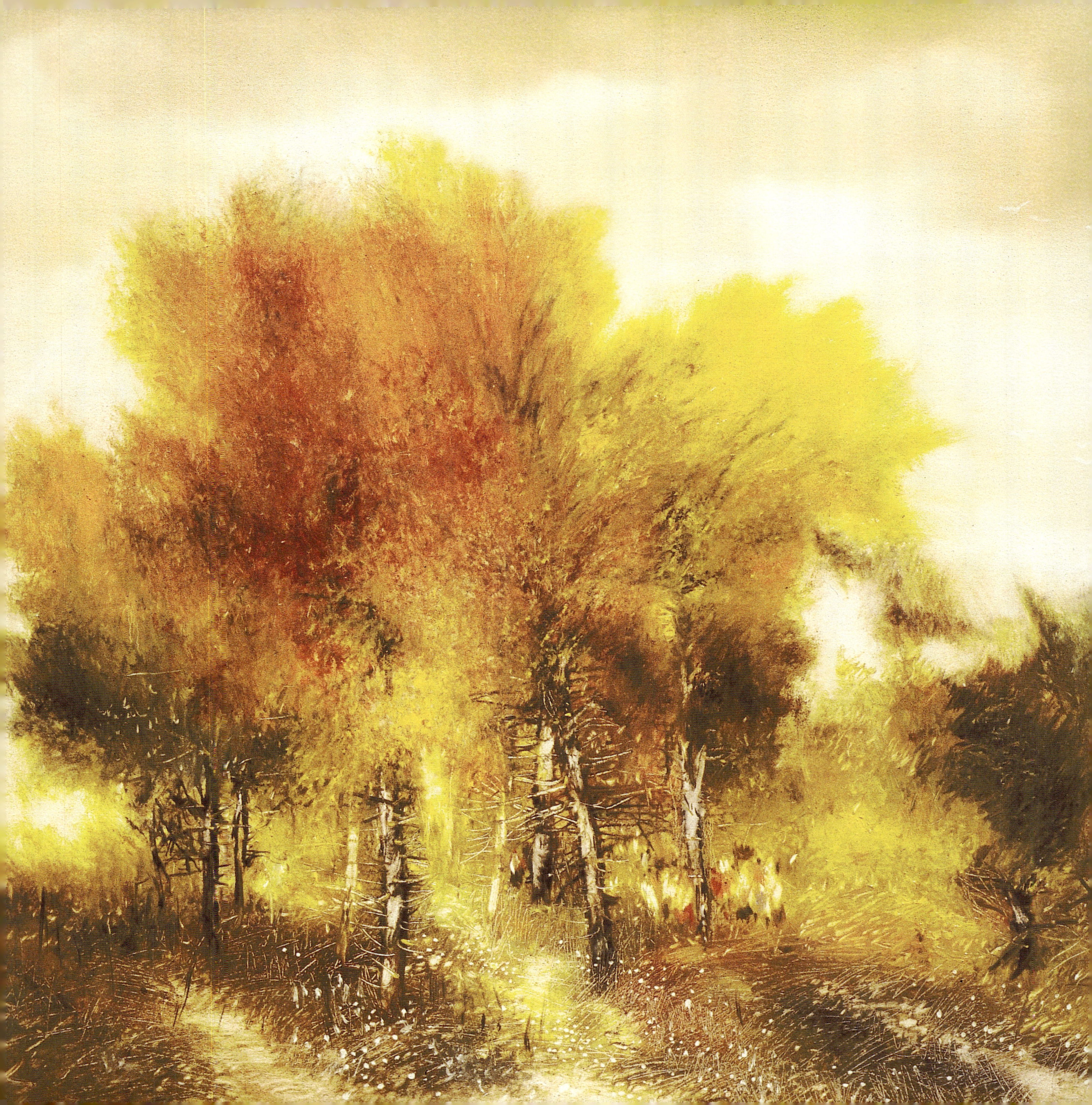

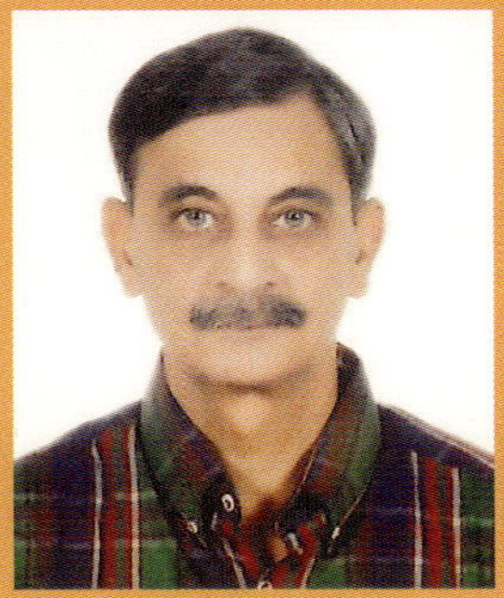

A Child-like Purity

Fasih Ahmed
Friend

My first meeting with Satish bhai is distinctly etched in my mind, or rather, upon my conscience. It was a chance rendezvous at our common friends Sunita and Kanchan's place during the summer of '95, when my wife Andaleeb and I had driven down from Kanpur to attend one of those frequently hosted 'evenings' by Sunita. Amidst the usual party babble, I chanced upon someone who was to leave a deep impact upon me – someone who would hereafter introduce me to the myriad colours of Nature and possibly one day transform me into a better human being. He

Facing page: Oil on canvas, 1989.

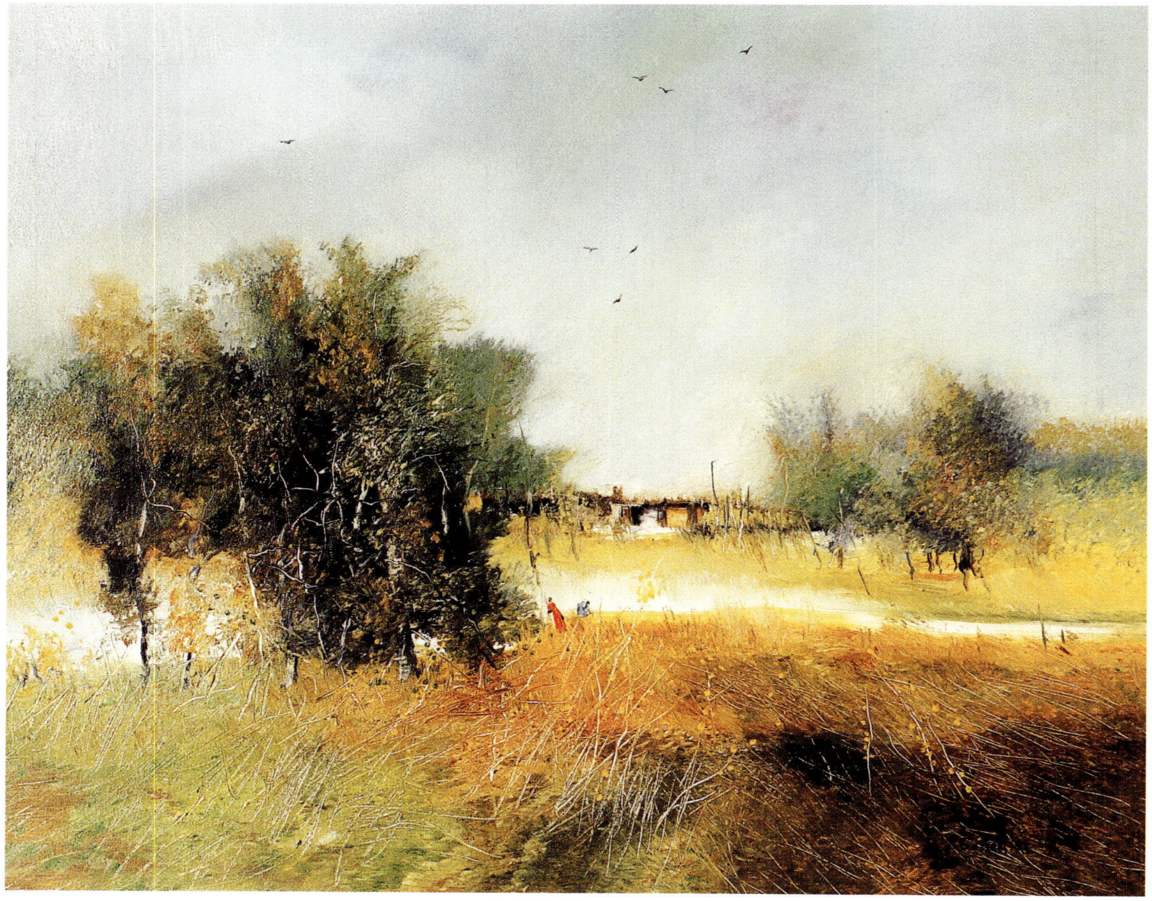

Oil on canvas. *Facing page:* Oil on canvas.

appeared to be the most silent of all in the crowd, yet far too eloquent than others in many ways. What struck me instantly about Satish bhai was his childlike innocence.

I had heard a lot about his accomplishments as a painter. Yet at that point in time I hardly possessed an eye for appreciating art or artists. It was his persona that attracted me.

For the next three years we met whenever I was in Lucknow. However, every such chance meeting was sufficiently invigorating to find reasons to meet again. Familial bonding between us occurred only after I hung my boots and returned home to settle down in Lucknow. Our usual haunt was Sunita's or Sharat's place where we would get together on the flimsiest of pretexts. Satish bhai and Meenakshi bhabhi were an integral part of the 'gang'. Satish bhai, although a person of few words besides being older than us, was always ready to energize us. Very soon we as a group became notoriously famous for our 'riotous' singing and merrymaking. I remember our common friend P.L. Punia fondly christening us as a "bhajan-mandli" –

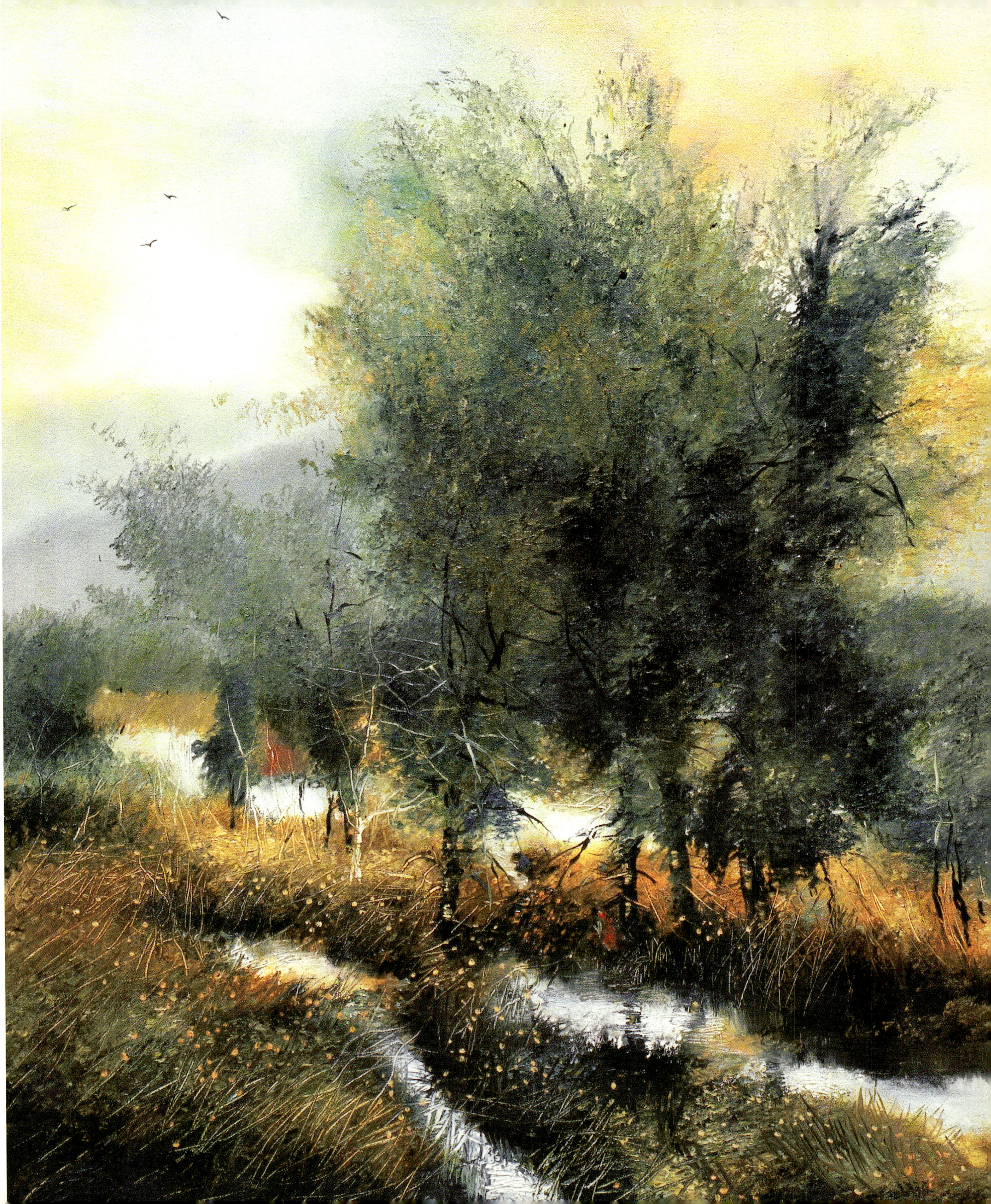

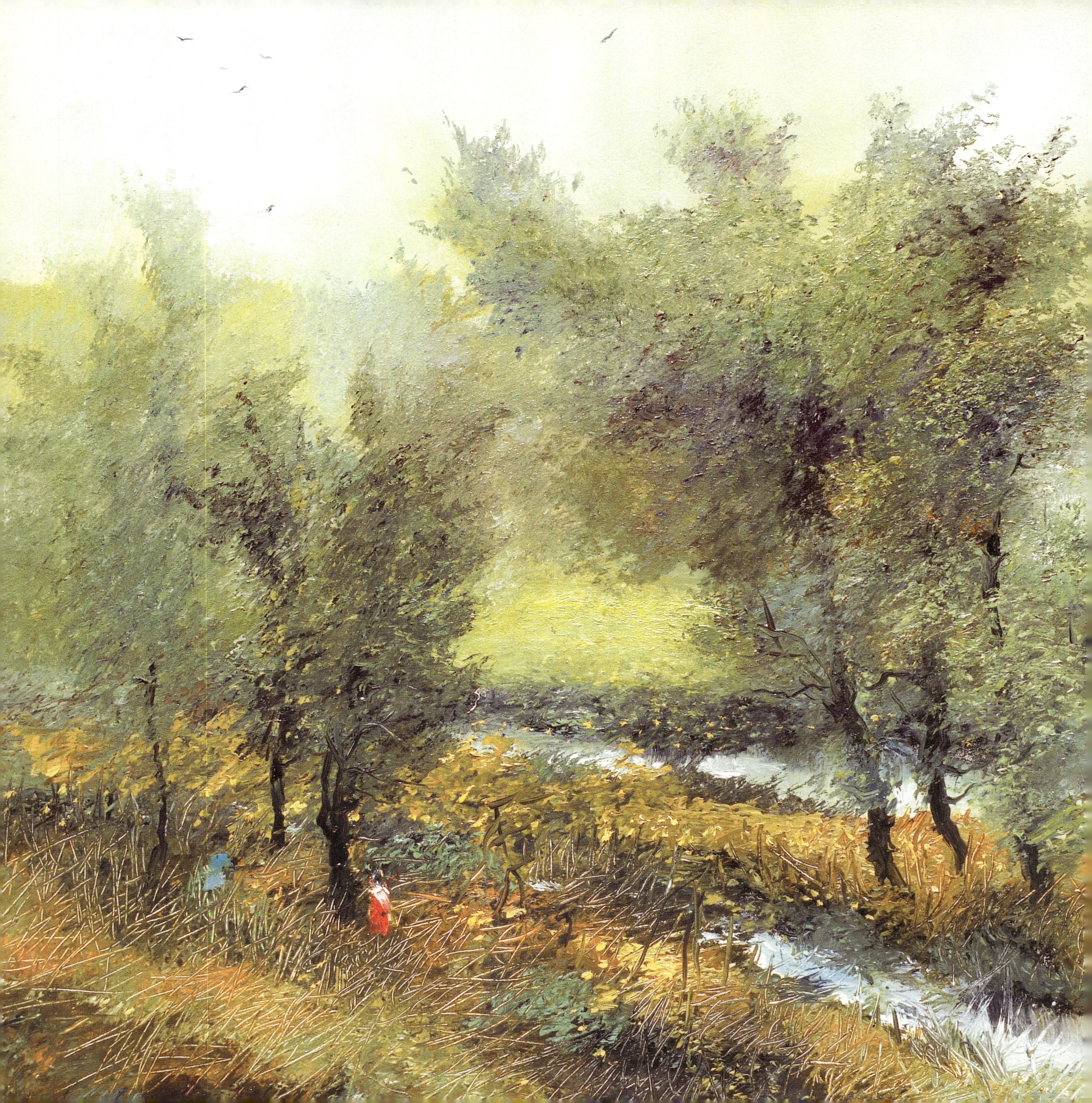

Satish bhai was essentially its Zubin Mehta. Looking back, I feel he possessed an uncanny knack of pushing and pumping us all to our limits of harmless frenzy. Since Sharat and I would invariably become the lead performers at all such musical soirees, Satish bhai, I felt, was always biased towards the two of us, never ever failing in lavishing heaps of praise upon us.

Yet, despite the growing mutual admiration, what intrigued me for a long time was the reason for his fondness for me, because at some level there was a strange dichotomy between us. Professionally we couldn't have been more diversely placed since a large part of my life as a soldier had been spent in honing skills to kill, so to say, while here was a man who had the deftness to breathe life into a dead piece of canvas. Temperamentally too, while I was often brusque and impulsive, he was always overly serene,

Facing page: Oil on canvas, 1998.

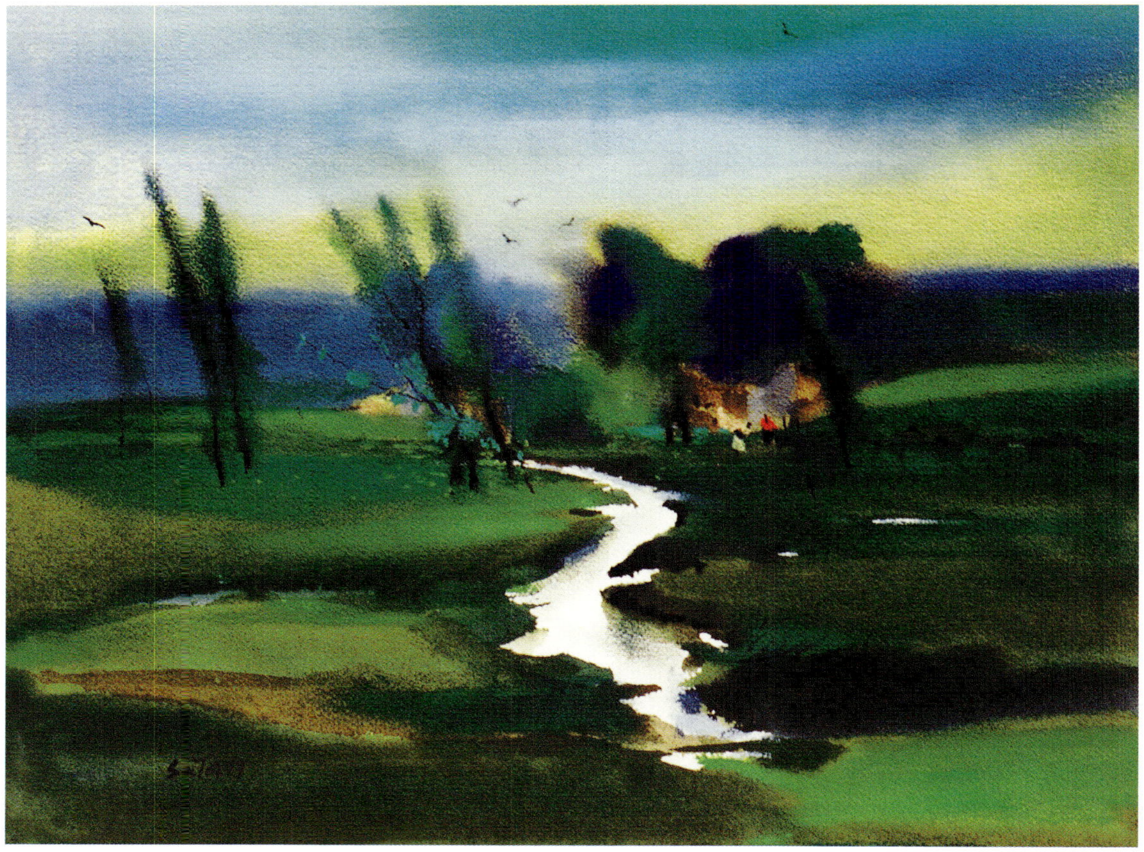

Watercolour on paper, 1999. *Facing page:* Mixed media on paper.

soft-spoken and reassuringly calm. Perhaps this Nature-lover was simply meant to share goodness with anyone who came in his contact.

His abundant humility was another attribute to be imbibed, for on every occasion he would make the other person feel very important. He handled relationships like porcelain, giving far more care and attention than what would be considered adequate by any other well-meaning person. This rare quality has evidently rubbed off with similar intensity on Meenakshi, Siddharth and Pooja.

I remember Siddharth's wedding,

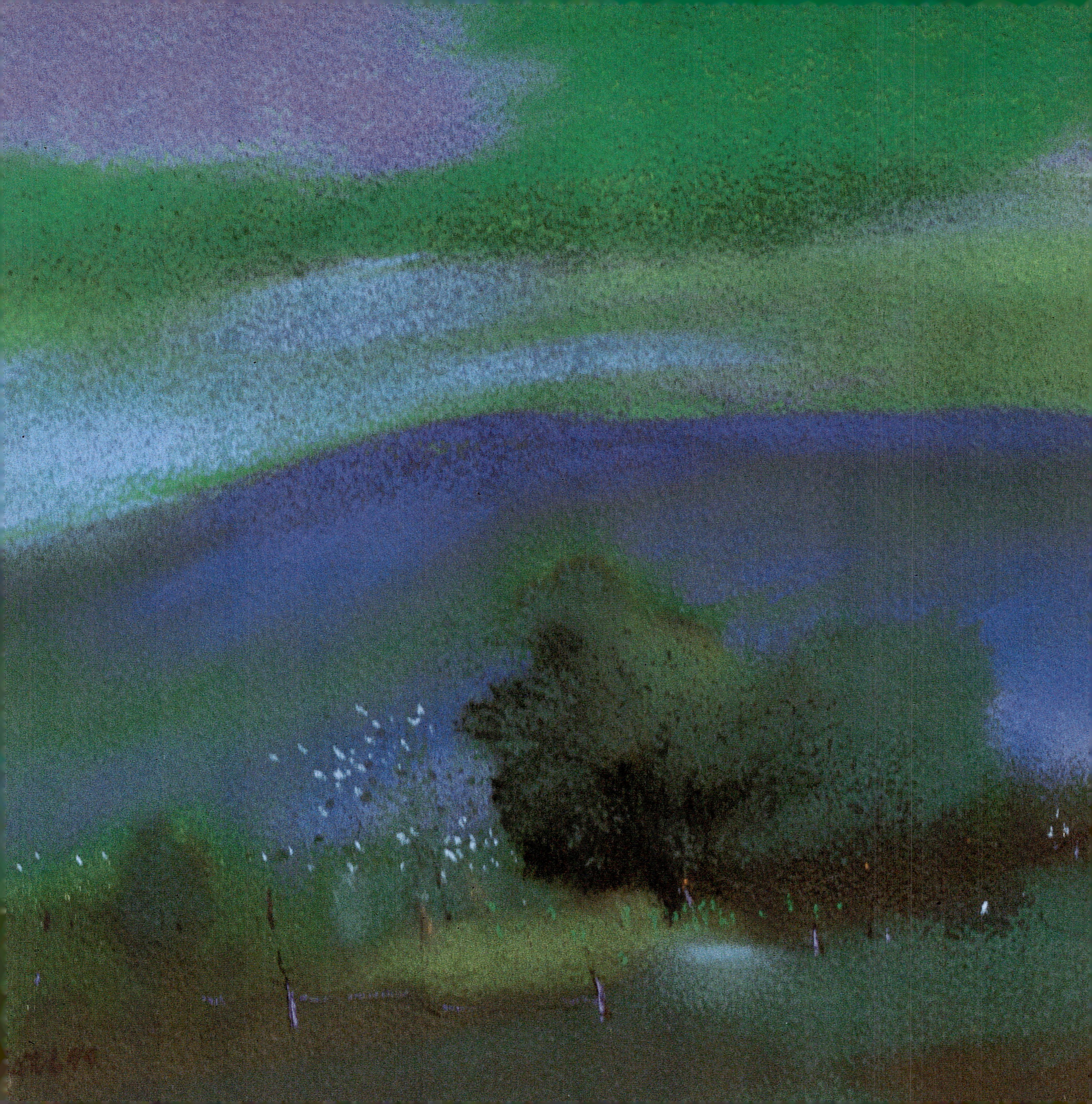

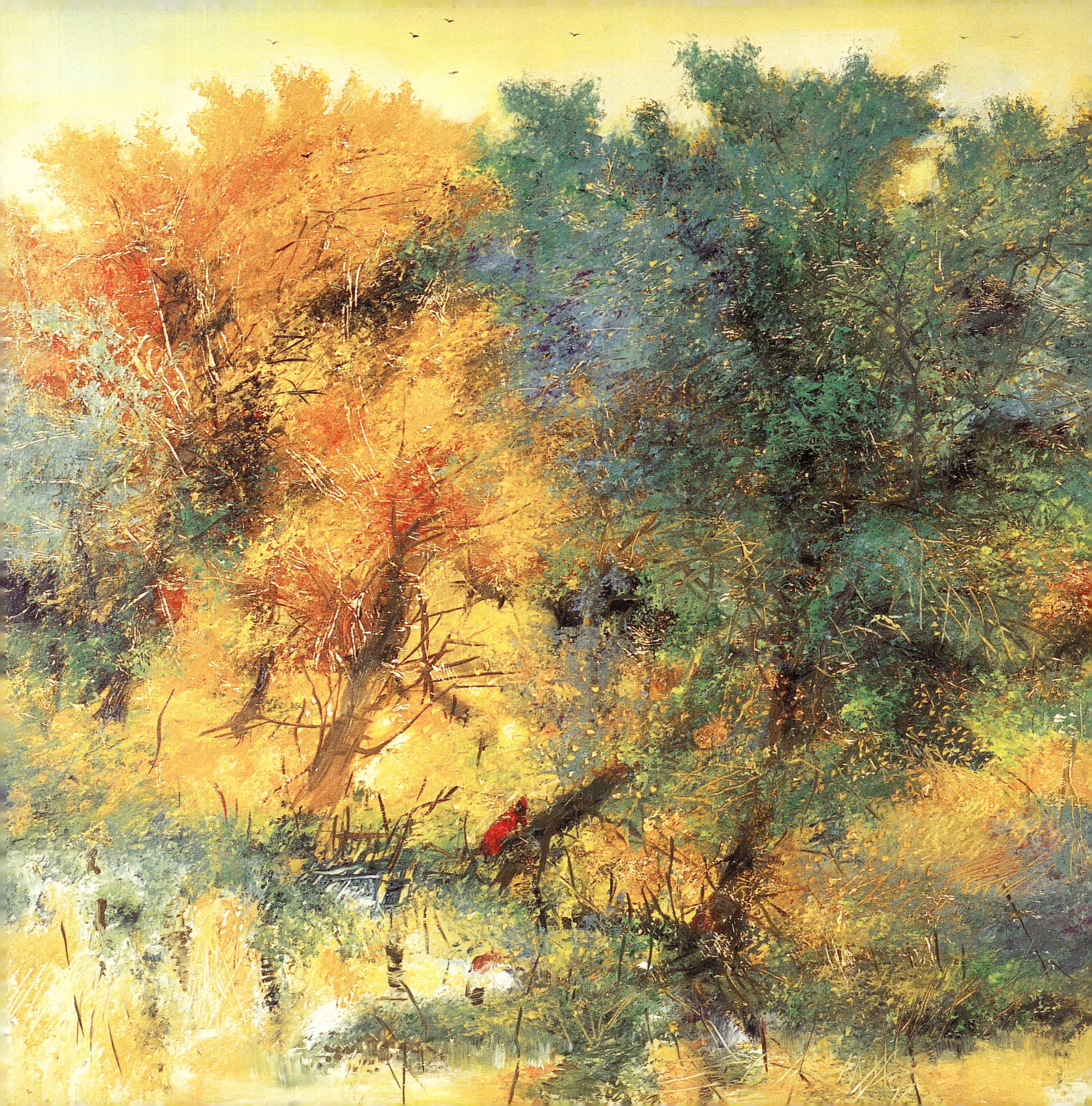

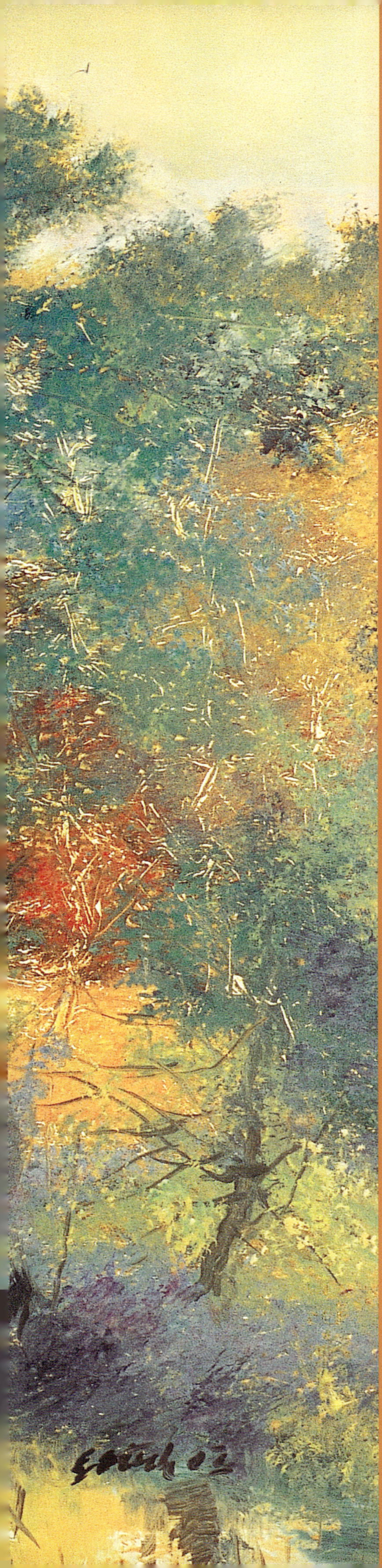

the painstaking details that Satish bhai had gone into despite pressures, to make sure that we were more than comfortable. Very soon we were savouring the coveted status of 'baratis', enjoying the importance that came our way.

Until the very end I could not unravel the many dimensions to Satish bhai's personality. He always said that he drew inspiration from the small wonders of Nature that normally went unnoticed. Every facet of his life was undoubtedly a direct manifestation of Nature in its purest form.

Facing page: Oil on canvas, 2003.

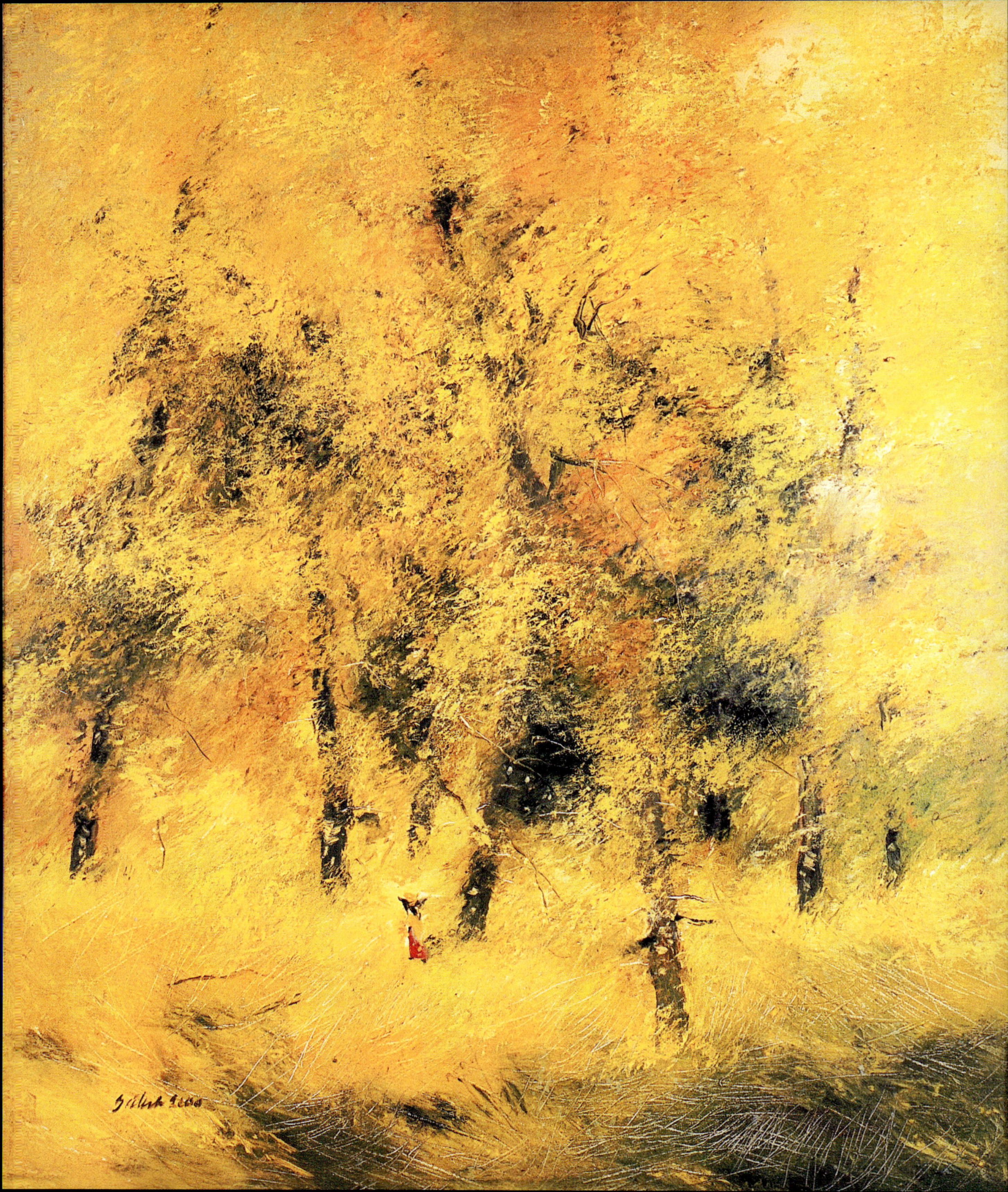

Oil on canvas, 2000.

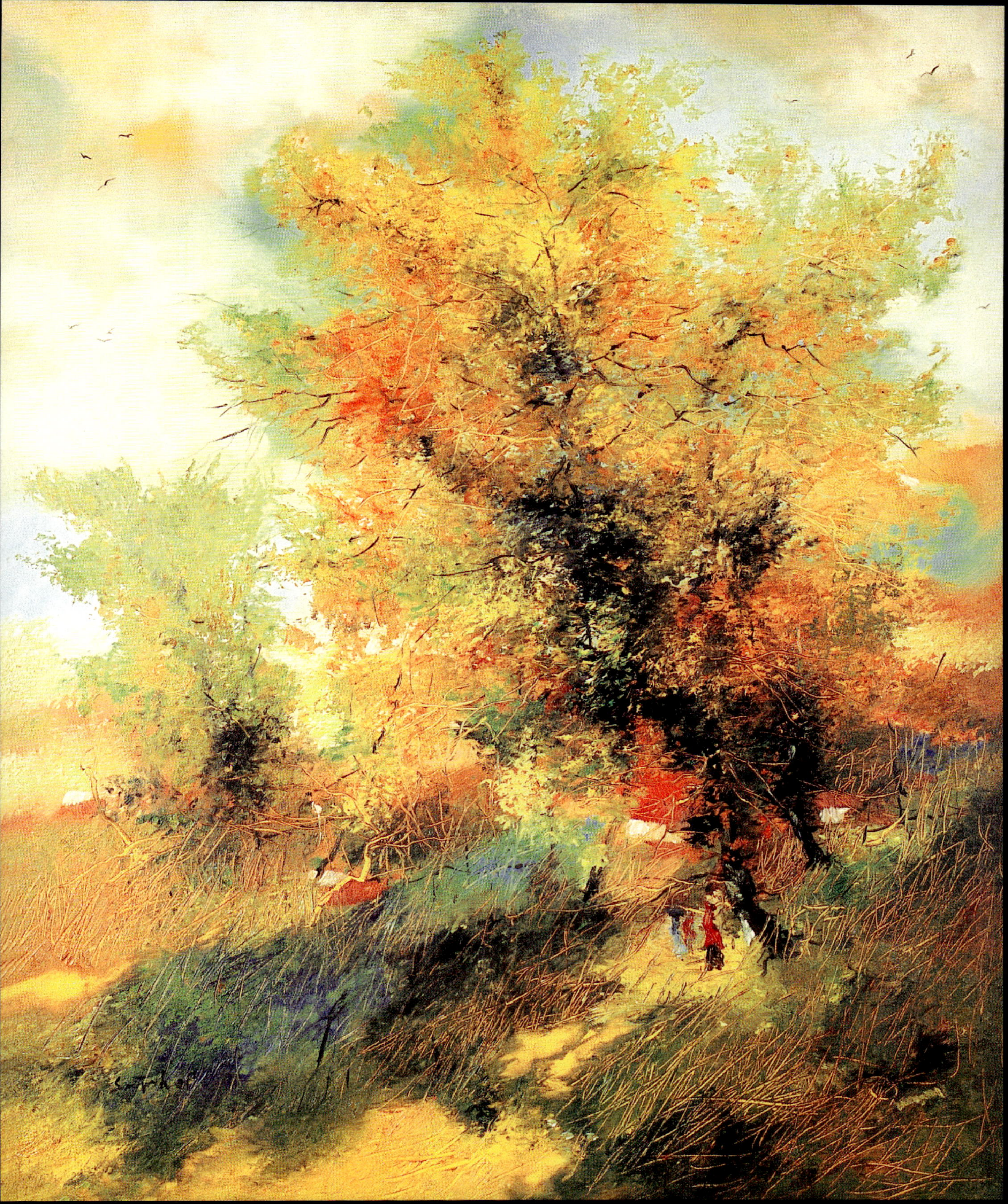

Oil on canvas.

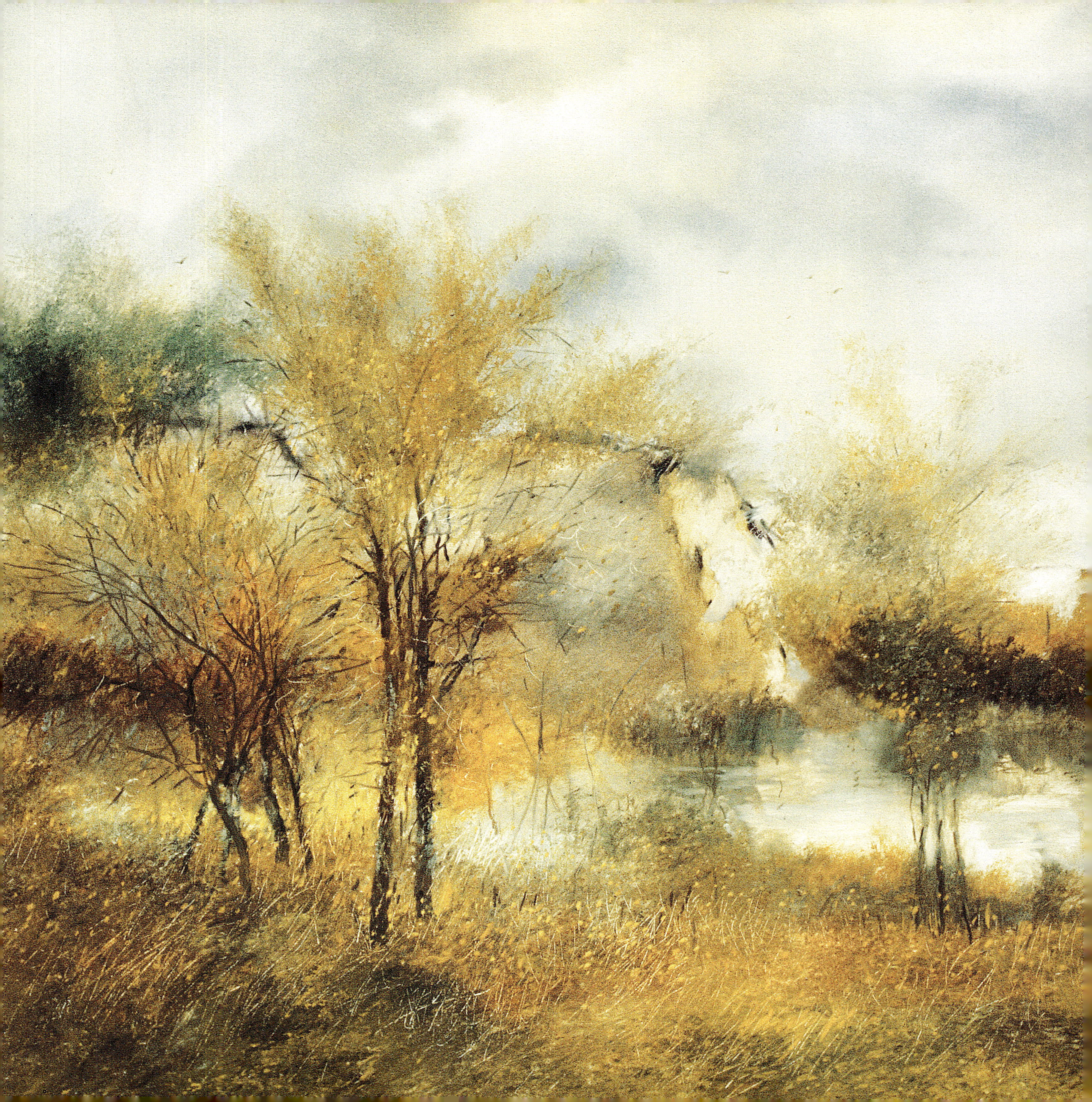

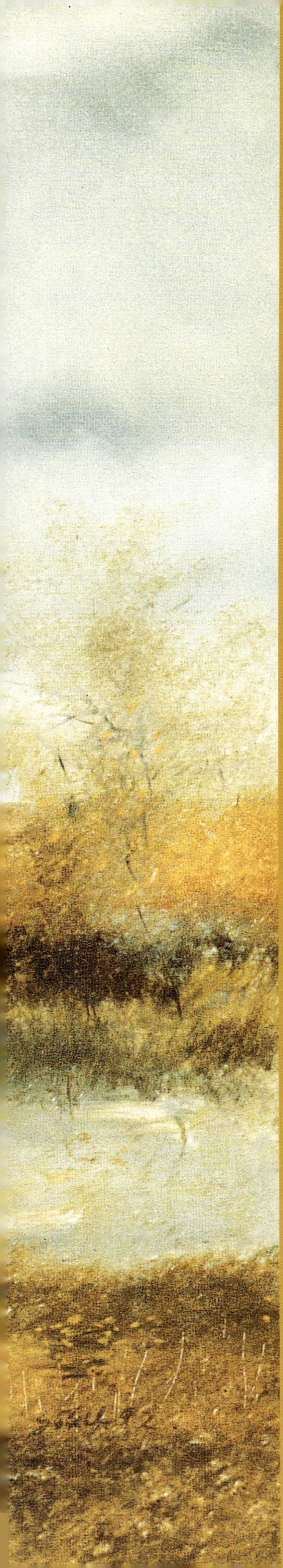

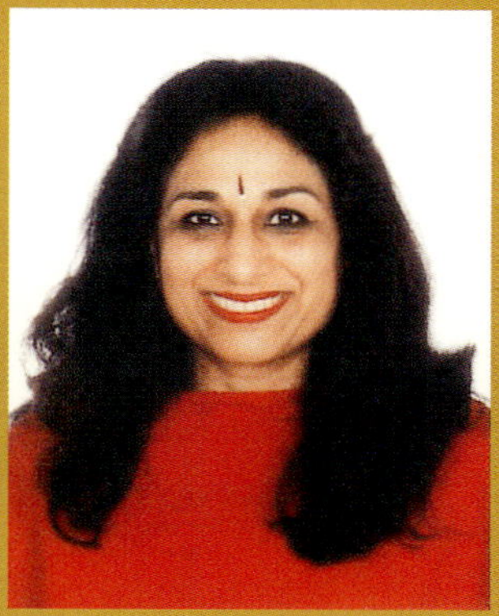

A Friend Indeed

Rita Sinha
Friend

Whenever I see a painting done by Satish, I get a feeling of inner peace. Nature seems to be at its calmest best and yet there is a subtle movement in every frame and virtually in every stroke of the brush. What fascinated me the most about his paintings was the tiny speck of red seen in the backdrop and yet quite prominent. When I asked him about it, he admitted shyly that this red dot represented Meenakshi. This gives us an idea how deeply involved Satish was in both his paintings and his family.

He told me that he had stopped putting up exhibitions of his paintings

Facing page: Oil on canvas, 1992.

in Uttar Pradesh. But when I was posted as director, North Central Zone Cultural Centre (NCZCC), Allahabad, I pleaded with him to exhibit his paintings at the NCZCC art gallery. Without a moment's hesitation, he complied with my request. He got his paintings framed and packed and then transported them himself to Allahabad. Needless to say, the exhibition was highly appreciated. There was nothing that Satish was not willing to do for a friend.

It was around this time that I was having some problem in retaining the house allotted to me. Satish went out of his way to help me retain the house, which I was legally entitled to.

Meenakshi has an excellent wardrobe. Whenever I complimented her on the beautiful saree or salwar suit that she wore, I always got the same reply, "a present from Satish". Meenakshi once told me a very sweet story about a birthday gift from Satish. Knowing how much she loved chocolates, Satish bought her a huge

Facing page: Watercolour on paper, 1993.

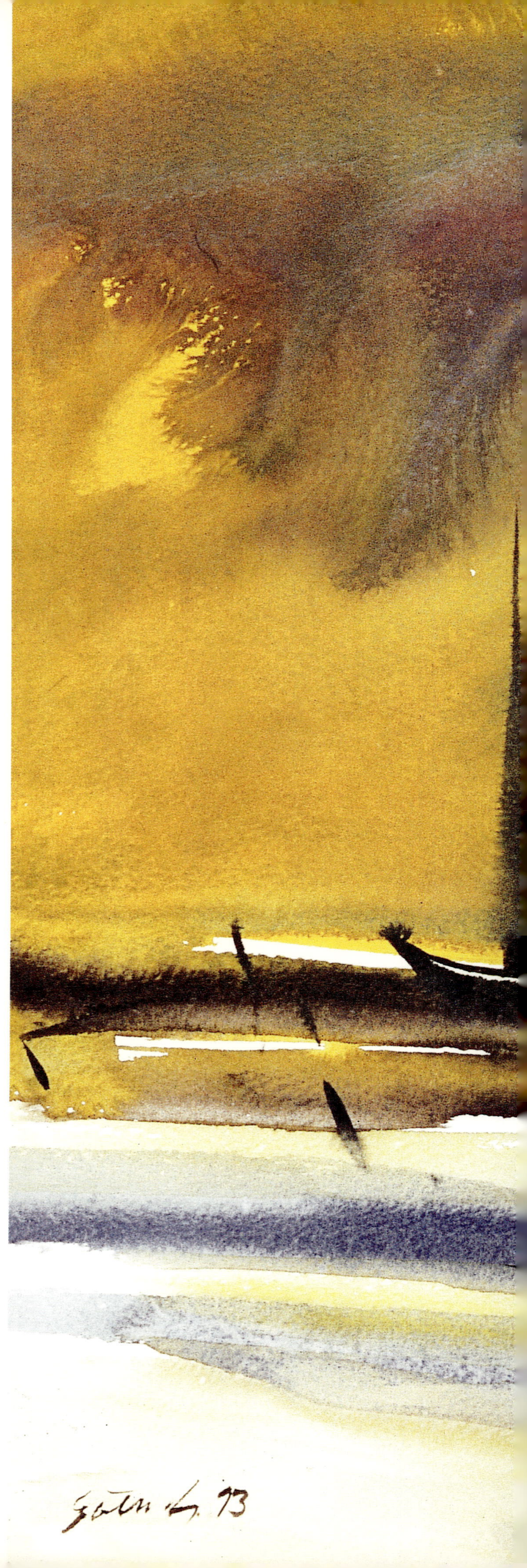

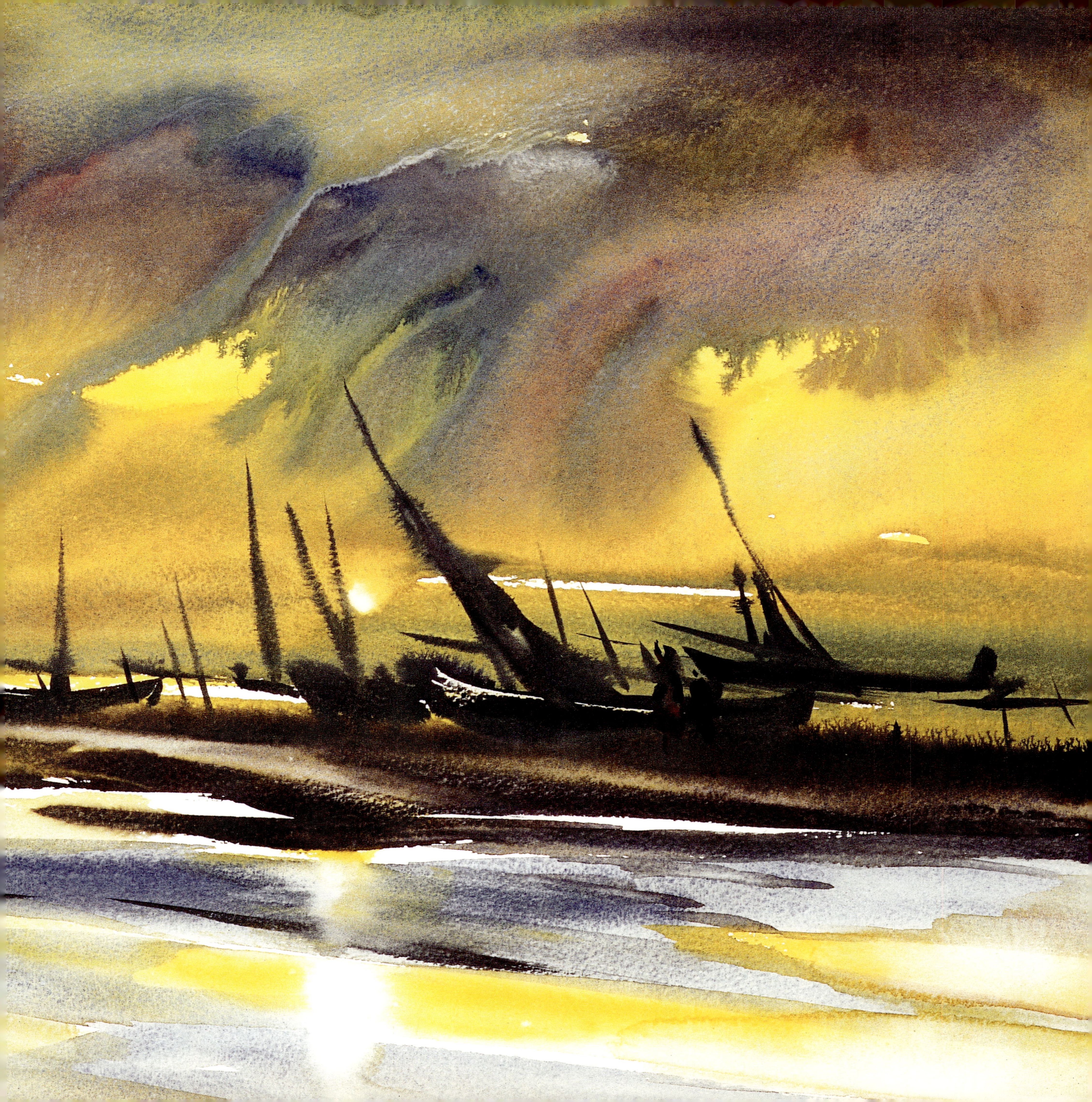

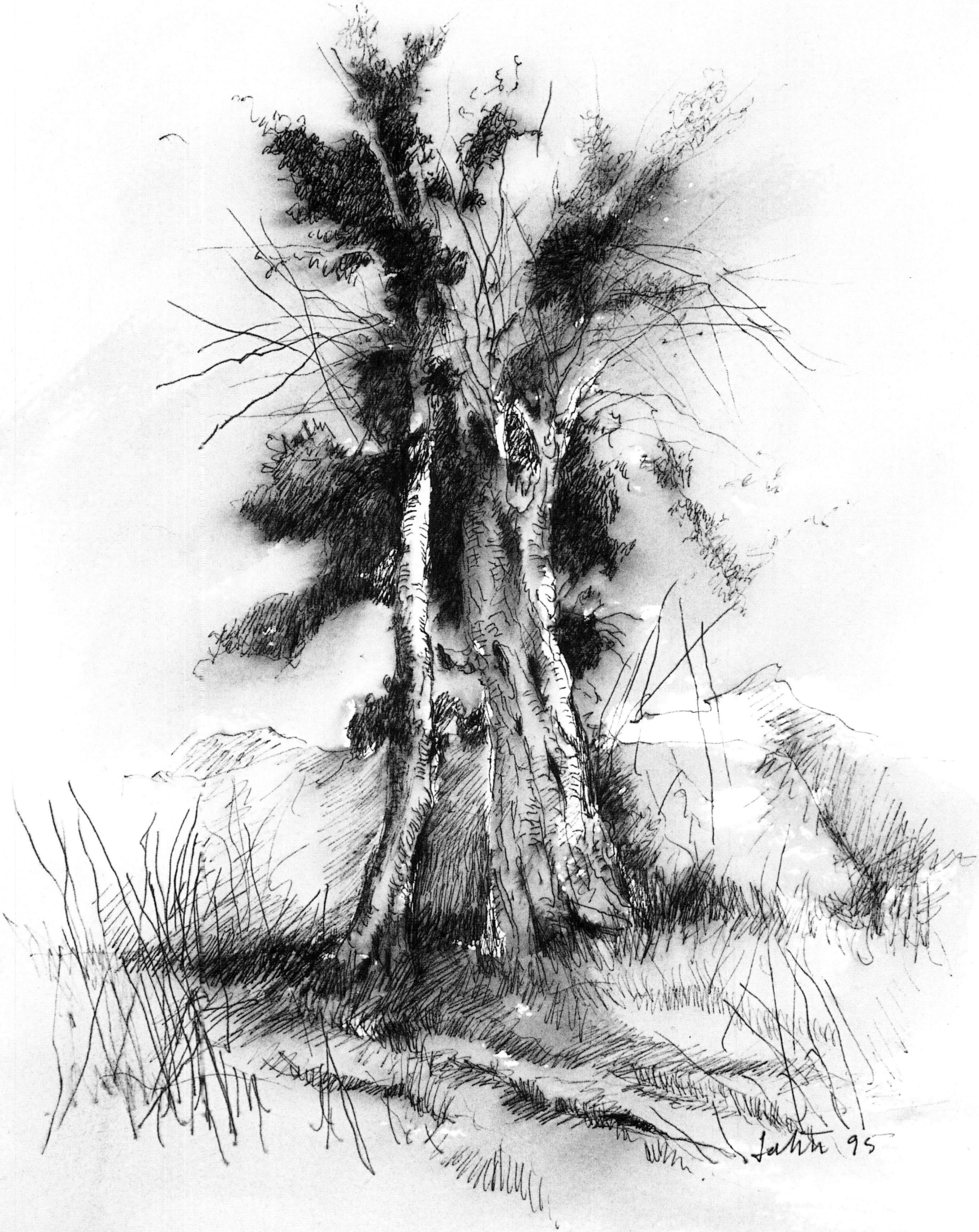

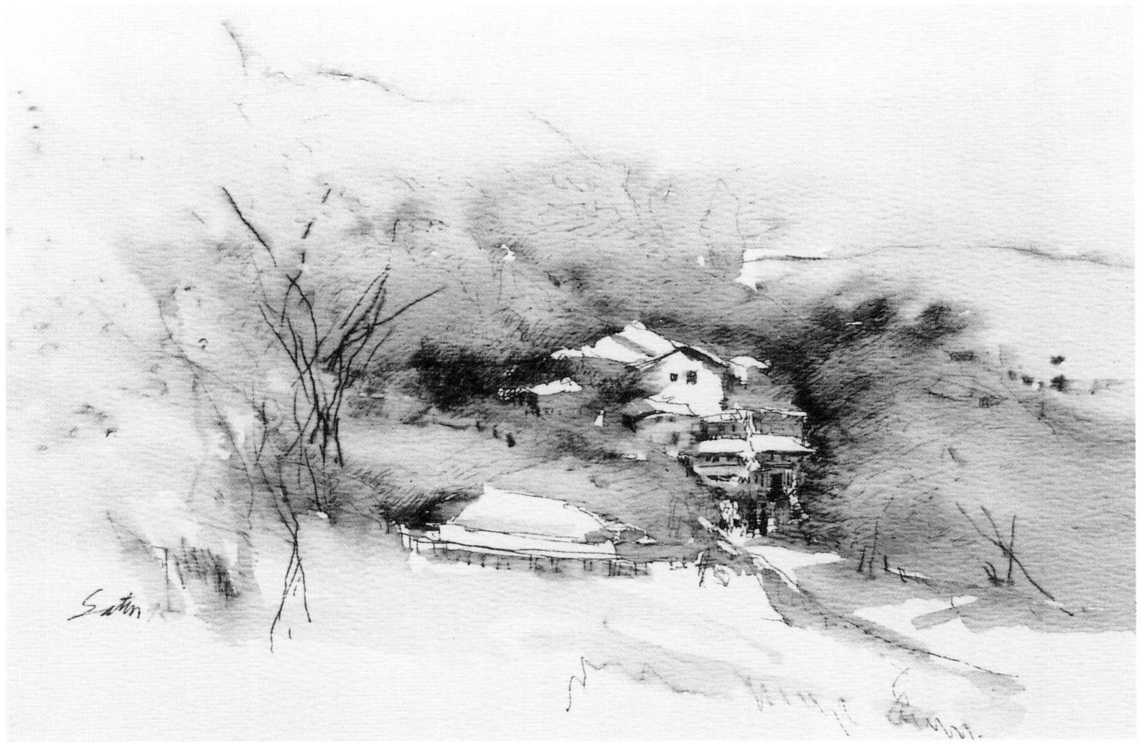

Pen and Ink on paper.
Facing page: Pen and Ink on paper, 1995.

box of exquisite chocolates. But those days the doctors had put Meenakshi on a strict diet. So, while handing over the chocolates to Meenakshi, Satish pleaded with her not to eat them!

When it came to art, Satish had boundless energy and great organizational skills. As chairman of the UP Lalit Kala Akademi, both these qualities came to the fore. It was during his tenure that the academy started several activities, and the art galleries were made air-conditioned and modernized. He also started the emporium in the basement of the academy after clearing up the great mess there. He was the first one to bring out presentation sets of reproductions of great masters.

Satish's paintings will always remind us of him. May his soul now rest in as serene a place as his brush always painted.

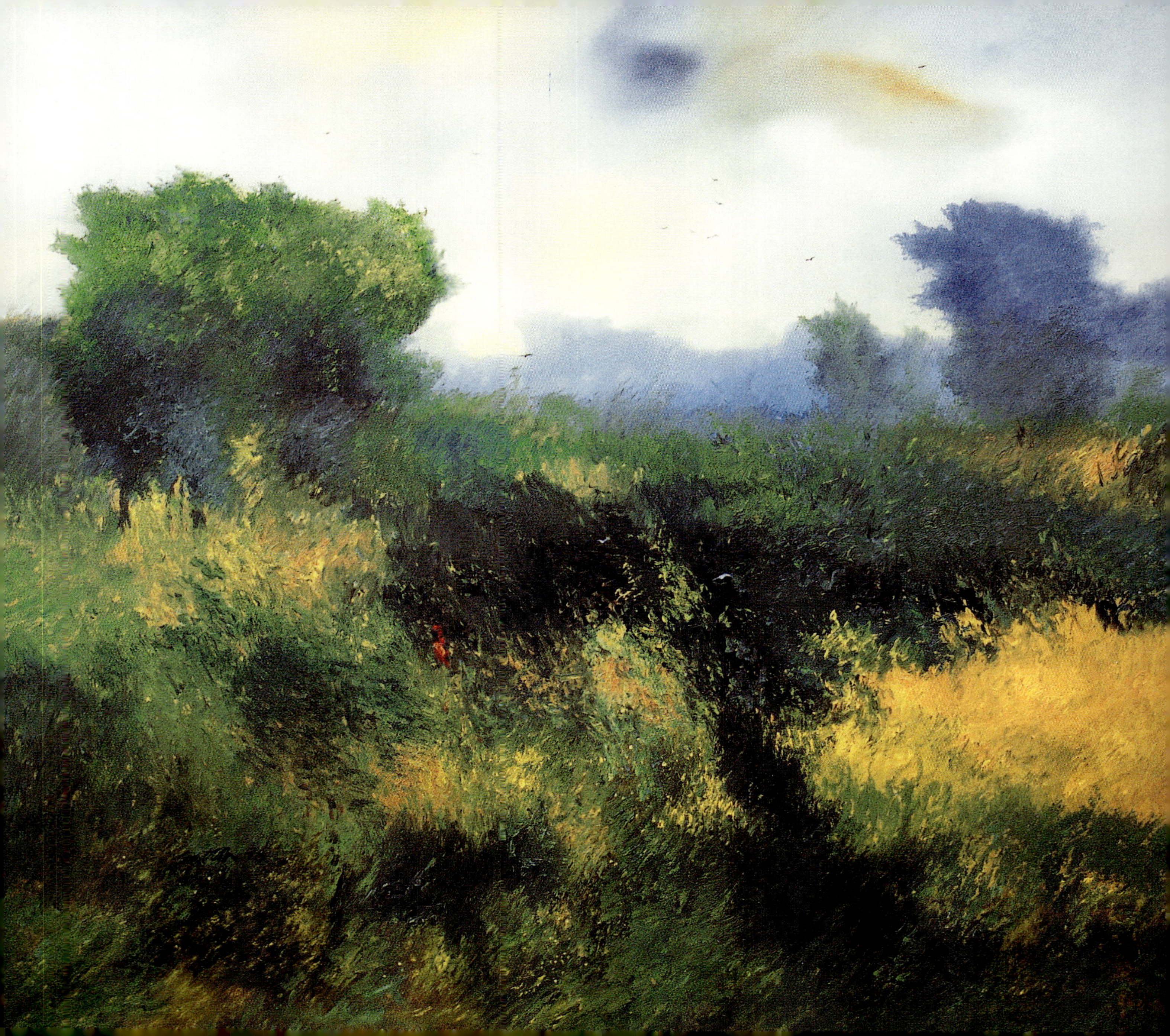

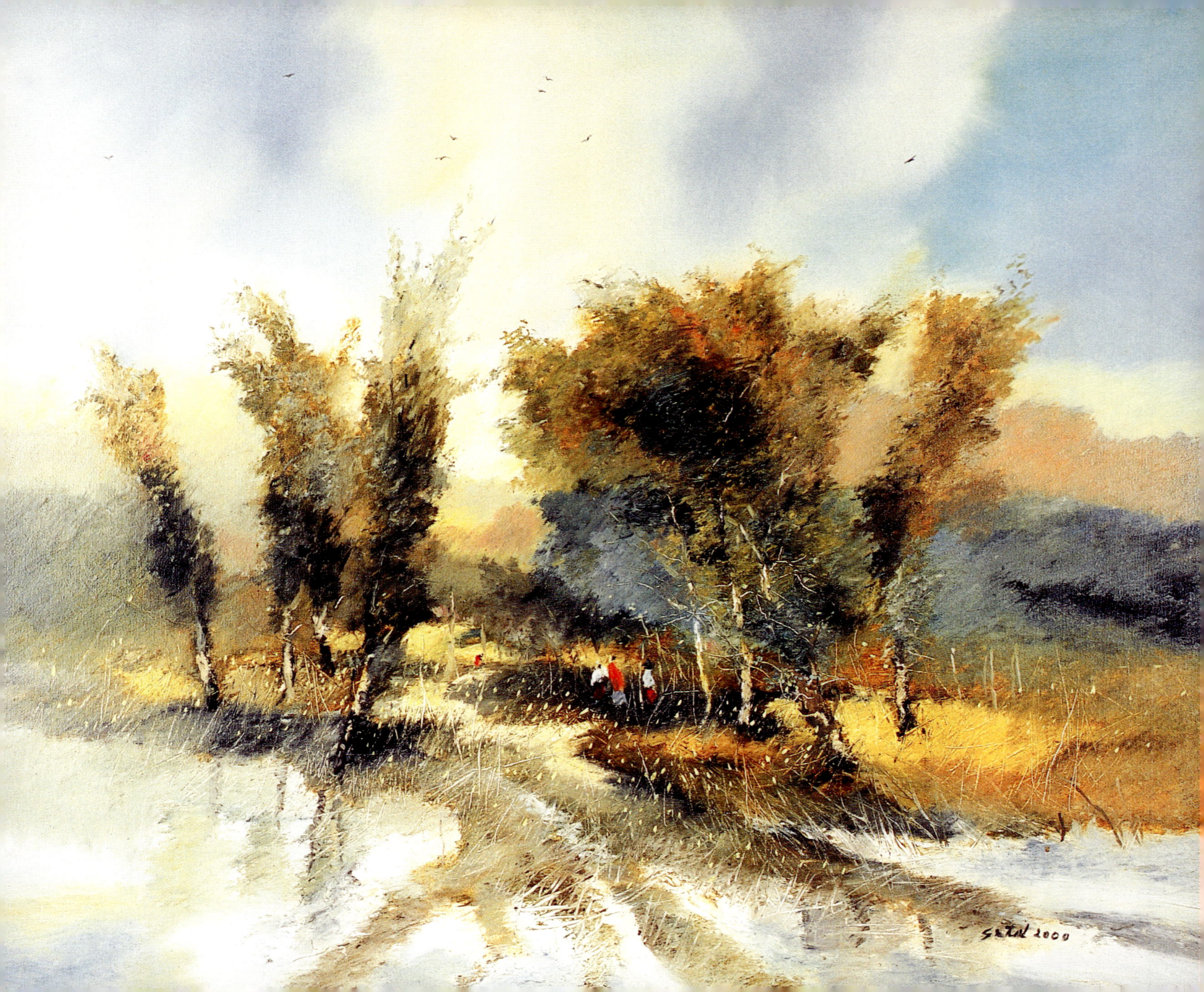

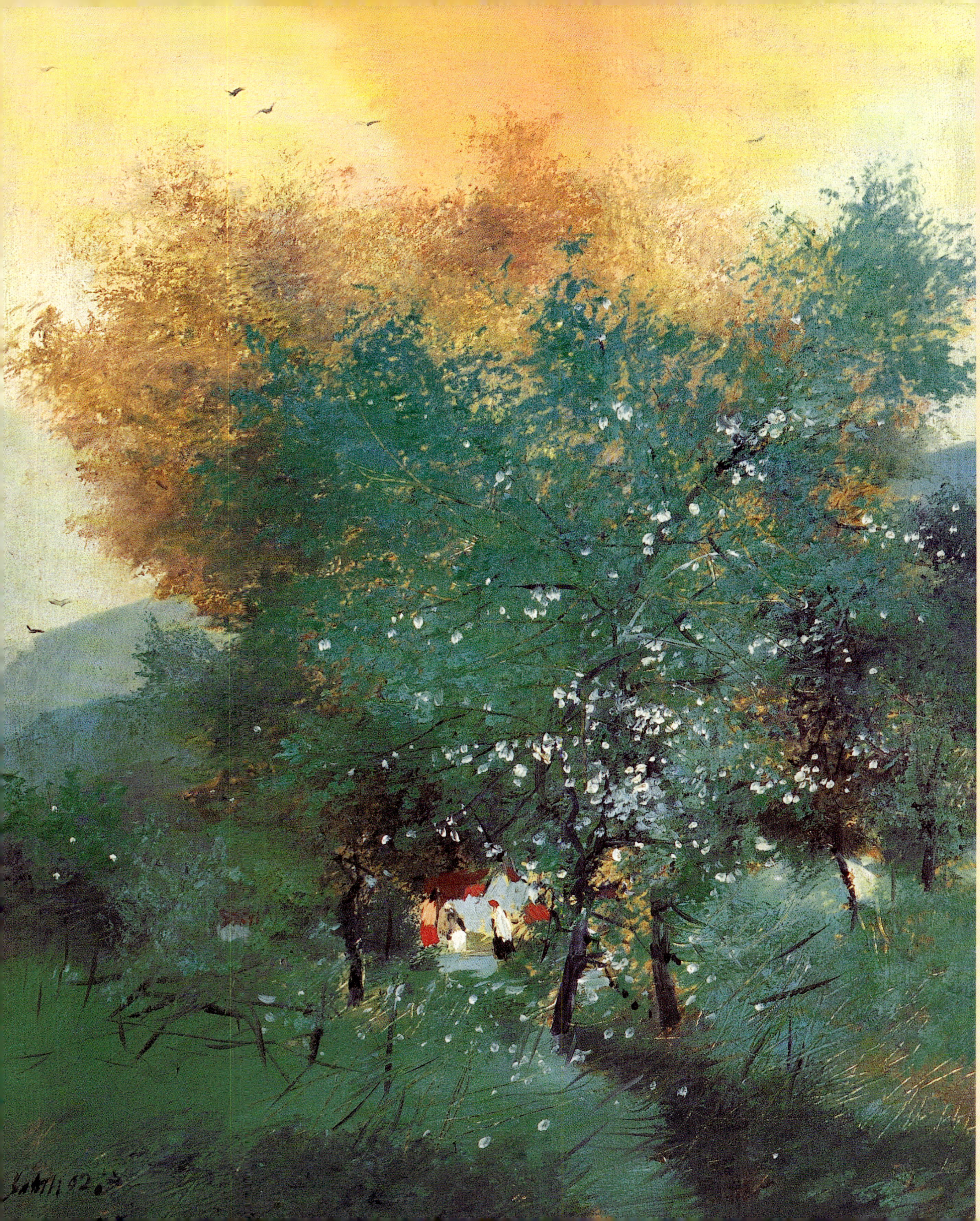

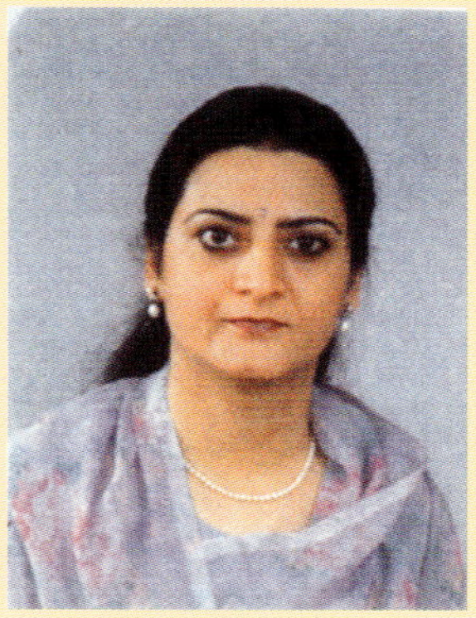

A Remarkable Resilience

Meenakshi Pahwa
Friend

The first time I met Satish bhai was at our common friend Meera di's place. After the routine introduction my husband Sudhir and I settled down for a nice chat with him. Sudhir knew him and had always admired his work. I had often been told little tales about how he had overcome the vicissitudes he had faced as an artist. Yet, when I met him, he seemed to be unscathed.

When Meera di shifted back to Delhi, we frequently met up at Rita's. By then, he had reached greater heights in his profession, yet he never flaunted his achievements. To talk to him was a veritable education – he could talk easily on any subject. Though we were fully aware of his stature as an artist, yet Sudhir and I never felt small in his presence. He would never talk down to people. Also, we never felt the age difference.

Satish bhai was magnanimous – his paintings graced the homes of his innumerable friends. As an artist, he never pandered to the dictates of commercialism, but let his heart rule his head.

He was essentially a very simple man with very expensive tastes. He was always immaculately turned out – an enthusiasm that he kept up till the last. He bought the finest selection of sarees for Meenakshi – which could only be the prerogative of an aesthete.

Facing page: Oil on canvas, 2002.

We remember very fondly some nice evenings spent in his Gulmohar Apartment. It was very well-appointed, with every little thing in it a virtual insignia of his presence.

Satish bhai valued human beings for their worth. As an employer too, he was caring and thoughtful. His old, trusted driver Shafi was the beneficiary of his munificence. It was absolute anathema for Satish bhai to contemplate Shafi's dismissal despite the latter's failing eye-sight. In today's age, where we celebrate perfection and excellence, where anyone who is fallible is dropped like a hot brick, Satish bhai embraced the imperfections in Shafi the same way as he achieved perfection in his paintings.

As a son he was extremely devoted, particularly to his mother. He would often remember how she had played a stellar role in his having taken to the fine arts. It was she who persuaded Satish bhai's father to let him opt out of an engineering college in which he had been enrolled.

 Facing page: Oil on canvas, 1992.

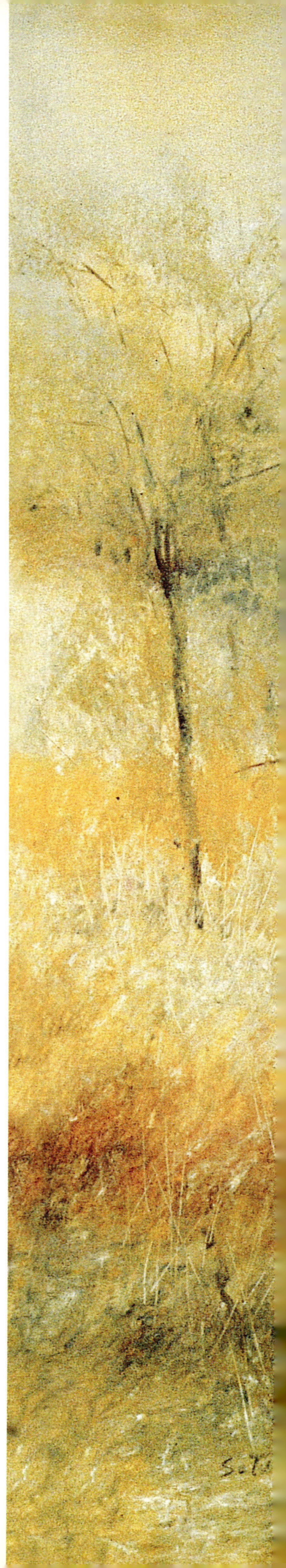

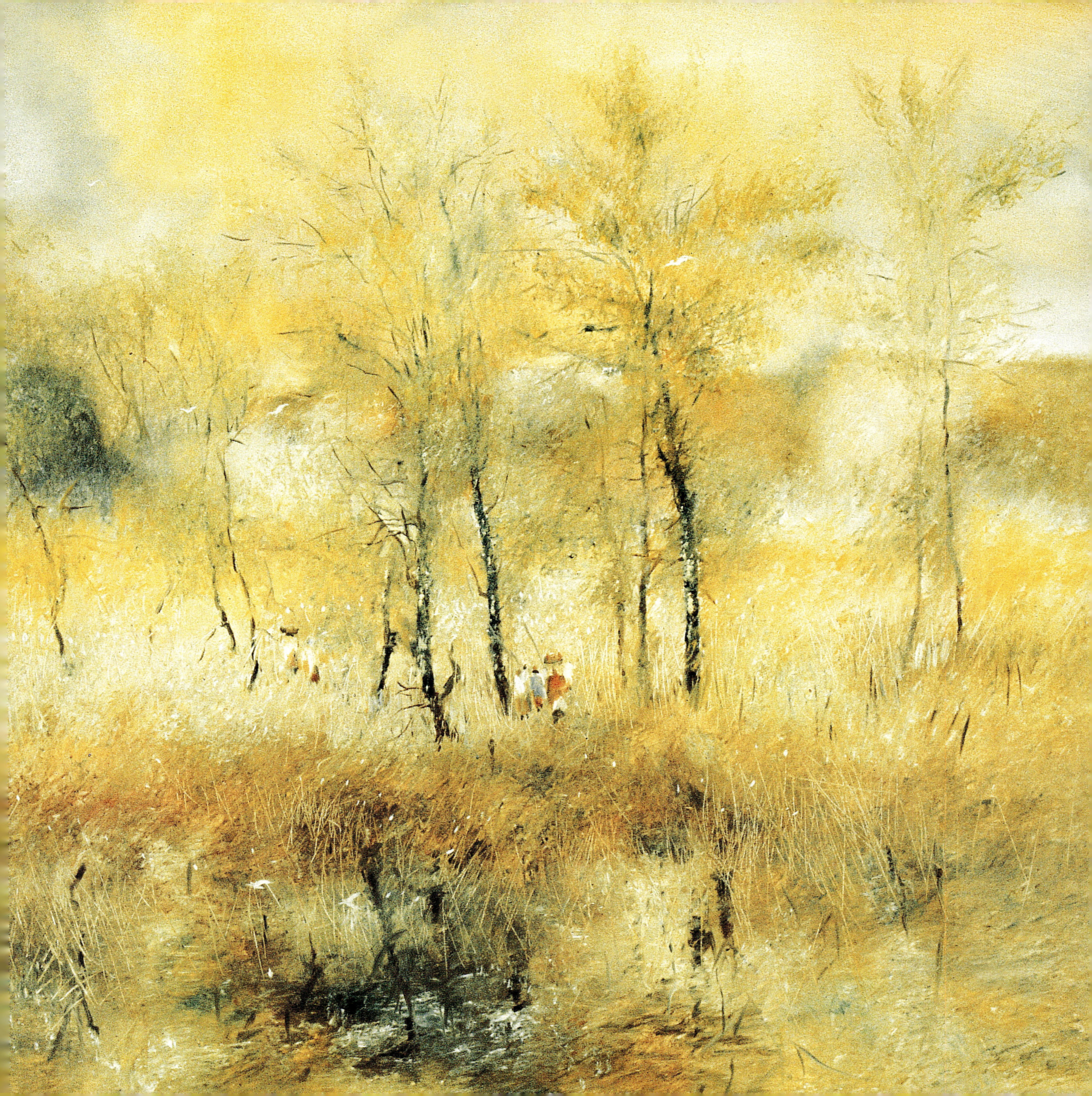

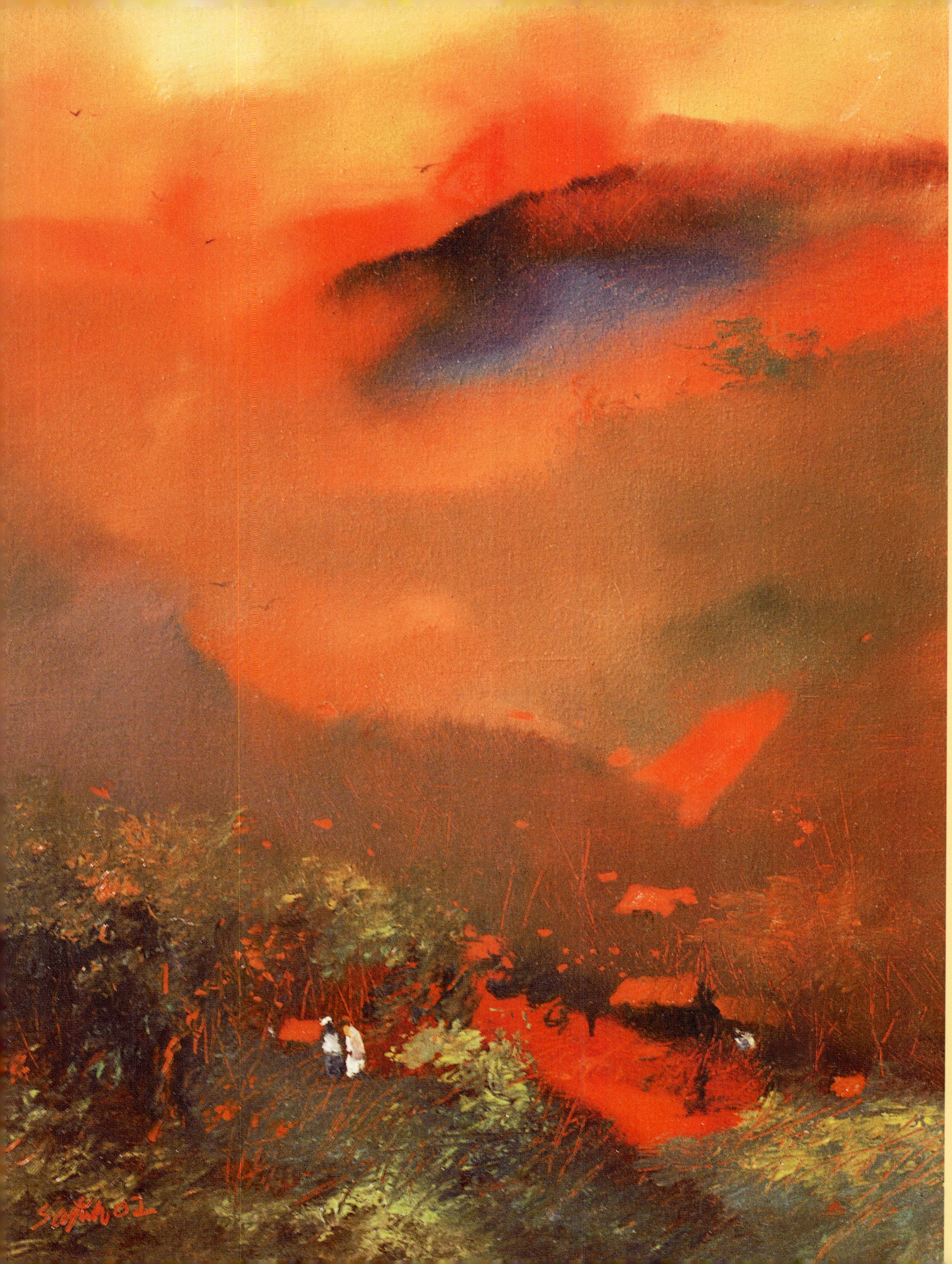

In the marriage of Meenakshi and Satish bhai, we often witnessed a happy togetherness. He went along with her just as she went along with him. In fact, it is this togetherness that has sustained Meenakshi in her irreparable loss, as she is so rich in her memories of him. She is a woman of resilience and stoicism. During his long period of illness, she ministered to his needs with a smile. Thinking about both of them, I am reminded of what I read sometime ago, which very aptly sums up their relationship:

"Lost love is still love... It takes a different form, that's all. You can't see their smile or bring them food or tousle their hair or move them around a dance floor. But when those senses weaken, another heightens. Memory. Memory becomes your partner. You nurture it. You hold it. Life has to end, love doesn't."

We collectively admired Satish bhai's indefatigable will in combating his ill-health. The most unique thing about him was that despite his various health setbacks, he would never let the conversation veer towards it. He would very imperceptibly steer it towards yet another engrossing detail about something or the other. In fact it was his will power that gave him those 'added' years. Medically, his prognosis was very bleak. Yet he surprised everyone around him when he took his own time to get Siddharth married to Pooja.

All of us noticed the serenity with which he went about his business. All the doctors in town thought that time was running out for him – yet Satish bhai had no such etchings on his mindscape! He went about his job with a resilience that did yield the requisite results.

Knowing a man like Satish bhai was indeed a blessing. As there were a myriad hues in his paintings, so were these present on his emotional palette.

Facing page: Oil on canvas, 2002.

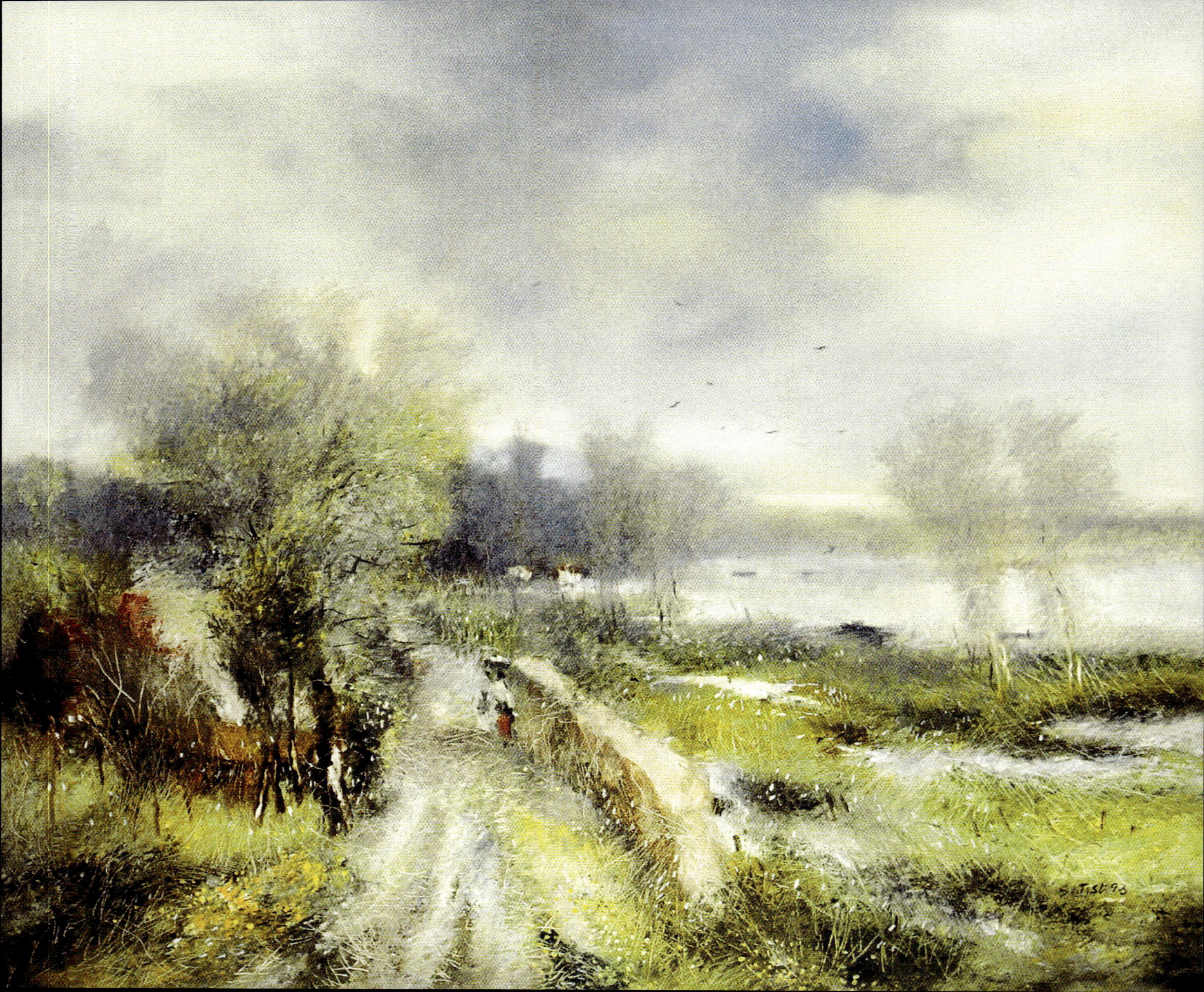

Oil on canvas, 1993.

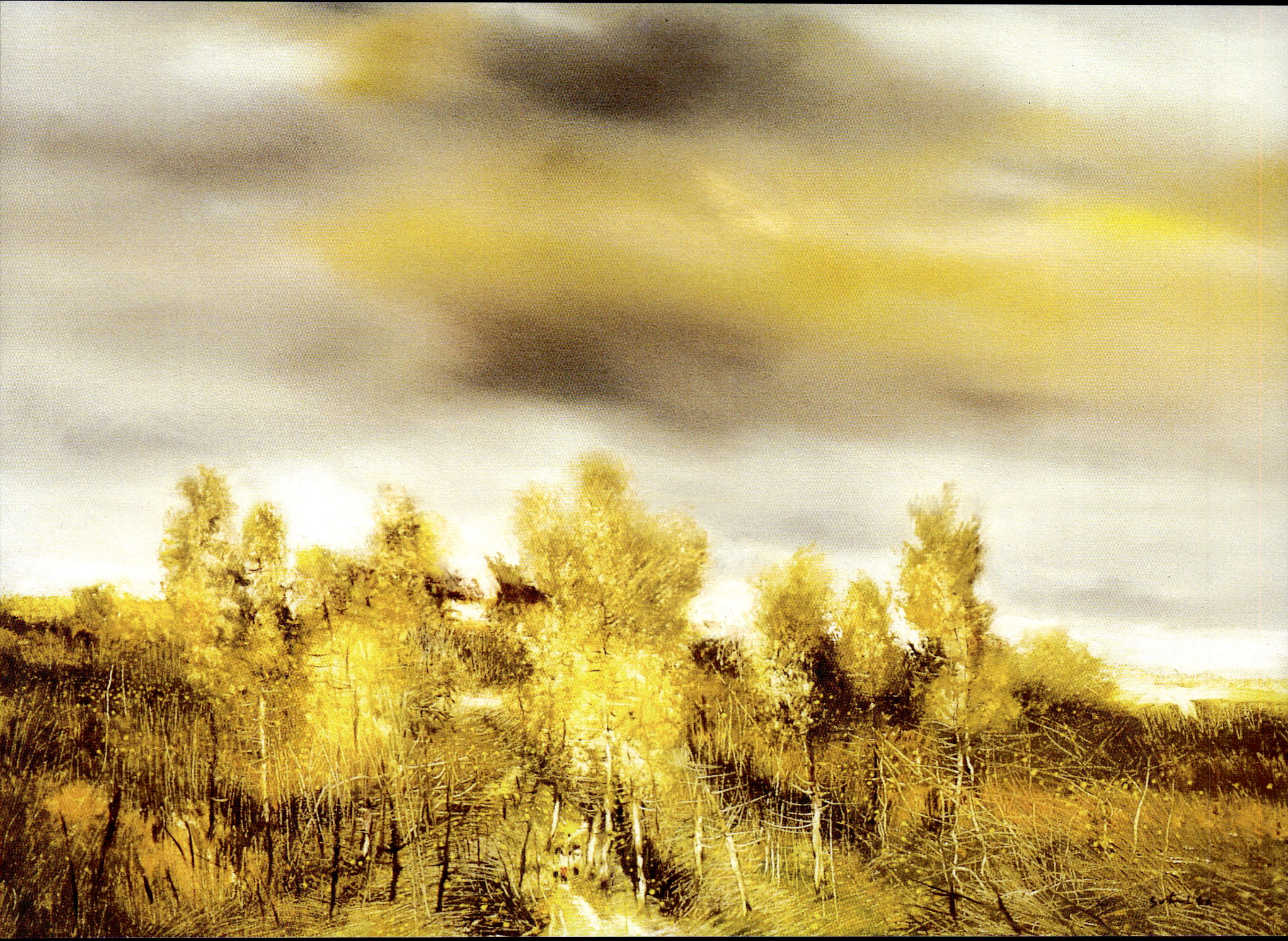

Oil on canvas.

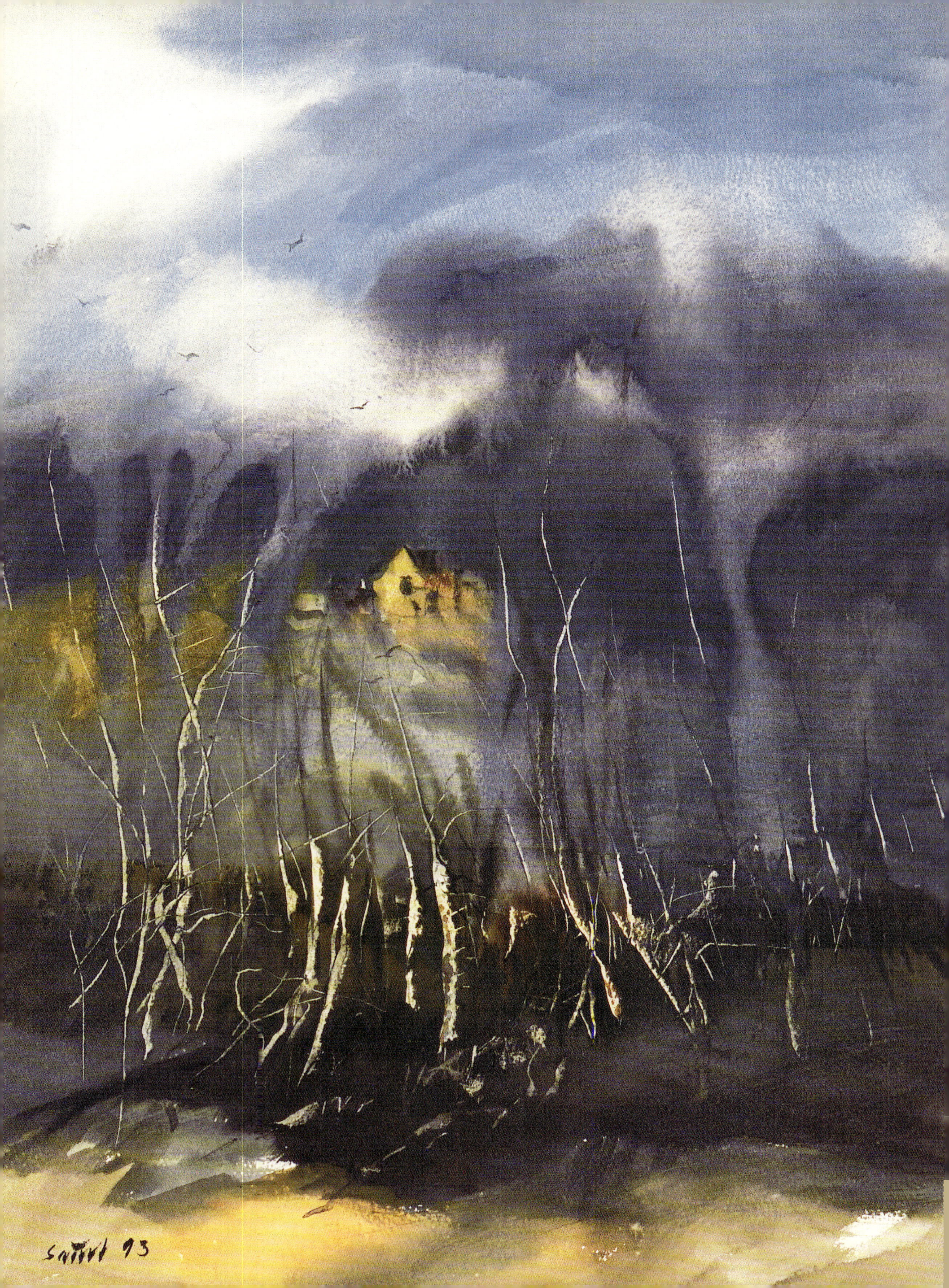

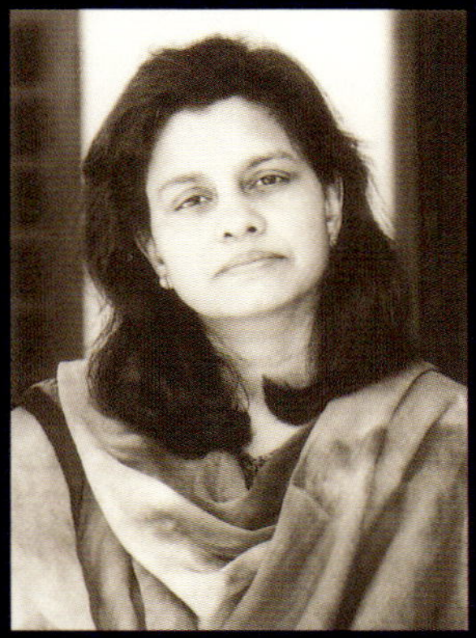

A Fond Teacher

Manju Tayal
Friend

Marriage brought me to Lucknow, and a love for art brought the artist Satish Chandra into my life.

It was in the 1970s that I moved to Lucknow. I was passionate about painting and was looking desperately for a guide to help me with my work. I went to meet Satish at his home in the campus of the Arts College. He was very warm and encouraging but firm that he would not teach me! I requested him to the point of begging, but in vain.

Three years later I visited him again with the same request and was pleasantly surprised when he said, "You're still looking for a teacher? You must be really serious and I shall train you." That was the beginning of a beautiful relationship, one that brought joy, creativity and colour into my life.

He had his way of encouraging people. One time he told me that he believed young married girls painted only to do up their homes and that I had proved him totally wrong. There was another time he said that if he put his name on my paintings, they would all sell.

He was unassuming, down to earth, open-hearted and straight-forward and never pretended to be something he was not.

One incident stands out in my mind. We were working on an oil.

Facing page: Watercolour on paper, 1993.

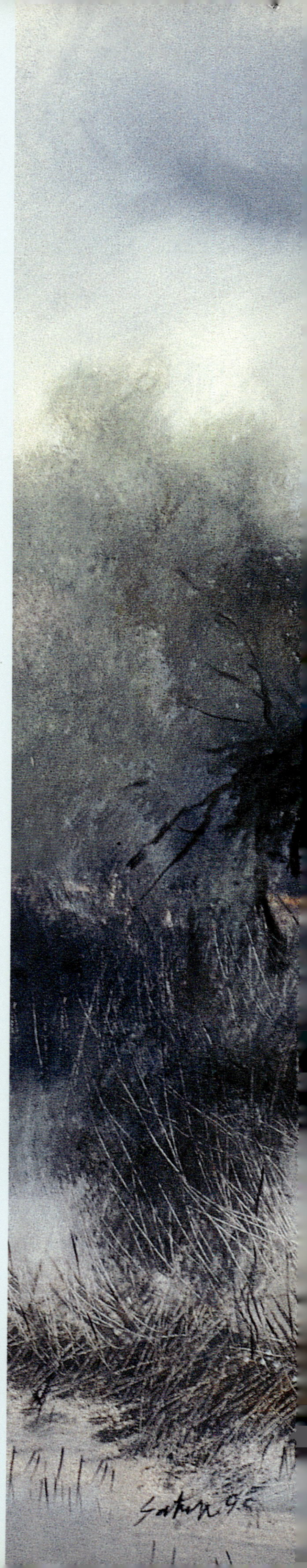

The sky had turned out breathtaking and both of us stood before the canvas mesmerized. Someone walked into the room and said, "What is this? Why have you put yellow for the sky, it ought to be blue." The artist in Satish Chandra disapproved of any kind of directions and restrictions in art. Before I could even react, Sir (that's what I called him) had picked up a brush and covered the sky with blue paint! I still haven't gotten over that – neither the sky, nor the interference, nor Sir's reaction.

A man of convictions, he believed that while creating and expressing his emotions, an artist needed to be left free, bound by no norms, no preconceived notions or ideas, no expectations. If he met with any such preconception his reactions would be erratic and unpredictable.

His other passions included his love for plants and children. He interacted with them in a childlike manner and they naturally responded, and yes, he felt his plants too spoke to him.

Facing page: Oil on canvas, 1995.

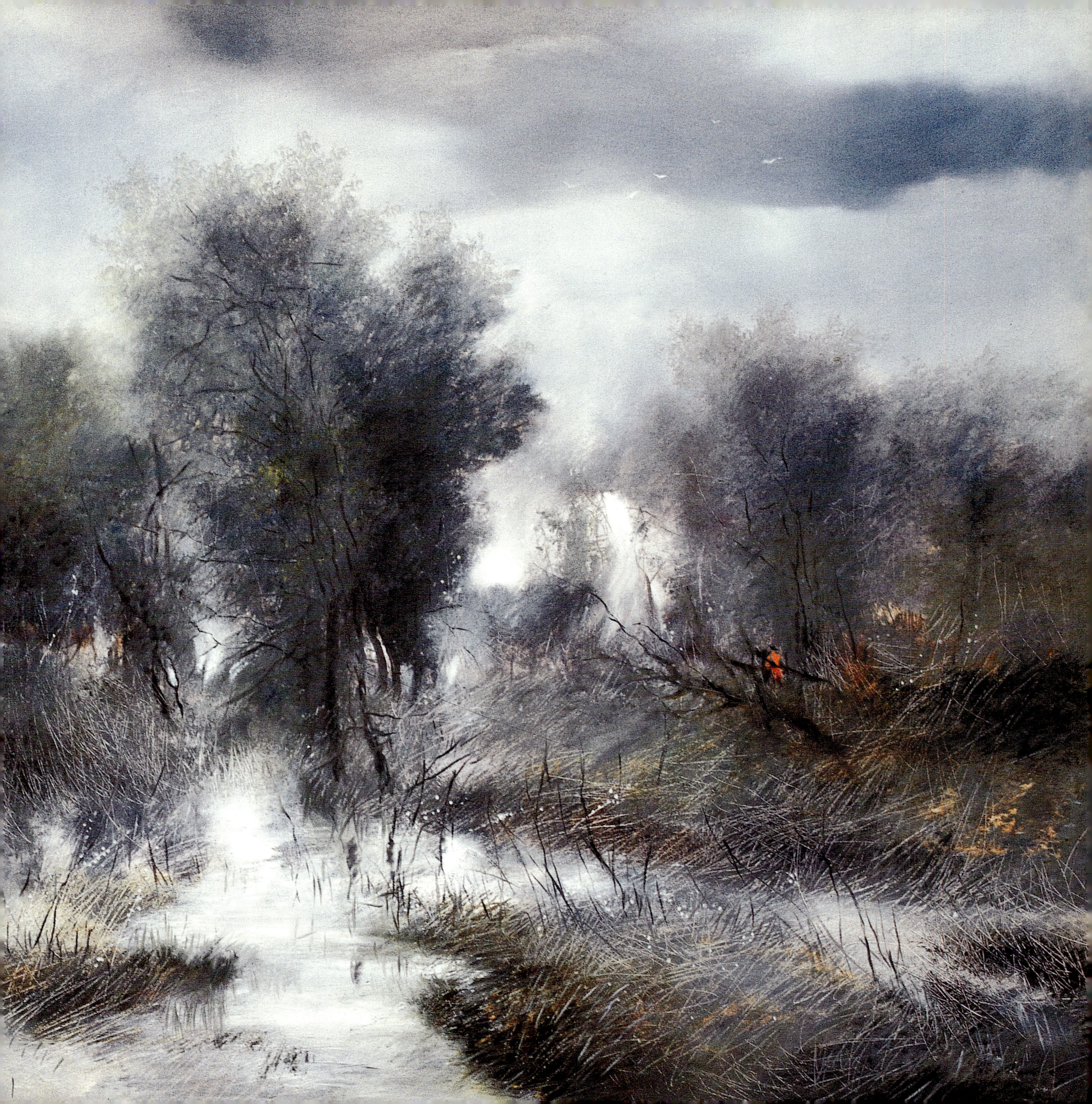

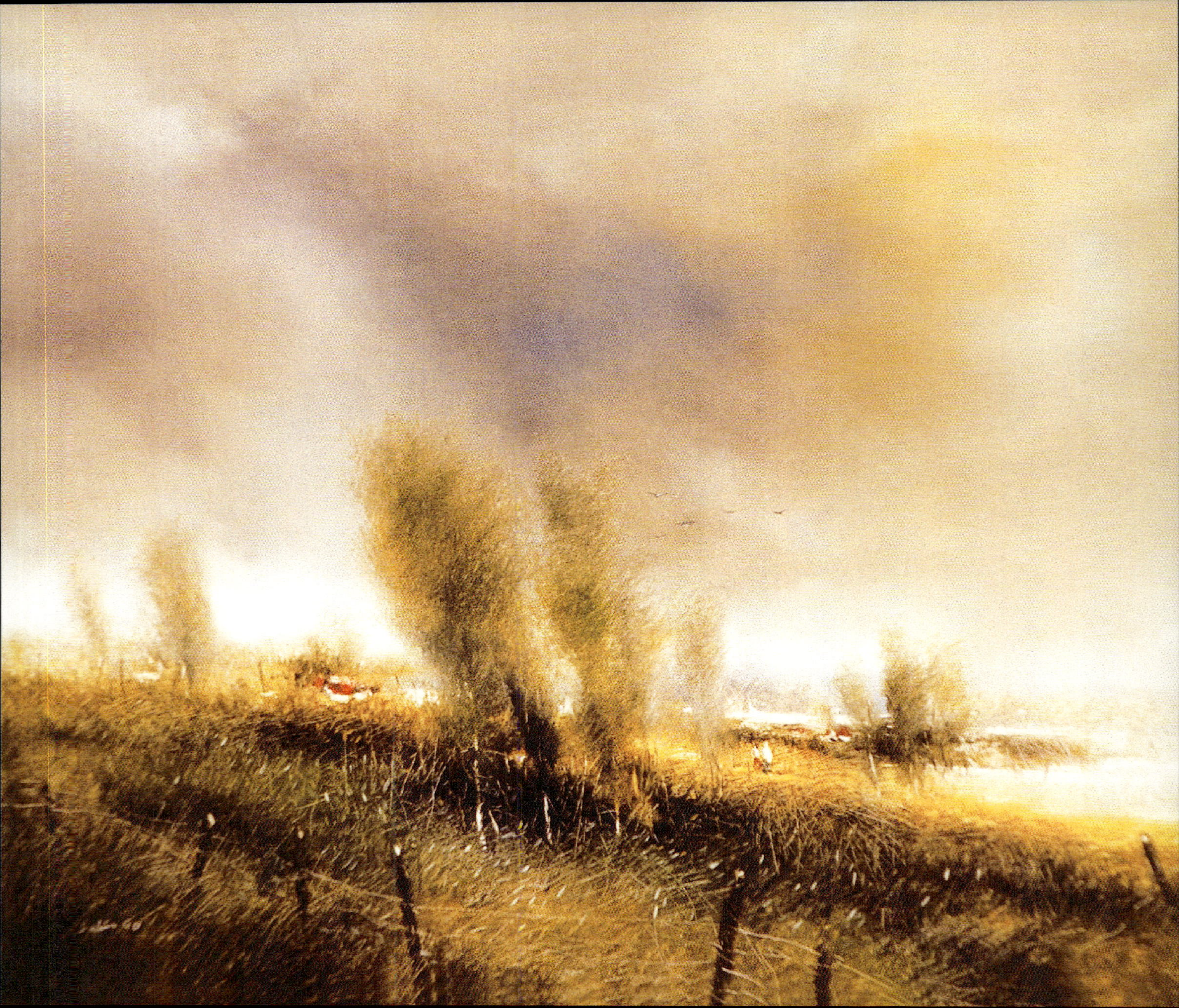

Oil on canvas, 1990.

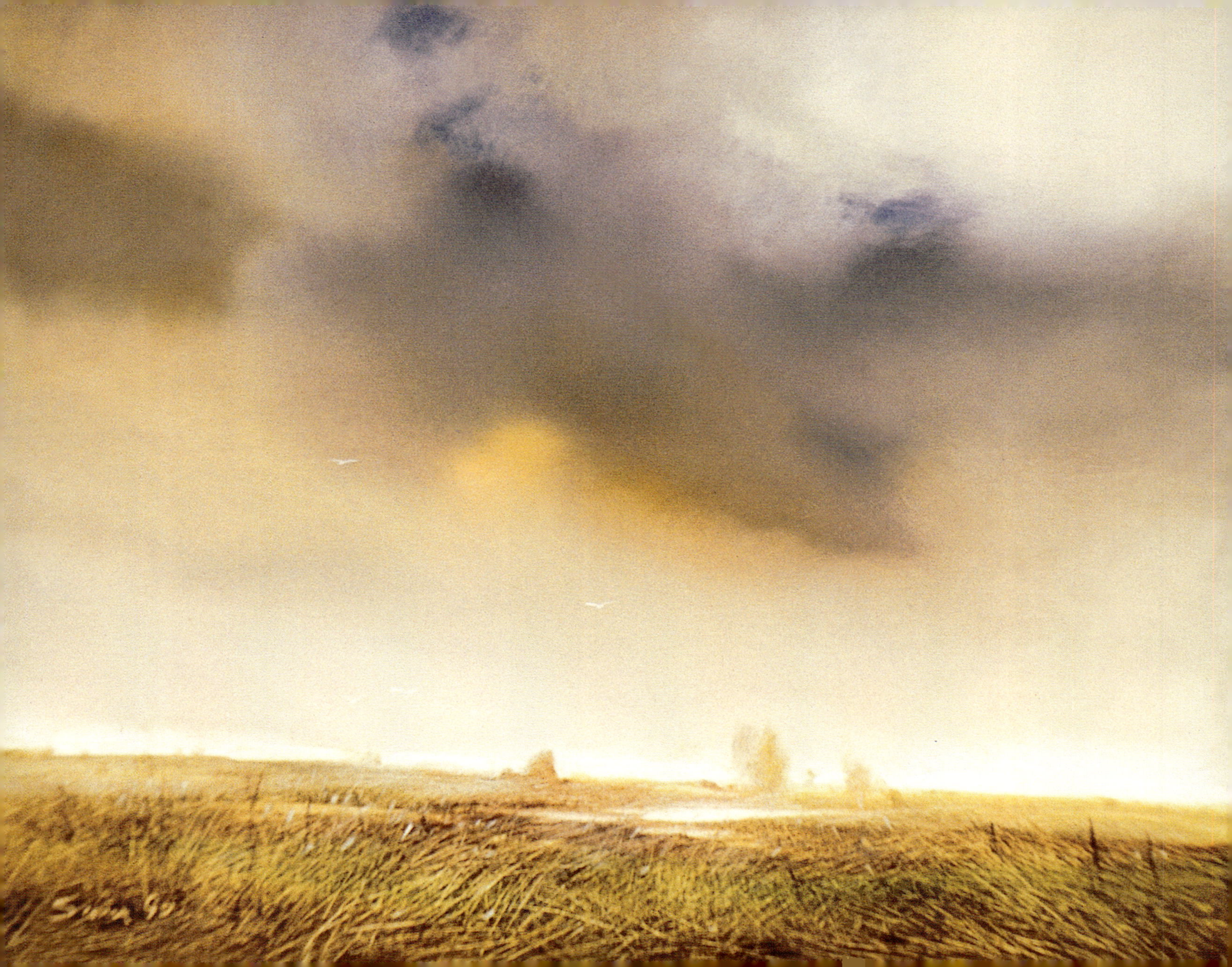

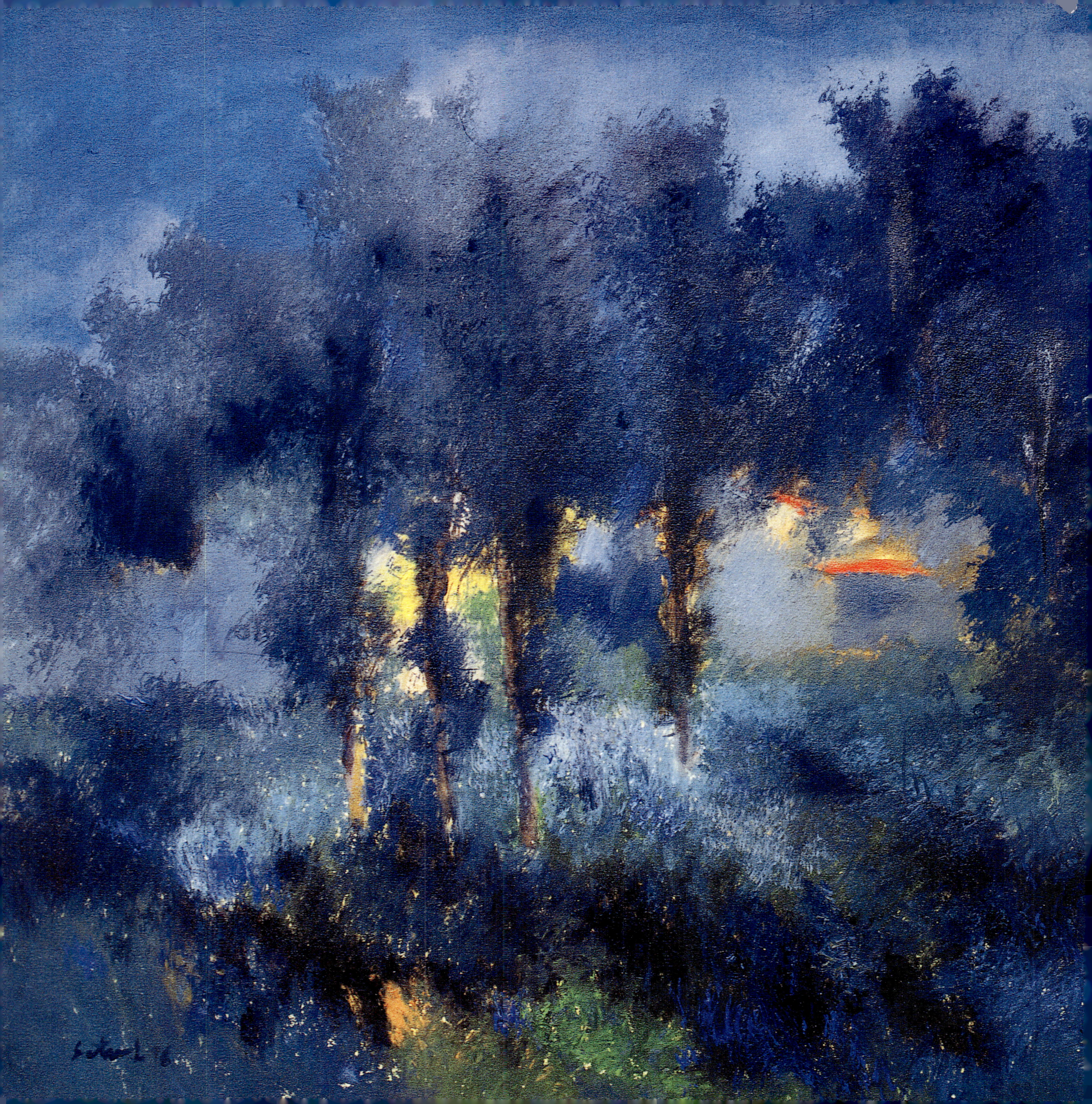

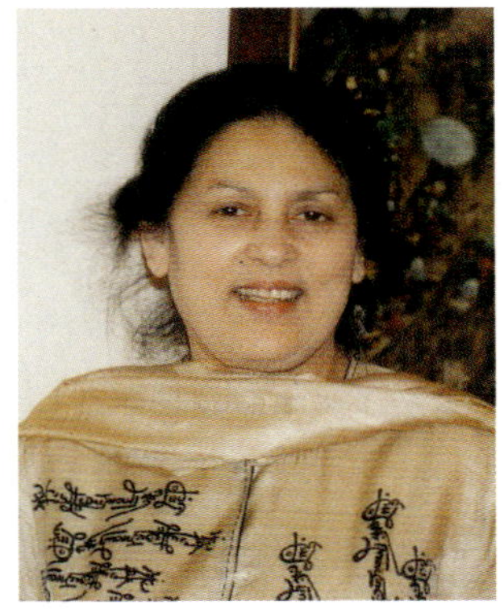

Love Thy Neighbour

Sehba Ali
Friend

We returned to settle in Lucknow after three-and-a-half decades in the West. Much had changed, naturally, but not as much as we apprehended.

The morning after our arrival, I woke up early and made my way to the kitchen to prepare a cup of tea. Just at that moment, the door-bell rang. There was a man at the door with a large covered tray in his hands. "I am your neighbour Mr. Satish Chandra's servant. They noticed you were up and they thought you may not have all you need for breakfast today so they have sent you this." I was deeply touched. I took the tray, and offered him a tip. He looked at me surprised, nodded his

Facing page: Oil on canvas, 1996.

head in refusal, gave me a little bow and left. I felt ashamed and instantly found my old Lucknow back.

In the tray, along with the breakfast, there was a note welcoming us to the neighbourhood and inviting us to meals till our kitchen was operational. Later in the morning we dropped in to meet the Chandras. We instantly became friends. Meenakshi and I had a teaching career in common and Satish and Liaqat enjoyed a drink together in the evenings.

We were delighted to know that Satish was a very accomplished artist. When we actually saw his paintings at his home and in public places, we were overwhelmed by his talent. His landscapes reminded me of Aristotle's saying. "In part, art completes what Nature cannot elaborate and in part, it imitates Nature."

What I also liked most about Satish was his courage to defy social evils such as religious bigotry, caste and class divisions, and the dowry system. Satish had a large circle of friends from all creeds and classes. He was a true believer in secularism.

 Facing page: Watercolour on paper, 1996.

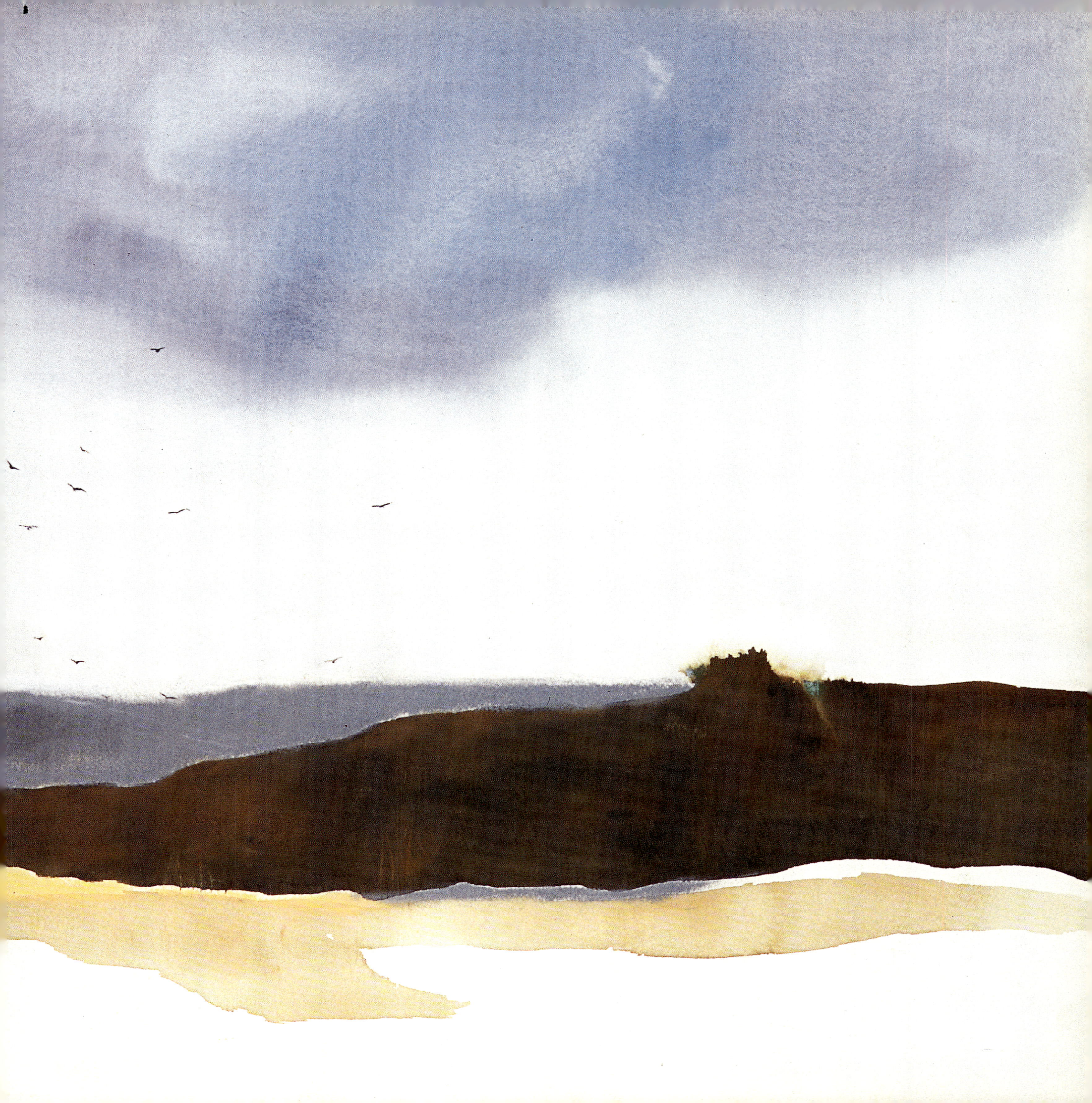

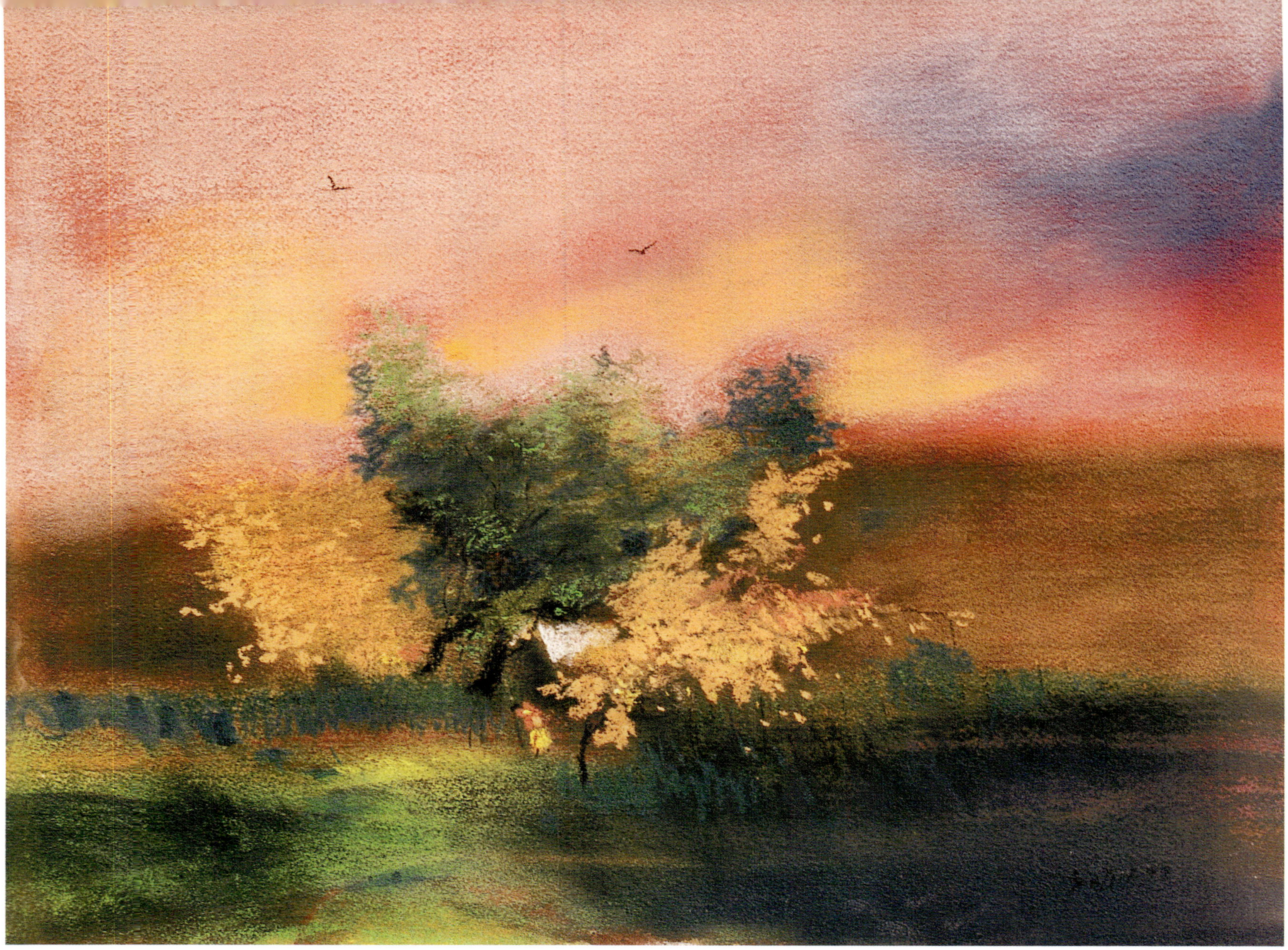

Mixed media on paper, 1999.

It was a pleasure and privilege to know this family and I regret that we only had a short time together with Satish.

Following are some lines from a poem I wrote in Urdu. These lines hold true for Satish.

Marg-e-Nagehan

Zehn me vusat kahan samjhe jo marg-e-naghan
Kyon hai zeb-e-dosh ek hansta hua karyal jawan
Kyon yeh aaya tha yahaan aur ab yeh jaata hai kahaan?
Mod kar apno se munh, chhod kar bazm-e-jahaan
Tum to thhey pyarey sabhi ke tum thhey fakhrey khandaan
Tum to thhey mehfil ki raunak, tum thhey jaan-e-dostan
Ilm aur fun ke khazaney tere seene mein nihan
Buzla-sanji aur zahanat terey chehrey se ayan
Kub tumharey ahl thhey yeh zamaan

Bus ki tumne pa liya ek maskan-e-haft
aasman

A Sudden and Untimely Death

Our minds are incapable of
understanding a sudden and
untimely death
Why a youthful and lively young man is
being carried on shoulders?
Why has he come here and where is he
going now?
Turning away from the near and dear
ones and leaving behind this world
You were the apple of everybody's eye,
you were the pride of the family
You were the soul of the party, you were
the favourite among friends
The treasures of knowledge and art,
hidden in your chest
Wit, humor and intelligence obvious in
your face
Perhaps this land and these times did
not deserve you
So you found a place in the Seventh
Heaven.

Mixed media on paper, 1999.

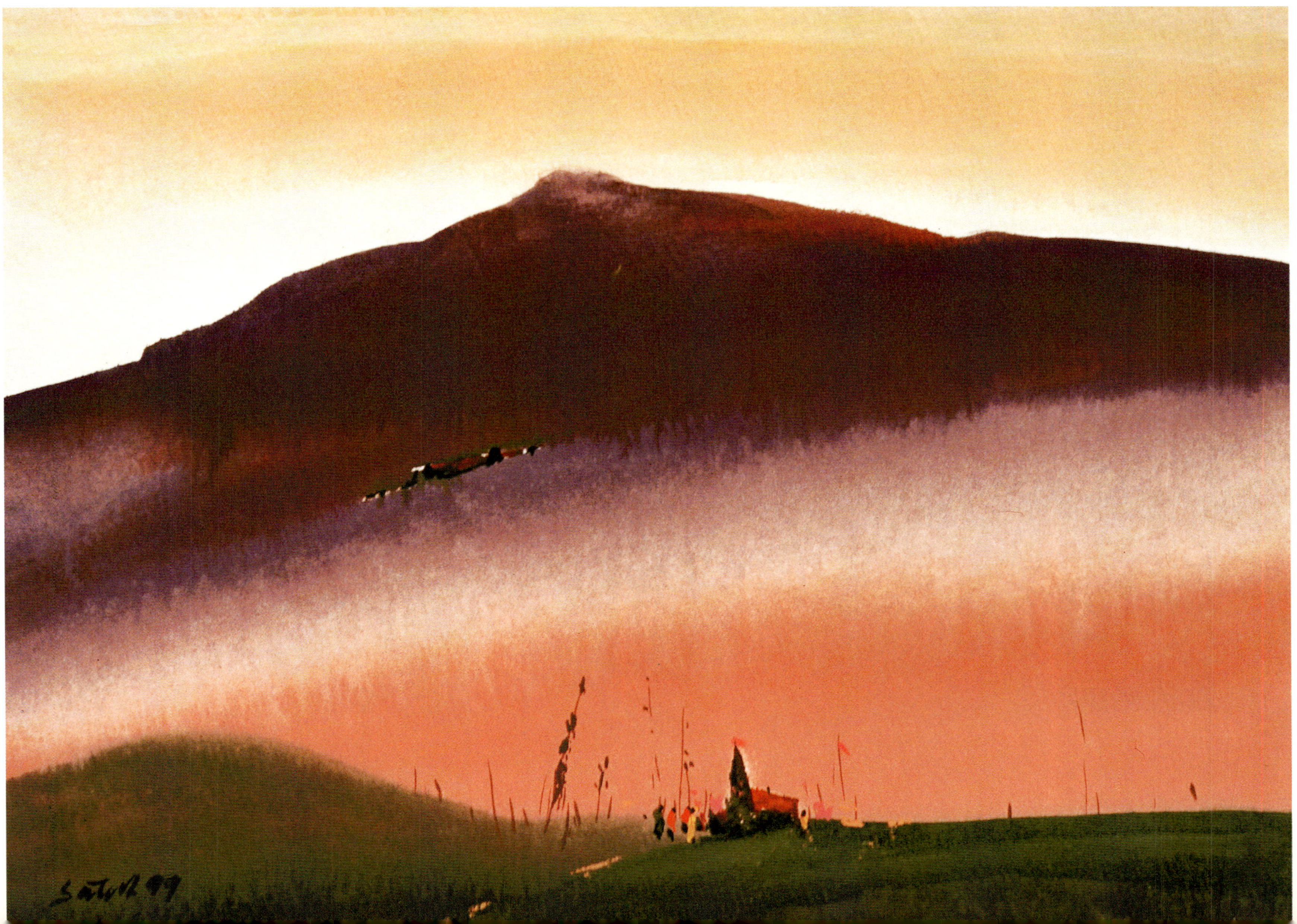

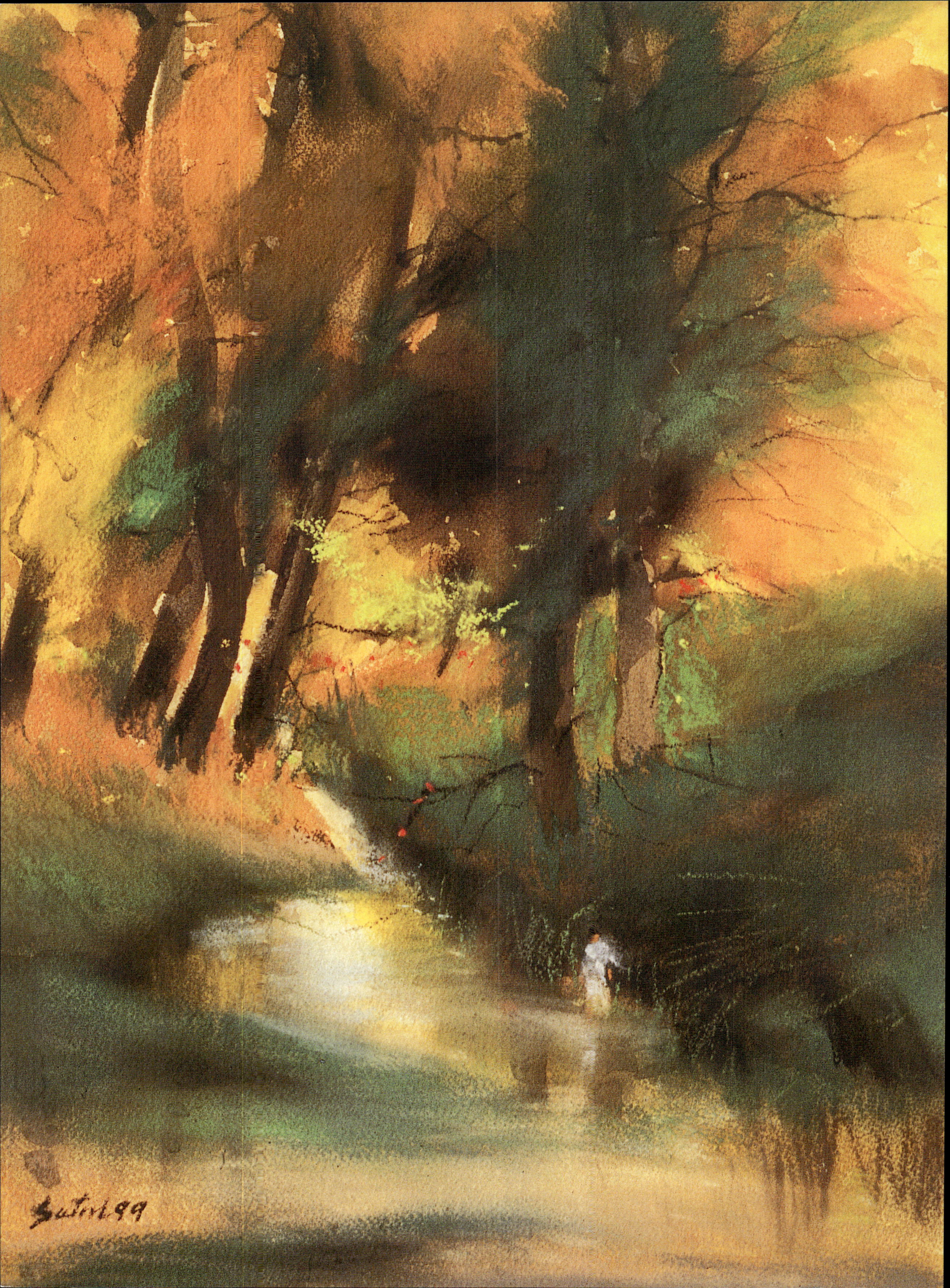

Hushed Whispers

"... Satish brings us different tonalities and moods to ponder over. While the azure blue sky becomes the most refractive idiom, it is the hint of habitation and the dense precipitation of the leaves that at once brings on prismatic fantasies. Earth and sky rejoice in these oils. While the sky smoothens and thins itself out like a stretched tissue, it is the earthy crustacean feel of grass that thickens with life. So comfortable and so much at ease with the scene of the pastorale is Satish that you can actually tether your mind to the responses that he evokes in you. Interestingly these large canvases have a heightened shade of colouration, while the whole scene can make you drift into a dream.

However, what entrances is the sky, its ability to draw you into its maw and keep you in the gaps of the crevices on earthy terrain. Then there is also the feeling that when you look at these works, you need to be alone, to be with yourself to listen to sounds and inner responses that matter.

That is precisely what Satish himself is, an artist who can sit for hours and study the quality of nature's many distinctions and its diminishing deviances as the light fades into the night sky. There are no harsh sounds here that ripple through the grasses. There are only hushed whispers of impaled sequences that stand the test of time.

Other than the large canvases, there are three oils in the smaller format of Kerala. Your gaze can begin anywhere on these small gems, so mesmeric are they, that they can be the personification of a tapestry of perfection. In these three works the sea and the sky both become like a thin amorphous blanket of sheer satiety. Not

Facing page: Watercolour on paper, 1999.

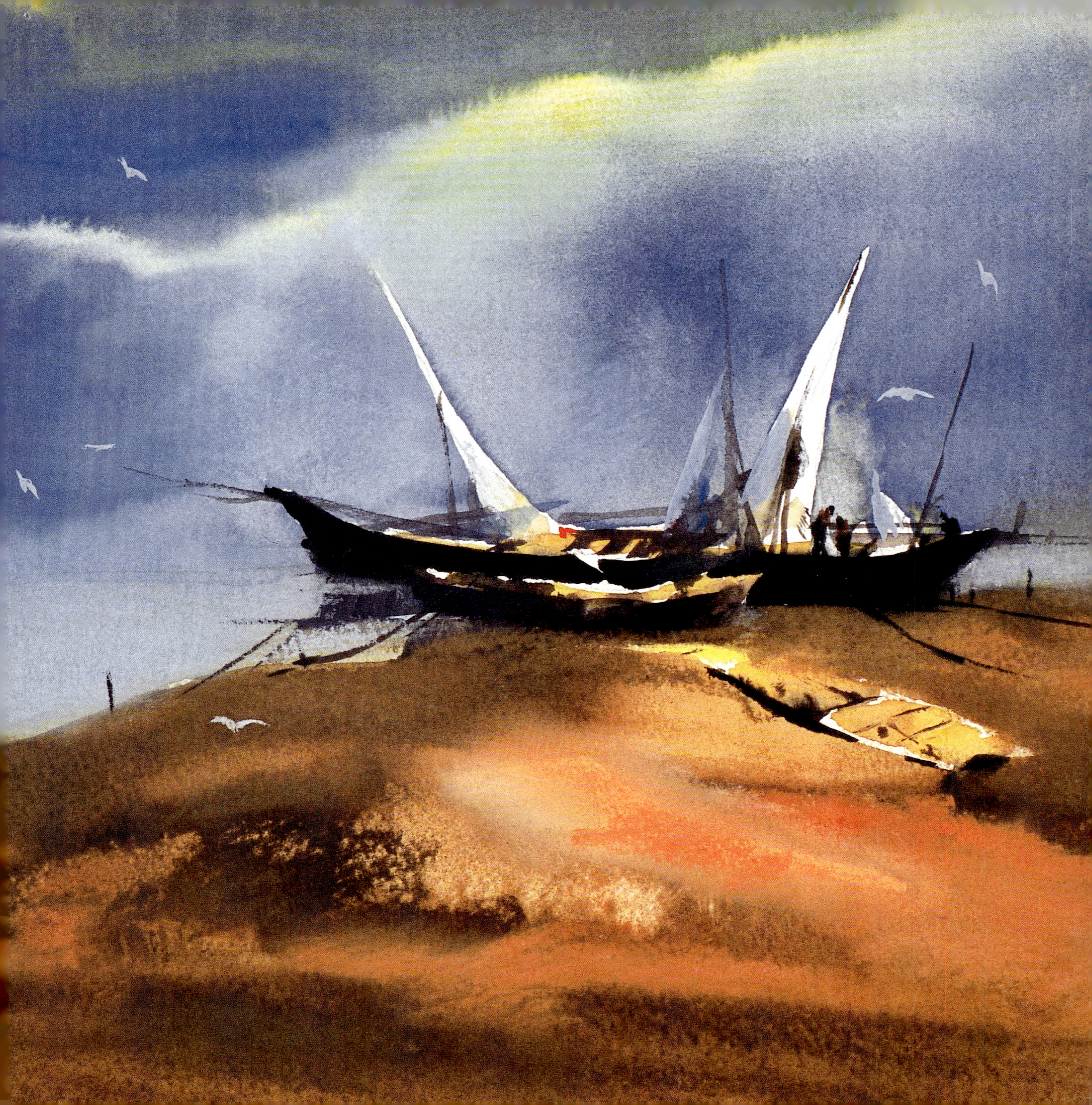

A Biographical Sketch

ACADEMIC PROFILE

Graduate in Fine Arts, College of Arts and Crafts, Lucknow.

Post Graduate in landscape and specialization in watercolour painting, College of Arts & Crafts, Lucknow.

PROFESSIONAL EXPERIENCE

1965-2002	Artist, Department of Architecture, Roorkee University.
	Reader, Department of Fine Arts, College of Arts and Crafts, Lucknow.
	Professor & Head of the Department of Fine Arts, College of Arts and Crafts, Lucknow.

AWARDS

1964	UP State Lalit Kala Akademi Annual Award
1964	UP Artists' Association Silver Medal
1966	UP State Lalit Kala Akademi Annual Award
1967	UP State Lalit Kala Akademi Award
1968	UP State Lalit Kala Akademi Radhakamal Mukherjee Gold Medal
1977	UP State Lalit Kala Akademi Annual Award
1977	UP Artists' Association Annual Award
1978	All India Academy of Fine Arts, Kolkata, Annual Award
1989	National Award, National Akademi of Arts, New Delhi
1994	Yash Bharti Samman, Government of Uttar Pradesh, India

SOLO SHOWS

1963	UP State Lalit Kala Akademi, Lucknow
1964-65	Mussoorie (Savoy Hotel) and Roorkee University of Architecture
1965	Kanpur British India Corporation Club
1964	New York City
1966, 68, 70, 72, 74, 76, 80	Lucknow
1975-97, 99	Taj Art Gallery, Mumbai
1977, 78, 81, 93, 95	Various galleries in Delhi
1994, 98, 99	Gallerie Ganesha
1998	North Central Zone Cultural Centre, Allahabad
2005 (posthumous)	Palm Court, India Habitat Centre, Delhi, sponsored by Gallerie Ganesha
2006 (posthumous)	Visual Art Gallery, India Habitat Centre, Delhi, sponsored by Gallerie Ganesha

GROUP EXHIBITIONS

1967, 1982	Four Contemporary Painters of UP, Lucknow
1976-77	Visual Art Society, Lucknow
1978-79	Various art galleries in Delhi
1985	UP Artists' Association All India Exhibition, Lucknow
1987, 98, 2001	Exhibition of Contemporary Water Colour Painters of India, Gallerie Ganesha
1999	Mirage Art Gallery, Delhi

PARTICIPATION

New Delhi	National Exhibition of Art 1963-67, 1970-71, 76, 78, 81, 84, 85, 87, 88, 89
New Delhi	Dhumimal Art Gallery 1964, 65, 66 (till 2002)
New Delhi	Kala Kumbh: Organized by Panchamrit in collaboration with Indo-Soviet Nicolai Roerich Art Club, 1991
New Delhi	Gallerie Ganesha
Bombay	Chemould Art Gallerie, 1987
New Delhi	AIFACS Exhibition, 1965, 66, 70, 78
Bombay	Bombay Art Society, 1965
Kolkata	Academy of Fine Arts, 1968, 73, 77, 78, 79
Lucknow	All India Drawing Exhibition, 1976
New Delhi	National Kala Mela, 1978
Kolkata	Birla Academy of Fine Arts, 1978, 81, 82, 83, 84 (continued upto 2005)
New Delhi	National Lalit Kala Akademi Contemporary Miniature Painting Exhibition, 1980
New Delhi	Trade Fair Exhibition, 1980
London	The Nehru Centre, 2002

INVITATIONS

New Delhi	6th Triennale India 1986, National Akademi of Art
Dhaka	4th Asian Biennale
New Delhi	Nehru Centenary Exhibition organized by Lalit Kala Akademi, 1989
New Delhi	Mirage Art Gallery
New Delhi	Delhi Art Gallery
Japan	Japan Biennale
Kolkata	Birla Akademi, 1982-2004
Bhopal	Bharat Bhawan, 1992

COMMISSIONED WORK

1967	Posters for UP Department of Tourism
1971	Mural Ceramic 24″ x 8″ UP State Electricity Board
1974	Mural Wood 18″ x 12″ UP State Bridge Corporation
1974	Paintings calendar published by Indian Explosives Ltd, Kanpur
1975	Paintings calendar published by Indian Explosives Ltd, Kanpur
1978	Mural Kwality Restaurant, Lucknow
1998	Murals for Ambedkar Park for Government of UP
2001	Paintings calendar published by Helpage India
2002	Murals for Ambedkar Park for Government of UP

COLLECTIONS

New Delhi	American Embassy
New Delhi	British High Commission
Lucknow	State Legislature Council House Building
Lucknow	State Chief Minister's Residence
Roorkee	Central Building Research Institute
Lucknow	State Information Director's office
Lucknow	Carlton Hotel
Lucknow	UP State Lalit Kala Akademi
Bombay	Indian Oil Corporation
Bombay	Taj Group of Hotels
Bombay	Air India Collection
New Delhi	National Lalit Kala Akademi
Lucknow	Indian Overseas Bank
Modinagar	Modi Rubber
Kanpur	Indian Explosives Limited
USA	California University
New Delhi	Taj Hotel
Lucknow	Government House
Bombay	Bhaba Atomic Research Centre
New Delhi	National Gallery of Modern Art
Lucknow	Dr. Mansoor Hassan
USA	University of California
Canada	University of Toronto

CAMPS

1973	Painters' Camp, Dehradun: Organized by UP State Lalit Kala Akademi
1977	All India Painters' Camp, Bhubaneshwar, organized by National Lalit Kala Akademi, New Delhi
1985	Painters' Camp at Nainital, organized by UP State Lalit Kala Akademi
1987	All India Painters' Camp, Regional Art Centre, Lucknow, organized by National Lalit Kala Akademi, New Delhi
1989	International Artists' Camp at Regional Art Centre, Lucknow, organized by National Lalit Kala Akademi, New Delhi
1992	All India Artists' Camp organized by NCZCC, with collaboration of Indian Academy of Administration, Mussoorie
1994	NCZCC All India Painting Camp, Lucknow
1997	NCZCC All India Painting Camp, Udaipur

BOOKS & CATALOGUE PUBLICATIONS

Four Decades Art of Uttar Pradesh by UP State Lalit Kala Akademi

Indian Contemporary Drawings by State Akademi UP, 1976

Sangrah by State Akademi UP, 1992

National Lalit Kala Exhibition Publication, 1992

State Lalit Kala Contemporary Artists of UP, 1990

Kalakumbh International Exhibition by Panchamrit, Delhi, 1991

The Downtrodden and We, Dr. B.R. Ambedkar Birth Centenary Exhibition by National Lalit Kala Akademi, New Delhi, 1991

National Exhibition of Art Award Winners 1995-1999 by National Academy of Art, New Delhi

Sixth Triennale India 1986 by National Akademi of Art, New Delhi

Bharat Bhawan Biennale Bhopal, 1992

Birla Akademi of Art and Culture Silver Jubilee, 1967-1992

Asian Art Biennale Bangladesh, 1989

Nehru Centenary, 'Nature and Environment' by National Akademi of Art, New Delhi, 1989

Indo-German Workshop, New Delhi

National Akademi of Art, New Delhi, 1989

ORGANIZATIONAL WORK AND ADMINISTRATIVE POSTS

1972 onward	Secretary, Visual Art Society, Lucknow
1979-82	Member, General Council, UP State Lalit Kala Akademi
1985	Member of the jury in UP Artists' Association, All India Exhibition
	Vice-President, UP Artists' Association
1988	Co-ordinator, UP State Lalit Kala Akademi Artists' Camp
1989-91	Member of the executive council, Lucknow University
1989-92	Member of the Jury in UP State Lalit Kala Akademi
1989-92	Member of fellowship committee in UP State Lalit Kala Akademi
1990-92	Member, North Central Zone Cultural Centre (NCZCC)
1991	Member of the publication committee for UP Contemporary Art
1992-94	Member of the executive council, Lucknow University
1994 onward	Member of the governing body and programme committee, NCZCC, Allahabad
	Member of the board of studies, Department of Fine Arts, Kumaon University
	Member of the executive and general council, Ayodhya Shodh Sansthan
1994-98	Chairman, UP State Lalit Kala Akademi, Uttar Pradesh
1998	Jury member, Birla Academy, Kolkata.